THE CUNNING OF UNREASON

THE CUNNING OF UNREASON

MAKING SENSE OF POLITICS

JOHN DUNN

HarperCollins*Publishers*

Endpapers show 'The Charge of the Light Brigade – Lord George Paget heads the Fourth Light Dragoons' by John Charlton (1889). Reproduced courtesy of Mary Evans Picture Library.

HarperCollins*Publishers*
77–85 Fulham Palace Road,
Hammersmith, London W6 8JB

Published by HarperCollins*Publishers* 2000
1 3 5 7 9 8 6 4 2

A catalogue record for this book is available from the British Library

ISBN 0 00 255647 2

Set in PostScript Monotype Bembo by
Rowland Phototypesetting Ltd,
Bury St Edmunds, Suffolk

Printed and bound in Great Britain by
Clays Ltd, St Ives plc

FOR CHARTY

CONTENTS

PREFACE

What exactly is politics? Why does it occur? (Has there been politics ever since there were recognizably human beings? Might it just stop, even though there continue to be eminently recognizable human beings?) How has it come to take its present forms?

How is it best understood? What are the best approaches to understanding it? How far *can* it in fact be understood? What limits do human beings face in their attempts to understand it? What resources for understanding it do we now have? How far, if at all, do these resources derive from the professional study of politics? How successfully are they now incorporated into that study?

In the pages that follow I try to show readers how to answer these questions for themselves, and to make clear how closely their answers depend on one another. I try to show how politics has come to be a vaguely degrading and highly specialized occupation: the trade of Tony Blair and Peter Mandelson, of William Hague and Michael Howard, and until quite recently at least one of the trades of Jonathan Aitken: also, of course, the trade of Bill Clinton and Newt Gingrich, of Benjamin Netanyahu and Yasser Arafat, of General Suharto all too recently and, alas, still of Saddam Hussein as I now write. And vaguely degrading? Well, on the evidence of this list alone, plainly a career wide open to all but unmentionable talents and an occupation blatantly unfit for gentlemen – let alone gentlewomen. And this last was a complaint pressed from the beginning not merely against the cultural styles of conspicuously brutal and autocratic regimes, but also very much against the impact of democratization on the personnel who lead or govern a political society (cf. Plato 1930–5; Wood 1991).

But I try, too, to show why even today politics can still sometimes seem uniquely courageous, direct and even potentially effective in its assault on the misery and injustice of the great bulk of collective human life. Not just a career, but a true and noble vocation (cf. Weber 1948, 77–128). (A *noble* vocation? How undemocratic can you get?) I try to show why the impact of concentrated coercive power upon individual human life chances should vary so sharply from time to time and place to place. More immediately and pressingly I try to make clear why the politics of such a large proportion of states should have shifted so drastically to the right (in practice, if not necessarily in explicit political preference) over the last quarter of the twentieth century, and what that shift is likely to mean for the politics of the next few decades.

Whom can you trust to tell you the answers to these questions? (People who share your taste in political outcomes? People who plainly do not care what the outcomes are?) Why should you trust them, and not trust others who answer them very differently?

Why is politics so consistently disappointing? Why does it repeatedly nourish such high hopes, and why does it virtually never realize them? Few factors have more causal force in politics (do more to determine what in fact occurs) than how well we understand what we are doing. Disappointment is a mixture of dismay and surprise. If we understood politics better we would certainly be less surprised by its outcomes, as well as surprised much less often.

This would be partly because we had greater expectations of being dismayed by them (less readily anticipated that they would come out just as we wished). Replacing disappointment with dismay, a perspective of eager anticipation by one of chastened retrospection, would not be gratifying in itself. My claim is just that only this shift in attitude would place us as well as we can be placed to secure the outcomes we want.

All human action lies under the shadow of prospective regret. But there are few, if any, domains of our acting over which that shadow falls so darkly as it does over the huge, and ever more drastically consequential, field of politics. What this book aims to show is why this should be so and what it means. (What it *means*?

Well, let us say: what it meant for our parents and grandparents, what it has meant for you and me, what it is likely to mean for our children and children's children, and how we should see all three of these together.) You could think of it as a book about the inevitability of disappointment. But I prefer myself to think of it as a book about how (and how not) to hope.

It is not a book for advanced students in particular (though I hope that many of them may get something from it). But it very much is a book for those who read books. It asks to be read as a whole, and is most likely to prove instructive to those who do so read it. It presumes its readers to be intelligent and potentially interested, and trusts that they will prefer to be addressed as such (as a serious newspaper might). But it tries to avoid presuming anything much in the way of prior knowledge about politics. It makes bold claims, and seldom lingers to give adequate reasons for regarding most of them as valid. (It has a long way to go, and travels as fast as it dares. It hopes to blaze a trail, not to lay down a road.) But it does also try throughout to show an incredulous reader where she (or he) can turn to see just why I believe its claims to be valid. Few of the arguments which it advances are particularly original. But the relations which it tries to bring out between them are at times comparatively novel. It is here, if anywhere, that its capacity to illuminate lies: in the whole, not in the dismembered parts.

I have written it very much on my own. So its failures and follies are no one's but mine. But in writing it I have drawn wholesale and ruthlessly on what I have been taught, both as student and as teacher, in the three and a half decades which I have spent in the still great University to which I have the honour, the privilege and the more intermittent pleasure to belong. Any merits it has are mainly borrowed, not earned.

I am grateful to the Humanities Research Board of the British Academy for the term of research leave in 1998 which made it possible for me to finish this book, to the University of Cambridge for the sabbatical leave which made it possible for me to begin it, and to my colleagues in the Department of Social and Political

Sciences for the many burdens which they shouldered while I was doing so. I should like to express my warm thanks to Frank Kermode for inviting me to write it in the first place, to Stuart Proffitt, Philip Gwyn Jones and Toby Mundy at HarperCollins at earlier stages, to Georgina Laycock and Michael Fishwick for all their kindness, encouragement and help in ushering it at long last into the world, and to Peter James for his exemplary patience, skill, tact and taste in handling a very trying manuscript. I must also apologize one last time to Ruth, Charty and Polly for all that it has cost them. I can only hope that in some ways, in the end, it will have been worth it.

JOHN DUNN
King's College, Cambridge
July 1999

PART I

1

Starting Out

Defining the Task

What would I have to understand to be confident that I really understood politics?

WHAT IS POLITICS?

My first need would be to be sure that I knew what politics is: what it is that I was trying to understand. This is considerably harder than you might at first suppose. Beyond a certain degree of assurance, indeed, it is simply impossible. Any of us, if we bother to, can form reasonable beliefs about what politics is or isn't. But none of us can literally *know* what politics is. What stops us from knowing is the fact that the beliefs which seem reasonable to human beings about what politics really is, and about why it is as it is, have always differed very widely. As far as we can now tell, they will always continue to differ: perhaps, in the end, less widely than a thousand years ago, but perhaps, also, still more widely as the centuries go by. Some have recently been confident that they are bound to differ less widely in the centuries to come (Fukuyama 1992). Some have been equally confident that they will continue to differ at least as much more or less indefinitely (Huntington 1997; Gray 1998). But each, on the most preliminary inspection, is clearly just guessing.

We can criticize one another's beliefs about these questions, and learn to do so quite effectively. But none of us can sanely hope to replace most of other people's beliefs on this score with a plainly superior set of our very own. Political understanding modifies and sometimes amends the understanding of others; but it never simply supplants it. However clear-headed and well-informed we may learn to be, and however confident we may become, none of our understandings of politics will ever be more than one small voice in dialogue with an immense range of other voices. To be sure, we can often hear ourselves exceedingly well, but that is largely because we are so ill placed (and perhaps also in many cases so disinclined) to listen accurately to anyone else.

WHY IS THERE POLITICS AT ALL?

My second need would be a clear and accurate view of why any such field of activity as politics existed at all. What is it about humans, or about their present situation, which ensures that none of them today can ever fully escape politics? Does politics come from what they always necessarily are? Does it come merely from how they now happen to be, and might soon or eventually cease to be? Or does it come not from inside each of them (from their own minds or bodies), but from outside them (from the ways in which their human predecessors have shaped and reshaped their world over time, or from the cumulative impact of those reshapings on the minds and bodies of the present generation)? If it comes from all three, which parts of it come from which?

Agency

Why should we think of politics as an *activity*? Because human action is the centre of politics – its core, what makes it itself and not some other field of human experience (love, suffering, laughter). Politics can be moving. (It can elicit passion and even deserve devotion.) It is often weighed down with suffering. It is usually more than a little absurd. But passion, ludicrousness, even misery, are never the key to politics.

That key is always how human beings see their world (above all, the role and significance of one another in making it what it is), and how they choose to try to master it, to bend it to their wills. How they judge, and how those judgments impel them to act. Often, perhaps on careful examination always, mastering it[1] includes, and perhaps principally requires, subduing, eluding, persuading or enlightening one another.

Politics is an endless and highly unstable round of struggle and quest for understanding. None of us can ever be certain how obstinacy in struggle and effort to understand are balanced, within it or within ourselves, at any particular moment, and how far one is tipping decisively into the other. Because professional politics and routine political awareness are often banal and callow, and because most human beings have their pride and seek out occasions for feeling superior, all of us are permanently tempted to assume that we ourselves (unlike all too many of our acquaintances) understand politics at least as well as we have any good reason to bother to and that, insofar as we don't, this is essentially because we have chosen not to, and done so for pretty respectable reasons. One of the main things which I hope to show is why this is extremely unlikely to be true for any of us.

Scope

Why should we think of politics as a *field*? It is always the external setting of human action, the constraints this imposes and the opportunities which it opens up, which dominates human action. It is this setting which frames it, gives it much of its meaning, summons up its energies and challenges it to do its best or worst. And as of human action in general, so too of politics, our actions towards one another on the largest possible scale and over the great issues of life and death, prosperity and indigence, even more conspicuously and peremptorily.

FORMS OF POLITICS

My third need would be to see just why politics has come to take the distinctive forms which it has today, and to judge, more tentatively, how these forms are likely to alter, either in shape or in meaning, in the reasonably near future (the modest horizon of comprehension of the prospective outcomes of their own future interaction with one another which is open to human beings).

Note, again, the centrality of action, and the key significance of the unintended consequences of past human actions for the prospects for human agents in the present and the future.

THE RANGE OF ANSWERS

In the course of human history, the faltering and patchy memory of our species' progress through time, an immense range of answers has been given to each of these three questions (cf. Dunn 1996(a)). To be quite certain that we really understood politics, we might need to know all of these answers, and to see how far each was or was not valid. To assume that we do not need to know most of them is to assume at least that none of these contain elements which are distinctive, valid and of any real depth. And how, without even knowing what they are, could we reasonably be confident of this?

For most of the last two or three hundred years many European thinkers have assumed that all they needed to know was which answer was valid and what that answer was, since the rest of human belief on such matters could safely be consigned to the rubbish bin of history. More sporadically, of course, much the same assumption has been made by rather smaller numbers of thinkers over a far longer span of time and in societies scattered throughout the world. Today, for the most part, we have lost this confidence. In the main we are quite right to have done so. Modesty is more prepossessing than arrogance; and overwhelmingly rational modesty is more reasonable than preposterous arrogance. But even though modesty is an epistemic virtue (an *aid* in knowing), it is emphatically not enough. Extreme modesty in cognitive pretension (in the scope of what we claim to be able to know) is quite compatible both with utter confusion and with the abandonment of the slightest attempt to understand most of what we need to understand. More maliciously, it is equally compatible with abandoning the attempt to understand anything more exacting or useful than how to quarrel deftly and intimidatingly with one another in public (or private). Compare Thomas Hobbes's savage account of the pleasures of fellow citizenship in his great book *De Cive*

(Hobbes 1983), eminently applicable to the experience of any working academic.

The Academy, the Republic of Letters, even the day-to-day and very ordinary citizenry of the modern republic (or constitutional monarchy) need a more responsible and less self-indulgent approach than this (Fontana (ed.) 1994; Dunn 1990; Dunn (ed.) 1992). That is to say, *we* – you and I – need a more responsible and less self-indulgent approach than this.

If the key to politics really is how human beings see their world and how they try to bend this to their wills, it is vital to judge how far they see that world accurately and how far the ways in which they wish to alter it are ways in which it can in practice be altered. Insofar as they fail to see it accurately, they can scarcely hope to understand what they are doing; and they are exceedingly unlikely to alter it even broadly as they wish. Today we are pretty confident that the line between true and false beliefs about politics is not a clear and bright one, and that there is no single authoritative site, no privileged human, or supra-human but humanly accessible, vantage point from which it can be identified decisively or once and for all. (Even those, like the Iranian *ulama* or perhaps the Supreme Pontiff, who reject the first premiss, appear in practice now to accept the second.) Only utter confusion, however, could possibly lead us to believe that there is no distinction between true and false beliefs about politics (Dworkin 1996), or that false beliefs about politics will not, in most instances and over enough time, do great harm to their human believers or others whom they affect. (But compare Elster 1975, 48–64, with Plato 1930–5.) This is discouraging, since the most casual inspection of politics in action, or the most desultory attention to most people's political beliefs, shows at once that a very large proportion of political beliefs are predominantly false. Dispiriting or not, however, one thing which this could not reasonably discourage is the attempt to understand politics better.

In this book, I consider in turn the three themes which we most need to understand, if we are to learn to understand modern politics, the politics of our own day and of the epoch which lies just ahead of us, better than we yet do. Of these, the first is deceptively simple. What politics is, you might think, must surely be either obvious or else essentially trivial, a matter for more or less arbitrary definition. It is a term which we can look up in a dictionary, and for which we can, if we wish, trustingly take the dictionary's direction. Or, if we are less trusting, we can write our own dictionary entry instead, taking care that the latter responds fully to our own impeccable reasons for viewing politics as we do. Neither of these two approaches, however, has the slightest chance of providing us with the sort of dependable control which we need. If we do not know what politics is we cannot even know what we are talking about or trying to understand. If we incorporate the full range of other people's usage of the term (even within our own natural language community: English, French, Korean, Hindi), we merely reproduce in our own understanding all the confusions and equivocations in their understandings. If, instead, we purge their understandings ruthlessly and rely firmly on our own, we beg the question of whether we ourselves really do understand what we are talking about, and do so at the most disabling of levels: the level at which we decide what we will even bother to consider.

THE KEY DILEMMA OF POLITICAL UNDERSTANDING?

There may be a real dilemma here: a choice between two profoundly unenviable alternatives, which at the same time appears to exclude the possibility of any other option. By the end of the book I hope that you will be better placed to judge for yourselves how far this is indeed a dilemma, and, insofar as it is, how far its two horns are accurately described. My own view, for what it is worth, is that it is not a real dilemma, since the most prudent way to proceed is to adopt both approaches resolutely, alternating the vantage points which they provide, and interrogating ourselves sternly throughout on the imaginative opportunity costs of the strategies of understanding which we find enticing. We can only see through our own eyes; but it is merely stupid to suppose that any of us will not still have almost everything to learn about politics up to the time that we die.

For the moment we must simply register the imaginative discomfort and the sense of external intellectual constraint of this potential dilemma, because each has strong implications for the strategies of understanding which it can make sense for us to pursue. What they preclude, we must notice at once, is the sort of confident allegation about what politics really is and why it occurs at all with which didactic accounts of it, *Introductions to Politics, Introductions to Political Science*, often begin.

Consider, for example, the initial formulae from a pair of recent British textbooks. 'The term "Politics" is used to describe the process through which individual and collective decisions are made' (Selby 1995, 1). 'People are social beings. They choose to live together in groups. Because people live together in groups, there is a need to make decisions . . . The study of Politics is the study of how such decisions *are* made. It may also be the study of how such decisions *should be* made' (Bentley, Dobson, Grant and Roberts 1995, 2). Neither of these, we can be sure, was intended to be controversial. Yet each contains quite surprising judgments.

In Selby's case, if there is a clear contrast between individual and collective decisions, it is surely that the former are taken by single individuals and not infrequently for single individuals. With many of the decisions which you or I take for ourselves it is most unlikely that we think of the process of deciding (however protracted) as an instance of *politics*. (Is it to be mangoes or strawberries? Shall I wear my jeans?) Sometimes we may be badly wrong in thinking as we do. But surely not always.

Bentley and his associates introduce their readers to British politics with a more elaborate and ambitious train of thought. But they too make at least one striking assumption: that the group character of human life which occasions the need for collective decisions is a product of choice. No doubt there is some sense in which this is true. Most individual human beings could probably live in a far more solitary manner than they do, if only they wished to with sufficient intensity. But it is certainly not true that they could all (the populations of Greater Tokyo, Mexico City, London, Bangkok, Beijing and so on) still simultaneously live in a far more solitary manner. Geography, the history of technology and the population history of the world, taken together, by now just preclude this. It is not a plausible description for most of us even by late adolescence that the groups in which we in fact live are ones which we have chosen for ourselves. More importantly still it is never true for any modern population for more than a fleeting moment that the sovereign political units in which they live are ones which most of them have chosen (Dunn 1997).

Consider now a series of bolder allegations, in some cases plainly intended to provoke controversy. Politics, Max Weber assures us, 'comprises any kind of independent leadership' (Weber 1948, 77). Politics, says Isaac D'Israeli, has been misdefined as 'the art of governing mankind by deceiving them' (quoted in Crick 1964, 16). What it should be seen as, Bernard Crick himself insists, is neither:

> a set of fixed principles to be realized in the near future, nor yet . . . a set of traditional habits to be preserved, but . . . an activity, a sociological activity which has the anthropological function of preserving a community grown too complicated for either tradition alone or pure arbitrary rule to preserve it without the undue use of coercion. (Crick 1964, 24)

This is less clear or economical than the definition which D'Israeli rejects (what exactly is a sociological activity? What is an unsociological activity?); but it is also considerably more appreciative.

Compare, again, the more astringent viewpoint of the German Carl Schmitt, writing under the Weimar Republic: 'The political is the most intense and extreme antagonism, and every concrete antagonism becomes that much the more political the closer it approaches the most extreme point, that of the friend–enemy grouping' (Schmitt 1996, 29). 'The specific political distinction to which political actions and motives can be reduced is that between friend and enemy' (Schmitt 1996, 26). Contrast this, in turn, with the list of eight possible ingredients of the idea of politics set out more ponderously by the American political theorist William Connolly in his widely used study *The Terms of Political Discourse*. The first six, in brusque summary, are (1) policies backed by the legally binding authority of government, (2) actions involving a choice between viable options, (3) the considerations invoked by participants in selecting options, (4) the impact of the choices on the interests, wishes or values of segments of the population, (5) the extent to which the outcomes of the decisions are intended by or known to those who make them, (6) the numbers affected by the decisions and the duration of their effects (Connolly 1974, 12–13). By politics these writers plainly mean many different things. The more urgent their reasons for selecting their preferred emphases, the less inclined they are likely to prove to defer to one another's habitual usage. Why should you be any more inclined to do so?

How, then, can I have the gall to assure you that human action is the centre of politics: a far from self-evident claim, and in the view of many not even a valid one?

I do so simply to encourage you to start thinking for yourselves, certainly not as an intellectual promissory note, a guarantee that you would be well advised to take the claim on trust.

SPECIFYING POLITICS: WORDS AND THINKERS

Let us take the question of what politics is (what it is that we are trying to understand) a little more slowly, and see what is going on as we try to answer it. One way of approaching it is to start off from dictionaries and see what they tell us. A second is to start off from some of the great European political thinkers who have tried to answer the question of what politics is, and whose answers, to varying depths, still mark educated understandings of politics in the world today. Why European political thinkers? Well, not just for old times' sake, but because politics is a European category and indeed a European word, and because European categories still have a dangerously privileged role within modern politics (Dunn 1996 (a)). Both the danger and the privilege are exceedingly important and need to be handled together and in relation to one another.

ARISTOTLE

If we adopt either of these approaches, we shall soon find that it intersects with the other. The history of words cannot readily be disentangled from the history of the ideas which the words are used to refer to; and the history of these ideas, in turn, cannot readily be disentangled from the seething turmoil of conflict and co-operation between human beings across their long history (Dunn 1980, cap. 2; Tully (ed.) 1988; Ball, Farr and Hanson (eds) 1989; Dunn 1996(a)). If we adopt either of these two approaches, we shall also soon discover that politics, the word itself in modern English and its transpositions into a wide range of other contemporary languages, is taken ultimately from the title of a single historical text, the *Politics* of the fourth-century BC Greek philosopher Aristotle, tutor to Alexander the Great of Macedon. It was a text, moreover, to which, as far as we know, the author himself did not even give a title. The word itself was not composed arbitrarily by Aristotle or his subsequent editors (by, for example, juxtaposing previously unconnected letters of the Greek alphabet). It was not a deliberate coinage, but a natural development of meanings already embodied in the Greek language. We have no reason to believe that it had been used by any previous Greek speaker (or writer) to pick out a field of human activity of particular importance, or one which posed distinctive problems of understanding. In our present understandings of politics, in all their confusion, it would be absurd to claim that Aristotle can in any sense have *started* politics. But it remains true that his performance as an author has placed an indelible mark on the entire cumulative subsequent effort to comprehend what politics is (an effort which could scarcely have had any integral momentum until politics had been picked out in this way as a distinctive field of activity). Whatever else Aristotle did, he certainly started something when he wrote the lectures we now call the *Politics*. At least some of our effort to understand politics, even today, whether we like it or not, indeed whether we *realize* it or not, must still take the form of a struggle with Aristotle's ghost.

The *Politics* is a complicated book, and not invariably clear. We do not, as noted, even know that Aristotle gave it a title, let alone the title it now carries. But that title is certainly closely related to the subject matter which it contains, and still echoes some features of Aristotle's own judgment about that subject matter. In particular, it echoes the judgment that there is a special sort of human association, one concerned with rule among free and equal human beings (Aristotle 1932, 1255b, p. 28) and at its best aiming at the supreme human good, that this association is deeply in harmony with what human beings and the world really are like, and how they ought to be (Aristotle 1932, 1252a, p. 2), and that humans who do not belong to such an association are sharply diminished by failing to do so (Aristotle 1932, 1252b, pp. 8 and 10; but compare Cooper 1975 on Aristotle's accompanying and not obviously compatible confidence in the priority of the life of the mind). Still more controversially, it picks out this form of association as virtually self-sufficient, as bound together above all, in its pursuit of a shared good, by the human capacity for speech and the unique concern of human beings with what is good or bad, just or unjust: not simply with the pursuit of given goals, but with how to value goals themselves, how to *choose* well (Aristotle 1932, 1253a, p. 10; cf. Taylor 1989, caps 1 and 2). More controversially still, it ringingly identifies this very grand conception of shared human public activity with a particular institutional and geopolitical format, the small self-governing *polis* (city state) of the fourth-century BC Greek world, and underlines the implication that the standing of such a *polis* is prior both in meaning and in value to any individual citizen within it, let alone to any of his female kin or slaves or its resident aliens. This is not an ensemble of convictions which anyone today really shares. But its power still pervades our conceptions of what politics really is (or should be, and hence perhaps could be), helping to shape these inadvertently even when we least mean it to.

One way of telling the story which culminates (if that is the word) in contemporary dictionary entries for the term *politics*, or in usages of that term today by television commentators or newspaper journalists, would be to see it as a protracted sanitization of the term that came to serve as the title of Aristotle's book: as a more or less steady depletion of its meaning, and a corresponding enlargement of its potential scope of application. There is nothing wrong with this judgment in itself. But for our purposes it is not the most instructive way to see what has happened. For us, it will be better neither to adopt Aristotle's viewpoint in its entirety (an option probably not really open to us anyway: cf. Williams 1981, cap. 11), nor to ignore the fact that he ever existed, but to try to understand the significance of some of the tangled imaginative history which lies between his formulation of his conception and the conceptions, in all their variety and disorder, which we ourselves hold today.

In the end we shall have to decide how much of Aristotle's conception it is still wise to embrace, and how far that (perhaps very shrunken) residue needs to be supplemented by types of consideration which did not, and perhaps could not, have occurred to Aristotle himself. The view that a truly political association can and should verge on self-sufficiency (Aristotle 1932, 1252b, p. 8), for example, seems practically precluded for us by the central facts of our increasingly globalized economy, though its echoes remain audible enough in the present anxieties of the right wing of the British Conservative Party. The conceptions that women have no clear place in politics or that slaves are a natural and acceptable feature of the social and legal landscape (cf. Garnsey 1996) are no longer avowable in polite company, though distinctly shiftier traces of each still play a pretty prominent role in practical life. But, by the time that we have decided which features, if any, of Aristotle's conception we should still adopt, we shall have had to think our way through virtually the whole of modern politics (perhaps, indeed, through literally the whole of it). Or, to see the matter another way, we shall have come to realize that our starting point and our hoped-for destination are massively confounded with one another: that we cannot hope to answer any of the three broad questions which we initially posed without answering *each* of them:

that their answers are interdependent. In the end, we must answer them together, or give up any attempt to answer them at all.

A century or so ago it was easy for any educated European to suppose that Aristotle's vision of politics (along with his views on the character of human existence as a whole) did carry a general significance for the denizens of any country. As a founding text of the continuing and still increasingly self-confident tradition of evaluation and judgment which Europeans liked to suppose lay behind their conspicuously growing power, its status was both emblematic and agreeably reassuring. Today the reasons for judging it central in the same way must be very different. But they may nevertheless still be extremely powerful. Strongest of all, perhaps, is the fact that a state form (the modern representative democratic republic) which draws its ideological charter from the claim to be uniquely equipped to provide rule for and among free and equal persons has fought its way to clear primacy in all the wealthiest and most of the most powerful societies in the world (see Chapters 6 and 8 below). The sheer power which has been won through, and exercised within, this state form stems from the human authority of that claim; and no other extant civilization has a comparably historically deep tradition of interpretation of the nature and sources of that authority. Aristotle was, at most, a severely qualified democrat. But the merits which he felt unable to deny in the democracy of the *polis* remain surprisingly close to the cool, unexhilarating advantages which it is reasonable to ascribe to this ever more commonplace and widely diffused state form.

The least controversial feature of his viewpoint today is his presumption that politics (both what he called 'politics' and, anachronistically, what we ourselves call 'politics') is inherently concerned with rule, the regular exercise of ultimately coercive authority by some human beings over others. (Cf. Finer 1997.) Virtually every feature of his viewpoint, however, has been controversial at one point or other in the many centuries which separate us from him: even the judgment that there is a sharp and telling contrast between the rule of free and equal human beings and rule over the unfree and unequal. Some features of his viewpoint are probably more controversial (or, at any rate, less widely acceptable) today than they have been at any point in the intervening period. Especially inflammatory today is his confidence that rule over unfree and unequal persons, the rule of a master, is not merely to be contrasted with genuine politics (rule not *over*, but *among*, free and equal human beings), but also wholly appropriate to the structure of a household. Aristotle did not, on the whole, think well of the absolute authority of barbarian monarchs, Greece's non-Greek neighbours to the East, whose territories his great pupil Alexander was to conquer wholesale. He viewed their political arrangements as uncivilized and their public belief systems as profoundly superstitious. But he also explicitly regarded the type and scope of authority which he scorned in their (as we would say) political arrangements as acceptable enough within the households of his own Greek communities: as the proper form for relations between an invariably male household head and the younger males, the women and the slaves who also belonged to that household.

The view that the authority of masters over slaves was natural and readily justified was already under fierce attack in Europe and North America two centuries ago (Davis 1966, 1975 and 1984), and now lacks public defenders in most parts of the world. But the view that male household heads have natural authority over female household members, and the extraordinarily elaborate range of more discreet practices of subordination still etched into the conventional domestic divisions of labour in most societies in the world, have only come under effective frontal attack on any scale in the last few decades. While their defenders in many settings are now more sheepish than they used to be, it must be said that the practices themselves continue for the most part to hold up with some tenacity. Because of the sheer numbers of human beings involved, it is likely that this particular enlargement in the scope of politics, this drastic politicization of some of the most intimate and pervasive features of collective human life, will prove in retrospect the most important single change of the last century in the scope and agenda of politics. Whatever we may in the end choose to agree with Aristotle over, we can hardly hope to see eye to eye with him on this. Some of us may still share many of his feelings (however surreptitiously). But none of us could now muster, on this score, the same unruffled public blandness.

THREE INTERCONNECTED QUESTIONS

What is the pivot of this great (and still startlingly recent) shift in the political agenda? A prudent answer would have to be that we are too close to the shift, and far too deeply and confusingly involved in it (urging it on, trying as best we can to ignore it, or fighting discreetly or brashly to obstruct or even reverse it), to be in a position to tell. But for our present purposes a bolder response will be more useful, even if in the long run it is unlikely to prove wholly correct. ('In the long run,' as Maynard Keynes tartly observed in his 1923 *Tract on Monetary Reform* (Skidelsky 1992, 62, 156), 'we are all dead.' And in politics especially, as the British Prime Minister Harold Wilson once memorably noted, even a week is a long time.)

More bravely, then, we may say that the source of this huge expansion in the scope of politics has been the perception that rule can hope to be legitimate only insofar as it passes the test of acceptability to the free and equal (cf. Dunn (ed.) 1992), and that very much of the texture of domestic relations virtually everywhere in the world today, as for long in the past, still conspicuously retains the character of *rule*, and rule over unfree and unequal persons at that. Once again, we can see how forlorn it is to hope to separate our conception of what politics really is (what it consists in) at all sharply from our understanding of what has been happening in the course of modern politics, and why that politics has taken the course that it has.

The view that to understand politics we first need to know what politics is (what we are talking about whenever we mention it) has a certain immediate force. The view that, if we are to understand it, we shall in the end need to understand why politics today takes the forms which it does and has the consequences which it has is blindingly obvious. The view that these two elements of understanding depend on one another, while more surprising and perhaps more puzzling, can be defended with some ease. But why do we need to know (indeed *do* we really need to know) why there is any such field of human activity as politics: why politics occurs at all? This is an extremely important question, but it cannot be answered convincingly in a hurry. The book itself is my attempt to answer it. At its outset, all I can do is try to indicate why this third and intervening question earns its place in our schedule of responsibilities, and is in the end the key to our prospects of discharging these.

Why, then, do we need to know why politics occurs at all in order to decide what it really is or grasp why it takes the forms which it now does? We need to do so, essentially, because we need to select a strategy for addressing both of these questions. Only a clear and well-founded conception of why politics occurs at all can give us a strategy of any power for answering the first of them; and only a convincing answer to the first can give us the chance to identify a well-founded answer to the second. There is a structure of analytic priority between these three questions, and it is unobvious and somewhat counterintuitive. In this book, I try to formulate answers to each of these questions and to show these answers in action in relation to one another. Each of these answers could certainly be false (misinformed, misconceived, irredeemably muddled). But none of them, taken free-standing and on their own, could simply be true or valid. (If anyone volunteers to tell you what politics just *is*, disbelieve them without hesitation.)

Their claim is not to be *correct* (to carry epistemic authority), either prior to or in the aftermath of experience. It is merely to be useful: to aid in understanding something important and intractably there. That claim every reader who reads the book through can, must and unquestionably will judge for themselves. If they decide against it, that will be that. The claim simply falls (at least for them; and for them, that must be what matters). I don't, of course, mean that they must be right in rejecting my arguments – that they, or you, or any of us, are guaranteed to display perfect judgment. I only mean that, when it comes to understanding, each of us can only understand (or fail to understand) for ourselves. I can only hope that some of you will find that the book does help you to understand and, in this simple respect, that it is indeed useful.

Why Is There Politics at All? Four Answers

ORIGINAL SIN OR MORAL ERROR

Why is there politics at all? Why does it (or anything like it) occur? Many answers have been given to this question. Let us consider some of the more impressive and interesting. One is that that there is a way in which human beings should behave but in which most of them conspicuously fail to. You might call it the theory of original sin or, less hectically, the theory of moral error. Humans are very apt to be bad, or in more censorious eyes to be very bad indeed.

Almost anyone would agree that if there is indeed a clear and well-specified way in which human beings ought to behave, most of them lamentably fail to follow it, and very many give little, if any, sign of recognizing what it is. They deviate from the straight and narrow, do what they ought not to do, and there is little health in them. Not only do they behave badly: their bad behaviour is often linked directly to how they feel, and their feelings often appear not merely unedifying, but also very ugly. Politics, in this view, stems from human misbehaviour (of which there has always been, and will no doubt always continue to be, plenty). All this clashes discomfitingly with the terms of modern democratic belief systems, in which all adults are assumed to be entitled to behave as they feel inclined, at least within the scope of their incomes and the constraints of public law, and insofar as they refrain from damaging the opportunities for their fellow citizens to do likewise. But in this clash, for the present, it is still probably true that at least in European countries the older and essentially pre-democratic theme reaches deeper into the individual psyche than its younger rival. Despite Nietzsche's efforts, many of us still have a lot of guilt. Perhaps this is a disadvantage for you and me; but I doubt if any of us has much reason to regret it in most of our contemporaries.

There are two main limitations to this answer. The first (and analytically more immediate) is that it is unconvincing even on its own terms. If there were indeed a single coherent way in which human beings ought to behave and they all always punctiliously adhered to it, then politics (like most of human life) would certainly be very different from the way it is today. It is far from clear, however, that there would be no politics. If the humans who conformed to the one true Way with care and dependability were still recognizably human, they would certainly be more trustworthy than most of their current counterparts. But they would still face many decisions about what to do. They would take these decisions for themselves and have to cope with the consequences of one another's decisions. It is inherently unlikely, even if they always agreed on what to value and what goals to pursue, that they would also invariably agree on how best to act to realize these values, or attain these goals, in practice. Insofar as they thought, saw or felt differently about how to do so, they would disagree too in practical judgment: disagree about what is to be done, and need to decide yet again how to handle these clashes in judgment. Some of politics, certainly, comes from human depravity. (Think of the fates of Bosnia or Burundi: Lemarchand 1996.) But some, too, comes from discrepancies in practical judgment: disagreements on what is to be done to reach even the best agreed goals.

The second grave limitation of the theory of original sin (or moral error) is politically more fatal, though analytically less decisive. It could be expressed in many different ways. But one increasingly natural way of putting it is simply to say that it has become steadily harder to believe that the theory itself is literally true. It may, for many, have lost little in metaphysical resonance or rhetorical force. But few today can still contrive both to see it clearly and to believe it. That human beings are often very bad is an evident truth of experience; and no sane observer could doubt its political relevance. What is hard for us to make sense of is the view that there is a single coherent way for them to be good, and that this is a way which they all knowably have good reason to adopt. (Compare John Locke's famous affirmation that 'The candle of the Lord which is set up in us shines bright enough for all our purposes': Locke 1975, I, i, 5; p. 46; Dunn 1989(b).) I doubt myself whether this view can even be expressed coherently any longer; and I am quite certain that no possible expression of it could still reasonably hope to win universal assent. The view that there is such a way of acting has been strongly linked historically to the perception of the world as a whole (and of human beings within it) as fully under the sway of a single unified and directing moral intelligence. Without that link, it carries little credibility and perhaps barely even makes sense. The theory of original sin (or moral error) can explain some but not all of politics, and may not even explain the parts which it does cover in a very illuminating way. But for us and our potential successors its fatal weakness is not its limited explanatory scope or precision, but our increasingly strong grounds for supposing that it simply is not true. Human beings (*all* human beings?) are strongly inclined to behave very badly: some, of course, worse than others. The reasons why they feel so inclined (and act on their inclinations) may often involve failures in apprehension – in imagining exactly what it is that they really are doing. But we have no reason whatever to believe that there is a single way of acting which, if only they saw straight and had themselves fully in hand, they would have no option but to adopt. This is still a central myth of our culture, as of many others. But that does not make it true. It is not a reasonable belief about human beings as a type of animal (cf. Runciman 1998) that all of them are as a matter of fact capable of seeing consistently straight or keeping themselves permanently in hand. Try, if you doubt me, to see if you can believe that you have these capacities yourself.

And even if it were, how would we set about determining what it is to see consistently straight? Which of us is equipped to judge dependably? Whom can we trust to do so on our behalf when we ourselves have the misfortune to be in error? How can we tell when we *are* in error, and need to defer to judgments more reliable than our own? The great question in politics, as John Locke painstakingly explained, following, among many others, Plato, is: 'Who is to be Judge?' (Locke 1988).

The theory of original sin states that it is the aberrations of human passions and the distortions of judgment that these passions prompt which lead to the massive weight of crime and folly in human history. So, indeed, they rather obviously do. The less drastic theory of moral error presumes either that the passions in question could in principle often or always have a less malign outcome, or that the judgments which govern them or result from them might always be free from such distortion, or that sounder judgments could either harness more beneficial passions or subordinate the former dependably to the latter.

In its classic theological form, the theory of original sin is radically despondent. It presumes human beings to be profoundly corrupt and their corruption to be beyond human remedy. But the theory of moral error is far less pessimistic. It presumes, with varying confidence and precision, that humans could, if only they wished to, act far better, and that if they do not wish to, the fault is no one's but theirs. Both attribute much of the worst of politics (perhaps even all that is genuinely bad within it) firmly to human nature. But the first sees human nature grimly as fate; and the second sees it, more charitably, and perhaps more energizingly, as a site of continuing and real choice. It may accept the existence of (or even confidently predict) patterns in these choices; but it has no doubt that the choice in question is always entirely real.

As explanations of why politics occurs at all, both the theory of original sin and the less perturbing, and perhaps now less alien, theory of moral error are versions of a general theory of human nature. We have politics because we are human beings: because of the sort of creature (animal) that we are: because of what we are *like*. (A modern version of the viewpoint is the human application of the academic discipine of sociobiology: as yet pretty uninstructive on political matters.) At some level this certainly must be right. The question is how much, if anything, it really tells us about why politics occurs at all. In the last century and a half many thinkers (including, for example, Karl Marx and Michel Foucault) have claimed that it tells us literally nothing, because human beings have no definite nature (aren't really like anything in particular). This seems a shade extreme. It is not in general hard to distinguish humans from other animals. Their intelligence and social gifts – above all, as Aristotle pointed out (Aristotle 1932, 1253a, p.10), their gift of speech: the capacity to express themselves in language – make them in many ways markedly unlike every other animal. (Just *how* unlike? We do not yet really know. Some animals prove to be much better than expected at learning human languages and even at counting. Many types of animals, birds and even insects communicate extensively with their fellows and some modulate their behaviour very elaborately through doing so. We can be pretty certain that there are many more continuities than we have yet contrived to notice.) But the central sceptical objection that we know human beings to differ astonishingly from one another, across time, space, culture and occupation, remains extremely powerful. Since the forms which politics takes at particular times and in particular places are marked so strongly by this unimaginable range of differentiation, it will not be easy to see, underneath or within it, clear and stable structures, either in human agents or in their situations, which pervade it in its entirety and explain accurately why all of them have politics at all.

CONFLICT OF INTERESTS

Let us consider three other very different answers to this question. The first is that politics occurs among human beings because of, and only because of, historically created conflicts of interest between them. On this view, of which the most important exponent was Karl Marx, there once was a time (call it primitive communism) when there were no grave conflicts of interest between human beings. There will or may once again come a time when there are no grave conflicts of interest between human beings (call it full communism). In these two (in most ways so very different) times there was or will be no politics. Politics, accordingly, is not an inevitable product of a given human nature. It has come about in history and will or may pass away in history.

But in the lengthy meantime what it comes from and expresses harshly and durably is the deep clash between what is to the advantage of one group of human beings and what is to the advantage of another in the most fundamental practical activities of their lives.

Here it is important to be extremely careful. This is an approach which can (and often does) offer great explanatory power. It makes the clearest and most vivid sense of many particular conflicts. It can often show, in a steady hand, just why we have many of the sorts of political conflicts and solidarities which we do. On its own terms, too, it explains with some ease just why politics occurs at all. Politics appears, it claims, where the main contours of collective social and economic life set the principal interests of groups of human beings against one another: where fundamental human interests conflict deeply, predictably and durably. Where they do not so conflict, politics will not occur. This last judgment may not be correct. (I do not myself believe that it is.) But it *might* be correct; and if it were, its exponents could reasonably hope to find themselves able to explain not just why humans have politics at all, but also why the politics they now have, and have had in the past, has developed just as it has. In Marx's own version of the viewpoint, the interests which groups of human beings have arise above all from the ways in which they take part in producing; and production itself is shaped by the inherent dynamism of human powers. This is a bold and exciting theory (Lichtheim 1961; Kolakowski 1978), even if it may be hard (or impossible) to render it completely clear (Elster 1985; Cohen 1978). It has certainly prompted many of its exponents to disastrous misjudgments about the near future (Kolakowski 1978; Dunn 1984(a) and 1989(a); Harding in Dunn (ed.) 1992). But that might be at least as much their own fault as it is the fault of the theory itself.

Its principal limitation as an instrument of explanation is closely related to its main merit as an approach to explaining the historical contours of politics at different times and in different places. What makes it historically and politically illuminating is its diffuse suggestiveness – its radical openness to historical and political variety.

What limits its explanatory power is the vagueness or implausibility of its key assumptions. (In each instance, in my view, they can be vague and plausible, or clear and implausible.) In particular its conception of the nature of human interests is inappropriately clear-cut and rigid. The clarity sounds a clear intellectual advantage; but the rigidity offsets any gain which might result from this by its resolute insensitivity to the human propensities for fantasy, to the vagaries of our attention and to the unpleasant conspiracy between these features and their clever and energetic manipulation by those who hope to gain power from doing so. (Cf. Pascal 1962, 103, pp. 63–4.)

It is not hard to find apparent structural oppositions of interest between groups of human beings who interact extensively with one another: between, for example, masters and slaves, feudal lords and their serfs, capitalists and workers, perhaps in many instances even men and women, or the old, the young and the middle-aged. In every instance, however, the clarity of even these relatively stark oppositions depends upon causal judgments of how matters might otherwise be, about what exactly would have to be different if they were to be transformed into commonalities of interest, and about how reasonable it is to hope, and under what circumstances, for that transformation to occur. Because judgments of interest depend upon extraordinarily complicated and hazardous causal judgments, they are ineliminably controversial. (Not only will they provoke bitter quarrels. It is quite unclear how many of them can be settled decisively, even by the most careful and detached reasoning or the most painstaking inquiry. No wonder our judgments differ so widely.) Such conflicts cannot therefore ever be decided with authority once and for all, even if some (over the relations between master and slave, for example) eventually pass so solidly into history that it becomes hard to see where the need for judgment could have arisen. Even in this case, a little historical inquiry brings out how very hard-won such belated clarity has been (Garnsey 1996; Davis 1966 and 1984; Jordan 1968; Tuck 1999; Cohen 1997).

What cannot ever be adjudicated with authority once and for

all cannot hope to serve as a trustworthy instrument of final and external understanding – especially understanding of such an unstable and conflictual field as politics. On a sceptical view, there is no determinate and reliable answer, even from my own point of view, as to what exactly is in my interest: still less any reliable means for me to ascertain just what is in the interest of anyone else. We can, to be sure, make plenty of confident negative judgments. It is unlikely ever to have been in the interest of most chattel slaves to be slaves rather than free citizens. But positive judgments (the ones which we would need to pin the field of human interests firmly down) are inherently hazardous. There is something to this second answer to the question of why politics occurs at all. But it is too slippery, and in the end too inconclusive, to serve our needs on its own. In the end its key underlying weakness (epistemic as much as political) is that what the interests of any human being really are is a first-order political judgment in itself.

PARTIALITY IN JUDGMENT

What then of the other two varieties of answer? What hope is there that either or both of them may serve us better? The third answer turns not on the objective relations between human interests (what will be determinately there, if and only if human interests themselves are determinate in the first place), but rather on the force and idiosyncrasy of human judgment.

We may doubt that humans do have clear and indisputable interests. But we can scarcely doubt that the great majority of them judge their interests for themselves and take their own judgments with the utmost seriousness. This does not, of course, imply that nothing external to us affects these judgments, or that most of us have much insight into why we judge as we do. Still less that most of us are wise to feel such complacency about the quality of our own judgment.

It is not solely in assessing their own interests that most human beings take their judgments all too seriously. Over every issue of what is of value or what is to be done humans may choose to judge for themselves (with, to be sure, widely varying courage, inanity and incisiveness). Most attach great significance to the judgments which they do make, and fiercely resent the scorning of these by their fellows. Most side intuitively with themselves; and many pride themselves explicitly on the quality of their own judgments. For the most part, too, they take a distinctly less sanguine view of the quality of judgment displayed by their fellows, and are inclined to attribute the main deficiencies which they detect there largely to failure of character. (Compare, for example, in a work by a prominent modern social scientist, Gellner 1998.)

Human partiality is all but universal, keenly motivating, and productive of endless mutual enmity. But, even in the case of the nicer among our human fellows, those whose character is untainted by conceit, self-regard or condescension towards others, clashes in judgment remain important. If they believe a particular action to be wrong, or a particular line of conduct to be prospectively disastrous in its consequences for others as well as for the agent herself, the most saintly and selfless of persons has every reason to press their judgment with some vehemence.

Partiality, therefore, is no prerogative of the ludicrously self-satisfied. In their strong forms the theories of original sin or moral error volunteer to undercut explanation through human partiality, attributing the latter in effect to pride, and hence to culpable departure from the knowably good, induced by the corrupting impact of pride (or other dubious passions) upon the judgment. In their strong forms, however, each of these theories requires us to believe too much. We do not need to explain human partiality from below (at a supposedly more fundamental level) to recognize that it is there. It establishes its own presence all too effectively by direct experience; and very palpable features of human beings explain both its presence and its motivational weight, and do so all too readily. (The sociobiological explanation of human partiality, in contrast to the perspective of natural law (Dunn 1969 and 1989(b)), would be the same as, not the opposite of, its explanation of human intelligence.)

It is the intricacy of the context in which human beings act (social, economic, cultural, intellectual, political), and the complexity of the judgments on how to respond appropriately which that intricacy imposes upon them, which force human beings to take their own judgments so seriously. (Much of that intricacy, and much of the consequent complexity of the judgments for which it calls, comes needless to say from one another.) Neither intricacy of context nor complexity of judgments need render them smug about these judgments; and in the more diffident (and perhaps the nicer) it sometimes makes them humble and docile, eager to take the judgment of valued others for their own. But only the terminally diffident have literally no judgment of their own, while the more confident (who are also often the more determined) clash repeatedly and irritably with the very different judgments of many of their fellows. Politics (the civic experience unsentimentally considered: cf. Hobbes 1983) is saturated with these conflicts of judgment. Much of its bite, animus and sheer danger comes directly from that saturation. When human beings disagree deeply about what is good or evil, just or unjust, it is easy for them to take their disagreements all too seriously. Such disagreement may be a distinctively human activity (as far as we know, it is: cf. Taylor 1989, caps 1 and 2; Hobbes 1983). It may call on some of the grandest of human powers, but it certainly also calls on some of the most dangerous. It is characteristic of human beings to disagree deeply, sooner or later, on what is to be done and why (Hobbes 1983; Lenin 1970), and on how their societies ought to be: on, for example, who should rule, who should obey whom, who should own what. These disagreements can be, and often are, intensely felt. Collision in judgment, one can see by direct inspection, is the source as well as the site of much of politics. In the dominant world view of our own epoch, it is hard to see how such conflict in judgment could be eliminated, and far from easy, all too often, to see how it can readily be kept within acceptable bounds. The core of modern political thinking is a sustained reflection on just how and where (if at all) these conflicts in judgment can safely be contained.

THE LOGIC OF COLLECTIVE ACTION

The fourth answer to the question why politics occurs at all is less direct, less striking, but at least equally important. It is that politics comes from, and is endlessly reproduced by, the logical relations between actual and possible human actions. It is a product of the fact that human beings increasingly need to act collectively and on an ever larger scale, yet remain irreducibly individual. They remain individual both physically as agents (creatures who can alter the world through their own deliberate movements) and mentally in their reasons for acting as they do. The first individuality can reasonably be seen as primarily a fact about their bodies; but the second is plainly more decisively a fact about their minds (Williams 1981). The logic of collective action is a relatively modern preoccupation, though aspects of it were isolated by the French revolutionary Condorcet and even the great seventeenth-century French religious writer Blaise Pascal.

In the last half-century it has become the focus of extremely sophisticated formal analysis, above all through the application of a branch of mathematics known as the theory of games. This sophistication is not simply gratuitous. Very complicated relations between choices can be expressed accurately through this analytical apparatus, and can probably only be understood with real clarity and precision through its application. But it is much less clear so far how much the gains in analytical precision made possible by the development of the theory of games have really enhanced anyone's understanding of politics as this actually occurs, in all its clumsiness, confusion and opacity to direct observation. What was John Major really doing while he was Prime Minister? Did even he really know? What has Mr Yeltsin been doing since he first became President? A better answer in each case than any which could readily be expressed through the theory of games may simply be: hanging on for dear life.

The key perception drawn from the theory of games for political understanding is blindingly simple: that there are many circumstances in which an outcome clearly to the advantage of most or all concerned is blocked more or less conclusively by the fact that each, in their turn, has better reason to act in a way which will prevent it than they do to act in a way which will leave it still possible. All this can arise, of course, only in circumstances in which none can simply ensure it by acting all on their own. But such conditions, fortunately or unfortunately, are far commoner in politics than the apparently happier case. The best-known example analysed by the theory of games is the famous Prisoner's Dilemma (Hardin 1982, esp. 22–30).

We certainly need to take this source of politics and its frustrations very seriously indeed. But we also need, from the outset, to keep our heads and refuse to make a fetish out of the powerful technique of analysis which has been used so extensively to interpret it. Above all, we need to make sure that our focus upon it really is assisting us to understand politics better and not merely diverting our attention to elegant formal structures which require high intelligence for their mastery but in themselves provide no guarantee whatever of showing us anything at all about the political world in action.

The Centrality of Rule and its Sources

The least controversial feature of Aristotle's diagnosis of what politics really is, we have already noted, is that it is inherently concerned with rule (cf. Finer 1997), and how this can be made better or worse, juster or more unjust. And what *is* rule? Above all, compelling large numbers of human beings more or less systematically to act as they would not otherwise be inclined, whether or not to their own net advantage. Today, as the late Sammy Finer shows so well, there is far more rule than there used to be: so much more that he even doubts whether any population was really ruled in the modern way much before the nineteenth century (Finer 1997, 685).

ASSIGNING THE BLAME

There is one point to note at the outset about the three (non-moralizing) interpretations of the ultimate sources of politics which we have considered. Each answer to the question of why politics occurs at all offers a distinctive approach to the question of why there is such a thing as rule in the human world. The view that politics arises from (and only from) persisting structural conflicts between human interests attributes rule in practice to the defence of the interests of some (the powerful) against those of others (the weak). Marx may have been the most notorious and relentless advocate of this viewpoint; but it is at least equally well expressed by Adam Smith (Smith 1976, V, i, b, p. 715: 'Civil government, so far as it is instituted for the security of property, is in reality instituted for the defence of the rich against the poor, or of those who have some property against those who have none at all.')

If the structural conflicts between human interests in their turn derive, as both Marx and Smith supposed, from the ways in which they organize the production of goods and services, then the most important question about politics at any time must be how much real discretion a given group of human beings has over just how it organizes its production of goods and services. The huge significance of this question has been weighing more heavily on human imaginations for several centuries (Dunn (ed.) 1990). Over this timespan the balance of educated judgment has moved fairly steadily towards the conclusion that, for one reason or another, they have very little discretion indeed. (There has been far wider oscillation over just where that discretion is thought to lie.) In itself this movement is somewhat surprising, since the judgment in question cannot in principle be true. The individuality of human agency is a palpable biological fact and cannot coherently be denied from any potentially instructive viewpoint. Even if it is true, as it presumably must be, that all human action is comprehensively caused, there is no possibility in principle that humans will ever become aware of exactly how it is being caused at the time in question, whether in their own or in anyone else's case. At present, despite several centuries of intellectual bravado, they really do not have the foggiest idea of how virtually any of it is caused.

Since humans all choose freely all the time, one by one, there is no concretely imaginable limit to what they might collectively elect to do over time. But, of course, very many of the actions which they might conceivably choose to perform (like many of those which they have performed already) it would be completely demented of them to select in practice. A great deal of the understanding of modern politics consists in seeing why exactly it is that human beings today feel so effectively discouraged from even attempting bold and optimistic reorganization of the ways in which they produce goods and services: why they feel increasingly hemmed in in the main structures of their working lives and in the systems of ownership and control on which these structures depend (Dunn 1984(a)). (Hemmed in enough to elect politicians eager to compel them to draw these bonds still tighter, and increasingly uninterested in bothering even to garland them with flowers: cf. Rousseau 1964, 31 (1986, 4–5).)

RULE AND STRUCTURAL CONFLICTS OF INTEREST

The view which attributes politics to structural conflicts of interest must be understood at two levels. The first identifies the structural relation between the interests so opposed and the socio-economic or political setting in which these interests are located. The second (and deeper) level explains why that setting is as it now is, what has historically created it, and what now sustains it. In Marx's view, as in that of Adam Smith from which it largely derived (Meek 1976), what historically creates such a setting, and sustains it for as long as it proves sustainable, is above all the effectiveness with which it musters and deploys human productive powers. Ineffective productive structures succumb over time to more effective successors. They do so, characteristically, through violent and initially destructive conflict, and in some confusion. But seen over time, or in the calm of hindsight, their succession is remarkably insistent. It remains intensely contentious how (or indeed whether) this viewpoint can be expressed briefly, clearly and accurately. It also remains controversial how far the viewpoint itself is even broadly valid. It sounds surprisingly optimistic to the late-twentieth-century ear.

We do not need to try to settle either of these questions here. (Just as well.) But we do need to notice one feature of the viewpoint. Even if the viewpoint itself is essentially valid, its political implications depend decisively on whether there is or is not a clearly superior way of organizing production, a structure of ownership, work disposition and political control, through which that production can be sustained and enhanced, which is within the reach of a particular community at the time. It is the historical sequence in ways of organizing production (essentially from the less productive to the more) which is presumed to show that the structural conflicts between human interests on which they have all been founded (and which were in their time necessary for the communities in question) are necessary no longer. Structural conflicts of interest which are no longer necessary can no longer be readily excused. Because they cannot readily be excused, they also become far harder to defend in political practice: to protect against the energy and anger of their victims. No one now alive can sincerely believe that chattel slavery is a prerequisite for civilized life. Even serfdom has largely lost its social or economic plausibility. Unfree labour of a less legally explicit kind, however, still plays a very prominent role in many poor countries; and there is increasing imaginative and political pressure to view the division of labour between men and women inside households in the wealthiest of societies today as still resting on somewhat more discreet exactions of at best semi-voluntary labour.

A century and a half ago many were already convinced that the private ownership of capital was just as dispensable in an effectively working modern economy as chattel slavery or serfdom (Lichtheim 1969). The political and economic history of the twentieth century has been largely devoted to exploring whether they were right (thus far, with extremely discouraging results). If they were (and are) right, an economic, social and political order resting on the private ownership of capital is certain eventually to succumb. But, until we know that they are right or it does durably succumb, the view that a regime of private ownership of the means of production is now gratuitous (and so indefensible) remains a somewhat reckless leap of faith (cf. Przeworski 1985); and the view that, clearly understood, there are ultimate and internally irresolvable structural conflicts of interest between owners of capital and those who own only their labour remains unconvincing (true perhaps in much of what it points to, but dangerously false in what it strongly suggests). Few sincerely doubt that it is more convenient to be rich than poor, to enjoy a wider and less forbidding range of options than a narrower and grimmer range. But the main weight of judgments of structural conflict of interest cannot rest on the relative advantage of finding oneself at one point rather than another in the distribution of opportunities within them. It must rest on the assessment of whether or not the practices as a whole are or are not to the collective benefit of all their participants (cf. Rawls 1972), and above all on whether they could readily be replaced by others of palpably greater collective advantage.

The view which attributes politics solely to the existence of deep structural conflicts of interest is at its most plausible when it sees rule as the essence of politics, and especially so when it has in mind not rule between free and equal persons, but rule among the conspicuously unequal: rule of the palpably more free over the unmistakably less so. Where production does not require such sharp inequalities, it argues, there will be no comparably fundamental need for rule; and where there is no fundamental need for rule, rule itself will in due course wither away, disappear sheepishly from the human scene. We have seen at least two strong reasons for doubting that this cheery expectation is correct. But even if it is hopelessly misguided, there is no reason why the more despondent judgment of the basis of rule today should not be largely valid. Even if, to speak crudely, there is no practical alternative to capitalist production which is not manifestly inferior to this from a human point of view, it is hard (or, more probably, impossible) to avoid a capitalist society's distributing opportunities among its human members with such blatant capriciousness and insensitivity as to require a considerable amount of rule to keep it in working order. This is accepted, not challenged, by capitalism's clearer-headed and soberer champions (Hont and Ignatieff (eds) 1983, Introduction; Hont 1990; Hundert 1993; Gamble 1996).

Since this rule will be (and will be widely seen to be) very much the rule of some over others, of stronger and wealthier over weaker and poorer, it is most unlikely that the denizens of such a society will acknowledge that, for them, rule occurs solely between free and equal persons. Whatever the institutional apparatus of rule, many of them (and especially many of those who are plainly playing no active part whatever in ruling) will find it impossible to believe themselves either effectively equal to or as free as those who plainly benefit more directly and more handsomely from the ways in which economy and society work, or those who play a conspicuously more active part in the activity of ruling. (One important reason why some do not see politics as a field of *activity* is that being ruled can be an exceedingly passive experience.)

The view that politics in the societies to which we belong derives from, and expresses, a structural conflict of interest at the very core of these societies may not be analytically stable, or entirely clear under close consideration. But it is certain to continue to carry a considerable weight of social (and hence political) plausibility. As an all but universal perception within politics, if not as a dispassionate analytical judgment poised steadily somehow *above* politics, the view that politics for us still turns on massive structural conflicts of interest can be expected to endure for some time.

If rule derived exclusively from structural conflicts of interest which, in turn, derive (at least now or in the very near future) from organizing our economies in ways which we no longer need to, then it would be reasonable to hope that rule will pass away. It would also be reasonable at least to entertain the possibility of acting with some vigour to speed its passing. (The role of midwife was offered by Marx as an appropriate model for political actors in such a setting. To ease the birthpangs of history would be a generous and rewarding task. But to officiate at the outcome of a hysterical pregnancy has proved understandably less fulfilling

(Harding in Dunn (ed.) 1992).) It is easy to see that a theory which attributes the presence of rule to (now) avoidable structural conflicts of interest has implications for the attitudes we have reason to adopt towards the place of rule in human societies. They are markedly more optimistic than the implications of the other three theories we have briefly considered: the theory of original sin, the theory of individual self-righteous judgment (at individual or group level), and the theory of collective action. Unlike these, they promise an eventual end to politics, or at least a transformation which purges it utterly of every trace of rule and leaves it barely recognizable: hard to distinguish from the practice of moral philosophy or the pursuit of the least fraught forms of conversation. (There is a suspiciously close relation, from Plato in fourth-century BC Greece to Jürgen Habermas in contemporary Germany, between exponents of higher education and those who find this point of view compelling.)

For the moment all we need to bear in mind is that the weight of this promise to end politics falls squarely on the accuracy of its identification of an equally (or more) effective organization of production which is devoid of internal structural conflicts of interest, and which can readily be installed. Whether or not this idea can even be coherently formulated, which has yet to be settled one way or the other, the accessibility in practice of the outcome it envisages has so far proved a mirage. For the present, if we wish to understand politics, we are forced back, whether we care for it or not, to the other three broad theories (or families of theories) which we have so far considered. Structural conflicts of interest, apparent and real, remain of immense importance *within* politics; but the idea of a human world devoid of such conflicts has no clear and stable role to play in *explaining* existing political structures or conjunctures.

RULE AND ORIGINAL SIN

The first of our remaining three theories, the theory of original sin (or, less hectically, of moral error), gives the boldest and most implacable explanation of why there is rule in human societies at all. Humans need rule because none of them is fit to be free (Maistre 1994), or, more calmly, they need rule because any of them may always act very badly indeed. Rule is an activity in which, at best, some of the worse aspects of human nature are successfully subordinated to some of the less bad. At all events, it is an activity in which some of the very worst aspects of that nature are kept minimally at bay. Rule is above all the enforcement of law; and law is, among other things, the systematic spelling out of how it is or is not permissible for human beings in a given setting to behave towards one another.

Between human societies, the worst aspects of human nature are far harder to restrain. Law is less prominent, less definite in its sources, and in most domains for the most part still less likely to be enforced. Here, all too often, because there is not (or cannot be) rule, there is war instead: a perception which played a dynamic role in forming modern conceptions of the nature of politics (Tuck 1999).

The balance between the worse and the less bad elements in human psyches may vary somewhat over time and space. It may even vary through what it is natural to see as the initiatives and efforts of other human beings, from natural parents and siblings, through to rulers, priests, prophets or even United Nations officials. In the more secular variant of the theory, the skilful design of human institutions (their neat adjustment to the realities of human untrustworthiness, ingenuity, cruelty and greed) can even make some modest headway in keeping the worst dependably at bay. (For a notably sceptical example see Hundert 1993.) The history of government is neither aesthetically exhilarating nor spiritually inspiring; but it may nevertheless contribute immensely to the enhancing of human life (Forbes 1975; Finer 1997). The theory of original sin views human nature with alarm, perhaps even panic. It has no difficulty whatever in explaining why government is needed, and is distinctly relieved to find government present wherever it proves to be so (cf. Hobbes 1991). Where the theory does have difficulty is in explaining just why government should be present on any particular occasion, or in indicating why the aspects of human nature which make it so imperative on the demand side do not also render it prohibitively dangerous on the supply side (Locke 1988; Dunn 1996(a), cap. 4). If humans really do pose such hideous dangers to one another, why do those of them who can coerce their fellows wholesale and without impediment not represent a far worse danger than any less powerful competitors? This is a very serious question. It is not clear that it has any general answer which is both valid and at all encouraging. But a very large proportion of modern political thought, from Kant, Sieyès, Constant and Hegel to Bentham, John Stuart Mill, Tocqueville and even Hayek, is in a sense an attempt to answer it.

The theory of original sin (even the theory of moral error) may not be literally true. But both theories pick out components of politics which still matter (and are likely always to matter) very gravely indeed. As we have seen, the theory of original sin attributes these components essentially to two interconnected features of human agents: their motives (the impulses which goad them to act as they do) and their judgment (the ways in which these motives control and distort their assessment of how they have good reason to act). The theory credits human beings, as these now exist, with very unpleasant impulses: anger, pride, cruelty (Shklar 1984), greed, hardness of heart and the will to dominate one another (what St Augustine called the *libido dominandi*). In their cradles, as John Locke says, 'they cry for dominion'. Something of the kind certainly appears to be true. But then, of course, they also need a prodigious deal of help: and how else can they hope to get it?

Our very ordinary vices more than suffice to ensure that the human world is often very ugly indeed. Those who resist the theory of original sin, who find it imaginatively repulsive or simply ludicrous, do not necessarily see a wholly different creature. They merely focus on somewhat different aspects of that creature's performance: on the degree, in particular, to which its performance is never fully externally imposed upon it, and could always in principle (at least after a certain age) be modified by its own choices. This is the key contrast between the classic theory of original sin and the more etiolated modern theory of moral error. The former explains the squalor of human performance in the end by something external to, and plainly beyond the causal reach of, the members of the species itself. The latter attributes it unflinchingly over time to an endless sequence of choices firmly located within that reach. The two theories need not diverge at all in their predictions; but they differ quite fundamentally in their attitudes towards the species as a whole. The theory of moral error places the responsibility (and hence the blame) for human squalor fully on humans themselves. For its exponents, it has been literally true that each adult human being who has not been terminally damaged could always have behaved differently; and for as long as there remain human beings, it will always remain true that almost all of them could behave better than they actually will. While there is history, there is hope (also, of course, and for the same reasons, fear). For the theory of original sin, by contrast, any hope there might or may be for humans must lie outside human history (after it, above it, beyond it: in some quite other type of power and will and agency).

In each of its two main versions, this theory has major weaknesses. In its full-blown theological variant, it assumes a degree of shape and determinacy of meaning in human experience which there is no surviving reason for most humans to credit: a way the human world simply ought to be, which no one today has publicly defensible grounds for supposing. It is radically insecure in its very foundations. But even in its more tentative and secular version (of which the greatest modern exemplar was the eighteenth-century German philosopher Immanuel Kant) it makes one heroic assumption: that human choice is not fundamentally an illusion. What we experience in choosing – doubt, deliberation, even some degree of moral anxiety – really is the way it seems to be. We really are agents. We do act for, and as, ourselves. It is true that we always could have acted otherwise than we did and can always act otherwise than we in fact will. Human beings are plainly subject to fate. They are born, they sicken, they suffer or rejoice, they die. But they do not simply consist of fate. They make their own lives, even if conspicuously not in circumstances of their own choosing. It is hard to resist the sense that there is something profoundly right in this vision. But it has proved extremely hard to identify just what it is (though cf. Davidson 1980). The main limitation of each version, then, is that either may very well be false in its central assumptions. For my part, I think the first to be evidently so, if often salutary on initial encounter, and the second to be true but altogether vaguer and less instructive than it sounds. But you may judge very differently.

What makes the first potentially salutary, at least in the first instance, is the vigour of its psychological emphases: the strong colours with which it paints human nature in action. Human motives certainly matter in politics; and the ways in which they mould human judgment also matter very deeply indeed. The theory of original sin or moral error stands over against an academic programme of analytic explanation like rational choice theory, which takes humans as well-formed and inherently sensible agents. It explains, with some economy, why such programmes are virtually bound to ignore matters of the most pressing importance: why they are pre-guaranteed to misapprehend much of what drives politics or of where politics is likely to find itself driven (though cf. Hardin 1995). But if the strong colours signal something important, their standing is more rhetorical than it is scientific. Human beings are very dangerous, and often extremely nasty, animals. But the ways in which they will act cannot simply be read off even the soberest assessment of just how dangerous or nasty they are capable of being. They cannot, not merely because at least some human beings are intermittently capable of being very much nicer, but also, and more decisively, because the range of possible human action is so vast and so limitlessly intricate in variation. Almost all of politics may be compatible with the theory of original sin (literally all of it with the theory of moral error); and yet the theory of original sin, even if valid, contrives to explain very little of it. As a theory, it is too obsessive in its negative focus on the human psyche, and far too confident over the precision of its estimate of how that psyche works and how its bearers can thus be expected to behave. It is certainly of enormous political importance that human beings are so often moved to behave abominably, and that they can and frequently do act on their very worst impulses. But the force of this insight is weakly admonitory, not boldly directive. It warns of what there always may be to fear. It does not tell us what is going to happen (or even what is likely to happen), let alone what we would be best advised to do in the light of this judgment. Both because of the shakiness of its foundations and because of the inherent vagueness of its implications, the theory of original sin is far less instructive than it initially sounds. No more than the theory of structural conflict of interest can it hope to provide us, either now or in the future, with a steady intellectual instrument for the ultimate understanding of what is really going on politically at any time, or of how we would be wisest to respond to this.

How far can either of the two other theories we have noted, the theory which focuses on the self-righteous individuality of human judgment or on the logic of collective action, hope to step into the gap?

RULE AND PARTIALITY IN JUDGMENT

These two theories have markedly different shapes. Each has a lengthy history; and the history of the former plainly overlaps extensively with those of the theory of original sin or moral error. Over the last four centuries there have been a number of subtle and illuminating attempts to combine a focus on individuality of judgment with one on the logic of collective action: notably in the writings of Thomas Hobbes, Adam Smith, Immanuel Kant and Hegel. The relation is easiest to see in the pages of Hobbes (Gauthier 1969; Hampton 1986), though even there locating it accurately is far from effortless. I shall draw on each, as we move through the web of modern politics, seeking throughout to show just how it contributes to clarifying how things really are, why they have come to be as they are, and how far and in what ways it is reasonable to hope to change them for the better.

Even at this point, however, it may be helpful to say a little more about the theory which focuses on the self-righteous individuality of human judgment. A theory which focuses on the logic of action offers some immediate prospect of imaginative independence and analytical stability, of being able to take one's stand outside the seething and all too personally implicating turmoil of political conflict. One which, by contrast, chooses, not merely to focus on the individuality of judgment, but also to highlight the strong impulse to self-righteousness within the exercise of that judgment, seems all too implicated in the psychodynamics of political participation from the outset.

As we shall see, this is not a groundless suspicion. It is enough in itself to obviate Hobbes's confident project of deriving an entire strongly structured (and unflinchingly negative) conception of politics, with sharp and overwhelmingly cogent practical implications, from the drastic physical hazards which human beings can all pose to one another, and from the radical partiality of human judgment (Hobbes 1991). But it does not simply obliterate the potential instruction of Hobbes's line of thought. The recognition that humans are capable of great cruelty and hardness of heart is sometimes hideously important in politics. But it is scarcely politically instructive in itself. Human capacities are immensely varied. Everything in politics turns on which of them will be engaged when. Several thousand years of sporadic political reflection have made extremely little headway in identifying just when our worse capacities will be engaged and when they will be kept under some degree of restraint. We can make some educated guesses: more, on the whole, in wartime than in the course of peace (for why see Walzer 1978; Clausewitz 1976; Gallie 1978), more where rule is unchallenged than when its miserable victims dare to fight back (Moore 1978). But such guesses are far too vague and undependable to base any decision upon them: certainly too undependable to base on them a decision as vital as whether in the end to make war to defend a given system of rules or to fight back against oppression (cf. Dunn 1996(a), cap. 8).

Many thinkers today (following especially Macpherson 1962) assume that Hobbes's viewpoint depends for its force on peculiarities of culture or socio-economic organization: that it is crudely relative to the England or France of his day, or more slyly relative to a lengthy capitalist epoch which has reshaped the West, largely since he wrote. I do not find this judgment at all convincing. We can be confident, to be sure, that what enabled him to entertain the thoughts which he did, and develop them as he did, was, among other things, distinctive features of the intellectual culture and social, economic and political organization of the Europe of his day (Skinner 1996; Dunn 1996(a), cap. 1). But it emphatically does not follow from this that the arguments which he advanced or the conclusions which he reached have no bearing on the denizens of other cultures or of societies very much later. Critics of Hobbes who attribute his views to a distinctive (and spiritually corrupted) Western individualism, deformed by capitalism, or driven by initially unintended psychological implications elicited over time from Christian belief, contrast the Europe of Hobbes's day (and perhaps of our day) with its own presumed past, or with evaluatively more committed societies in other parts of the world. To see human judgment as inherently individual and partial, for them, is to embrace this corrupt historical condition, and turn one's back deliberately on the relative integrity and spiritual health of other forms of collective life elsewhere or at other times. For them, Hobbes was an accomplice in spiritual corruption, or at best a diagnostician of its increasingly endemic presence, while the point is to resist or reverse it (Macpherson 1962 and 1973). This is a delicate disagreement, and not prospectively resoluble in a hurry (if, indeed, at all). I shall simply state my own judgment on it tersely and dogmatically.

I do not believe that Hobbes's emphasis on the individuality (even the self-righteous individuality) of human judgment is an idiosyncratic and misguided Western misapprehension: perhaps true of us, but plainly false about other parts of the world or other times. I think it picks out a fundamental, permanent and biologically grounded feature of the human condition, which certainly can and does receive much greater cultural amplification and reinforcement in some settings than others, but which must be reckoned with wherever humans are to be found. If historians or ethnographers tell me otherwise, I disbelieve – at the very least – the hermeneutic skills (the direct human discernment) of my informants. I doubt that they have fully captured what was really going on. What can be true (and indeed palpably is) is that in some human settings, for a variety of reasons, the psychological pressures to judge one way rather than another are far more intense and painful to resist than they are in others. Both the capacity for autonomy (for judging for oneself) and the taste for autonomy vary considerably from person to person and place to place. It is entirely reasonable to think of their distribution as a causal product of the structure of different cultures, or the economic, social and political organization of different societies. But it cannot be true (and I have never seen the least reason given for supposing that it in fact is true) that there are cultures in which individual human beings simply never in any way judge for themselves: in which shared external reasons simply replace the internal reasons which all human beings always have for acting as they do (Williams 1981). But even if there could not be a human culture in which the denizens failed to judge many matters, however supinely or unreflectively, for themselves, it is both true and important (Carrithers 1992) that cultures vary greatly in how far they savour or revel in the individuality of judgment.

Here, Hobbes's brilliant books are perhaps a shade misleading even about the content of his own views. *De Cive* (1642) and *Leviathan* (1651) in particular are not best seen just as expressions of a would-be timeless truth about the human political predicament. Each also plainly responds to a keen dismay on Hobbes's part at what he saw as distinctive and acutely regrettable cultural features of the England of his day. While the political theories which they state have much in common, they focus on somewhat different targets. *De Cive* was above all a ferocious attack on the ancient concept of citizenship and on Aristotle's endorsement of the value of a politics of open public debate and committed participatory partisanship: on its irresponsible activism and feckless enthusiasm for the pleasures and exhilarations of public speech. *Leviathan*, by contrast, in the aftermath of England's dramatic Civil War, focuses principally on the political hazards of a bible-reading Commonwealth, in which, as Hobbes put it elsewhere, 'every man, nay, every boy and wench, thought they spoke with God Almighty and understood what he said' (Hobbes 1969, 21), and in which, in consequence, murderous factional quarrels about who had heard God correctly proliferated endlessly.

Hobbes's political theory, the common element of the two books, was in his judgment a sufficient remedy for each of these cultural ills (or at least it would have been if only it had been adopted by someone in a position to apply it in practice). Its targets were cultural deformations which he saw as located principally in the educational institutions of his society, and which carried dire political consequences. Hobbes was as well aware as Michel Foucault that cultures differ from one another, and that their differences can carry profound political consequences. Had he not been so, he would have had little reason to try so hard to change the culture of his own society. The will to purge a culturally induced self-righteousness has been a recurrent aspiration throughout modern Western intellectual history. It is instructive to compare the strategies which different thinkers have adopted for the purpose: Machiavelli, Hobbes, Kant, Foucault, Rawls. But culturally induced self-righteousness is no prerogative of the West. (Try discussing the future of China with any educated Chinese woman or man.) Hobbes was right, I am presuming, to see the potentiality for self-righteousness as inherent in the individuality of human judgment (compare Charles Taylor's analysis of 'strong evaluation': Taylor 1989, caps 1 and 2), and each of these features as of enormous political importance. But he was equally right to see that there is great cultural variation in how far this individuality is intensified or buffered by the cultures within which human beings form their judgments and learn to understand their social, political and economic worlds. It is a very important (and obscure) question about modern politics how far he was right to view the deliberate cultural intensification of individuality of judgment and its political expression (the fostering of autonomy) with such visceral political hostility, and how far we are right to view the same phenomena so much more blithely (not to say smugly). One way, for example, of seeing what is really at stake in the contemporary academic quarrel between philosophical proponents of liberalism and communitarians, and perhaps also in the grittier encounter between one wing of the American Republican Party and most of the Democrats is to see these as divisions over whether Hobbes or contemporary bien-pensant opinion shows sounder political judgment. (Both, of course, in either case, may well be hopelessly in error.)

THE ARISTOTELIAN AGENDA: THE CENTRALITY OF HUMAN VALUE

To understand politics, Aristotle was confident, we need above all to analyse how human beings are best advised to live together, in order both to judge how their common life could go best and to give it the best chance which they can to go well in practice. (These two objectives, as we shall see, can readily pull us in very different directions.) In public political profession, across the states of the modern world, this vision of Aristotle's is still very prominently avowed, if not usually either as a consequence of any effort of his or with any direct acknowledgment to him. But, widespread though the viewpoint remains, it can readily nowadays appear intellectually pretty callow. What makes it seem so is the pivotal role which it assigns to human evaluation: to what human beings care about and how they think about what they care about. Today, you might suppose, we surely know that evaluation is simply something which humans do, and do in very different ways, according to time and place and chance. It is not, and cannot now reasonably be seen as, a reflection, however faltering, of a pre-given order of value in the universe at large, external to them and in the end decisively authoritative over them. (Compare Taylor 1989 with Nussbaum 1985 and Lear 1988.) If evaluating is just one of the things which human beings do, we surely have better reason to see it as located within politics, as part of a single continuous causal field: not as a reality outside and above politics, to which the latter is conclusively answerable. Anyone who is wholly certain that this supercilious modern judgment is simply right – clear, steady and comprehensively undeceived – will inevitably regard the central strategic judgment of this book not merely as misguided but also as hopelessly out of date: both anachronistic and superstitious. In the end, you judge as you see. I see differently. I take the fact that human beings do value not as a blunt biological fact about the members of a particular species but as a key prerogative of that species, an aspect of its very special relation to the realities which surround it, and an index of its capacity in principle to respond deeply and accurately to these realities. It is important, in this view, that human beings are not merely open to depravity and folly but also capable at their best of resisting both: capable of acting well. Any vision of politics which omits these characteristics or portrays them simply as consequences of other and supposedly stabler and more fundamental properties of the members of the species will, in my judgment, deform our understanding of politics rather than enhance it. It will lead us to misjudge how we ourselves have good reason to act within and towards it, and do so with catastrophic thoroughness. Insofar as we succumb to it, it will ruin all our lives, and ruin still more dependably the social and political settings in which all human beings, from now on, will also always have to make their lives.

2

The State

Explaining and Appraising Rule

THE CENTRALITY OF RULE

Politics, for better or worse, has a special relation to rule (cf. Finer 1997). One dimension of understanding politics today (this virtually any student of politics would have to agree) is to grasp why rule now takes its present forms. A second (perhaps equally uncontroversial) would be to grasp why these forms have their current consequences. A third (as we have seen, drastically more controversial) is to grasp how far we (you, I, the people of Myanmar, Luxemburg, Indonesia, Brazil, Tibet and so on) have good reason to appreciate or regret the consequences that rule now has for us, and how far we may reasonably hope to alter these for the better. To take the three dimensions together, to bear each in mind in considering the other, is to adopt an Aristotelian approach, to conceive politics in ways discernibly connected to those in which Aristotle himself envisaged it.

If we proceed in this order, we begin with a problem of explanation. Why, for example, is there so *much* rule in the world today? Why does it often extend over such large territories and over so many people? Why does it occur to such a large degree within a common format, the legal frame of a modern state (Finer 1997)? Why, even, does it seek sanction to such a large degree (surely more than ever before in the history of human beings) through such a small family of apparently shared ideas (Dunn 1993; Dunn (ed.) 1992; Dunn 1996(a): cf. Fukuyama 1992)?

The last of these four questions is highly contentious at present, since many inhabitants of the modern world see any search for a common sanction as essentially spurious: either as patently insincere, or else as involuntary, externally imposed, and hence entirely inauthentic, a tracer of the West's imaginative imperialism or of its stunning capacity for self-deception. In any case, however sincere or inauthentic the apparent ideological commonalities of the modern world may be, even the appearances demand explanation. There is every reason, too, to suppose that a sound explanation of one of these four aspects must not only be compatible with, but also very probably illuminate, each of the others. One can approach the attempt to understand politics with the full range of human daring, from the most devastating (and prospectively suicidal) audacity to the most arrant cowardice. The more audacious and historically cosmopolitan, the ampler the opportunity for error, but the more passive and parochial, unsurprisingly, the slimmer the prospect of real illumination.

THE AMBIVALENCE OF RULE: DOMINATION AND GOVERNMENT

There are two broad ways of thinking about rule. One is detached and essentially historical: to see it as a condition engineered and sustained throughout by human action, the mustering of power by some over others, both a product and an instance of incessant struggle between human beings, a matter, in Lenin's brutal phrase, of 'Who Whom?' (Compare 'Great historical issues are resolved only by force,' cited in Harding 1977, I, 226; and 'In politics there is only one principle and one truth; what profits my opponent hurts me and vice versa,' cited in Ulam 1969, 295; see also, for example, in a very different cultural and political context, Meier 1995, 449, 483.) The second is more sympathetic and even partisan: seeing it teleologically, in terms of a goal which it serves and draws its authority from serving, the goal of aiding human beings to meet a key range of their needs. The first sees rule essentially as domination: the wilful exertion of control for its own sake, or for the benefits which can be extracted from it by those who bother to implement it. The second sees rule above all as government, as the steering of groups of human beings towards destinations at which they need to arrive and away from hazards which threaten them more or less acutely. The two ways of thinking offer starkly contrasting images of (or metaphors for) rule, in the first instance the relation between master and chattel slave (between a free agent and their effectively bound victim), in the second, that between the helmsman of a sea-going vessel and their largely dependent passengers. Each metaphor is of great antiquity. While the images differ notably in emotional tone, their practical and causal implications are not necessarily incompatible. Only a very sentimental view of government (one appreciably more sentimental than even the governors themselves are likely to manage to sustain) could see this exclusively as the service of human needs. Only an obsessively selective (perhaps virtually paranoid) vision of domination could see it as undeflected throughout by the slightest effort to provide services for anyone but itself. But the two viewpoints remain very far apart. The first sees rule as a structure of inequality, built and reproduced by strategic interaction between drastically unequal agents, and its human merit as permanently and acutely in question. The second sees government as essentially an instrument for expediting co-operation for human benefit. Not only do they offer rather disparate answers: they also address markedly different questions. (It is an important and conspicuous fact about modern politics that much struggle for power takes the form of competing claims to be able to supply benefits to large groups of people. Just how important, however, remains both hard to judge and very keenly disputed.)

The first viewpoint focuses principally on the techniques for control of human beings, and the factors which affect the practical availability of these techniques to different groups of actors. The second, more adventurously, focuses on the changing conceptions of the content of human needs over time and place, and the varying means which have become available for fulfilling these conceptions in practice. The first is more deeply and durably concerned with coercion: with making people do what they emphatically do not wish to. It broods on weapons and armies, on the facilities for finding out what the dominated are doing and for shaping their minds and dispositions (their psyches) to do as they are told (or as their rulers would wish them), and not as they might otherwise feel inclined. The second is more preoccupied with food and protection, and the provision of goods and services, with the ways in which economies do or do not work, with minimizing the dangers which groups of human beings pose to one another, and maximizing the benefits which they can hope to win from co-operating painstakingly with one another. For it, coercion is always an occasion for regret (a cost), and often also a sign of ineffectuality (a failure).

EXPLAINING THE INCIDENCE OF RULE: DEPTH, SCOPE, MODALITIES AND IDEOLOGIES

The four explanatory questions which we outlined look very different from these two viewpoints. The depth, scope, modalities and ideologies of rule all plainly require explanation from either viewpoint. They all matter. They are all unmistakably there; and none in any straightforward fashion explains itself. Each viewpoint must plainly acknowledge the force and pertinence of these questions (though it may do so with greater alacrity or reluctance). But the two viewpoints approach the task of explaining these factors in very different ways. To stylize this contrast, we may see their natural lines of approach as roughly the inverse of one another. The view of rule as systematized coercion begins by seeking to grasp why rule today should be so deep, pervasive and insistent: why it has become so hazardous or futile for us to resist rule at all comprehensively (cf. Dunbabin 1985, 277). But it must also in the end explain, with greater or less meticulousness, just why contemporary rule should be vindicated by its defenders, in the great majority of instances across the world, through such a narrow range of categories. It may not regard ideology, in the sense of publicly proffered justifications or rationales of rule, as inherently trivial or inconsequential. But it sees these as at best marginal and supplementary: an adjunct of rule, not a load-bearing element in sustaining its structure. The view of rule as principally a means for facilitating human social co-operation is more likely to start at the other end – to analyse its present historical contours through the changes over time in the services which it is able to offer (services which, naturally, remain as prominent as ever in the justifications or rationalizations which it now chooses to advance on its own behalf).

Approaching the phenomenon of rule from this angle, its principal contemporary institutional format (the modern state) can be presented as following relatively directly from the charter which it now chooses to offer for itself. The territorial and demographic scale of states in turn can be explained, with only slightly greater strain, as a prerequisite for this format to furnish these services for those who now need them. Even the depth of modern rule (its normatively queasiest aspect) can be explained, albeit with varying plausibility, as a product of the need to organize and concert deftly together the immense range of human activities, also addressed to providing services or fostering welfare for someone or other, which can only be prevented from colliding, and from frustrating one another, by a firm and mutually dependable framework of regulation. One of the two viewpoints is patently gloomier than the other. But it is less obvious whether this is a merit or a defect, a strength or a limitation. (It would not be surprising if, from different and untrivial human points of view, it turns out to be both.)

It is tempting to view the main contrast between the two viewpoints as lying between two conditions of pre-critical or inadvertent imaginative commitment. (At some level this must be the case.) But it is hard to pin down quite where that imaginative commitment occurs, or where exactly it is located. Some modern thinkers of real insight have equated the first view (the vision of rule as domination) with an approach characteristic of the natural sciences, and these sciences, in turn, with an approach in which human beings have at last escaped the limitations of their own humanity, and seen the universe and their own place within it, and their relations with one another, in ways which no longer depend on what they happen to be like as animals and how they happen to live their lives (cf. Williams 1978; Runciman 1998). It is reasonable to see a hope of roughly this kind as the inspiration behind much of the development of the social sciences (and of political science in particular) in the aftermath of the Second World War, especially in North America. The normative and teleological view of rule as facilitator of social co-operation would then be a superstitious residue, a mark of the imaginative incapacity of its all too human bearers to rise above the insistent pressures of their own hopes and fears.

The philosophical presuppositions of this view are no longer fashionable (Rorty 1979; Taylor 1985), though that alone is no reason to suppose them groundless. A more important reason for questioning this way of seeing the contrast is that each viewpoint in fact centres on human agency: on a view of what humans characteristically attempt to do. They differ, certainly, in their estimate of the goals of the agents in question, and hence in their view of what determines their choice of the actions which they decide to perform: personal power for its own sake, or the relentlessly ingenuous pursuit of collective benefits. But each specifies the outcomes which it is attempting to explain in terms of what at least some human beings steadily and predictably want, and of how they thus can be confidently expected to behave. Where they fail to do this explicitly, the conceptions with which they seek to fill in the explanatory gap (system, function) prove in practice to be analytically rescuable only if they are translated to back into terms of strategies or tactics which are reasonable for particular groups of human beings (Elster 1979, 28–34). When it comes to interpreting politics, and explaining why this takes its present form, we still have no conception of what it would be like to interpret this from a non-human (supra-human? sub-human? inhuman?) point of view. Nor has anyone yet shown why we (our particular, decisively embodied, all too human selves) should wish to do anything of the sort.

The sharpest contrast between the two viewpoints, accordingly, is not metaphysical (in what they assume about the nature of reality in general and how this can be known), but psychological (in what they assume about the characteristic purposes of rulers, or at least of those rulers whom they do not see as already irretrievably pathological). This last qualification is of some importance. You can (if you are historically fortunate) think about government, in the case of your own country and others with which you feel some sympathy, principally in terms of an effort to co-ordinate human activities for mutual benefit, without being in any way tempted to deny the record of Adolf Hitler or Pol Pot. In the political structures of electoral democracy, there is a strong, if intermittent, imaginative pressure to see at least one's own government in the near future as a potential instrument of one's own purposes: to identify with it and even aspire to direct it (Dunn 1980, caps 6 and 7; 1990, cap. 8). But electoral democracies have no particular difficulty in recognizing that there are also other, and very different, sorts of states in the world, and that these (or others) may well be deadly enemies to their own state.

There is something imaginatively and conceptually unstable (perhaps simply confused) in seeing government in this split manner, as divided into generous agencies of good and malign agencies of harm, or as divided within itself into benign and malign elements (the bits that are part of the problem and the bits that are part of the solution). Such divisions are real enough in themselves. They are immensely important (and in some ways devastatingly revealing) both for how we view ourselves, one by one, and for how we view our closer human acquaintances. Here, they lie at the very core of human experience. But any clarity and accuracy which they can hope to reach in these intimate and closely observed settings can hardly be retained when they come to be applied to distant and largely unknown political territories. What was the Third Reich really like?

How did most of its inhabitants perceive and relate to one another for most of the time for which it lasted? Just how different really was it from the home life of our own dear country? The urge to see politics in these split terms is as powerful today as it ever has been – we as against they, friend as against foe, the kindly pastures of the welfare state against the killing fields of Kampuchea, the torture chambers of contemporary tyrannies, the ethnic cleansing of Bosnia or Rwanda. It would be insane to doubt the depth of human meaning which lies in these contrasts. But, if we wish to understand politics, it would also be fatal to ignore their huge potential to distort our perceptions and aid us in deceiving ourselves, in putting us wrongly at our ease (cf. Hardin 1995 on epistemological imprisonment).

The psychological mechanism which gives them this power over our understandings is identification: identification with and, still more, identification against. (It may be hard for me to find a surviving British or American career politician with whom I can comfortably identify. But I can be very sure that I do not care at all for Saddam Hussein.)

The great strength of the vision of rule as domination is its resistance to identification (or at any rate to sentimental identification – an over-generous sense of oneself or of those political figures or agencies with which one feels most at home). It picks out one key aspect of what must be going on in ruling, an aspect that can never hope to be intrinsically ingratiating; and it asks tenaciously just how it works. If we choose to see rule (or politics in general) this way, we can be sure we shall at least be trying to locate and comprehend something which must be there, and must matter greatly. We can reasonably hope to avoid contaminating our perceptions and judgments too pervasively with our own hopes, or fears, or desires. It will not in the end exempt us from having to judge (or from feeling about) politics for ourselves. (Compare Max Weber, *Politics as a Vocation*: Weber 1948, 77–128.) But at least it will give us a chance to judge and feel *after* we have formed a coherent and sober understanding of what we are trying to judge, and not infect our understanding of this fatally and comprehensively from the outset.

If, on the other hand, we choose to view government in terms of its potentiality for facilitating human co-operation, and see this potentiality as the core of politics, we are plunged from the outset into an endless exercise in personal disapproval. We commit ourselves, not merely to recognizing the very many instances in which actual governments facilitate nothing of the kind, or facilitate the worst forms of human co-operation (shared banditry (Augustine 1884, IV, 4, vol. 1, p. 139), the fleecing of the weak, the wholesale and deliberate infliction of intense pain, genocide), but also to an over-eager embrace of such few governments as appear, on initial inspection, to be performing largely as we might like them to. We see them through their willed (or avowed) goals, not through their internal causal characteristics, the ways in which they operate and the mechanisms which make them operate as they do. It is not that the ultimate judgment of good or bad consequences is unreal or idle: still less the intervening judgment as to which of these good or bad consequences are secured deliberately and deftly, and which emerge merely from confusion or mutual frustration on the part of the agents concerned. It is simply that we see and apprehend the promotion of good or bad consequences too hastily and too impressionistically. We do so because we model their implementation too readily on our own actions, or on those of our dearest enemies. We see them as full-blooded and clear-cut choices. In real politics, seen as it is, little but genocide is ever full-blooded and virtually no choice, seen in the round, can ever be clear-cut.

Any fluently moralistic political judgment is irretrievably stupid, and the vision of rule as domination thus an indispensable impediment to such fluency. But it is no alternative to political evaluation in its entirety. A Martian might not need to decide which outcomes to favour in human politics and which to regret. But very many human beings, since long before Aristotle, have very much needed to decide. In the increasingly intercommunicative and interactive world of today, in which politics affects more human lives more deeply than it has ever done before, their need to decide (or at the very least to have others whom they can trust decide on their behalf) is more insistent and more urgent than it has ever been before. If they are not to decide through over-hasty and ingenuous identification with (or, for that matter, against) the role of governors, how else can they best decide?

The Implications of the Explanations

ASSIGNING THE BLAME

One of the deepest questions in politics is where the good and bad consequences in the end come from. Just why is it that some groups of human beings groan in agony and others saunter (or cruise) the streets in relaxed well-being? This is not a question on which the modern professional study of politics has much to offer. Political scientists today certainly cover a great range of material which is pertinent to answering it. But few of them now dare to confront the question itself directly and frankly. Nor, for the present, is any other body of modern thought equipped to address it with much courage or clarity of mind. (Closest to doing so, probably, is the inchoate rumination of the ecological movement, often very discerning in its diagnosis of urgency and hazard, but woefully apolitical in its grasp of the dynamics of a human world which is political all the way through, and often also more than a little confused in its grasp of economics.)

If we set our four principal themes up against this blunt question, they suggest very different strategies for answering it. They also suggest correspondingly different conceptions of how modern rule – its depth, its scope, its current formats or modalities, the ideologies or pretexts on which it claims authority – should feature in our answer.

Original Sin All on its Own

The theory of original sin (or moral error) offers the most flamboyant answer. 'Il le faut l'avouer, le mal est sur la terre,' wrote the great French eighteenth-century publicist Voltaire. We must acknowledge that evil is all around us (Voltaire 1968, 156). Voltaire's bitter apothegm was prompted by the Lisbon earthquake of 1755, and was directed in the first instance at religious apologists like the German philosopher Leibniz (Riley 1997), who tried to explain away the all too apparent evils of worldly experience in terms of the good intentions of a just, concerned and omnipotent Creator. But Voltaire himself certainly saw such evil as intractably present in human beings too (themselves, of course, on the Christian hypothesis, fully intended instances of God's good intentions). He hated, and struggled against, human cruelty in many different forms, and especially against those forms of it which were closely linked to the continuing factional power of organized Christianity, against the amalgam of cruelty and bigotry which he called the *infame* (Gay 1959).

The struggle against human infamy was the very centre of Enlightenment politics. It has a distant (and wholly admirable) echo today in the efforts of Amnesty International, the brave and diligent organization which struggles so determinedly and with such relative impartiality to protect the incarcerated victims of state authority across the world from the limitless cruelties which may so readily be visited upon them. For the theory of original sin, cruelty is permanently loose in the world. Almost every human is capable of cruelty, and some (the professional torturers whose handiwork Amnesty seeks to chronicle and restrain) become wholly inured to it: capable of very little else. Almost every human, too, is a potential killer: can kill if they really choose to. The great majority, too, will in fact choose to do so in the last instance, to protect their own lives, or the lives of those whom they hold dear, or even perhaps to forestall a pressing risk to the former or the latter. (The great majority? Well, I would certainly kill if I judged the alternative to be the killing (or perhaps even just permitting the death) of my own son or daughter. Are you sure that you would not too? Are you even sure that you should not?) This is a slope slippery with endless blood. Remember that only a decade ago the thermonuclear weapons systems of the two great world powers stood permanently ready (and in a very poorly controlled condition: Bracken 1982) to eliminate human life on earth, in the optimistic (though also, as it turned out, apparently successful) endeavour to defend their own populations. Remember, too, that the reason why they are not still in this atrocious condition is not any secure gain in collective human rationality, or any dependable edification of our own (or others') purposes, but simply that one of the two superpowers has effectively collapsed.

Cruelty, the late Judith Shklar argued, following the great sixteenth-century French sceptic Montaigne, is the worst thing which human beings do to one another: the worst of which they are capable (Shklar 1984). The capacity for cruelty exists in every human being who is capable of acting. But this is not likely to prove a politically illuminating thought. The very worst consequences of politics may simply consist in the exercise of cruelty. But if we wish to understand why these consequences in fact occur, what we need to grasp is not why any human being might in principle choose to do such things (even on the perhaps implausible hypothesis that this is actually true), but why these particular human beings have so chosen, and why they were not prevented from acting out their choice.

Cruelty and murderousness are ghastly vices – extreme instances of human depravity. But murderousness, at least, is not an ordinary vice. A large proportion of murders is in fact domestic. In Britain at least, most of us are likeliest to be killed by those whom we know best. (Who else could have as powerful motives?) But this is a potentially confusing statistical truth, not a profound insight into the horror of human intimacy. (It is not confusing, of course, on the comparatively low probability of being murdered elsewhere or by others. It merely fails to underline the causal significance of the vastly greater opportunities available for domestic implementation.)

This touches directly on an extremely important issue in contemporary feminism – and hence on an issue which matters greatly for all of us. Are all men not merely potential killers, but also potential murderers? (Creatures who may readily kill for wholly insufficient reasons: no killing for which there is sufficient reason – no killing which is on balance appropriate – can reasonably be viewed as a murder.) If they are, does this in any dependable way distinguish them from all women? Is heterosexual sex necessarily a form of cruelty and an act of degradation or subjugation? I, at least, think plainly *not*. But you may think very differently. If you do, it matters which of us is seeing more accurately.

Cruelty, however, is a very ordinary vice. It is at least as common in the practice of education or the exercise of religious authority as it is on the sports field or in the school playground. Bullying, whether flagrant or discreet, is a very prominent strand in social interaction: the nasty end of the endless human endeavour to get other people to behave as we would wish. We may like to think that we ourselves bully only on behalf of higher values (sharpening the exercise of the mind, deepening the awareness of God in the spiritually resistant, winning an argument or a struggle in which we are confident that right is firmly on our side). But those who can bully with any proficiency (those who are not irretrievably feeble) are apt to bully largely out of habit. We may like to think that *we*, at any rate, are cruel mainly to avoid worse outcomes: that only the compulsively cruel – the genuinely depraved – are cruel for the sake of being so. But cruelty has a constant tendency to get out of hand. In the areas of human practice where the capacity for cruelty is most directly engaged – in policing, in imprisonment, above all in warfare (Walzer 1976) – the control of cruelty (even the control of murderousness) is always pretty insecure. In such a milieu, there will always be many who go too far, whose actions vastly exceed any possible justification, even when the practices themselves are relatively easy to justify. There cannot be armies or police forces or gaols without cruelty. (This is a matter better treated by Augustine a millennium and a half ago than by any subsequent author: Augustine 1884.) Least of all can there be wars without cruelty. But there are very good reasons (and more than sufficient causes) why armies and police forces (Finer 1997), and even gaols (Foucault 1979) and wars, are still with us today.

Why are human beings capable of cruelty? Why are they often so fluent at it and so addicted to it? Why are some human beings at times so unmistakably murderous? The conceptions of what it is to be cruel, and of how far and when cruelty may be justified, are intensely culturally specific (cf. Geertz 1983). They depend upon (often lengthy) histories of thought and sentiment within particular human groupings. But the potentialities for cruelty or murder seem genuinely universal, certainly omnipresent in any human association of any scale. They appear to be simply features of the human animal. Why are they there? Every human culture has an explanation of its own. In the now widely diffused culture of the Christian and post-Christian West there remain today two principal answers. One is evocative, full of pathos, but now almost inaccessibly obscure: that something which need not have happened but did happen has blemished for the rest of human time the serene order of the universe and wounded in a way which humans themselves can never repair the relation between them and their omnipotent Creator. Their cruelty is the brand of their shame. This, very crudely speaking, was St Augustine's view, the view which enabled him to face the pervasiveness of human cruelty, as we ourselves manifestly no longer dare to (Brown 1967). It is not a view which has ever had much resonance in non-Christian societies (of which there have always been, and will now plainly always remain, more instances than there are of Christian societies).

Values

Once we have made this modest concession to our own reality (to what all of us simply are), the sheer human potentiality for cruelty or murderousness is not overwhelmingly illuminating over why there is politics at all, or why it takes its present forms, or even over what we would be well advised to do in order to modify these forms for the better. Only if we refuse to make the concession, if we begin by simply denying our own reality, will the core subject matter of the theory of original sin or moral error bear decisively on our prospects for understanding politics. If we deny that core subject matter (if we cannot face human cruelty and murderousness, and their potent traces in each and every one of us), we preclude ourselves in the first instance from any hope of understanding politics. We substitute a resolute misunderstanding of ourselves for any prospect of comprehending the wider human world which we need to grasp.

Original Sin, Partial Judgment, Conflicting Interests, Collective Action

There is still, however, one residual element in the explanatory target of the theory of original sin which requires attention. Zest for inflicting pain, or eagerness to murder, may need to be set in rather elaborate contexts for them to explain anything important about politics. But the capacity to kill, and the preparedness in more restricted circumstances to do so, are altogether less peripheral.

It is enormously important for political understanding just how this capacity and preparedness mesh with the self-righteous individuality of political judgment, the history of structurally conflicting interests, and the logical but all too practical problems of collective action. In the first place, it seems reasonably clear that they do not mesh at all directly with the problems of collective action. As with every other aspect of politics, they are likely to prove more intractable and baffling, harder to defuse and bring under reasonable control, because of the omnipresence of the puzzles of collective action. But while the latter may help to explain the forms assumed by the capacity or preparedness to kill in particular settings, they can do nothing to explain why either is present at all, and hence nothing to show where the very worst consequences come from.

In the last century and a half of Western political thinking, most explanatory weight has been laid on the history of structural conflicts of interest, perhaps inevitably so given the most obtrusive features of capitalist production (Hont and Ignatieff 1983). It is far from clear today that this emphasis has been wise. Struggle between classes certainly occurs. Only a fool could doubt either the energies and passions which it elicits or the scale of its potential impact. What is distinctly less clear is how far any class ever acts on a sound and reliably available judgment of what its own interests really are. (Despite David Cannadine, however, this is not a good reason for doubting that classes are there: Cannadine 1998.)

Underlying every political venture, individual or collective, is a necessarily precarious judgment as to what is or is not in the interest of the agent concerned. The capacity to kill is a biological property of reasonably mature members of the species. But the preparedness to kill on any scale whatever, from the individual members of a household to a global military and ideological bloc, rests on judgments of the balance of danger, on assessments of who is likely to menace whom, and how they can most effectively and affordably be deterred from carrying out their threats.

The Primacy of Partiality

Here the last century and a half of Western political thinking is less illuminating in its basic orientation than the perspective of a century and more earlier, the perspective of early modern natural jurisprudence, the theory of natural law and natural rights (cf. Tuck 1999). In that perspective, there is the most intimate possible link between the human capacity and preparedness to kill and the vagaries of human judgment: its ineradicable partiality. The dynamics of one simply map the dynamics of the other. As we judge, so we are ready to kill. But the urgency of judgment and the alacrity of response are each drastically exacerbated by the magnitude of the stakes at risk. Every human being can be killed. Most humans can and, if they feel it necessary, will kill. Since they were certainly not made (either by nature or by the God who perhaps made it) simply in order to be killed by one another, none has any reason (and few have much inclination) passively to accept another's mortal threat. So there is no worldly authority of reason, nothing beneath heaven, which can appeal beyond their perceptions of mortal threat from one another. Everything thus depends on their detailed assessment of the acuteness and immediacy of those threats. All human beings always, singly or in huge numbers, must and will judge such threats for themselves, many, of course, allowing their judgments to be determined for them by other human beings or institutions in whose opportunities to judge accurately they have more confidence than they do in their own. As they judge, so they will be prepared to act, and so, sooner or later, they very probably will act.

Even the structural conflict of interests looks more alarming, more like a force capable of producing the horrors of the last century, if it is positioned within (rather than offered as a replacement for) this older imaginative and analytical setting. The interests of the main board directors of a recently privatized utility in John Major's Britain were palpably not identical with those of their less skilled or more readily dispensable labour force, let alone their own customers, or fellow taxpayers or citizens helplessly dependent on the scale of social security provision. But the judgment that their enviable advantages were enough to kill for (or at any rate to kill against) could only carry conviction if it was evident that there was some other specifiable and potentially accessible organization of the utility in question which would benefit most of these other concerned parties more generously and equally reliably while cosseting its principal organizers less offensively.

Usually, of course, there are endless ways in which any human institution could be organized differently, not merely in principle but very much in practice. But it is also usually hard to improve on every aspect of a given human arrangement at the same time. (This is why the principle of Pareto optimality is such a savagely conservative criterion for the modification of economic or social arrangements: Barry 1965.) Decisions to attempt to improve institutions pass through (and rest upon) judgments as to how such improvement can be secured. These judgments are strongly influenced by the roles occupied and experiences previously undergone by the agents in question. They are inherently perspectival and correspondingly likely to differ.

Because the judgments plainly matter, each agent has good reason to place a high value on their own best judgment, however that judgment was in fact derived (formed actively by and for themselves, or incurred passively from their political, industrial or military leaders, their priests or *ulama* or shamans, their spouses or favoured daily newspapers). The social or political source of a judgment is often a ground for others to doubt its validity; but, once you have made the judgment your own, you cannot also doubt its validity merely on grounds of its source. (And least of all so, no doubt, when you most should.)

The higher the stakes, the more committing the judgment, and the stronger the reason to back it to the hilt: if necessary with your own life, or, less discouragingly, with the lives of as many others as prove to be necessary. This is not a matter of epistemology: of how to recognize, and thus to avoid, false beliefs (but cf. Hardin 1995). Beliefs derived from inherently unsound authorities, to be sure, are more likely to mislead than they are to enlighten. The higher the bets placed upon them, the more disastrous the misjudgments they are likely to prompt. But this tells us nothing whatever about how to establish which authorities are in fact sound.

It very much is, however, a matter of politics. One alternative to politics, much favoured over the centuries by philosophers and religious leaders, is the replacement of corrupt misjudgment on the part of political agents by the authority of those who know, are uncorrupt (or even incorruptible) and hence incapable of misjudgment. No political issue has proved as inflammatory across the millennia as the judgment of just who these superlatively authoritative beings really are. The partiality of judgment is a central and ineliminable feature of all politics everywhere. Meshing directly with the capacity and preparedness to kill and the rather steady human stake in preferring killing to being killed, it has made, and will assuredly continue to make, a great deal of the history of politics.

Perhaps, though, thinkers have hoped at intervals throughout the intellectual history of the globe, it may be possible to *tame* the partiality of judgment, first cognitively and then practically, by pinning down just where judgment comes from, what governs it, what partiality ultimately consists in. If we could explain first the form and then the content of the most partial of judgments, then surely we could break their spell and turn history and politics (and human choice more generally) into a march of Reason.

It is easy enough to see why this hope keeps recurring (why it revives for a time in virtually all of us, if we think about politics for long enough and care enough about it). But it is vital to see why it can never hold its ground. Where judgment comes from, alas (or wondrously), is the whole breadth of human experience and human history. What partiality rests on is the lives which each of us live. It is not that most of us necessarily think very hard, or think very much for ourselves even when we do think. It is simply that all of us live our own lives, experience them for ourselves, think, feel and judge as ourselves, and have no option (despite the efforts of Buddha or the Stoics) but to live them very hard. To live is to judge. We can be bullied into concealing this. But we cannot be bullied, at least as ongoing societies, into ceasing to do it. If this is a Western individualist dogma, so much the worse for any culture which contrives to remain blissfully obtuse to its validity.

The State as Idea and as Fact

THE STATE AS A POLITICAL SITE

Only massive selective inattention could stop anyone recognizing that states today remain (as they have been for some time) the principal institutional site of political experience. The modern state is an idea with a distinct history (Skinner 1989; Dunn (ed.) 1995; Finer 1997). (In Stone Age Europe no one had that idea; and even if they had had, there was no set of human institutions to which it could have been plausibly or accurately applied.) But whatever role political institutions or practices have played in shaping that idea, it is clear that the idea itself now has many concrete referents in the world. The French republic is a state today. The United Kingdom, for the present, is still a state. The constitutional empire of Japan, for all the presumptively divine ancestry of its ruling house, is very much a state. Even the Kingdom of Saudi Arabia is a state. In imaginative heritage, as in many other respects, they differ notably from one another. But each is a state in essentially the same sense (cf. Khilnani 1997). The states which now actually exist are each marked more or less deeply by the idea of the modern state; and that idea is modified incessantly, if erratically, as features of these states come into sudden focus or pass effectively from view. It is a matter for extremely sophisticated political judgment (probably for unattainably sophisticated political judgment) just how much of modern politics is still caught in the format of the modern state. Indeed it is none too clear even now whether that proportion is still increasing (as it plainly has since the idea first began to come into focus in sixteenth- and seventeenth-century Europe: Skinner 1978 and 1989; Franklin 1973; Tuck 1993; Ertman 1997; Mann 1986–93; Tilly (ed.) 1975; Finer 1997), or is now beginning more or less steadily to decline. Getting some grip on this question is a clear prerequisite for mustering any understanding of politics today. But, even to try to get such a grip, we need to be very clear just what it is that we are talking about.

What then *is* a state? Or, more tamely, what would we for the present be well advised to mean when we use that term ourselves?

Max Weber

Two connected but distinguishable answers are worth considering. The first, the answer of the great German sociologist of the turn of this century Max Weber, is that a state is a certain sort of factual entity: that entity which 'successfully upholds the claim to the *monopoly* of the *legitimate* use of physical force' in enforcing its order within a given territory (Weber 1968, 54: and see 54–6 passim; for Weber's career and importance see Beetham 1974, Mommsen 1974, Bendix 1960, Breiner 1996). The claim to exclusivity in the use of force (to outlaw or explicitly license all other usages of it), and the initially territorial restriction of that claim, both apply illuminatingly to modern states as these actually exist, though they feature more steadily in their public and official self-conceptions than in their practical habits. Where political claims clash fundamentally with this today (as, for example, in the case of the Iranian *fatwa* against the British writer Salman Rushdie), what startles is less their sheer malignity or the depth of hatred which they express than their frontal collision with the central official premisses on which political relations between human populations now take place.

What is elusive in Weber's conception is the proviso that the claim in question should be successful. States certainly vary today (as entities which we would now call states must have varied across history: cf. for example Nippel 1995, esp. Conclusion; Coogan

1995) in just how successfully they realize this claim in practice. Some states confront more thoroughly pacified or subjugated populations than others. But no state has ever confronted a wholly pacified or subjugated population. (This was one of the main complaints levelled at the political precision or realism of the category of totalitarianism: that it promised, or threatened, what is simply impossible.) Success in implementing this key claim forms a factual continuum and must always in practice have been severely incomplete (some distance short of one end of the continuum). It cannot sanely be regarded as a constitutive property (a defining feature) of states as these have ever actually existed.

Bodin and Hobbes

The second answer is distinctly older. Its two great intellectual architects were the sixteenth-century French jurist Jean Bodin (Franklin 1973) and the seventeenth-century English political philosopher Thomas Hobbes (Skinner 1978 and 1996; Tuck 1989). It is that the modern state is in the first instance an idea – an incisive and adventurous intellectual construction – and that the point of that idea was to transform the political relations between human beings for the better. The state was a structural relation between three elements: a ruling power, a historically given set of human subjects, and a particular territory (Skinner 1989). It was not a government. It was not a people. It was not a country or homeland (a *patria*). Rather, it was the structure which related together all three at any one point in time, and, because it did so, could outlast quite drastic alterations over time in any, or even in all three, of them. The central motif of this idea, its intellectual emblem, is the notion of sovereignty, of a unified and internally unchallengeable site of authoritative judgment to which every other aspect of the state is clearly subordinate and answerable. This was never intended to be a description of how things were, a simple statement of fact. Rather, it was a deeply motivated political aspiration, with evident attractions for some, and at least equally evident menaces for others. Through it, for most of the centuries which followed, has flowed a constantly increasing proportion of the political energies and hopes of ever larger areas of the world. Territorially today its scope is all but universal. Antarctica, and what is left of the great shrinking common of the oceans, still belong to no state in particular. But what can be done to or in them now depends more nakedly than ever on strenuous bargaining between states.

DISTINGUISHING DOMINATION FROM SOCIAL CO-OPERATION

Each of these two conceptions (the state as sociological fact and the state as normative political proposal) must relate in some way to most of the entities which we now call states, but neither makes clear quite how to apply it in practice. Each has some natural affinity with a vision of states as instances of domination, and some with a vision of them as human devices for facilitating co-operation. If we are to decide for ourselves which of the two is more reliable or more illuminating, we shall first need to be much clearer about just what we are seeking to understand *through* them: what questions we really need them to aid us in answering.

It has been a recurrent complaint against the state since the term came into use in its modern sense that its role in human political history has increased, is increasing and ought to be diminished (if not, indeed, eliminated): an attitude common to Marxists, anarchists and libertarians. The judgment naturally links with the conception of the state as a structure of domination (with Weber's or Lenin's view). But it has a natural antipathy for the conception of the state as a facilitator of social co-operation. It suggests that social co-operation is readily available and thus needs little (if any) facilitation. In recent decades (as for much of the nineteenth century) it suggests, more concretely, that such facilitation as human co-operation plausibly does still require it can be confident of securing from other types of human agency, notably the large-scale business enterprise, the cosmopolitanly professional non-governmental agency, or the institutions of popular political, social or economic struggle.

Defenders of the state, seen as a facilitator of social co-operation, are strongly attuned to the dilemmas of collective action, and tend to view the self-righteous individuality of political judgment as a permanent source of instability and acute danger. Opponents of its claim to serve as anything of the kind, would-be clinical diagnosticians of its role in domination, tend to be unperturbed by the challenge of collective action and to underestimate the degree to which political judgments simply do and always will differ across human populations. The former are plainly apt to be over-charitable in their perceptions or expectations of states; but the latter are just as apt to be over-sanguine in their perceptions or expectations of large-scale business enterprises, NGOs, institutions of popular political struggle or any other materials which they trust to maintain shape and security in human collective life (Dunn 1996(c)).

It remains, however, more misleading than illuminating to see political attitudes or expectations as though these were free-standing sources in themselves of how we choose to envisage either actual or possible states. The choice of how to envisage actual or possible states is a political attitude in itself. It embodies political expectations and could scarcely fail to be modified by these. But the interpretative leeway between actual and possible states – the space which the contrast between actual and potential necessarily opens up to active imagination: to hope, to fear, to desire, as much as to judgment – precludes our political attitudes from ever becoming robust and stable features of the universe at any point in time. What drives them is something which is in some ways beyond or beneath politics, the movements of our psyches. But, however urgent the personal imaginative pressures behind political attitudes, the attitudes themselves are never dependably immune to political experience: never fully sealed against it. The more broadly we conceive politics, the less plausible the claim that even the movements of our own psyches, one by one, are in any sense external to it. Consider, for example, the relations of power and opportunity (and resignation) between men and women. It is easy to imagine that few citizens of Britain have found their imaginative life deeply marked by the experience of Mr Major's premiership. (There is some evidence, drawn from the ravages of Alzheimer's disease, that the same was far from true of his formidable predecessor Margaret Thatcher, whose name still carried clearly to some patients who had forgotten the significance of most of the more personal elements in their own lives.) But none of us can reasonably be confident that our sense of our self, our shames and aspirations, has not been deeply shaped, over the last generation or two, by the law of marriage and divorce, or the legal framework governing access to education or employment, still less by the legal regulation of property. We are all who we are, in quite large measure, because of the history of politics. Each of us sees politics, as we in particular see it, through our own idiosyncratic sensibilities: not as it just happens to be. And those sensibilities in turn bear a deep impress of the political past within which we have grown up and become our selves. (For essentially the same point expressed in a very different intellectual format, see Hardin 1995.)

There has been much professional study, especially over the last half-century, of political psychology and political culture (the ways in which individual psyches react to, or enter into, political experience, and the broader patterns of political perception and sentiment characteristic of particular populations). Some of this has been quite illuminating in detail. But over the gross question of the ultimate relations between the individual psyche and political reality no detectable headway has been made since the days of the ancient Greek philosopher Plato.

It is a reasonable hypothesis (though in no sense a professional research finding) that the sharp contrast between these two images of the state, and the varying plausibility of the two to different sets of human beings, derives not from rational inductive learning from clearly discrepant streams of political experience, but from attitudes which are chronologically prior to (since they emerge earlier in the life cycle than) any experiential encounter with states or their historical predecessors (Solomon 1971, 28–153). The view that a state is a structure of political domination cannot conceivably be refuted by political experience, and has seldom so far been seriously discouraged by it. But the view that all states have been, are or could be nothing but structures of domination cannot have been derived merely from experience. It vastly exceeds the scope of any possible personal, or even collectively available, experience. It can be defended, if at all, only in large measure by terminological fiat (arbitrary restriction of the use of the word 'state'); and it can be kept plausible only by crudely selective attention to social, political or economic causality. What drives such views is a distaste for being subjected to alien will: a raw dislike for either authority or power, precisely the impulse which has given democracy its extraordinary cosmopolitan appeal today (Dunn 1996(b)). To impede or block such views in an individual, either authority or power must intrude, and intrude effectively, into their psyche: must transform how they see and feel.

LEGITIMATION THROUGH PERSONAL CHOICE

All human beings wish to live as they choose. This is a necessary truth, not a daring historical speculation. But how they feel able to choose – the breadth of their range of choices, and the ease and relaxation of the choices themselves – varies immensely across time and space. Some structures of choice (the life of a Trappist monk or a Hindu ascetic) leave little room for sensual gratification, for acknowledged whim, or for the quest for physical enjoyment or comfort. More societies today than ever before in history seek to validate their claims to authority over their members by their prowess in extending the range of personal choice and augmenting the opportunities for comfort and physical enjoyment. (Note the contrast here with the attitudes of seventeenth-century French or Japanese rulers at the prospect of their peasant subjects living at their ease: Richelieu 1947, 253–5; Church 1972; Elliott 1984; *The Keian No Furegaki*, Sansom 1963, 99; Berry 1989, 167; Elison 1988, 74–6; Ooms 1985.)

This, charitably interpreted (Hont and Ignatieff (eds) 1983, Introduction; cf. Thompson 1993), is what the history of capitalism has been all about, though it requires very charitable interpretation to incorporate the history of chattel slavery comfortably within it. Capitalist societies today (by now a very large proportion of the human societies there are) vary in how uninhibitedly they embrace the goal of expanding what Benjamin Constant christened the liberty of the moderns (Constant 1988, 313–28), the personal freedom to live as one individually pleases. But none can afford (or have good reason) to reject the goal as such. Their success in attaining that goal is an important source of power over their own members. Over time, too, it is increasingly a necessary condition for being able to reproduce that power effectively.

Causality

It is extraordinarily difficult to see clearly and steadily quite what is at stake in this drastic shift in the conditions of collective human life. Some of the judgments required are essentially causal. They are judgments of how one aspect of social, political or economic organization depends upon and affects other aspects. Such judgments, as we have already noted, are enormously complicated and inherently highly uncertain. Despite the professional efforts of hundreds of thousands of would-be social scientists, the only such judgments which carry real authority thus far (which it is reasonable to trust implicitly) are essentially negative: that one particular practice will not dependably support another, that some institutions will certainly not work at all as they are intended to do. Such negative guidance is practically helpful. In most instances it is better not to do something the predictable but unintended consequences of which are immensely harmful and clearly outweigh any prospective benefits which can reasonably be anticipated from it. But, helpful though such negative guidance can be, it will always be woefully insufficient to direct human practice: to show us how best to act in circumstances in which we simply must. Much of understanding politics just consists in improving our practical judgments of causal relations of this kind: raising them from the lamentably ignorant and silly to the at least minimally informed and coherent.

Values

Improving our practical judgment of political causality and extending the range of relevant information of which we are aware

are by no means the only prerequisites for understanding politics. A further prerequisite of a very different kind is to clarify and learn how to apply a number of extraordinarily important relations between human values.

If we merely wished to explain why particular individuals conceive states as they do, we could perhaps afford to confine our attention to their own personal experience of states thus far, and to how they became the sorts of persons they are. That might be as full an explanation as could in principle be given. But, if we wish to understand politics ourselves, we certainly do not merely wish to understand why others view states as they do. We also wish (and need) to judge how best to view states ourselves. This judgment will certainly, over time, contain elements of choice and decision. But it is an error to put these elements first. I can choose a strategy of understanding for myself; and defining (or conceiving) states in one way rather than another is a key element in any strategy for understanding politics today. But it is demented to choose a strategy for understanding, in the end, for any reason but the reasonable expectation that it will prove effective. I cannot coherently decide what to do to understand something, unless I already have many beliefs (as almost all sentient human beings plainly do) about what is likely to contribute to understanding and what is likely to impede or frustrate it. In seeking to judge what strategy for understanding to adopt towards states, we need to become more aware of why we in particular are likely to prefer to see them one way rather than another, or why some sorts of strategy are likely to appear to us more plausible and others less. We need to deepen our understanding of our own sentiments and our own thought processes: to introduce some discipline into their often unedified, and always somewhat unedifying, dynamics. To fail to do so is to imprison ourselves inadvertently within our own parochial horizons of political experience and make ourselves passive victims of our personal psychic histories. (The view that parochialism is the happy essence of political experience, and that passive reiteration of our own psychic histories is an existential right, or even duty, strongly pressed in many societies today and in the latter case closely linked to the unfolding history of capitalism, is both corrupt and stupid.)

Power and Authority

DISTINGUISHING POWER FROM AUTHORITY

Here a simple contrast between power and authority is illuminating. Both power and authority are subject to at least as wide and as fierce a controversy in application as the term state. They, like the terms in other languages by which it is natural to translate them, appreciably predate the appearance of that term. There is no way, either philosophically or historically, in which we can reasonably see ourselves as *compelled* to use them one way rather than any other.

The contrast which we need to clarify our thinking, however, does not require a decisiveness of authorization which it cannot in any case be given. Power, in one useful sense, is a relation between two or more human wills, in which one will can for some purposes effectively control the other will or set of wills. The idea of control implies the possibility of freedom from control (of independence), and hence of regret at loss of independence (at succumbing to alien control). Authority, in one useful sense, is a relation between specifiable human values, particular human understandings, and the wills guided or determined by those understandings. From the point of view of those subject to power or authority, the relation of power is an external relation between wills, and the relation of authority is an internal relation between a particular human understanding, the will which it guides, and the values to which it responds. It is the values which have authority; and any other human interpreter of these values who claims their sanction is entitled to such authority only insofar as they do in fact speak for the values themselves: insofar as their interpretation of them is valid.

All states in some measure claim authority and exert power. But to understand a particular state, it is necessary to ascertain not merely how securely it controls the wills of those who are subject to it, but also how far its claims to authority are justified. Neither exercise is at all easy. But they are difficult in very different ways.

The contrast between viewing a state as a structure of pure domination and viewing it as a facilitator of social co-operation is a contrast between interpreting it solely through the concept of power, in this simple understanding, and interpreting it through one modern variant of the concept of authority. This is not, as should now be clear, a factual disagreement; but neither is it just a matter for arbitrary decision. Each viewpoint responds to a schedule of questions and prompts a range of answers to these questions. Neither schedule of questions can possibly be irrelevant to understanding politics today; and neither range of answers could be any kind of substitute for the other.

To establish some control over these two contrasting schedules, we need to grasp two key points. The first is that the choice between viewing states exclusively as structures of domination and seeing them also as potential or actual facilitators of social co-operation cannot be settled merely by past or present fact. It is not a question about human history thus far, let alone a question about the broad balance of experience within that history. It cannot be settled in this way because the choice between these two viewpoints will certainly enter into the interpretation both of history and of present fact, and because what has been true about the past or is true about the present does not dependably indicate what will (or even may) prove true about the future. In the case of politics it is of very great importance that, as such conceptions enter into the interpretation of history or present fact, they may always, and not infrequently do, modify what that future would otherwise be. An historically important instance of this effect was Karl Marx's assurance that, with the coming of full communism and the comprehensive transformation of social and economic relations hitherto dominated by class struggle and class subjugation, the state (an especially dense and capricious structure of class domination: see Marx, *Draft Plan for a Work on the Modern State*: Marx and Engels 1975(b), IV 666) would wither away, and the government of men (and women) give way to the administration of things (Kolakowski 1978; Harding in Dunn (ed.) 1992). In the political history of countries which underwent political revolution under Marxist auspices in the course of the twentieth century, this forecast has appeared either as a massive practical miscalculation on Marx's own part or as a brazen pretence on the part of the most dedicated and ruthless of dominators who claimed his mantle (Dunn 1989(a)).

The second key point is that the pertinence of the concept of authority to understanding what states really are has nothing to do with its role within their own preferred self-understanding or public self-advertisements. It is not principally because authority is an internal ideological property of states that it bears decisively on the question of what they are. Rather, it is because authority is, however precariously, an internal psychological and evaluative property of individual human beings, and because it alone can serve to bridge the gap between how they themselves see and feel and what possible arrangements of their social, economic and political surroundings they have good reason to welcome or to seek to secure. The recognition that all human beings wish to live as they choose is less instructive than it sounds, because it ignores the fact that every human being, besides experiencing a present of their own, also faces an equally personal future. Only the most twisted of human beings looks forward to regret. Most would certainly prefer to live as they please in the future as well as in the present. To have the chance to do so, they need to modify their present choices, what they feel immediately attracted to doing, more or less drastically, in the light of it. The shadow of the future reaches back a very long way in the human life-cycle, forcing on the attention, even of very young children, an intermittent need to sacrifice intense and immediate purposes for richer but later rewards. Adult, and above all parental, rationales for such sacrifice stress the urgency of the need to respect the prerequisites for effective agency, for a child to increase its own personal powers. To the child, however, these rationales are often indistinguishable from the direct application of alien will. The parental and adult rationales are frequently offered in bad faith (for less elevated motives – the desire for a less turbulent home or a quieter classroom). They are also often predicated on extremely poor practical judgments: superstitious mistakes about what will in fact develop personal powers, and what will merely render the children concerned less perturbing or exhausting to their adult companions. The age-old struggle between adult and child is not a just war with a predestined victor or vanquished. But it is always right to see it in part as a struggle about, and hence *for*, authority in which neither party is guaranteed to be in the right, even on balance.

To define states simply as structures of domination is either to deny them authority or to refuse to consider the relation between human institutions and the meeting of human needs. Some particular states at every point in time (perhaps Myanmar at the time of writing, as for some time in the past: Taylor 1987) approximate closely to pure structures of domination. Insofar as human needs are still met within their territories, the institutions or expedients which enable them to be so have no direct dependence on the state and owe it nothing whatever. But the most important political fact about these states is always that the range of human needs that can be met while they remain in this condition is far narrower and less dependable than the range that could readily be met if the states concerned were altered for the better. A state in which this is true can be quite powerful. (It can, for example, succeed in reproducing itself as a structure of domination for lengthy periods of time.) But it has no authority whatever. Such authority as there is within its territories rests in other human institutions (religious, familial, even on occasion the leadership of an opposition political party). But the pertinence of the idea of authority is no less peremptory in conditions as sad as these than it is in the most impressive and humanly prepossessing of political communities. To stress the absence of authority in these settings is to focus the scale and contours of unmet human need within them (above all, the unmet need for protection and sustenance), and the historically feasible and accessible political, economic and social structures which could meet these needs effectively. It is to link an ugly present to one or more better possible futures.

One cannot say with confidence that all of us view states as we do just because of our own personal experience of human value over time, or just because of our own direct or indirect encounters with political causality. We do not know that it is the combination of personal experience of value with strictly political encounters that determines how we all view states. (That claim is too vague in content and too complicated in possible application to test at all decisively.) But what we can say with some confidence is that every human being has good reason to draw their assessment of what states just are (what they really consist in) from each of these two dimensions of their experience: that both bear on the choice of an appropriate strategy of understanding. So the question of what states really are is not going to have a single univocal and comprehensively valid answer. Its sense will vary for each of us and alter over time, and its appropriate answer will alter with its sense. To pose it usefully, we must do so more patiently and cautiously from the outset. One reason why it is hard to learn to understand politics is because none of the possible approaches to understanding it can simply be adopted and pressed with vigour and confidence from the start. It is not a subject matter which succumbs to direct assault from a single angle. It cannot be taken by storm.

Some past answers to the question of what states really are, however, still have far more claim on our attention than others. Weber's is certainly one of them; and, while it has an obvious elective affinity with a vision of the state as a structure of domination, it in no way discourages us from posing other and imaginatively more demanding questions about how we should envisage the states within which we live, or other states which affect these more or less deeply from the outside by their actions. What is less clear is how directly Weber's conception can *aid* us to understand politics as this is today or is likely to be tomorrow. It encourages us to focus on the history of states rather than on their future destiny. Within that history, it encourages us to focus on the accumulation of power and the concentration of control by some wills over others. On any construction of what states have been, are and will be, this must be an important aspect of them. But, as we have already seen, it is far from being the only feature of them which we need to understand, if we wish to understand politics. If we turn to consider the initial shaping of the modern concept of the state this can help us to grasp something rather different about the modern entities which now bear its title.

The Formation of the Idea of the State

Quentin Skinner has argued that the modern idea of the state was developed, slowly and with some difficulty, to defend a set of specific political interests and to subvert older political ideas which its exponents saw as politically harmful (Skinner 1989). In particular, it was developed to facilitate the construction of a single integrated system of authoritative political and legal decision-making over a given territory and subject-population, and to offset the continuing subversive potential of the longstanding (Greek, Roman and medieval) viewpoint which derived political authority in the end from the people over whom it was exercised. As Skinner shows, this was not simply a matter of backing rulers against their subjects. The state was no more to be identified with its present rulers than it was with its existing subjects or territories. But the new conception plainly favoured rulers against subjects whenever the two came into conflict, as, in sixteenth- and seventeenth-century Europe, they very frequently did (Skinner 1978; Zagorin 1982). The core of the new idea was the conception of sovereignty, of ultimate worldly authority over people and territory, and its firm location in particular human institutions and decisions: the right to be obeyed without challenge. The entity in which that right inhered was no longer envisaged as a particular human being (pope, emperor, king, lord), however, but as a continuing structure of government, decision-making, legal interpretation and enforcement, which was sharply distinct from its current human incumbents. Such a structure could take in or lose subjects or territory without altering its identity. It could change its system of rule or legal adjudication almost beyond recognition, and yet remain intractably itself. In the end, this conception proved inhospitable to many, or even most, of the political, social and indeed economic assumptions of the world within which it was devised. It had little natural affinity with ideas like dynastic legitimacy: the view that the rightful monarch at any point in time was the nearest lineal descendant, under existing rules, of the rightful monarch immediately preceding. But these effects were slow in coming; and their eventual arrival plainly owed at least as much to a wide variety of other forces, as it did to the inherent potential of the idea itself. Louis XIV, the Roi Soleil, notoriously equated the French state with himself (Rowen 1980, cap. 4; Rowen 1962). Even his successor Louis XV, more than half a century later, had no hesitation in insisting that 'L'ordre public entier émane de moi et que les droits de la Nation, dont on ose faire un corps séparé du Monarque, sont nécessairement unis avec les miens et ne reposent qu'en mes mains': The whole public order emanates from me; and the rights of the Nation, which some have the nerve to turn into a body distinct from the Monarch, are necessarily united with mine and rest solely in my hands (Flammermont and Tourneux 1895, II, 558; Viollet 1912, 78; Rowen 1980, 126; and, for the political context of the King's emphatic proclamation at the Séance de la Flagellation, Swann 1995, cap. 9).[2]

If we view states merely as structures of domination, it is plain enough what the principal impact of the idea has been. Over time, and wholly unsurprisingly, it has served to intensify, systematize and deepen subjugation: to subject huge numbers of human beings more and more decisively and inescapably to the crude pressure of alien will. This was the task for which it was invented; and this is the purpose which it has unrelentingly served. As an assessment, this cannot be said to be false. But it is certainly incomplete, and, because of its resolute incompleteness, more than a little myopic. What else, of a less bleakly discouraging character, lurks within the modern conception of the state so understood and has also, over time, made its historical presence felt? There are two powerful and far from contemptible ideas which formed part of the conception from its very beginning. One was an idea about the nature of law, the other a judgment about the prospective consequences of different ways of organizing political institutions. In the conception of sovereignty the two ideas blend in an evocative but perhaps irredeemably confusing mixture.

The State as Authoritative Law

The legal idea is that any sound body of law requires a single authoritative and effectively enforced site of ultimate decision. It requires this in order to aim for (or hope to reach) ultimate clarity and consistency of self-understanding. It also requires it in order to realize the claim to authority without which law is little more than a rhetorical medium or a range of publicly expressed good (or bad) intentions.

In the sixteenth-century France of Jean Bodin or the seventeenth-century England of Thomas Hobbes, in which the idea was first worked out, this viewpoint was at odds with much of the practical reality both of the law and of politics. It failed to describe with the least plausibility either the content of many of the different bodies of law then in existence, or the contours or workings of the institutions whose task it was to interpret these bodies, or the major institutions of political decision-making or authority. Yet its point, of course, was not to describe one or any of these, but to change them, and change them all. Not only was that its point (the purpose of those who best understood what they were doing in forging the idea in the first place). That has also, over time, been quite unmistakably its consequence: the effect it has in fact had.

The State as a Mechanism of Security

The second idea was not a quasi-logical conception of what is required for something to be a well-ordered body of authoritative law, but a vividly political assessment of how institutions must be organized if human beings are to have a reasonable prospect of living with one another in a modicum of ease and security. The combination of both ideas proved peculiarly attractive in face of a social and political world in which laws were characteristically vague, confused and indeterminate in scope, and personal life was massively insecure for virtually everyone. Each idea has an imaginative force and a capacity for illumination of its own. Combining the two offered the prospect of compounding these strengths. It also had the attraction of picking out, through this combination, a common set of hazards and prospective enemies, and a joint and agreeably emphatic remedy for each.

The ideas themselves, however, were (and remain) very different in kind. The presumption that they belonged indissolubly together (formed part of a single clear and overarching idea: the idea of the modern state) has never been wholly convincing. Certainly they could be (and often have been) deployed together, to deepen subjugation and build state power, to conceive and develop the extraordinarily elaborate institutions of legal and bureaucratic regulation within which modern populations live. But there is no reason to expect to understand the impact of either accurately, whether for the better or for the worse, by considering them together and as a single unit.

Authoritative Law, Security and Political Obligation

The idea that for there to be valid law at all there needs to be determinate and ultimate decision remains as controversial today as it has always been in the past (Hart 1961; Dworkin 1986). It is not, in itself, either a prudential recipe or a precept of justice. But it fits quite harmoniously with other conceptions which are clearly marked by each of these concerns: with, for example, John Locke's celebrated insistence in his *Two Treatises of Government* of 1689 on the need for known standing laws, with impartial adjudicators and trustworthy agencies to enforce the latter's judgments (Locke 1988). The idea of a rule of law must certainly be incoherent if there is no reason to suppose the laws themselves coherent in the first place. Its appeal as a political formula lies in its firm promise to ensure justice (at least within the terms of existing law), and in its relatively specific proposals for how justice can be ascertained and implemented. But it must attempt to retain the initial imaginative force of the idea that for law to be systematic and coherent it must be articulated through a single and necessarily hierarchical structure of decision, while yoking this idea to more concrete proposals for how justice is to be assessed and implemented. In practice, decisions will be made by particular individuals or sets of individuals at particular times, on the basis of their own limited insight and for their own not invariably irreproachable motives. Any plausible view of what it is for a given decision to be just, or for a particular set of institutions to be serving rather than menacing human interests, will be bound to diverge, sooner rather than later, from what the court of last instance within a particular jurisdiction happens to decide. It is clear that even the most adventurous intellectual pioneer of the logical conception of sovereignty, Jean Bodin, found it hard to resist this realization (Franklin 1973).

In the pages of Hobbes, the arguments for locating sovereignty somewhere definite in the first place and for the folly and injustice of opposing it once it has been so located, also combine a concern for justice with a concern for security and ease. They form a classic theory (perhaps *the* classic theory) of political obligation (Dunn 1996(a), cap. 4). Hobbes volunteers to prove (and insists in conclusion that he has succeeded in proving: Hobbes 1991) the validity of political obligation: that states (except under various extreme conditions) are fully entitled to the obedience of their subjects, and that their subjects have a corresponding duty to obey them. Why?

His theory is complicated and subtle. But its principal ingredients are as simple as they are striking. Both states, and the conception of political obligation which is an intrinsic part of them, are imperfect remedies for the threat of violent death. They are imperfect in a number of different respects, most decisively because all they can ever hope to do in any case is to postpone the inevitable. But imperfect though they are and always will be, no fuller or more dependable remedy is in principle available. Since death is, in the vast majority of cases, acutely unwelcome, and in virtually all cases unwelcome where it is also wholly involuntary, the view that it is prudent to go to considerable lengths to avoid involuntary death at the hands of other human beings has great force. So too, for much the same reasons, the view that to be coercively deprived of one's life by another human agent is, other things being equal, a peculiarly gross and humanly urgent form of harm, almost the worst thing that human beings can readily do to one another. The state, in Hobbes's construction, is a rationally eligible human device for protecting its subjects against each of these dangers. That is both its charter and its main and most pressing task.

To fulfil its charter and discharge its key task, it needs to be able to control three very turbulent domains of human activity, two of them domestic and one effectively international. It needs to be able to stop its subjects, individually or in groups, from directly menacing one another's lives: to pacify its own domestic arena. It also needs to establish and maintain control over two aspects of their behaviour which, unless they are effectively controlled, will spill over constantly into their mutual relations and disrupt these lethally: over the public expression of their opinions and over the judgments as to what does or does not by right belong to them on which they feel entitled to act.

It also needs to muster the power to ensure that no foreign agency can threaten the life or security of its own subjects: to exclude foreign coercive power permanently from its territory, by threatening retaliation and mustering sufficient power of its own to make that threat credible. The task of external defence (of guaranteeing its citizens' lives and personal security within their own territory) is as widespread and uncontroversial as any attribute of the modern state, even if the extent of its practical provision, and the means by which this is provided, remain acutely controversial.

What is still especially contentious about Hobbes's conception of political obligation is the trenchancy of his insistence that the state cannot hope to be able to provide the core services for which it is imperatively needed unless it can decide for itself without internal impediment just what opinions may be publicly expressed, and just who is to own what and why. Neither of these views is well regarded at present in Western societies (or, for that matter, in a country like Japan). But both remain deeply implicated in the idea of the state, as they do in the practices of many existing states. To see how far we have good reason to view the idea of the state in the end with categorical sympathy or hostility, we need to judge how far Hobbes was right to regard the appropriation of these powers as essential to the state as such, and how far his decision so to regard them was a remediable error of prudential judgment.

State Authority and Popular Consent

The demand that the state be in the end able to control the expression of opinion collides frontally with one of the most prominent contemporary candidates for a criterion of political right: the judgment that only states which accurately express the opinions and judgments of their own citizens can be fully entitled to the latter's obedience. It is enormously important for the understanding of modern politics to grasp why this principle of political right has come to enjoy the normative authority which it now carries. But it is also essential, for the same purpose, to judge how far the principle really does shape the workings of modern political institutions, and why it does not (and perhaps could not) shape them more decisively.

Over the last two decades especially, the presumption that it is proper or desirable for the state to decide, on its own best judgment, who should own what and why has been subjected to intense and highly effective (if also often somewhat confused) political assault. These two prominent features of Hobbes's conception of the state, in each instance emphatic assertions of the necessary scope of its powers, have become acutely disturbing today to some of the most influential bodies of political opinion (as, of course, they already were in Hobbes's own day). The first is profoundly unacceptable (at least at first sight) to any modern interpreter of the state as a mechanism for ensuring the human rights of its citizens. The second is almost equally discomfiting for any serious believer in the unique virtue and efficacy of a capitalist organization of production. A capitalist economy, in this sense, is one organized comprehensively through markets, in which most factors of production are privately, not publicly, owned, and in which the role of the state in relation to property must consist principally in facilitating the workings of markets and guaranteeing the ownership of whatever is privately owned.

In this perspective, Hobbes's conception of the state appears a pure structure of domination, and some of its most obtrusive features as categorically incompatible with fundamental human entitlements and basic preconditions for economic flourishing. But this judgment is definitely largely mistaken. Hobbes's causal assessment of what threatens and sustains political institutions is very different from our own. It arose from a very different experience and prompts very different practical conclusions. But it is wrong to see it either as implying or as intending to encourage a conception of the state as a structure of pure domination.

The powers which Hobbes insists that a state requires it requires not because it is agreeable for rulers to possess them, and still less because rulers themselves may come to feel personally entitled to exercise them, but because, in his causal judgment, they are prerequisites for it to discharge its core responsibility. That responsibility is to its subjects. Hobbes's theory was not, at its foundations, a theory of the entitlements of states. It was a theory of why individual subjects had good reason to obey their own state: a theory of the indispensability of the services which it, and it alone, was in a position to render to them. It was above all by guaranteeing to them peace, by excluding the imminent threat of violence from their lives, that it provided this service. On Hobbes's analysis, the clash of self-righteous opinion about who does or should own what, or about what God commands, directly and constantly jeopardizes the state's capacity to exclude violence from the lives of its subjects, and can readily imperil its own capacity even to continue to exist.

Where the state sees no clear and present danger in its subjects' voicing of their opinions, or in the patterns of property-holding and use to which they believe themselves to be entitled, Hobbes does not, of course, recommend that it should interfere in either domain (Ryan 1988; Tuck 1990; cf. Lund 1992). To do so would be perverse and inequitable. But it is the state's responsibility (and not the subjects' right) to judge this degree of jeopardy in every instance. It carries (and must carry) the authority of its own subjects' will and choice to make that judgment on their behalf, and to act decisively upon it. Indeed each subject has a right against every other subject that it should do just this. That is precisely why (on Hobbes's account) they were right to authorize it, and did in fact authorize it, in the first place.

What makes Hobbes so illuminating about what states really are is not the quality of his judgment about political causality: of what causes what in politics. That judgment was deployed on states very unlike those of today; and it may in any case have been quite erratic even in relation to them. What makes it still so illuminating is the decisiveness with which he rested his draconic insistence on the scope of the state's entitlement to dominate on the prerequisites for it to deliver to each and every subject the services which they most urgently needed. More precisely, it was the clarity of his argument that even the most emphatic structure of publicly self-righteous domination would be better understood not as an instance of subjugation to alien will, but as an outcome of potential rational choice on the part of the subjects' own individual wills.

THE STATE AND HUMAN RIGHTS: SOVEREIGNTY AND PERSONAL AUTONOMY

To part company decisively with Hobbes's conception of the state, it is not enough to conclude that in the right country at the right time (over very many, though not all, matters, Great Britain at the time of writing) there is no danger whatever in according to its citizens an unfettered right to think and say what they please. Still less is it enough to conclude that much of the economic life of its inhabitants will go better if it is left to the choices of a wide variety of other agencies acting for their own perceived advantage than it is likely to do if the officials of the state itself attempt to concert and control most of that life for what they judge to be the collective good. Genuinely to reject Hobbes's conception of the state, what is needed is a firm decision that there are no other values (harm to others, the danger of violent death) which a state has a prior responsibility to take account of in choosing, for example, how far to regulate public expression or how far to tax.

The American philosopher Robert Nozick's celebrated argument that taxation is equivalent to forced labour has convinced few readers who did not already presuppose it (Nozick 1975). But he was certainly right to insist that there is no clear dividing line, from the viewpoint of ownership, between being taxed and having one's property confiscated. Taxation at 100 per cent simply is confiscation; and taxation at over 100 per cent is confiscation with punitive damages.

In practice, the entities which we now call 'states' can approximate quite closely to structures of pure domination, in which relatively small numbers of human beings dominate relatively large numbers, and do so for no clearly identifiable, independent and potentially justifying purpose. (Few states today neglect to offer at least a façade of justification. Even the worst purport to defend the nation against its internal or external enemies, or to serve the people, or perhaps Allah. But in some cases – Myanmar, for most of its independent history Nigeria – that pretence has become pretty perfunctory.) These cases demonstrate conclusively some of the worst domestic potentialities of the idea of the modern state. But it is less clear that they cast light on the implications of the idea itself. To focus the idea more clearly, it is more helpful to begin from Hobbes and to register the direct tie between the interpretation which he gave to it (one which played a key historical role in defining the term in the first place) and what he saw as the *rights* of its human subjects.

The idea of the modern state and the idea of human rights are not two clear and diametrically opposed conceptions. Each is distinctly hazier than this suggests; and the two, on any careful historical or conceptual analysis, are very elaborately interrelated with one another. This can be shown readily enough by elementary study of the historical development of European political thinking, from Hobbes, to Locke, Montesquieu, Rousseau, Kant, Hegel and John Stuart Mill (for example, Tuck 1979, 1993 and 1999; Skinner 1978; Dunn 1969, 1985 and 1996(a)). But it can also be shown, at least equally decisively, by studying the political, social and economic histories of particular human populations over the last two hundred years. In those histories the ideas of the state and of human rights interact ceaselessly, and do so with increasing momentum and urgency. Through each flows an immense variety of human initiatives and patterns of political action. On any coherent and remotely adequate interpretation of what has been happening in modern politics and what has given it its present shape, these are two of the master ideas of modern politics.

What we need to see about them from the outset is that these are ideas which will always be in some tension with one another but which also belong deeply together. Anyone who is an enemy to one will sooner or later prove an enemy to the other (Dunn 1990, cap. 3; Lukes 1985; cf. Taylor 1982). Seen sympathetically and from the viewpoint of potential agency, the relation between the two is one of means to end. The state is a means; the securing of human rights the end. The state, it is still reasonable to believe, is thus far a necessary means, however woefully insufficient particular examples of it may prove in practice. If we will the end of the securing of rights, this is (at least one of) the means we must, for the moment, will too. (If we cannot bring ourselves to will it, we must find some other at least equally effective and more dependable means to will in its place. So far we have failed to do so.) But, of course, many states have no claim to be viewed sympathetically. Whatever they are a means to, it is certainly not the securing of the rights of most of those whom they affect. One key question of modern politics is how states (or other types of political institution with newer names and superior properties) can be built so as to ensure human rights rather than violate them. This is the question which modern theories on a variety of topics from constitutional republican representative government (Fontana (ed.) 1994; Manin 1997) to the radical transformation of gender relations aim to help us to answer. The answers they suggest, however, cannot any longer rest on their own. Once discovered or chosen, they must articulate, too, as deftly as they can, with answers to a very different sort of question, the question of how economies can operate most efficiently: increase the supply of goods and services as handsomely as possible, while doing as little damage as possible to other, and sometimes longer-term, human interests at the same time (Dunn 1994).

We need not be surprised that no master theory of just how this articulation can be caused to come out consistently beneficial has worn very well over the last two centuries (compare Dunn (ed.) 1990, Dunn 1990, 1993 and 1999 with the experiences reported in Haggard and Webb (eds) 1994). Either question is exacting enough on its own. Discerning a clear and dependable relation between compelling answers to both has so far proved beyond the wit of interpreters of modern politics, or economics. This is not the sort of gap which it would be sane for an individual to hope to fill. (Nor does the present book have any such ambitions.) But it is important from the beginning to have some conception of where it is that we are for the present astray, of why it is that we have so evidently lost the thread, and of why we cannot reasonably hope to find that thread once again.

(Of course, the metaphor of the thread is misplaced in the first place: no Ariadne without Theseus. There is no sound reason to suppose that human beings have ever been fortunate enough to hold such a thread. But they have sometimes in the past been quite confident that they did. Some at least feign to believe that they do so even today; and some will almost certainly continue to suppose this throughout any human future that lies ahead.)

If we wish to understand politics, I would argue, this is a hope which we must firmly abandon, a promise of ease which we must refuse to offer ourselves. Not only must we abandon it, we must also grasp why it is essential for us to do so, why the ease which it offers, however solacing in other ways, can only be premissed on political illusion, and will thus on balance certainly expose us to quite gratuitous dangers.

The most reckless follies, it is true, can sometimes succeed. But, despite Lenin, this casts distinctly more light on warfare than it does on politics. Illusion can foster the brazenness of political actors and give them nerves of steel. But they will seldom profit for long just from being fools, or blithely unaware of the risks which they are running on their own or others' behalfs.

Conclusion

States have an insistent ideological impulse towards coherence, efficacy and the pursuit of edifying collective purposes. They also have a relentless availability for ad-hoc appropriation for whatever purposes groups or individuals happen to find compelling. Professional analysts of politics often suggest or presuppose that the first of these features is simply an imposture, and the second its permanent and necessary reality. But this is not a sound judgment. What is true is that the first is very much a reflection of the *idea* of a state, and the second an ineliminable potential of its practical instantiation. Neither, therefore, can simply be dismissed; but neither, also, offers a trustworthy basis on its own on which to judge the politics of anywhere in particular at any given time. Each must be kept permanently in view and assessed carefully for its weight and substance *in situ*. Judging politics is always judging where and how the two line up.

3

Political Understanding

Political Understanding as Guide to Political Judgment?

WHO NEEDS TO UNDERSTAND POLITICS?

It is not because political understanding is intrinsically encouraging, or because informing ourselves about politics can be relied upon to prove agreeable, that we have good reason to try to understand politics. A soberer judgment would have to be that much of politics is always likely to be extremely depressing, and that for most (though not all) of us the quest for political information will impose more personal costs than it will yield rewards. This thought has been formalized at some length by American political scientists (following Downs 1957; cf. Barry 1965 and 1970) in the conception of information costs: costs not merely in money itself (spent or left unearned), but also in the other and more vividly enjoyable activities which we must forgo if we are to search for political information. It is easy to be over-solemn about this. Some of us become deeply addicted to politics, and find the deprivation of political information acutely distressing. Even for the better balanced, political gossip can be as gratifying as any other kind of gossip. But in the main politics is not one of the more rewarding human preoccupations, either aesthetically or materially, still less libidinally.

What might make it worthwhile to understand politics is the effect of doing so on our political judgment, and hence on our political actions. The less we understand what is really going on, the less likely we are to act, individually or collectively, in a well-advised way. The very best of understanding will never show us quite what to do. But reasonably accessible levels of understanding can and should help us to judge better what to favour or oppose, and what courses of action to avoid like the plague. It is a fair (and very common) complaint about political thinking that its lessons are predominantly negative (and somewhat discouraging): fair, insofar as the complaint itself is largely true. But, fair though it may be, it is better understood as a complaint in the end against the universe and the place of human beings within this than as a complaint against political understanding itself. Types of understanding which are less discouraging and more positive in what they offer do not show us better how to deal with one another or with the external world. At most they show us how to deal more successfully with ourselves, given our very limited capacities to deal successfully with one another or the external world. They may reconcile us to (make us more at home within) the universe; but they do so essentially by psychic sedation.

There is no reason whatever to anticipate that psychic sedation, whether on a large or a small scale, will have a benign effect on politics, and some reason to fear that it may have extremely sinister consequences. These are, of course, complicated and somewhat opaque political judgments in themselves. It is especially instructive to try to make them, as teachers are constantly prompted to do, about the political dispositions and cultures of different educational cohorts of schoolchildren or university students. What, then or later, are the net benefits or costs of an activist or of a more politically quietist or indifferent generation? On the whole those most moved to make such judgments are too psychically involved themselves to do so with much reliability. In the turmoil of twentieth-century political and economic change these shifts in generational attitude have often been prominently associated with major national crises, and especially so in the case of some of the more symbolically evocative and responsive of twentieth-century states (China in 1919, in the Cultural Revolution, and again in Tiananmen Square; France, above all in 1968; Indonesia, in the late 1990s).

As yet, however, social scientists have made little, if any, headway in assessing their overall consequences.

THE CASE AGAINST POLITICAL UNDERSTANDING

There is a strongly conservative case against political understanding – in essence, that most human beings (all human beings?) are too dangerous, too malign and too silly to be trusted with anything as menacing as true beliefs about what is really going on in their lives. But if this is offered as a rational case, and not simply as a mood of spiritual submission (a due humility, in place of an odious pride), it is either incoherent or it goes much too far. If most human beings are too malign to be trusted, why should any human beings prove dependably trustworthy? Who among them is to judge which of them is trustworthy (and when) and which is not? If human understanding is inherently treacherous, why should we trust in any understanding but God's? (God, for this purpose, *defines* right understanding. Unlike us, God cannot see or judge or feel wrong.)

The deepest and steadiest versions of this line of thought, especially the great conservative revulsion in face of the French Revolution – Joseph de Maistre (Maistre 1994), Louis de Bonald, perhaps Hamann (Berlin 1994) – offered as comprehensive surrogate for human judgment an unflinching trust in divine Providence, a direct submission of the mind as well as the will to God himself. But they made this offer, of course, in the form of a personal recommendation of a line of conduct, and did not themselves hesitate to give extensive practical grounds for their judgment. Nothing at the time, still less in what has happened since, gives the slightest reason for supposing that God shared their judgment (even on the hazardous supposition that He was and is there to do so). Among human beings themselves, the case for apolitical resignation is merely a recklessly over-general instance of political judgment. How aptly it applies is a question which will itself require permanent and highly particular political judgment to answer, wherever it is entertained or evoked. The case in favour of seeking to improve our political judgment is tentative and unexhilarating. It could never be conclusive, especially as against other possible uses for our time and hope and imaginative energies. But the case against seeking to do so is not only feckless; it is also superstitious through and through.

UNDERSTANDING, ENGAGEMENT AND SELF-DECEPTION

There are two very different senses of political understanding which we need to distinguish as sharply as we can. Once we do distinguish them, they suggest two very different trajectories towards (or away from) political understanding, and two very different ways of viewing the history of politics. The first prompts us to view that history dispassionately and without engagement (as so much blood under the bridge). The second prompts us to view it actively and with engagement: above all, as our sole repository of potentially decisive evidence on what, on any scale of human interaction above the most intimate, we ourselves have good reason to try to do in response to the broader human setting of our lives.

The first is in one sense the simpler. It takes politics as, even from our point of view, just one element within the history of the universe, to be understood in principle in just the same sorts of terms and by just the same methods as any other element in that history. On closer consideration, however, this air of simplicity has proved largely illusory. Much energy has been expended in the effort to understand politics in this way. But there is little agreement as to which of the efforts have been even minimally successful, or even as to what has enabled these to succeed insofar as they have done so. Even the assumption that the inquiry itself can in principle be coherent has been questioned quite effectively (Taylor 1985, cap. 2), essentially by casting doubt on whether the element of the history of the universe which is at issue can be identified in the first place in a way independent of our own concerns.

There is an obvious point to seeking to understand politics dispassionately and without engagement. If we are to understand it, and not merely fantasize about it, we need to understand it the way it is, and not the way we would like it to be. We need to grasp its causal dynamics as these really are and to keep our hopes and fears as firmly as we can out of our belief about these dynamics. But this obvious maxim is not a purely epistemological point: not just a matter of applying sound rules on how to know and how to avoid false beliefs. It is also, and rather obtrusively, a political point – a point which bears directly on our engagements, tangles unavoidably with our passions and fantasies, and carries pressing implications for what we do or do not have good reason to do. If there is no means of identifying politics in the first place (no means, for example, of distinguishing it clearly from the rest of human activity, or from the entire causal interaction between humans and the rest of nature), any attempt to understand it dispassionately and without engagement is bound to prove futile. Any sense of epistemological security predicated on such efforts would be wholly illusory. On this view, then, the contrast between the two viewpoints is best seen not as a clash between two distinct conceptions of how to know (one modern and rational, and the other pre-modern and superstitious), but rather as a far less clear-cut disagreement over how best to handle our own passions and worldly commitments (conscious or inadvertent), as we attempt to understand as best we can.

What there in the end is to understand, on either view, is a very complicated and concrete segment of reality with an urgent bearing on human interests. One perspective suggests that it is best understood by ignoring this bearing on human interests (or by attending to it only as it shows up unmistakably within the causal relations themselves: for example, by prompting particular human beings to act in one way rather than another).

The other perspective assumes that since it is the bearing of politics on human interests which gives us our strongest reasons for wishing to understand it in the first place, it would be perverse, even if it were practicable, not to understand it as steadily as we can *through* its relations to those interests. If we seek to understand politics (a somewhat indeterminate range of human activity), while ignoring its bearing on human interests, it is hard (or perhaps impossible) to know quite how to begin: what to take as our core subject matter, or how to proceed in establishing intellectual control over that subject matter. Even if we do attempt to understand politics in relation to its bearing on human interests, it is far from clear that this gives us either a determinate core subject matter to understand or any reasonably trustworthy rules of intellectual procedure, through which to grasp this.

What we can draw from this perspective is an initial schedule of questions which will in the end need to be answered: if not a method, at least an outline intellectual agenda. In politics, human beings act to achieve immediate purposes and, less steadily, to serve or secure their more enduring interests. The relation between the immediate and the longer term is seldom very clear or especially reassuring. The main grounds for doubting the quality of human judgment today, from the most intimate and personal of settings to their most extended economic and political performances, are, as they perhaps always have been, doubts about how far immediate purposes dominate longer-term interests. Ecological panic is the most prominent and consequential example of such anxiety at present. It is at least possible that it, and any other particular focus of fear at present (demographic, ethnic, military), will in the end prove largely unfounded. But this has hardly been true of the human record thus far; and we would be stunningly fortunate in our day if it proved true for us. Nor are there clear traces, as we encounter one another in everyday life with its endless quarrels and confusions, that our collective grip on practical rationality is any more impressive than that of our predecessors. Most of us have discarded some false beliefs which were quite widespread in the past. But we are virtually certain to have acquired numerous other relatively novel beliefs, most of which will also in due course prove to be largely mistaken in their turn. Most of us most of the time, too, do not seem notably more temperate or clearer-sighted over much of our own lives than the human beings of earlier generations.

CONCLUSION

Political understanding, then, has a triadic structure. It is always understanding *of* a subject matter *for* a person or set of persons *in relation to* the questions of how they might have good reason to act, or to welcome (or fear) others acting on their behalf. These three elements naturally vary in salience; and the last of them varies greatly in urgency. Where there is little to hope for and nothing much to fear from politics (however understood: cf. John Locke to Edward Clarke, 17 October 1690: Locke 1979, 148), the third element is, *ex hypothesi*, nugatory; and the second loses significance along with it. But, while there may always be many circumstances in which most of us have nothing much to hope for from politics, it is hard to imagine a world in the future in which the great majority of human beings no longer have anything to fear from politics. Would it perhaps be the world foreseen by Goethe on his Italian journey: 'I am sure that he [that is, Herder] will have set forth very well the beautiful dream-wish of mankind that things will be better one day. Speaking for myself, I too believe that humanity will win in the long run; I am only afraid that at the same time the world will have turned into one huge hospital where everyone is everybody else's humane nurse' (Goethe 1970, 316–17)?

Understanding Human Interests

WHAT ARE HUMAN INTERESTS?

I have no clear idea of how it would be wise to attempt to understand politics independently of its bearing on human interests. But it is much easier to see some of what we must try to understand if we wish to understand politics as it does bear on human interests. In the first place, truistically but decisively, we must try to understand what interests human beings really do have.

This has proved a very treacherous venture. So treacherous, in fact, that much of the imaginative energy of the search for an understanding of politics independent of human interests plainly came from rational despondency at ever determining what those interests are. Many of the greatest political theorists have begun from that question (perhaps all the greatest political thinkers – Plato, Aristotle, Augustine, Hobbes, Rousseau, Kant, Hegel). It is fashionable today to regard their efforts as ludicrously over-ambitious, and their failures, accordingly, as eminently deserved. But fashion is seldom a trustworthy epistemic guide. No doubt their failures have been far from surprising. But it does not follow from this that it would have been (or is, or will be) more salutary to eschew any such attempt. If anything is inherently objectionable about these great adventures of the past, it is not the enormity of their authors' presumption in addressing the questions which they asked, but the assurance which some of them mustered over their success in answering these questions, and, still less surprisingly, many of the elements on which they relied in formulating their answers. We shall certainly continue to have ample grounds for modesty about our own success in answering such questions; and it is entirely reasonable to doubt the trustworthiness of many of the assumptions which we may make in attempting to answer them. But that is no reason whatever for declining to ask the questions in the first place, nor for not seeking to answer them as bravely as we dare, and with as much intellectual energy and care as we can.

If we do press the questions with any energy, we are unlikely to settle for any of the many well-established intellectual devices for taming the problem of identifying the content of human interests. (For thoughtful and contrasting discussions see, for example, Geuss 1980; Barry 1965; Parfit 1984; Griffin 1986.) We will not be tempted, for example, to equate them with the preferences unmistakably revealed by the actions of others. A moment's reflection is enough to make clear that our own actions are a singularly unreliable guide to what our preferences really are, let alone to what we might seriously suppose to be in our own interests (too flustered, too confused, too offhand, too indolently and myopically greedy, too obsessive, too clumsy, too sly, too endlessly silly). Only the very inattentive can suppose that anyone is a consistently sound judge of their own interests, and only the hopelessly ingenuous are likely to suppose that most human behaviour dependably reveals even what its perpetrators are up to, let alone the full range of potentially pertinent considerations which cross their minds over time.

It may be hard to tell for sure what is in anyone else's mind; and there have been vigorous and interesting philosophical arguments intended to demonstrate that to *know* what is in anyone else's mind is simply out of the question. But it is taking philosophy altogether too seriously to be prompted to doubt that anything at all is in the minds of others over time. (For a compelling interpretative strategy see Davidson 1980. For an introduction to the field of philosophy which seeks to clarify these issues see McGinn 1982.) Since the most promising grounds for doubting that we can ever know what is in the minds of others strongly suggest that we are just as much at sea when it comes to identifying at all reliably what is really going on in our own minds, this line of scepticism is too internally unstable to sustain with any consistency. (Even the youthful David Hume found it only intermittently credible: Hume 1911.) Since politics proceeds on its violent and dangerous way with minimal attention to doubts of this character, it is not a wise approach to taking the measure of politics to linger over them too protractedly. We can be relatively confident that the problem of how to identify human interests will never receive a conclusive solution. But that is no reason whatever for ceasing to try to identify these interests in the arenas which do (or may well) affect our own lives, let alone for embracing what are patently pseudo-solutions, the main charm of which consists in their deference to particular patterns of philosophical nervousness.

If we are prepared to accept the risks of attempting to understand politics actively and with engagement – of understanding it in relation to human interests – what will that commit us to seeking to understand?

An understanding of politics as it bears on human interests cannot hope to be a unified vision from a single point of view. For one thing, it must seek to do justice to the full heterogeneity of human points of view. At a bare minimum it must do its best to allow for the causal significance of their presence (for what can and cannot happen in politics because all of them are there). More adequately, it must also try to register the implications for what the interests of human beings really are of the bewildering variety of human imaginings across cultures, across space, across time and across the lifetime of every individual.

It must acknowledge not merely the absence of a single plainly authoritative standard of value to which all human beings should plainly defer, but also the painful clashes between values in everyone's life, and the tensions and incompatibilities between the pursuit of different values on every scale of collective life from the couple or nuclear family to an entire civilization (Berlin 1990; Williams 1985; Huntington 1993 and 1997).

Human interests patently conflict with one another. Human purposes clash repeatedly, within individual lives and between them. These clashes readily prompt not merely enmity but also, as Hobbes underlined, a moral and aesthetic contempt for one another, and an unreflective self-regard.

HUMAN INTERESTS AND RATIONAL CO-OPERATION

As analysts of collective action have repeatedly insisted, it is often with the best will in the world hard or impossible to locate clear and dependable bases on which we do have good reason to co-operate with one another. Simply registering the causal significance of this immense array of grounds for mutual impatience, intolerance and animosity (grasping the ways in which they are likely to move us to behave) is unlikely to generate patience, trust and co-operation. The urgency of the need for the co-operative virtues is no guarantee of their availability. Even the most accurate and level-headed registration of the practical significance of the grounds for mutual hostility in the ways in which human beings view their world is little direct aid in muting that hostility. It is only when this recognition affects our sense of our own purposes, and above all our sense of the resemblances, or the categorical contrasts, between our own purposes and those of others, that registering the presence of difference can lead to its acknowledgment, let alone its appreciation.

TOLERANCE

Tolerance is a conceptually precarious virtue – permanently poised between indifference and appreciation. Once appreciation is firmly in place, tolerance has become a misnomer. It is for what is subjectively intolerable that tolerance is required. If I like or admire someone, I certainly cannot helpfully be said to tolerate them – although I almost certainly will have, sooner or later, occasion to tolerate something about them which is (to me) distasteful: few humans are comprehensively agreeable, and none at all is consistently admirable. But tolerance which simply consists in indifference (tolerance untouched by any hint of appreciation) is a distinctly fair-weather virtue. As soon as the indifference cracks, the tolerance will go with it.

To move from a minimal registering of difference to a reasonably robust tolerance requires the mechanism of identification, a recapturing of resemblance at a slightly more abstract level. It requires, too, an acceptance of the applicability (at least for some purposes) of the principle of reciprocity. It is more than most us can manage to view any other human beings with quite the delicate sympathy with which we view ourselves. (A more frequent, if often unwelcome, possibility is to be compelled to view ourselves intermittently as others routinely view us. Cf. Strawson 1968.) It is a less heroic achievement, however, to recognize that every other human being (Michael Portillo, O. J. Simpson, Mother Theresa) has a life to live of their own. In a great scene in Marcel Proust's novel, the dying Swann bids farewell to his old friends the Duke and Duchess of Guermantes, who are on their way to an appropriately grand dinner:

> 'But whatever I do, I mustn't make you late; you're dining out, remember,' he added, because he knew that for other people their own social obligations took precedence over the death of a friend, and he put himself in their place thanks to

> his instinctive politeness. But that of the Duchess enabled her to perceive in a vague way that the dinner party to which she was going must count for less to Swann than his own death. (Proust 1983, II, 618)

We cannot hope to match Swann's politeness. But if we wish to understand politics, we shall certainly need to grasp what Swann knew. At the very least, we must get as far as the Duchesse de Guermantes.

INTERESTS AND IDENTIFICATION

To judge what politics implies for what we have good reason to do is only a crisply defined task if the *we* in question is extremely narrow (perhaps, indeed, if it is a rhetorically misleading way of referring to a single person: a singular masquerading as a plural). But the referent of *we* is never pre-given. It has an insistent tendency to spread out from individuals to families and friends, communities and cultures, nations, civilizations, even the species as whole, at least in the present and the future. (It is psychologically peculiar to identify at all wholeheartedly with our ancestors in the Old Stone Age. But many of us have been brought up to profess, however flippantly, an identification with the future of our species as a whole, if not indeed with that of endless other species also. On the puzzles and force of this orientation, see Parfit 1984.)

The causal substance of politics, as this exists at any time (the patterns of practical interaction between human groups and their prospective consequences) must lie at the centre of political understanding, however broad or narrow the human identification which drives our efforts to reach such understanding. For any *we*, it will tell us, among other things, some of the limits to what we could have good reason to do. It will show us, insofar as anything can, the degree of plasticity in our collective fate at the time, the range within which it can, or might be, modified by our own or others' actions. It will indicate, too, for any given *we*, the commonality or contrast of our predicament with those of other groups, and may well over time modify our identifications by so doing. It will show us how far some of our purposes, and the conceptions of our interests which inform those purposes and may well have derived from them in the past, are in fact coherent and well conceived. What it cannot do is to show us how far the purposes themselves are creditable or defensible, or how narrowly we have good reason to confine our identifications. In the end this is simply a question *to* each of us, one which no one else has either the authority or the power to answer for us, however many and imposing the claims which have been advanced across history to be in a position to do so.

UNDERSTANDING AND DEMOCRACY

The fact that this is a question to everyone does not give everyone's answer to it equal force or insight. Indeed it does not give any particular answer any authority at all (though it certainly gives it a minimum of political weight). Some answers are manifestly evil. Very many are exceedingly stupid. To deny this is to carry tolerance to the point of indifference (as we have already seen, a highly insecure foundation for political co-operation). Over this point, there remain, as there have been since self-consciously critical political thinking began, acute tensions between democratic and aristocratic elements in political understanding. The very idea of attempting to understand something which is recognized to be hard to grasp has pronounced aristocratic elements. But any interpretation of democracy as a political value which repudiates the need to understand what is hard to grasp (what many at any given time have palpably failed to grasp) will preclude coherent understanding of interests, and make it exceedingly unlikely that the democrats in question do in fact grasp their own interests with any accuracy. Every reflective and seriously entertained interpretation of democratic politics throughout the history of the idea of democracy (Thucydides 1919–23; Finley 1983; Farrar 1988; Ober 1989; Hansen 1991; Manin 1997) has needed to incorporate counterbalancing and plainly aristocratic themes. With the growing normative weight and political power of the idea of democracy, this has become harder (and politically more costly) to acknowledge at all frankly (Dunn (ed.) 1992). But the failure to acknowledge it frankly has poisoned modern political thinking almost in its entirety, reducing it more and more radically to professedly morally engaged stupidity or bad faith, or to openly morally unanchored instrumental calculation. To learn to understand politics, what we need above all is to learn how to avoid either horn of this unappetizing and essentially delusory dilemma.

THE BEARING OF UNDERSTANDING ON POLITICAL JUDGMENT: CAUSALITY AND VALUES

What has all this to do with understanding politics? How might it help us to grasp why the unlikely figure of John Major, the precarious leader of the Conservative Party at the time, was Prime Minister of the United Kingdom in the summer of 1996? Or to judge why his party's principal opponent at the time was still the Labour Party? Or why the Kingdom of Scotland has been politically united with the Kingdom of England since 1707 (Levack 1987; Colley 1992; Nairn 1977)? Or why, while the United Kingdom still has its monarch, it has also become a representative democracy, with much in common with its fellow members of the European Union? Or why the very wealthy in the United Kingdom, as in the United States, should on average have become so much wealthier since the early 1980s, while many of their fellow citizens so plainly have not (*Independent on Sunday*, 21 July 1996; cf. Gottschalk and Smeeding 1998; Gottschalk 1993; Danziger and Gottschalk 1995).[3]

We need to understand our own values, if we are to judge how we in particular have good reason to act. But, even to judge the merits of these values, we need to understand a great deal else as well. To grasp the significance of what has been happening in politics, we need, for a start, to be far less egocentric: to understand the values of very many others too. Most political understanding consists not in direct insight into values, but in assessment of causality: of how existing circumstances have come about, of what leads to what and what prevents what, in politics. There is some temptation to see political causality just as obstruction to our own personal values: to see what we happen to want and care about as a free-standing force and value in itself, and to see how the rest of the human world inhibits its realization as not merely alien (which it plainly is) but also devoid of value. Yet this is not a reasonable view (Scanlon 1982). If anything which any human values is of value merely because they happen to value it, then everything which all humans value must be of value in exactly the same way. Much of the way (I would say most of the way) in which the rest of the human world inhibits the realization of our own values is best understood not just as alien force but also as alien value: as the shared presence of the values of our human fellows.

If we can learn to register this co-presence accurately, we shall not merely have made some headway in grasping political causality, we shall also have begun to grasp much of the human significance of politics in a less egocentric way. To understand political causality, then, can also be morally educative. But its capacity to educate is permissive, not compulsive. Highly skilled and utterly morally unanchored instrumental calculation is a real and relatively stable possibility. In politics everywhere always there are those attempting to develop this skill, to deploy it on their own behalf, and to market it to those who can afford to pay handsomely for it. There is a long and often lurid history of the cultivation of such skills, from classical Greece, China or India, through Machiavelli and the early modern European analysts of Reason of State (Meinecke 1957), to the nuclear strategists of the Rand Corporation or the Hudson Institute, the more ambitious National Security Advisers to America's post-war Presidents, and the media strategists of contemporary electoral campaigns. These people may not ever understand quite what they are doing. But it would be absurd to deny that they grasp some aspects of political causality far more deeply and accurately than you or I can ever hope to do. They do so, of course, mainly through intelligence, natural aptitude and a certain lack of fastidiousness, but also through a high degree of attention and energy. It would be nice to believe that nothing in this book could impede anyone with equal intelligence, natural aptitude and opportunity for energetic attention from getting equally far. But it is less clear whether greater fastidiousness is merely likely to limit energy and attention, or whether it would sooner or later prove a handicap to understanding in itself. Machiavelli, for example, certainly suggests that most human beings cannot endure very much political reality. What one cannot bear, one has extremely fierce motives for refusing fully to comprehend. One hazardous hope in seeking to understand politics is the hope of facing Machiavelli down, even of showing him to be wrong. It is a very nice point if anyone has ever succeeded in doing so. But that alone may be no reason not to try. (What would give a good reason for not trying is his simply being right.)

THE INSTITUTIONAL AND PRACTICAL SCOPE OF POLITICS

To begin to understand politics, we first need to see what range of institutions and practices we must consider. It is easy to start such a list, if never possible to know that one has completed it. If we attempt to understand politics today, there will be many prominent items on the list which simply could not have figured on it if we had been attempting to understand politics a thousand years ago. A thousand years ago, we should remember, no one, as far as we know, was using the term *politics* in any language to refer to the field of human interaction which we now so name. Politics, you might even say a little flashily, was not even there to understand. In AD 1000, there were certainly no modern states. There was no genuinely global market, and few effectively national markets, in any goods or services. There were no political, diplomatic or legal institutions spanning the world as a whole. Coercion, ownership, exchange and normative interpretation of each of these were all very different from the ways they are today. Political agency itself was often all but unrecognizable to us (cf. for example Bloch 1973). Even in two hundred years' time it will be surprising, unless the conditions of human life have already deteriorated spectacularly, if there are not many equally novel institutions and practices at the centre of politics. Political understanding for us, however, must obviously consist principally of understanding of politics today (and perhaps tomorrow), *from* today: from where we now are.

Understanding States

THE SCOPE AND LIMITS OF STATE POWER TODAY

For this, the list must still begin with states as these now are (Dunn (ed.) 1994). It must try to capture both their form (why they have their present institutional shape and the public conceptions of value which now inform them) and their content (their internal operating dynamics, the main pressures which act upon them from the outside, and the principal components of collective life, inside and outside their own territories, on which they exert a more or less steady pressure). It must separate out their main components (coercive, legislative, adjudicative, administrative, protective, educative) and make clear why these components link together as they do, or interfere with one another over time. It must display them as structures both of law and of power, as sites of at least partial authority, as arenas of struggle, but also as zones of bemusement, frustration and the relentlessly cumulative weight of unintended consequences of vehemently intended actions. Even such a perfunctory list as this makes it luminously clear that what we need, if we are to succeed in grasping this substantial component of modern politics even in outline, is not some would-be integrative theoretical conception of the state which reduces this multiplicity of relations to a single pre-given and supposedly necessary order. There could scarcely be any such overarching order at any point in history in such an intensely contested zone of human experience. The quest to find one has largely proved, and could scarcely have failed to prove, a wilful exercise in superstition.

(i) Challengers and Limits to State Authority: Supranational Authorities, Markets, Subjects

Seen through their own master self-conception of sovereignty, all states must and do deal with at least three other quite distinct sites of power and potential authority. They must deal with territorially wider claims to be entitled to act, with their own peoples (their subjects) and with markets (sites of residually free economic exchange). All three of these sites challenge the sovereign pretension at the heart of state power: the claim to decide for its own subjects and over its own territory in the last instance what is to be, or not to be, done, what may, or must, or cannot be permitted to, happen. A few tentative supranational sites (a set of international or supranational courts, for some purposes the United Nations) claim authority to adjudicate from above on what states may or may not do. (For the background to their presence see Bull and Watson 1984.) They claim to apply to states a law which the latter have in some degree already acknowledged. Their central premiss is the existence of a valid international law to which all states are legally subject. This assumption has always been hard to reconcile with the core conception of what a state is. In the course of the twentieth century, the conception of the existence of a valid international law has made inroads, however erratically, into that core conception. We can be reasonably confident, and perhaps also reasonably determined, that these inroads will deepen in the future.

Markets, by contrast, are processes (or, at most, sites), not agents. In themselves they claim, and can claim, no authority whatever. Yet much authority has been claimed for them by their human admirers, and with important consequences. In the late twentieth century few would be fool enough to deny that markets are sites of immense power: sites which limit, sometimes very starkly indeed, what a given state can or cannot bring about. They do so by pricing goods and services and the investment of capital in such a way that the former can exchange freely and the latter yield on balance and over time greater profit. Markets, however, require structures of ownership, and both clear entitlements to use and effective control over resources on the part of human agents. These, in turn, increasingly require states to specify, guarantee and protect them, both internally and internationally. Much the most effective and densely used component of international law is the international law of commercial transactions. It is effective because, and insofar as, states accept its authority and enforce its implications.

Subjects, by contrast, are nowhere a very effective constraint on the power of their own state: an unsurprising consideration given that denial of the ultimate authority of the people was the central conceptual point behind the invention of the idea of the modern state in the first place (Skinner 1989; cf. Skinner 1978). Most states in the world today, however, claim confusingly to act in accordance with the will of these same subjects. Even in their own eyes they draw the authority they hold from the endeavour to do as their subjects would wish them to. Very many states claim that their actions are directly and reliably determined by what their subjects wish them to do. In claiming to be democracies, they do not merely acknowledge an ultimate authority on the part of the people (their subjects). They also claim to be doing as that authority (their subjects) tells them. In most states most of the time this claim is more than a little brazen. But the fact that the claim is advanced so extensively by states on their own behalf is a clear index that the people do indeed have some power. It is not a meaningless gesture of normative self-abasement, but an enforced index of at least some degree of constraint (Dunn (ed.) 1992).

Each of these sites is both a source of power and potentially effective agency and a locus of value. Authoritative agencies of international law (the United Nations, the International Court of Justice) claim to apply a law which does a justice to all human beings which the law of no single state could be fully trusted to deliver. Transnational agencies of opinion formation, propaganda and charitable disbursement (Amnesty, Greenpeace, the Red Cross, Oxfam) fight for human interests which they judge that particular governments (sometimes all governments) are incapable of serving, or conspicuously failing to serve. Transnational agencies of economic regulation establish frameworks for trade and monetary relations which facilitate at least some forms of economic exchange. Multinational corporations shape much of the changing economic activity across the world. By acting on state territories and populations wholly or in part from the outside, all achieve goals which probably could not be attained otherwise, and which they see as every bit as legitimate as those directly intended by the governments of the states in question.

Markets also, while they cannot accurately be said to do anything themselves, certainly foster the capacity of the most potent agencies in the world today to act as these now can, already limit the capacity of states to achieve many of the goals at which they have recently aimed, and emphatically constrain the range of policies which they can now pursue with reasonable hope of success. They do so, in the eyes of their admirers, by establishing (and enforcing) the price at which it is appropriate for goods and services to exchange. In rhetoric, this due equivalence is often presented as though it were a contemporary version of the medieval just price, as not merely their precise exchange value but their due reward. But the core idea at issue is theoretically more ambitious and evaluatively less committed than this. The view that markets can and should compete with states as candidates for authority has had immense political influence in the last two decades of the twentieth century. But it is hard to formulate clearly without self-refutation. What is compelling about it is better expressed as a judgment about lines of policy which states would be ill-advised or vicious to adopt than as a collision between two comparable contenders to define what truly is of value for particular human populations.

Citizens at large, singly or in groups, are certainly agents; and their capacity for agency has always placed some limits, significant if seldom clear-cut, on what the holders of state authority can bring about within their own suzerainty. As the eighteenth-century Scottish philosopher David Hume drily noted: 'Principles or prejudices frequently resist all the authority of the civil magistrate; whose power being founded on opinion, can never subvert their opinions, equally rooted with that of his title to dominion' (*Of the Origin of*

Government (1777): Hume 1985, 110). The claim to be obeyed is in the end just a claim; and its force over time depends upon the way it is heard and felt by others. (Not, to be sure, by all others within earshot, but at least by those others who can ensure that it is in the end obeyed or disobeyed.) Both the consolidation or deepening of state power and its weakening or dissolution have been erratic over time. Neither has ever developed in a simple linear fashion. But, in a variety of ways and for a miscellany of reasons, the revulsion from state authority and the practical faltering of state power have been especially pronounced since the mid-1980s. Why should this have been so (cf. for example Scott 1998)?

The core of the answer must lie in the exigencies of the Cold War, and in the outcome of that conflict in the collapse of the political pioneer of effective socialist revolution, the Soviet Union. In the eyes of its opponents, the Soviet Union had always been the very essence of excessive state pretension: a tyrannical state lording over a comprehensively subjugated people, and reshaping the whole of its society to fit its own odious taste: a profoundly pathological part taking itself for a potentially virtuous whole: a paradigmatic totalitarian state (Schapiro 1972). In a less historically and geographically specific form, the answer might be better put as the historical failure of socialism: the intellectual and practical collapse of the longstanding claim to provide a palpably superior economic, social, and hence political, order (Dunn 1984(a) and 1996(a), cap. 14; Bergounioux and Grunberg 1996). But underlying, and perhaps in the end undercutting, both of these answers is a different sort of process. The outcome was not just a product of geopolitical struggle, or of the refutation of an always somewhat hazy hypothesis about the prospects for comprehensive social and economic transformation for the better. It was also a product of a profound mutation within the domain of opinion: a transformation in the understanding of human value itself (Dunn (ed.) 1992, Conclusion; Dunn 1997). This transformation did not derive directly and automatically from specific changes in economic, political, or even social, structures and relations. It had a clear internal logic and a remarkable imaginative momentum. But its impact upon political processes and outcomes was always uneven and intermittent. It is still hard to judge quite what the transformation itself really means, and quite how deep, consistent and steady it is reasonable to hope for its impact to become. What is clear already is that in this instance the scale of the impact goes back not just to the imperatives of economic or political organization, but to the insistent, and in part autonomous, workings of the human imagination itself. (One way of conceiving the outcome is to see it as a substantial faltering in the presence of authority in societies: cf. Hont 1994; Bell 1976; Dunn 1985, cap. 3.) Here, at least, any ultimate separation between human evaluation and power would be simply incoherent.

(ii) Explaining, Assessing and Striving to Edify States

One helpful way of analysing modern political causality (what is really going on today in politics and why) is to map out these four distinct sources of power and sites of value (states, markets, transnational agencies, subjects) and consider how they bear upon one another. A second way is to attempt, independently, to judge their respective consequences at present for human interests now and in the future. This moves beyond the assessment of causality into an analysis of human value in itself, and raises many further questions as it does so. A third way, far less determinate and placing severe demands on the political judgment of the analysts, is to try to judge, on the basis of an assessment of these interests, quite how the four sources of power and sites of value might feasibly be modified to serve the interests more effectively.

I shall attempt all three. But to do so I need first to focus on each of the four sources of power and sites of value. Let us first consider the state. Whatever may have been true in the days of the Emperor Justinian, or in those of Martin Luther or Thomas Hobbes, how is it appropriate today to conceive what a state really is?

This, as we have seen, is a deceptively simple question. It does not have a single clear and plainly appropriate answer. But there are a number of comparatively promising approaches towards answering it. There certainly are states in the world today, and have, on a loose understanding of the term, been such for some time. Why are there such entities? (Cf. Finer 1997.)

EXPLAINING THE EXISTENCE OF STATES?: COERCION AND WAR

One approach to explaining the existence of states is to consider them as at least partly intended products of a great deal of energetic and manifestly intended action. To see them in this way does not necessarily privilege the public rationales for their creation or maintenance offered by those who lead or control them, or hold formal authority over them. But it does privilege a number of areas of state activity: the concentration and deployment of coercive power, the extraction of financial and other resources needed to sustain this power in face of potential enemies at home or abroad, the elaboration and operation of systems of law and adjudication, the establishment of administrative control over people and territory, increasingly the attempt to maintain or enhance the range and price competitivity of goods and services which their subjects can offer on the global market (Weber 1968; Dunn and Hont in Dunn (ed.) 1990; Dunn 1984(a); Finer 1997; Mann 1986–93).

Because of the dynamic destructiveness of modern weaponry, virtually all states today control a level of coercive power of which no human ruler could reasonably have dreamed even five hundred years ago. The history of the arming of states, the specialization and expansion of their coercive agencies for use at home or abroad, and their armed collisions and alliances (McNeill 1983; Kennedy 1988; Finer 1997) form the centre of the history of states in the classical realist view (the view of Machiavelli in the sixteenth century, and of Max Weber, Otto Hintze and E. H. Carr in the twentieth). This is an ugly picture. Over the centuries, too, it has been deeply implicated in the doing of appalling evil. War, as General Sherman said, is hell. It always has been so; and it is still conspicuously failing to become any less horrible. With the invention of thermonuclear weapons it reached a new threshold of destructive potential: one which could literally eliminate human life.

THE SOURCES OF MUTUAL THREAT

The interaction of human coercive power is inherently competitive and unstable. As the power itself grows, the potential destructiveness of the interactions into which it enters grows with it. We still have every reason to fear the state, to fear what states can and will do to one another, and what, in so doing, they may do to any, and now to all, of us. Where does this ghastly momentum come from? Does it come from us, or from something outside us (Waltz 1959)?

It certainly comes in part from the sort of animal that we are, from our biological history, which still equips (and often prompts) us to fight or to flee, to dare, to fear and to kill (cf. Runciman 1998). But, if this was the only identifiable source for our mutual threats, we would probably by now have learnt to handle these with more dexterity, since it has also equipped us to think, and to notice what is going on.

Besides stemming from each of us, one by one, in virtue of our animal nature, war also stems from a distinct field of our interaction: from politics itself. Part of its incidence, no doubt, can be illuminatingly explained through what I have called the theory of moral error – the recognition that some humans at particular points in time act in ways which they need not have done, and very plainly should not have done. Some wars, perhaps even most wars, can be traced to patently vicious purposes and actions (cf. Locke 1988). A better grasp, as already suggested, comes from the three main components of political understanding: from historically created and reshaped conflicts of interest, from the self-righteous individuality of political judgment, and from the logical difficulties of collective action. Wars do not come just from individual criminality of disposition in high places. They come also from quite reasonable conflicts over access to scarce and attractive goods (land, natural resources, human artefacts), from the fierce partiality with which the powerful (like the weak) see the actions of others in relation to their own, and from the inherent difficulty of identifying clear and stable bases for rational co-operation.

In the permanent choice between peace and war, if peace were clearly and steadily more eligible for all parties at all times, even such curmudgeonly creatures as human beings would be unlikely to fight each other on a large scale with any frequency. But peace is neither clearly nor steadily more eligible than war for many humans at many points in time. That is why there are so many wars. Historical divisions of interest and the structural partiality of political judgment are more than enough to ensure this.

Wherever peace is not both clearly and steadily more eligible than war, it is extraordinarily difficult for the very many humans for whom it really is more eligible to identify and establish a basis on which they can hope to co-operate confidently and dependably to avert war. This is an old and discouraging story, but not a wholly desperate one. In the aftermath of this century's two world wars, major efforts were made to create such a basis for co-operation. The first of these, the League of Nations, was in the end an unremitting failure. Even the second, the United Nations, fashioned in the aftermath of the Second World War, has proved at best a patchy and muted success. It is probably still true that most of such success as it has had can be fully captured by the sternest of realist interpreters: correctly identified as the product of the predictably effective pursuit of great-power interest. But the United Nations is a more sustained and less calamitous attempt at genuinely global co-operation to avert war than any made earlier; and we may still out find how to make it more effective in the future. Then again, we may not: and what is devastatingly clear is how acutely we need to do so.

THE CORE ROLE OF COERCION

Coercion is the core of states: what they have to be able to do and go on doing if they are to exist at all, and hence to be in a position to do anything else. The capacity they must create and maintain is the capacity to make each of their subjects in the end act as they direct and not as the subject in question would otherwise be inclined. This is an overweening claim; and it is not, of course, a capacity which any state (however totalitarian the inclinations of its rulers) has ever fully realized. What backs the claim in the end is control over weaponry: comparative firepower, or as Machiavelli more simply put it, 'good arms' (Machiavelli 1988, cap. 12, pp. 42–3). But the arms, naturally, need to be in the hands of those who can be trusted to use them as the rulers would wish. Commands are nothing without obedience. 'For if men know not their duty, what is there', Hobbes asked in the aftermath of England's seventeenth-century Civil War, 'that can force them to obey the laws? An army, you will say. But what shall force the army?' (Hobbes 1969, 59). Many countries in the course of the twentieth century, in Europe, Latin America, Africa and Asia, have found themselves, for one reason or another, effectively occupied by their own professional armed forces. Some, notably Nigeria and Myanmar at the time of writing, have found it extraordinarily difficult to re-establish effective civilian control over these forces. If political power, as Mao Zedong claimed, grows out of the barrel of a gun, it must be less easy than we normally assume to explain why soldiers do not rule in most places most of the time, why military regimes are not the rule rather than the exception. The fact remains, however, that today military regimes are by and large the exception. Even in the epoch of colonial empire, when political authority over much of the world rested rather nakedly on foreign conquest, it was not usually the case that formal rule, even locally, rested with military officers. Weapons may still be indispensable for rule; but they are evidently far from sufficient for it.

Four centuries ago, in the European cradle of modern political thinking, most presumptively legitimate political authority over territory or subjects could be traced back directly either to accident of birth or to military seizure. Even the accident of birth (a bewildering basis on which to claim a title to rule for most of us today) was in the majority of cases only intelligible as a rationale for legitimate authority if it, in its turn, ultimately led back to military conquest. There were, to be sure, other motifs deployed to present rule in a more engaging light, aligning it more tactfully with interpretations of God's purposes, or with the consent of the people, expressed through their appropriate representatives (Tierney 1982). But these seldom amounted to a genuinely alternative explanation of why the powers in question should have been in their present hands, still less of why the territories over which they were exercised should have been just what they were.

SUBJECTS AND TERRITORY

Modern political thinking has addressed with some energy the question of how states can legitimately claim rule over particular groups of subjects. The idea of the modern representative democratic republic is an important attempt to answer this question. But it has been decidedly less energetic, and notably more discreet, over the question of how a state can legitimately claim rule over a given scope of territory. As the government of the United Kingdom has painfully discovered, this is important, since disagreements over the title to rule particular groups of subjects are at their most intractable when expressed as claims to control territory. Ethnic cleansing is an ugly but far from irrational response to this dilemma. If I do not wish to be ruled by you, and you control the territory on which I live, I have in essence three options. I can leave the territory. I can accept your authority, however resentfully. Or I can attempt to capture that territory from you. If you resist my attempts (as you no doubt will), and if you can secure the co-operation of many others in your resistance, I face a pressing temptation to expel not merely you but also a substantial proportion of your collaborators from the territory. If war is hell, ethnic warfare in a multi-ethnic territory is likely to prove hell of a peculiarly intimate and ghastly kind. Very few territories in the modern world are not in some measure multi-ethnic in the composition of their populations. The idea of a nation state, a state composed of those who palpably belong together by birth, is an extraordinarily hazardous presence in modern history (Dunn in Dunn (ed.) 1995).

ARMIES AND POLICE

There cannot be political control without the capacity to coerce. The first right of the ruler is the right to use the sword (the *jus gladii*). Pacified and civilized states use the sword sparingly (Gilmour 1992(a)). A state like contemporary Japan, whose social foundations go back to the extraordinary level of social pacification achieved under the Tokugawa *bakufu* early in the seventeenth century, provides to its subjects even today a level of physical security in comparison with which the streets of most great American cities are haunts of rampant barbarism. But even the Japanese state, as the nerve-gas attacks of 1995 have underlined, needs the capacity to coerce whatever groups of its own subjects choose to flout its authority and threaten the lives of their fellows. In the geopolitical struggle between states today, long-distance missiles, aircraft and blue-water navies are at least as important as land forces. But the two key coercive institutions on which modern state power has been built, internally and externally, have been the standing army and the civil police force. The second of these is more recent than the first. Its political significance (like that of its companion institution, the modern prison) has yet to be explored entirely convincingly (cf. Finer in Tilly (ed.) 1975). (In this respect, the television police series probably offer a more sensitive barometer in the British case of shifting political awareness, in all its confusion and ambivalence, than the public discourse of Britain's career politicians.) By contrast, the standing army, separated from the populace at large and kept permanently ready for use, was clearly identified as a major political innovation as early as the seventeenth century (McNeill 1983; Pocock 1972; Schwoerer 1974; Robertson 1985; Ralston 1990). A standing army, set over against a disarmed people, was a state instrument for subjugating that people to its rulers: seen domestically, an instrument of explicitly alien authority. If the rulers themselves could not always be wholly confident of its allegiance, their peoples were still less likely to view it with implicit trust. In contrast with the military format of an armed people (the militia), standing armies, for all their potential professionalism and consequent efficacy in warfare, were hard to credit as guarantees of popular security.

COERCION AND TAXATION

An armed people, even a militia, do not require much expenditure or consume many additional resources over and above what is otherwise available to their members in everyday life. But standing armies, navies and civilian police forces (still more air forces or the increasingly rapidly changing weapons systems made possible by modern technological development) are exceedingly expensive. 'An army', wrote the seventeenth-century English republican James Harrington, 'is a beast with a great belly, which subsisteth not without very large pastures . . . and the beast is theirs that feeds it' (Harrington 1977, 411: *The Prerogative of Popular Government* (1658)). Besides the immense enhancement of their coercive powers, modern states also need to extract growing resources from their subjects, to fund the creation and maintenance of these unnerving powers.

Taxes, the taking of private resources by the state for supposedly public purposes, are just as central to the history of modern states as professional armed forces (Mann 1988, cap. 3). Few welcome the compulsory loss of their private resources. The history of taxation, throughout, has been closely bound up with the capacity to coerce, as well as somewhat more loosely interwoven with the political negotiation of relations between rulers and ruled. Within the format of the modern representative democratic republic, forms and levels of taxation are determined by the institutionalized consent of the people. But the exactions themselves are still, in detail, coercively enforced at least in the later instances. Coercion, too, is supposedly regulated by the institutionalized consent of the people. But in most European states, and in virtually all existing states in Africa, Asia and Latin America, both reasonably effective coercion and extensive taxation were plainly in place before anything which could plausibly be regarded as the institutionalized consent of the people had been established.

As political sociologists and historians have reminded us, there are extremely close links between the expansion of coercive power, the level of extraction of resources from their subjects by the state, and the deepening of state power (Mann 1986, esp. Index *sub* Taxes, and 1993, esp. Index *sub* State Revenues; Ardant in Tilly (ed.) 1975; Finer 1997; and in an analytically simpler format Levi 1988). Up to 80 per cent of English public revenues over very long periods of time were devoted to funding the military capacities of the state at home and abroad (Mann 1988, cap. 3). The main motor behind this development was the bitter competition for land, subjects and eventually markets with other states (Hont in Dunn (ed.) 1990). Seen from this angle, few presences in modern history can have been less reassuring to an individual subject than their own state at home. Even when its energies were directed abroad (Brewer 1989; cf. Colley 1992), it was often hard for its subjects to see their state as a reliably public good, rather than a series of reckless adventures on its own behalf, which might or might not on balance eventually redound to their (or their descendants') advantage.

This is in no sense a world which we have left behind. In the course of the last two centuries, however, it has gradually become more abashed in public avowal of its purposes and preoccupations. Few states today (not, alas, none) acknowledge an uninhibited zest for territorial appropriation as such. Even Saddam Hussein claimed that Kuwait, when he seized it, already belonged to Iraq and had been illegitimately appropriated by its then (and now) ruling house. Even the Serb leaders across the former Yugoslav republic presented their programme of conquest and ethnic cleansing as an attempt to ensure the rights of the Serbs. The Spratly Islands and Tibet, from the viewpoint of China's rulers, are just part of a single seamless heritage (the Central Kingdom a century on), which they have long claimed for, and liked to think of as, their own. The professional armed forces and weapons systems of contemporary states are presented, with few if any exceptions, as instruments for defending the interests of their subjects against enemies who might threaten them at home and abroad. Today, even coercion and taxation, the least immediately seductive aspects of the state, are ever more deeply submerged in the endless political negotiation of relations between rulers and ruled. From an alien and predominantly disagreeable reality, set clearly over against the lives of the huge bulk of its denizens (Zagorin 1982; Elliott 1984; cf. Womack 1968; Scott 1998), the state in consequence has become an altogether hazier entity, far less determinately located and often vigorous (however implausibly) in its efforts to ingratiate itself to its subjects. It is far harder today for most of these subjects to form a balanced judgment of just how their state relates to their interests than could have been the case in the seventeenth-century Europe of the Thirty Years War or the England of the Civil War (Underdown 1985, 154).

LIMITING GOVERNMENT FOR BETTER OR FOR WORSE

All states have at least some power to coerce; and most still have quite coercive habits. If it is true that the power of states today is limited in different ways by international and transnational agencies, by markets and by the capacities for agency of their own subjects, how far is this a limitation simply in their capacities to coerce, and how far should it be understood in quite other ways?

This is an extraordinarily difficult question to answer, and not simply because of the factual complexity of the issues involved. It is also exceptionally important, since it goes to the heart of the disagreement over whether states really are best understood primarily as structures of domination, or primarily as more or less errant instruments for serving the interests of their subjects. Many of the greatest modern political thinkers have set themselves to answer this question (even if none of them has expressed it in quite this form, and all have had many other matters on their minds as well): Grotius, Hobbes, Locke, Spinoza, Montesquieu, Hume, Rousseau, Kant, Hegel, Marx, Bentham, John Stuart Mill, Weber. Only Marx fully accepted the polarity (and even he, arguably, in the end more in the terminology he employed than in the structure of understanding which he developed). It would be a mistake to suppose that we now possess a clearer and more effective way of answering this question than these great figures contrived to offer (Dunn 1996(a)).

Taken together, those who make a profession of political understanding in the world today – career politicians, public bureaucrats, journalists, university teachers and so on – have access to, and some degree of control over, vastly more pertinent information than was available to single individuals in the past. But this bewildering volume of potential knowledge is not available as a cognitive resource to anyone in particular. It could hardly be further than it is from providing us with a clearer and more robust strategy for answering the questions addressed by Hobbes and Hegel than the latter hit on for themselves.

In what other ways are the powers of states limited, over and above their capacity to coerce: to make their subjects, in particular, act as these would not otherwise choose? The most striking and potentially important respect in which they are so is in their capacity to reach the goals for which they claim authority in the first place. These, plainly, differ from state to state. The avowed goals of the present rulers of Tehran are not those of their counterparts in Baghdad, Jerusalem or Cairo. Those of the contenders for authority in Washington DC differ from those of their counterparts in Havana, Mexico City, Westminster, Paris, Madrid, Athens, Belgrade, Tokyo, Seoul, Jakarta or Beijing. But, seen with a little historical distance, the differences are on balance less striking than the similarities. Not merely do all of these rule (or at least contend for the opportunity to rule) a state which is densely immersed in a common legal, diplomatic, administrative and economic structure. But all, also, for all the variation in their supplementary objectives, at least profess a degree of concern for the welfare, and even the human rights, of their subjects. On any coherent understanding of what rights humans have, it must be true that very many states violate some of these rights wholesale and most of the time. But it would be genuinely surprising if any state which had chosen to sign the United Nations Declaration of Human Rights (as the huge majority of existing states have firmly done) should have subsequently decided to cancel its commitment by tearing up the document in question.

Modern states, virtually without exception, claim to rule their subjects for the latter's own good. The rationale of the state's right to coerce is its need and duty to serve that good. To express this duty in the terminology of rights sounds more natural in some languages than it does in others. 'Human beings have rights,' says Robert Nozick (Nozick 1975, ix). There are things which no one can do to them without violating those rights. That human beings have rights may seem to an American, as Thomas Jefferson famously put it, a self-evident truth (Becker 1959, 175). If so, it is a truth which it has proved hard to translate convincingly into Chinese. This is not merely a matter of the immemorial savagery with which those who have held power in China have chosen to deal with dissidence and popular obstruction (Balazs 1965). The use of torture by those in authority, for example, while it might strike an American as a genuinely unAmerican technique for securing the co-operation of fellow citizens, has long been as Chinese as *dim sum* now seems. To an American, human rights, from their first appearance in a distinctively American national political history, have been as much rights against the state as against any other source of potential hazard. Since 1776, and more especially since the formal foundation and early years of the American republic, their so being has come to be incorporated indissolubly into the legal structure and informing belief systems of the American state itself: above all, in the key role within that state allotted to its highest institution of adjudication, the Supreme Court. Chinese political thinking, both a far older and a much more interrupted tradition than the American, has many elements critical of state pretension and supportive of the immediate human interests of groups of subjects. But it has never contrived to incorporate these elements at all robustly into the institutional structure of the Chinese state.

External Limits on Domestic Coercion

Both international and transnational agencies exert some pressure on the ability of states to coerce their own subjects, effectively by imposing additional costs from the outside on governments, over and above the costs intrinsic to domestic repression itself. Important examples in the final decade of the twentieth century include Myanmar, and, even less successfully, Indonesia in the case of East Timor. But there are often quite sharp conflicts of interest in such cases between non-governmental pressure groups (like Amnesty) and multinational corporations, so that the net balance of support and impediment often does more to sustain the regime than to induce it to change its policies. For a very brief period at the end of the Cold War, the United States government flirted with the prospect of establishing a new world order, a Pax Americana, imposed under the flag of the United Nations, and based upon the now overwhelming superiority of American military, naval and air power. But it took very little time for it to become evident (once again) that the possibility of devastating any other power in all-out military confrontation had limited bearing on America's capacity to get its own way in face of intimate and committed local enmities in most of the rest of the world: in Somalia, in Bosnia, even a modest distance offshore in Haiti (Dunn 1996(a), cap. 8).

Virtually nothing about another state is as hard to constrain effectively as its approach to domestic coercion. To control this requires full-scale conquest and effective pacification, neither a feasible nor an attractive venture for most states today except in dire necessity. What certainly can affect the capacity of a state to coerce is military intervention by one or more other states powerful enough and sufficiently committed to the outcome to dismember it, either by annexation (as in the case of India's occupation of Goa), or by creating a new state (as in Bangladesh). But such episodes are better understood simply as struggles between states than as instances of a single field of external judgment and power determining how far a given state may coerce its own subjects.

In the case of markets, the position is even simpler. The market position of a state's economy may well make it unwise for its rulers to pursue particular coercive policies. (The most important recent example must be the last decade of apartheid in South Africa.) But, since markets are not agents, they can never compel any state to forgo the core of its capacity for agency, the ability to judge for itself when and how to exert coercive power on its own subjects.

Internal Limits on Domestic Coercion

The one locus of agency which plainly does constrain any state's capacity to coerce is the domestic object of the coercion in the first place: its own people. In routine politics, the elements of that people which most palpably constrain the state's coercive capacities are seldom the elements which it most urgently wishes to coerce. The most obvious example is the coercive agencies themselves, the human instruments of coercion. But in extreme crisis or revolution the simple contrast between a body of rulers, a set of instruments of rule, and a far larger body of the ruled characteristically collapses (Dunn 1989(a); Moore 1978). Many factors affect the decisiveness of the outcome on these occasions (Skocpol 1979 and 1994; Dunn 1980, cap. 8, and 1985, cap. 4). But one indispensable factor, often extremely prominent, is the refusal by larger and smaller groups among the people to be coerced any longer. Revolution is the limiting case of constraining a state's capacity for coercion: the removal of that capacity from the hands of those who have been exercising it, and often its removal precisely through the exertions of large numbers of its habitual victims.

This is one reason why those who view the state as a structure of domination attach so much importance to revolutions. What revolutions reveal (they would like to believe) is what is always the case: the state's hidden truth. But this is a bit too brisk. In the aftermath of revolutions, always, sooner or later, a new state comes into being: usually pronouncedly more coercive than its predecessor, and not infrequently also heavily engaged in coercing not just a number of fresh segments of the society (those still aligned with the old regime), but also very many which were just as heavily coerced before. The core claim of the state is that clearly established capacity to coerce, firmly located in given hands, is a precondition for stabilizing many other aspects of collective life, and that such stabilization, in its turn, is a precondition for securing many obvious interests of the great majority of its subject population. This claim is strongly supported by the historical experience of revolution (Dunn 1989(a); and for a striking example Pinkney 1972). Revolutions may for a time feel, as Marx and Lenin proclaimed them, like festivals of the oppressed; but they never remain festive for very long.

Law's Empire

LAW AS COERCION AND LAW AS A SYSTEM OF LEGITIMATE RULES

Besides coercing and taxing, states also adjudicate and implement a structure of law. This too can be understood simply as an exercise in domination: as the systematization and detailed specification of an inherently coercive structure, which is itself effectively secured elsewhere (by the direct threat or use of violence). But, insofar as its detailed specification, its incidence in detail, really is systematic (Hart 1961; Dworkin 1986), it cannot be fully understood just as the remorseless impact of alien will. In any enduring legal system there will always be something else to understand besides its links with coercion. To judge what this further element really signifies for the human beings to whom it applies, it is essential to see how it bears in detail upon their interests, and thus to identify what their interests really are in the first place. What certainly cannot be assumed from the start is that this relation to the interests of the human beings affected can be read off the fact that the system of law itself is coercively secured: from its being enforced rather than merely suggestive or advisory.

ADJUDICATION AND PARTIALITY

The weight and human urgency of adjudicating and implementing a structure of law was clearly recognized by European political thinkers well before the modern conception of a state was first elaborated (Ullmann 1946 and 1961). The claim to be the mere vehicle of an authoritative law (in many instances a law of more than human authority) was the strongest entitlement which medieval thinkers recognized on behalf of holders of political power. It pervaded medieval political conflicts, in both ecclesiastical and secular fields. The claim itself implied the pre-existence of a structure of valid law, the standing of which in no way depended upon the properties or activities of its current custodians and interpreters. Often, too, it cast doubt upon the propriety in any circumstances of strictly human law-making: of the creation of law by purely human judgment or will. It is still controversial today how far medieval understanding of the nature of law in action involved and depended upon a conception of rights (Tuck 1979; Tierney 1983 and 1989; Oakley 1995). But it was certainly clear to many throughout the middle ages that even a law which had an indisputably supra-human source needed human interpretation in practice, and that it was the duty of the human interpreter in question to submit their will and judgment fully to that law's authority: to follow its requirements, avoid contaminating these with their own personal tastes or purposes, and train their intelligence and discipline their wills to capture just what those requirements were. Seen in this way, the law, properly speaking, should operate as a pure structure of constraint upon its human interpreters, directing them, of course, on their proper conduct, but doing so precisely by foreclosing for them the many lines of aberrant conduct which might otherwise appear to them excusable or even justifiable.

Within this structure, what restrains human partiality is the authority and content of the law itself. There is a close tie between the invention of the modern concept of the state and the reluctant acknowledgment that law, as human beings encounter it, can never constrain all of them, whether by supra-human or by extra-human features. In the modern concept of the state the permanent threat of human partiality is fully accepted, and the state itself is offered not as a site of humanly dependable impartiality, but as an artificial substitute for an impartiality of which no human is ever dependably capable. For an impossible unanimity in the content of judgment, and a prospect of peace which depended upon such unanimity, the modern state offered (as its exponents suggested) a possible, and potentially stable, majority agreement over the form of judgment: the recognition that it must in the end be determinate for it to be of the slightest human use. This way, and this way alone, a more modest but less unstable peace might at last be cumulatively secured.

The state conceived as a systematic structure of authoritative law is plainly not the same as the state viewed as a structure of practical coercion. As structures of practical coercion, states can be very unsystematic indeed: hard, at the receiving end, to distinguish from the state of nature, if not, indeed, the state of war. General Mobutu's Zaire, for example, was often at least as chaotic as it was brutal (so too, unsurprisingly, President Kabila's). But it would be hazardous to draw any direct inference from this to the character of its legal code. In every state there are gaps between what its laws, ingenuously interpreted, prescribe and what its courts in detail decide, its police force or army enforce, and its prisons or public officials exact. Where these gaps are large and relatively stable over time, few of its subjects are likely to view the state as a structure of law.

Where the gaps are much narrower, however, or even when they fluctuate greatly over time, any explanation of state performance which views this solely as a set of coercive outcomes is likely to confuse or mislead. In such states the gap between the rights which their subjects hold under the law and the treatment which they have meted out to them in detail by their rulers is likely to loom large in local understandings of politics. What a subject has a right to under the law is determined, except in the still relatively marginal case of international law, by the decisions of their own sovereign political authority. However objectionable these decisions may be, they are seldom genuinely inconsequential. If no state ever fully furnishes its subjects with all that they have a right to under its laws, few states today find it convenient or attractive for long to ignore these laws comprehensively in practice.

EXTERNAL DEFENCE OF DOMESTIC RIGHTS

Yet the rights in foreign countries in which the American government (like Amnesty International) at present takes such an active diplomatic interest are less often rights which the subjects of these countries plainly hold under their own laws than they are rights accorded under American law, and which it is natural for Americans to suppose that all legal systems should accord.

There is little evidence as yet that international or transnational agencies (let alone markets) have much control over sovereign states when it comes to enforcing their own understandings of the appropriate content of human rights upon the latter. To do so, they have to be in a position, in those respects and over that range of cases, either to supplant the state's sovereign judgment or to coerce its coercive agencies effectively from the outside. As already noted, this is unlikely to work in practice and hard to justify convincingly in theory.

Somewhat more leeway may be available when it comes to rights to which foreign subjects are clearly entitled under the laws of their own country. The preoccupation of the international credit agencies, especially the World Bank and the International Monetary Fund, with 'governance' in the 1990s has been an attempt to pursue this possibility in practice. On the most disabused understanding, the project of holding a state to its own hypocrisies by judicious bribery seems less extreme than one of forcing on it a self-abasing capitulation of sovereign taste to the taste of wealthier or better-armed foreigners. More charitably, a state in which law is still made firmly at the apex of state authority but adjudication and implementation have been effectively surrendered to an uncontrolled mêlée of lower officials might well, at least at the very top, welcome a degree of external discipline. If that discipline could be supplied in practice, some of its subjects might well come to welcome it too.

But, of course, in those states in which adjudication and implementation have dissipated most comprehensively into the hands of subordinates, and holders of state authority and people alike would have most to gain from the state being held to its avowed commitments and purposes, any attempt to hold it responsible inevitably involves virtually reconstructing the state, rebuilding it from top to bottom. International and transnational agencies may be able to assist in such a process (in Kampuchea after the Vietnamese withdrawal, for a bit even in Bosnia); but they can hardly hope either to enforce it or to carry it through by their own efforts alone. If they could do so, the thin barrier between residual sovereignty and imperial subjection would already have collapsed. The limited restraint on sovereign powers exerted by international or transnational agencies is a product less of shifting ideological fashion than of the practical difficulty of sustaining avowedly imperial rule in the late twentieth century.

It is not altogether clear why this difficulty should have proved so acute. There are plenty of examples of protracted empire in the twentieth century: Britain's rule over India up till independence, the Soviet Union at home and in Eastern Europe, China's control over Tibet (Dunn 1980, cap. 8). But the process of unravelling in the first two cases indicated clearly enough how precarious that rule had long been; and the comparative solidity of the last case is more a function of the continuity in Chinese state territorial pretensions and the formidable demographic dominance achieved by Han settlement than of any shift in attitude among the indigenous Tibetan population themselves.

What seems clear in the late twentieth century is that far more effective pressure on sovereign power now comes either from economic processes or from below than from other sovereign powers or from transnational agencies of opinion. Pressures from below can at times be unmistakably coercive. At the limit, they can involve the direct overthrow of a long-hated state authority. But over most of the relevant range they assume a quite different form, whether they emanate from external economic structures or agencies, or from the ranks of the subjects themselves. The main way in which either markets or subjects constrain state power is by altering more or less abruptly the incentives of those who control that power to act in one way rather than another. This is every bit as clear if we find it more natural to view states themselves as structures of domination directly controlled by those with a personal stake in their own dominion, or as clumsier devices for limiting the damage for most members of a polity from partiality of judgment or the inherent difficulties of collective action. This brings out the inherent inadequacy of this polarity. States do indeed combine these two aspects or factors, in widely varying proportions; but it is never accurate to view any state at all as simply consisting of one rather than the other. If all actual states consist in part of both, neither on its own can offer a very illuminating account of what a state really is.

Summary

What exactly is politics? It is, first of all, the struggles which result from the collisions between human purposes: most clearly when these collisions involve large numbers of human beings. But it is not, of course, only a matter of struggle. It takes in, too, the immense array of expedients and practices which human beings have invented to co-operate, as much as to compete, with one another in pursuing their purposes: most clearly, once again, when these expedients and practices involve co-operation between very many human beings. Anything about which human beings have come to care is apt to become part of politics: to enter its field, and modify its dynamics and outcomes.

Why does politics occur? What humans care about varies bewilderingly over time and space; and the expedients and practices which they adopt vary, only a little less bewilderingly, with it. Do they co-operate only to compete more effectively (in a perpetual and restless desire of power after power, that ceaseth only in death: Hobbes 1991, cap. XI, p. 70)? Or is competition forced willy-nilly upon them, because only by competing can they get what they urgently need, or what, whether they do really need it or not, they cannot help desiring with even greater urgency? In a sense, of course, each. Both the conflict and the co-operation are implacably there. Neither explains the other away. Neither can be explained without taking the other into account.

So are Machiavelli and Hobbes and Lenin and Carl Schmitt simply right? Is struggle and enmity what politics must always be really about? Or does the truth lie more with Plato, or Thomas More, or Rousseau, or Fourier, or Karl Marx, or for that matter with Confucius or the Buddha? Could our lives together all be completely different – orderly, temperate, just, organized around co-operation in service of a shared good? (It is unclear just how far, in the end, even Plato or More or Rousseau or Marx contrived really to disagree with the judgments of Hobbes or Schmitt. But at least, in their very different styles, Plato and Rousseau and Marx made a protracted and spirited attempt to do so: to summon up a less bleak picture of what human collective life really could be like, and make this practically credible.)

Wherever it has been clear to human beings that the actions of very many others affected their own lives deeply, their purposes have clashed drastically. Today a very large majority of the human beings in the world not only are affected very deeply by the actions of very many of their human fellows, often extremely far away; they are also at least dimly aware that this is so. This has been going on for a very long time (Dunn and Robertson 1973). The academic name for this central fact of contemporary experience is globalization. But this is still too vague a term to make the experience itself any clearer; and the practical organization of academic life and modern journalism virtually precludes it from being transformed into a conception which really could clarify what is going on. It is the name of a cognitive challenge, not of a potential solution to a cognitive problem.

Might this process of globalization, in all its chaotic heterogeneity, simply stop or go into reverse? It *could* well do so, in face of further intensification of human conflict (a third, a fourth, a fifth world war) or large-scale catastrophe, whether natural or humanly induced (asteroid strikes, accelerated global warming). None of these is a plainly unlikely eventuality; and they are, of course, all threats which have already come to our attention. There will be plenty of other (and sometimes wholly unanticipated) threats to come.

For the moment, in any case, globalization is in full swing. Human beings today struggle against one another and co-operate together (however irritably or bemusedly) on a far larger scale than they have ever done before. Politics fans out over and engulfs more and more of human life, along with the lives of ever more humans. This might cease to be so; but it is hard to see how it could without taking a prodigious number of human beings along with it. Perhaps there has not been politics ever since there were recognizably human beings. (This is principally a matter of semantic fiat and of no obvious continuing importance. Cf. Fortes and Evans-Pritchard 1940.) What is certain is that, in our sense (if less uncontentiously in Aristotle's), there has been politics ever since recognizably human beings became aware that relatively large numbers of other human beings were seriously affecting their lives in ways that really mattered to them.

Perhaps politics could just stop. (Perhaps it *will* just stop.) But it is far from clear that it could do so, while there continued to be recognizably human beings on any substantial scale.

What these answers assume is that human purposes have an insistent tendency to conflict with one another, only partially offset by a weaker propensity, and a still in practice more precarious range of capacities and facilities to induce and enable us, to co-operate in their pursuit. Speaking crassly, you might say that over time and space human beings have tried very hard to learn how to co-operate with one another and been only moderately successful in doing so. Why should their success have been so modest? Principally, it seems clear, because they have tried even harder (perhaps very much harder) just to get their own way. The forms which politics takes today are the outcome of the interaction between these two streams of effort. Where human purposes conflict sharply, you can expect human beings to clash extensively also (Hardin 1982 and 1995), and for there to be little justice in the results (Barry 1989).

But *need* human purposes conflict? *Why* do they conflict so? One hallowed and deeply serious answer to this question is that they conflict because, and solely because, humans value wrongly. If they recognized the Will of God or the Form of the Good, they could and would value rightly. Then there would be no real clashes between their purposes (just potentially muddling co-ordination problems: Lewis 1969). There is nothing incoherent in imagining human beings recognizing the Will of God (if God has a Will and is there for the recognizing, within human visual range and so on) or the Form of the Good (if that is there to be discerned: cf. Williams 1985; Mackie 1977; Blackburn 1981; McDowell 1981 and 1996). But the fact that we can coherently imagine a state of affairs is not a reason to expect it to occur. When human beings in any great numbers come to live together in a milieu in which all their purposes are consistently and effectively subjected to the Will of God or the Form of the Good (or any analogously comprehensive normative ideal drawn from another culture), I would say, they will have ceased to be recognizably human beings. This is a causal judgment, not just a stipulative definition. It might prove just wrong. But actually it won't.

The forms which politics now takes are the product of the history of at least two great forces: the conflicts between our purposes, and our endeavours to co-operate to pursue these more effectively. Thus far they have plainly been more a product of the conflicts than of the co-operation. For the foreseeable future we can expect this to continue to be so. The politics of the future will be a continuation of that history. (It will start off from where that history now ends.) It will also continue to express the most fundamental features of the human animals who have made that history what it was. For co-operation to bulk larger in that future (as in some ways it already does in our present) what alone can enable it to do so is the perceived requirements of the purposes themselves: not a faltering in their motivational power, or a chastening of their imaginative sources, but a widespread judgment of the practical prerequisites for realizing them.

How has politics come to assume its present forms? The history which would answer that question is as wide as the world and almost as long as the timespan over which we know with any intimacy how any humans have seen their world. Most of it we simply do not know, and now never will (even though we are better placed to see it in shadowy outline as a whole than any of our predecessors ever were). Even the little that we do know is unmanageably intricate and extensive, and obstinately resistant to compression. The best human understanding of politics there could be would be the endless trudge through that history, in all its wandering irresolution. But the epistemic excellence and ontological solidity of that understanding (its exhaustiveness, its patience, its stalwart refusal to omit) are offset by its stupefying price: its radical unconcern for what any human being might want or need the understanding *for*. For human purposes political understanding needs to be immensely simpler than this. Precision and comprehensiveness must be discounted ruthlessly for the time required to attain them. To see more clearly why this discounting needs to be done and how it can be done, let us consider a very practical problem of political understanding for British citizens now: why exactly the politics, economy and society of Britain came to be transformed as they were during the Prime Ministership of Mrs Thatcher.

PART II

4

Understanding the Constraints on State Power: The Case of Britain since 1979

British Politics since the Coming of Mrs Thatcher as an Explanatory Problem

How far is it true that the British state during Mrs Thatcher's tenure of the premiership was a structure of domination directly controlled by someone with a personal stake in her own dominion? There were certainly times when it looked very like this. But then how did it ever come to be under *her* dominion? If it was a structure of domination at all, how far was that structure in fact controlled by severely impersonal forces of a very different kind? Exactly what were these forces, how did they secure their control, whatever led them to pick on *her*, and how exactly did they manage to place her *en poste* once they had done so?

Or is it better to see Britain's state in those years not as a structure of domination at all, but as an altogether clumsier sort of device for limiting the damage to most British citizens from one another's partiality of judgment, and from the problems which they faced in acting together, in the circumstances in which history had left them (and they had left themselves) by early 1979?

To see why and how the British state over the eighteen years between 1979 and 1997 changed the structure of its economy and the distribution of wealth and income within it as it did, what we need is not to opt resolutely for one of these views rather than the others, but to work out exactly how to combine them and fit them together (no doubt with some pruning along the way).

Why did the British state (whoever and whatever it was at the time) choose to shift, and why did it prove able to shift, such a large proportion of wealth from some groups to others? Why did it contrive to transform the ownership and effective control of such large areas of the economy? Why did it effectively blight the power and conviction of the trade unions and decimate their membership? Why did it contrive, distinctly more recently, to lower the national rate of inflation to roughly the European Union norm? Why, by contrast, has it notably failed to diminish the proportion of national income expended by the government itself? Why, despite its repeated self-advertisements, has it had so little success in raising the dynamism and the cumulative economic growth of the national economy?

All of these, of course, are complicated historical questions, none of which could have a pat answer that is also at all dependably valid. But, both analytically and from the viewpoint of the British electorate, they also constitute a single explanatory puzzle: a common, and very practical, challenge to political understanding.

In the first place they consist of an at least superficially puzzling pattern of success and failure in a single political programme. It was a programme not merely implemented with varying energy, skill, conviction and success by a single political agency, the Conservative Party in government, but also indelibly associated with a single political actor, Margaret Thatcher.

Why, for example, was Mr Major, of all people, Prime Minister of Britain in the autumn of 1996? Firstly, because when Mrs Thatcher at last fell, he was to both her and her admirers the least unacceptable of the three candidates who offered themselves as her successor (the least unacceptable because at that point the least provenly prone to independent political judgment and commitment). Secondly, because however much they may have loathed and despised each other, and yearned to cast one another aside, there was still no other candidate for party leader whom more of the Conservative Members of Parliament would even grudgingly have followed than preferred, however reluctantly, to sustain him. This, of course, may have been as much a consequence of the modesty (or cowardice) of potential candidates who failed to offer themselves as of the relative prominence of those who did. Remember how Mrs Thatcher herself came to lead the party.

Why Major was Prime Minister at this point, you should note, is a far more complicated and less clear question than it sounds. At one end of the continuum of cognitive ambition, it is simple-minded to a degree and relatively tractable by the methods of contemporary political science (Cowley and Garry 1998). Why did which groups of Conservative MPs, those who could and did decide at this point, vote for Major, rather than for Michael Heseltine or Douglas Hurd? The answer, it appears, is that more of them minded – or minded more – about the attitudes of the candidates to the European Union than about any other issue. At the other end of this continuum of ambition, it becomes hard to distinguish from the problem of theodicy (Gilmour and Garnett 1997, memorably epitomized by the front cover of the dust jacket). In between lies all political understanding. On the whole the methods of contemporary political science do not come out well in the face of this challenge. They do nothing to explain why there should have been three male candidates at this point to succeed this redoubtable woman, why any of the candidates should have been who they were, how the winning candidate had ever got anywhere near being a candidate, or why he had already held two of the great offices of state, let alone why the MPs of the Conservative Party, with its long record of effective concentration on the requirements for winning and holding governmental power (Ramsden 1998), should have come to loathe one another with such intensity over the issue of Britain's participation in the European Union (cf. Young 1998). To be satisfied with this explanation of why Major became Prime Minister is to set the standards for political comprehension dismayingly low.

In the second place, this was a programme which, for all the inevitable vacillation in its interpretation and implementation, had always had, and very much retained, a single political and economic rationale. It was certainly never a programme which shrank from the idea of domination, and least of all in the face of active challenge, whether from the IRA or the National Union of Mineworkers. A 'free economy' was to be allied with, protected by and in the last instance enforced by a 'strong state'. The crack military unit, the SAS, was an appropriately emblematic instrument for such a state; and the tenure of the Ministry of Defence by Michael Portillo (still apparently in her eyes the authorized heir to Mrs Thatcher's mantle) an altogether suitable *terminus ad quem* of the Thatcherite road. But it is important here to distinguish symbol from substance. The programme of Mrs Thatcher was an eminently nationalist programme throughout, and many of its exponents were always ready to express a more or less belligerent chauvinism, whether in the South Atlantic or just across the Channel. But a zest for crushing one's enemies, at home as well as abroad, is no index of the content of a political programme.

THE THATCHER YEARS AS A WATERSHED IN POLITICAL JUDGMENT

The main outlines of that programme have been hard to mistake throughout and could scarcely by 1998 have escaped the notice of anyone minimally interested in British politics. The key political fact about the programme was that it had been on balance accepted, under the prevailing electoral system and in the competitive conditions imposed by the existing party system, by more electorally decisive voters than rejected it, and on four consecutive occasions. (This, of course, is very far from saying that it was ever voted for by a literal majority of those who chose to cast their votes.) Those who disliked the programme and its exponents throughout naturally feel that this record casts grave discredit either on the electoral system or on the party system or indeed on both, and perhaps at least some discredit on the electorate itself. In each case, they may well be right. But it is at least as important to recognize that such a pattern of political triumph has scarcely been paralleled in Britain since anything remotely resembling modern political parties came into existence. There is no compelling reason to suppose that the combination of electoral and party systems has ever registered the political tastes of British citizens with much precision. But haphazard and approximate though their combined incidence certainly proved in the two decades after 1979, it can hardly be denied that between them they did indeed register a massive shift of political judgment among the citizenry at large, and one as easy to pick up in the political platform of the principal party of opposition (the Labour government elected in 1997) as in the residual programme of the then Conservative government itself.

ELECTORAL CHOICE AS POLITICAL JUDGMENT

To identify a massive shift in political judgment among the electorate is not by itself to refute the presumption that the state is a structure of domination. Some of the subtlest and potentially most illuminating presentations of the view that this is what a state always is and must be focus precisely on the ongoing manufacture of public opinion, the moulding and control of popular belief. But in doing so they also bring into focus the precariousness of the assumption that a society and polity can ever consist integrally of domination.

Many of the beliefs of all of us are certainly false; and some false beliefs palpably disadvantage their holders in competing over given interests with other social or economic groupings. But it is seldom convincing to distinguish anyone (or for that matter any social group) too crisply and radically from what they happen to believe. We can certainly, of course, distinguish their bodies quite readily from their beliefs. But it is harder to sustain the distinction in relation to their minds. Some of our interests are naturally specifiable in relation to our bodies: food, warmth, sexual release. But very many of them can only be aptly specified in relation to our minds: to how we think of ourselves, what we care about, what we hope for, and fear, and dream of.

A modern democratic electoral system is an exceedingly crude device for relating what a given set of human beings hope for, fear and dream of to their selection of a set of temporary rulers. But, crude though it is, this relation gives it considerable political authority. Modern social and political theories (theories, for example, of the state as a structure of domination) need not be at all crude. But in themselves they carry no political authority whatever (Dunn 1985, cap.7). Any political authority which accrues to them they must either win by winning the hearts and minds of citizens, in the end through just the same crude electoral structure as any other aspirant politicians, or seize by direct conquest: by establishing an effective domination of their own. In the period since Karl Marx began to write publicly in the early 1840s, the pros and cons of these two lines of conduct have been very extensively debated among his admirers. The more confident have often favoured the high road, the road through formulating accurately the true theory of modern history, and placing this unflinchingly in power. On the whole, this gamble has worn poorly, even where it has appeared initially to triumph. The low road, the road through the attempt to convince a plurality of fellow citizens in the course of electoral struggle (Schumpeter 1950), has certainly proved frustrating and has palpably not ended up at all at the destination which Marx envisaged (Dunn 1984(a); Przeworski 1985). But, of the two, it has on balance worn far less badly. For exponents of the high road the state was always a structure of domination, to be destroyed and replaced, if with anything determinate at all, at least by something far less explicitly described. But exponents of the low road have been compelled to view the state throughout as something far more plastic and inherently less malign: an instrument which they themselves could reasonably hope to employ to pursue their own presumptively desirable purposes.

The view that any modern representative democratic state in normal working order can be aptly understood as a structure of pure domination is closest to breaking strain when applied directly to moments of sovereign popular electoral choice. (Even Jean-Jacques Rousseau repudiated it at this point in the case of the distinctly less representative state of mid-eighteenth-century England: *Du contrat social*: Rousseau 1962, II, 96.) Whatever may be true at other points, of which, as Rousseau underlined, there are always very considerably more, the state at this point is more plausibly seen as a structure through which the minimally participant citizen body (those prepared to take the trouble to vote) select from the meagre options presented to them those they hope will best serve their several interests. In that selection, the meagreness of the range of options is always important and sometimes absolutely decisive. In the elections of 1979, 1983, 1987 and 1992, across the set of national constituencies, there were an appreciable number of other political parties, some of them locally highly effective contenders. But there was only one reasonably effective and widely distributed option, which could hope to present a genuine alternative to the Conservative Party as a potential national government: namely, the Labour Party. In its way just as remarkable as the Conservative Party's achievement in winning these four consecutive elections was the Labour Party's achievement in losing all of them.

If we set aside Northern Ireland, which has other and more pressing matters permanently in mind, and ignore the fluctuations in nationalist party voting in both Scotland and Wales, which in this period never deeply affected the overall electoral performance of the Labour Party, it is easier to attribute the dismaying Labour share of the vote to the party's own powers of repulsion than to the Conservative Party's powers of attraction. Only in the last of these elections did the party go to the polls with both a political agenda and a potential team of government which might plausibly have governed effectively in the event of victory. In the first two elections in the sequence, the party was still riven by acute factional struggle. Even when Neil Kinnock took over as leader of the party his overall control of it was for long highly insecure; and the centre of gravity of party policy was not merely a very long way from that of the electorate but also wholly at odds with the viewpoints conveyed over the great bulk of the public media of communication.

It is possible to view this orientation of the party in a number of ways: as a stalwart disregard for political reality and a contempt for the judgment of most of the electorate, as an ingenuous misapprehension of how most electors did in fact view and judge its avowed policies, as a courageous affirmation of socialist principle in the teeth of the well-entrenched power of British capitalism's resolute defenders. (For a contrast with the first view compare the staggering judgment of a senior member of Mr Major's Cabinet, incautiously conveyed to the *Financial Times*, that the British electorate 'has become too cynical to be persuaded to vote for us in return for a penny off tax': Robert Peston, 'Treasury Ministers Oppose Pre-election Cut in Taxes', *Financial Times*, 30 July 1996, p. 1). These are better seen as contrasts in personal attitude than as differences in analytic judgment or disagreements about political or social fact. What they have in common is a sense that the weight of domination in governmental selection must lie outside the electoral process itself, and that the principal mechanism through which it is reproduced is the deformation of the electors' judgment of what really is in their interest. The first of these conclusions fits very comfortably with the image of the British state as a structure of pure domination, and certainly suffices to indicate that no modern British election closely resembles a free and open encounter between ingenuously conflicting interpreters of the political truth. But the second, the focus on the supposedly deformed awareness on the electors' own part of the content of their interests, has less felicitous implications. If the demos (you and I) cannot be trusted to judge for ourselves, if we are palpably unfit so to judge, then someone else must judge for us. If this is not to be, as it now sadly is, the indefatigable and devoted servants of the requirements of capital, then it will have to be capitalism's clear-sighted and resolute enemies. To prevail in the end, too, these must not merely judge on behalf of their chosen clients, they must also be willing to enforce their judgment against those who judge differently. In place of an existing and well-entrenched structure of domination, they must offer instead, as slyly and unobtrusively as they can, at least a brief interlude of alternative domination of their own – a liberating domination which will come to an end when their clients at last recognize that matters are as their patrons claim. (Cf the judgment of Auguste Blanqui, *Critique sociale* (1885), I, 207, cited in Spitzer 1957, 139.)

In 1979 (and, as it has turned out, for the next two decades) British voters, acting as they were compelled to do through the existing political parties and electoral structure, changed their collective judgment quite sharply about what types of economic policy (and, perhaps rather less clearly, about what type of society) would best serve their interests. Individually, to be sure, many of them no doubt modified their judgments little, if at all. Each, too, must have changed theirs, insofar as they did, to different degrees, and for a somewhat different balance of reasons. But the scale and brusqueness of the overall shift was unmistakable. We can also be sure by now that the consequences of the shift, for worse and for better, have already been very great (Gilmour 1992(b)), and that in the longer run they may well prove even more drastic (cf. Gilmour and Garnett 1997).

On any unified and comprehensive vision of the state as a structure of domination, this shift in judgment would have to be conceived, given the scale of its consequences and its direct bearing on the ways in which state power has been exercised, as an internal feature of the state itself. For purposes of political understanding, it is hard to see this as an advantage. To fathom what is going on in modern politics we need both clarity and analytic distance: the capacity to distinguish different aspects of our collective predicaments and to judge how each modifies the others. The view that the state is a single determinate structure, located within a single determinate history, can be held in a highly sophisticated form. But it is too narrow and obsessive in focus, too presumptuous about its own power of understanding, and too hasty in bringing that understanding to bear, to capture at all dependably just what our collective predicament at any particular time in fact is. It offers a severely premature answer to a set of questions which we first need to learn how to pose at all clearly.

THE FOCUS ON ECONOMIC EFFICIENCY

The central element in this great shift in judgment was its focus on the relations between the government and the national economy, and above all on the impact of these relations on the international competitivity of the vendors of goods and services within that economy. This was in no sense a novel preoccupation. But under Mrs Thatcher it dominated the political agenda to an extraordinary degree. Other issues came and went. But the supposed imperatives of economic transformation lowered over the nation's workforce (both potential and actual) throughout. From a torpid, feather-bedded, corporatist economy, with a large public sector, fostering welfare-dependence and privileging organized labour, Britain's industries and services were to be transmuted into a dynamic, lean, competitive economy, scorning weakness and ineffectuality in every form, lavishly rewarding those who proved capable of strength, and undercutting foreign competitors in market after market. Some of the economic techniques invoked to effect this huge change failed quite fast, especially the successive versions of detailed monetary control.

The anticipated surge in economic dynamism, viewed over twenty years, conspicuously failed to appear. But much did change, and some of it, almost certainly, irreversibly. Trade unions became much smaller, appreciably poorer and in most instances far weaker. The public sector shrank drastically and is still under some pressure to shrink further. Electricity, gas, telecommunications and water supply are now overwhelmingly privately owned. The upper echelons of corporate management are dramatically better paid. The rich are taxed much less, the majority of the population, if anything, slightly more. A far larger proportion of the adult population is involuntarily unemployed, many for lengthy periods of time, or indeed permanently. More surprisingly still, most of these changes seemed every bit as secure when the government itself fell into the hands of their long-despised opponents.

It is not easy to pin down just why an electoral majority should have found these changes consistently attractive over such a long period of time. Detailed analysis of opinion movements, naturally, shows that there is no reason whatever to believe that a majority of the adult population did view the changes, even on balance, as at all consistently attractive. Rather, on four distinct occasions, they chose, under the restrictive conditions of a national election, one of the two effectively contending national parties to be the party of government in place of the other, often by omission rather than by commission (Butler and Kavanagh 1980; Butler and Kavanagh 1984; Butler and Kavanagh 1988; Butler and Kavanagh 1992). Only in 1997, when the Labour Party, under its new leader Tony Blair, had painstakingly committed itself to virtually identical policies, even at the level of distribution, did it at last change its mind (Butler and Kavanagh 1997). Why did Britain's electors choose as they did?

Some elements which had an important impact upon public opinion at particular times were essentially fortuitous. The Argentinian decision to invade the Falkland Islands, for example, the degree to which this came as a surprise, and the promptness and in the end the triumphant success with which Mrs Thatcher gambled the destinies of much of Britain's remaining armed forces on rescuing her political career had little bearing on the history of Britain's post-war economy or the longer-term interests of the huge bulk of its inhabitants. But three types of factor together explain much of the politically decisive patterns of choice. The most important, unequivocally to Mrs Thatcher's credit, however contingent the pattern of personal acquaintance which first pressed it on her attention, was the recognition of the acuteness of the long-term competitive predicament of the British economy, and the clear practical priority for most of Britain's inhabitants of addressing that predicament effectively over pursuing most other potentially competing aims.

It is simply wrong, as we have seen, to think of markets as one type of agent, constraining or obstructing states (as another type of agent). But it is in no sense wrong, and has not been for many centuries, to think of markets as the decisive setting in which the life chances of modern populations at least in peacetime are determined. The scale of Britain's post-war economic failure is not a blunt matter of fact. It depends wholly on the standards with which you choose to compare it. What was crucial by the time that Mrs Thatcher came to power was that a large proportion of the British adult population had come to be aware, through one means or another (above all travel and television), that by standards which clearly did bear on their own lives (an experiential, not an analytical judgment: Runciman 1967) post-war Britain had indeed failed economically in comparison with most of its closer neighbours, with the United States of America, with the rest of Western Europe, with Japan and even some of the latter's Asian neighbours. The saliency of that perception naturally varies over time. (In the Japanese case it has looked steadily less intimidating ever since the collapse of the bubble economy; and with Japan's Asian neighbours, late in 1997, the comparison became for a time positively gratifying.) But in many ways the judgment itself has become harder either to resist or to ignore with the scale of international economic deregulation over the succeeding decade and a half, and the dynamic response to this of many of the world's economies (though scarcely of most of Britain's European partners).

In retrospect Mrs Thatcher's most decisive political act was the complete dismantling, at the very beginning of her first term of office as Prime Minister, of all controls over capital movements into or out of the economy. What this did was to establish a space of political competition between capital and organized labour in which, in the end, the latter could only lose, and in which it was relatively simple to present its predestined loss as unequivocally in the interest of the national population at large. It is easy to exaggerate the degree to which the post-war Attlee welfare state was ever fully accepted by the Conservative Party as a whole. But for almost three decades the political format established by the Attlee government did define an arena of political competition in which organized labour was at least as well placed as capital (privately owned invested wealth) to equate its own interests with those of the nation (Addison 1977; Morgan 1985).

Securing the shift in practice took more than a decade of (sometimes tense and hazardous) political struggle. It is hard to pin down even in retrospect how far the decisiveness of the outcome depended upon the almost equally dramatic international shifts over the same period in the institutional regulation of foreign trade and credit flows, or on the political collapse of the great-power embodiment of a presumptively socialist alternative. But it is simple enough to locate the impact of the outcome itself. Where it came to bear most painfully was on the relation between the national distribution of income and the terms of participation in international trade (cf. Hont in Dunn (ed.) 1990; Wood 1994). In a world of effortless capital mobility, intensifying international trade flows, intermittently drastic currency volatility and falling tariff barriers, it was hard to deny that the welfare of a national population must depend directly and immediately on the overall competitive efficiency of its economy. This was the core political perception on which Mrs Thatcher gambled; and, in this stark outline, it was hard to deny its force. Accepting it strongly encouraged a prioritization of overall economic growth over justly distributed personal welfare, and of production over distribution (in Thatcher's presentation, a precise inversion of the central premisses of the welfare state as William Beveridge had defined it and Clement Attlee had brought it to fruition). Describing the change in objective remained politically delicate, since at no point was there evidence that a majority of the British population intended or welcomed a dismantling of the welfare state so understood. But some features of it became clear extremely rapidly. The welfare state, as Beveridge envisaged it in the years of the Second World War, would offer full employment in a free society (Beveridge 1944). Mrs Thatcher felt no inclination to present herself as an enemy of a free society (whatever that might be). In contrast to the rulers of the Soviet Union, indeed, she was at some pains to identify herself as its stoutest and most resolute defender (*fidei defensor*). But what she did contrive to do, fast and thus far decisively, was to remove the goal of full employment from the national political agenda.

THE FAILURE OF THE THATCHER POLICIES

What proved altogether less felicitous were her hypotheses about how the economy could be rendered efficient in practice. The vehemence with which she identified the problem, and the massive subsequent reinforcement of public awareness that this was not merely urgent but also becoming steadily harder to solve, gave her a commanding political platform. (Only her party's need to claim some degree of success in meeting this challenge blurred over time the sharpness of her case.) Not until she herself had been forced to resign, and her political opponents had fully and effusively accepted the priority of tackling the problem, was this decisive comparative advantage at last offset.

Once it began to be offset, however, the relative ineffectuality of many of the techniques for promoting the economy's competitive vitality chosen by her, or by Mr Major after her, became far harder to ignore (cf. for example Thompson 1996). In particular, the focus on lowering labour costs by shrinking employment and lowering wages wherever possible became increasingly exposed, both analytically and politically, in face of a potential workforce whose overall skill level was already in numerous respects comparatively modest by international standards, and of a fiscal burden of maintenance for the already disemployed which had also become increasingly heavy. It was not that there was some other proven set of techniques for meeting the problem, applied perhaps in Scandinavia or East Asia, which was plausibly available to the British government (cf. Wade 1990; Esping-Andersen 1984; Wood 1994). It was merely that the techniques at the disposal of a still consciously Thatcherite government in Britain eighteen years on were themselves more and more evidently threadbare: incapable of meeting the problem which Mrs Thatcher herself had long and emphatically diagnosed.

FROM SEIZING THE COMMANDING HEIGHTS TO TARGETING THE KEY VOTERS

If this first element in explaining the Thatcherite impact upon British politics is essentially valid, it is gross enough and sufficiently definite in shape to provide much of the explanation required. But it is also excessively general, and manifestly unequipped to capture fluctuations in opinion over time, and especially in the decisive circumstances of an election campaign. In the condensed conflict of such campaigns, much of the explanation of what is happening simply consists in the detailed narrative of more or less well-considered manipulative efforts; and the assessment of which manipulative efforts are in fact well or ill considered is hard to distinguish clearly from their immediate outcomes (MacIntyre 1973).

But there is something else, most prominent in the closing phases of the 1992 election campaign, which is important too, and which is also politically more instructive. In that campaign, very clearly, the electoral strategists of the party picked out and concentrated with some vehemence on a very simple objective (Butler and Kavanagh 1992). They located, and addressed themselves narrowly and vociferously to, a relatively small majority of potential supporters, under the prevailing electoral arrangements, whose support would be sufficient to deliver victory. They sought to convince these supporters of just one thing: that they had good reason to fear that their own post-tax incomes in the event of a Labour victory would be lower than would be the case under another Conservative government (principally because the level of direct taxation would be higher under the former).

This was not (even in intention) a noble line of persuasion. It made little appeal to their political intelligence or (as Edmund Burke, for example, might have wished) to their feeling for the fate of their own society over time. It appealed instead, unflinchingly and exclusively, to their short-term greed. Backed by the uninhibited support of most of the national press, the appeal, it seems, went home (see for example Sanders in King et al. (eds) 1993, esp. 205–11; and Newton in ibid.). The best explanation of the outcome of the 1992 election, accordingly, has little in common with the best explanation of that of its three predecessors. The weight of the explanation has to fall somewhere quite different. How much more so would this have been so if the fourth successive victory had been succeeded by a fifth (cf. Butler and Kavanagh 1997).

IDEALIZATION VERSUS CARICATURE IN THE ANALYSIS OF ELECTORAL CHOICE

Even so, the complete (if perhaps somewhat caricatured) contrast in the two explanations highlights an important weakness in the first. Each is a notably rationalist explanation. They present the electoral outcome as a natural product of the agents' conscious reasons for acting as they did. The second attributes to them a very simple (and at its limit a mildly imbecile) structure of choice, a chillingly narrow range of sympathies and a bewildering simplicity of mind. It is, one might hope, too nakedly offensive to capture the full truth about one's fellow citizens at any point in time. But the first surely errs too far in the opposite direction. In a revealing passage in his mid-nineteenth-century *Considerations on Representative Government*, the utilitarian liberal philosopher John Stuart Mill insists at one point that citizens selecting their political representatives by casting a vote ought under no circumstances to choose essentially because they hope to benefit personally from the latter's performances. Instead they should choose with exactly the same would-be impartial concern for human goods and for the truth as should govern their decision as a member of a criminal jury on the outcome of a trial. To allow their vote to be deformed by thought of personal advantage would be every bit as disgraceful in the first case as it plainly would be in the second (Mill 1910, cap. 10, p. 299).[4] This is a luridly high-minded doctrine, which must have struck most of Mill's readers as very strange even in the heyday of Victorian public piety. Can it really be true that Britain's electors in the more raffish days of the late twentieth century exercised their franchise in the end with the same lofty austerity? Few, presumably, would answer yes; and nothing in the professional inquiries of contemporary political scientists into the determinants of voting indicates anything of the sort.

What transformed an impartial concern for the public good into a potentially pressing motivation for many of the unmistakably partial was the combination of a convincing identification of long-run commonality of interest (an outcome, if accessible, plainly in the interest of virtually everyone) with a refusal to recognize that commonality, or a manifest lack of either will or capacity even to attempt to secure it, on the part of Mrs Thatcher's main immediate antagonist. Under these conditions, the Conservatives, a party united around the recognition of a key problem of collective action and a real (if often crass and ugly) attempt to resolve this, confronted a party which for much of the time was not united around anything, many of whose members were strongly motivated by habit and imaginative pre-commitment to deny the reality of the problem, and committed to defending practices which made it virtually impossible to resolve. Under these conditions, the comparative advantage of the Tory Party proved overwhelming. But these conditions no longer obtain; and they were already ceasing to obtain by the time of the 1992 election. In 1997, the Conservatives, a party held increasingly precariously together by habit and the memory of their own self-righteous and protracted ascendancy, faced a party whose recognition of the scale and urgency of the predicament was, at least in public expression, every bit as acute as their own, which was now, at least superficially, united (if largely by the initial prospect and subsequent enjoyment of power), which had internalized much (probably too much) of the Thatcherite diagnosis and many of the Thatcherite remedies, but was at least at liberty to pursue other lines of practical thought at the same time. In this setting, only the narrowest concentration on locating a potential majority coalition of very short-term beneficiaries, or a pure gift of fortune, could readily offset the disadvantages of an overwhelmingly salient and increasingly unflattering comparison. It was wholly unsurprising that the Tory Party failed to win a fifth time in a row (civically reassuring, too).

In this twenty-year history of government, punctuated at intervals by electoral choice, government itself was unmistakably an attempt at domination, but electoral choice was not aptly seen as the deliberate choice of a dominatrix. In the passages of electoral choice many elements came to bear on one another: party machines, opinion researchers and professional advertisers, journalists and newspaper proprietors, political and economic theories, even the harassed citizenry in conversation with one another. Any account of what occurred which simply omits any of these elements is liable to mislead seriously. But no account of what happened which conscientiously included all, and did so more or less on their own terms, could hope to be very illuminating. What it would show is something true and important: that the government of a real country over many years is a confused and complicated business, and that the activity of popular electoral choice is an even more complicated, and probably on balance an even more confused, business.

It is more complicated because it involves so many more persons directly as agents. It is likely to prove more confused, not just for this reason alone, but also because so many of those whom it does involve have little motive to consider it at all attentively, and are hence unlikely to impose much clarity and order even on their own concerns in relation to being governed. The actions which issue from relatively perfunctory attention and hazily conceived concerns are unlikely in practice to be especially deft. But the very idea of deft voting can scarcely apply to a national election. (Where it is at home is in the tactics of small committees or in the modification of agendas.)

Political scientists have been disagreeing for a good century about how damaging the evidence of electoral participation really is to the intelligence and moral qualities of the mass electorate (you and me, in the polling booth). Sometimes the choice made is effectively beyond defence: the German elections of 1933, for example, with their appalling gift to world history, or for that matter the Italian national elections of 1994, with their more parochial defilements. But the cumulative evidence of voting studies is not especially damaging. Many citizens everywhere certainly know little about the struggles of career politicians; and a good many care even less. But this is a setback for the *amour propre* of those who consign their lives to the practice or study of politics. It is no proof of misjudgment on the part of the voters (or non-voters) concerned. For those who find it so, politics can be genuinely compulsive; but for those who do not it can be formidably unrewarding. It is entirely reasonable for most electors almost always to assume that there is no way of casting their ballot by which they could confidently further even their most prominent and fundamental interests.

No doubt every voter in every contested election always faces what are objectively better and worse options from the viewpoint of their own interests. It is sometimes easy to show by external analysis that a particular choice was virtually certain to cause great harm, not infrequently even to those who deliberately made it. But most voters have no rational motive to attempt an external analysis (which may require much information, developed analytical skills, considerable allocations of time and quite hard thought), and which is extraordinarily unlikely to issue in any identifiable and intended effect. Even were they to attempt one, their personal recognition of the infelicity of the choice that faces them can scarcely be expected to affect the outcome; and this solid prospect of ineffectuality in turn casts some doubt on the good sense of wasting time, money, effort and the opportunity for more agreeable experiences on sharpening their awareness of just how infelicitous the choice is. Why aggravate an objective impotence (which in any case cannot be overcome) by a readily avoidable despair? These lines of thought, of course, are not necessarily decisive even on a relatively despondent sense of what it is for a human being to act rationally. If there are indeed grounds for political despair, these may have strong implications for how (or where) an individual has good reason to pursue the rest of their life. Consider the position of a Jewish citizen in Germany in early 1933, or that of a Hutu or Tutsi citizen of Ruanda or Burundi in the wrong place and the wrong week for much of 1994–6, or, alas, ever since.

ASSESSING THE RATIONALITY OF VOTERS

Critics of the rationality of electors are usually (perhaps always) too ill informed about the latter's preoccupations, purposes or beliefs to grasp quite why they choose to vote or not to vote at all, let alone what leads them to vote just as they do. What prompts the criticisms they offer is never their own demonstrably superior grasp of considerations which the electors in question grasp feebly, if at all. In most cases it is simply their disapproval of what the electors have in fact done, or their fear of what the electors may well do in future. The second type of disapproval appears earlier in the modern history of electoral politics and is strongly connected with resistance to the expansion of the franchise: to even the marginal incorporation of most adults into the political life of the country concerned. Its main animus was the presumption that most of their fellow countrymen (let alone women) were unfit to be citizens, and that any claim to be so which they chose to offer on their own part could only be an index of unwarranted vanity (cf. Burke, *Letter to a Member of the National Assembly* (1791): Burke 1989, 313).

This line of thought has not worn well, since vanity is not plausibly a prerogative of the hitherto politically excluded, and there is no inductive reason to believe that large electorates are politically any stupider or more selfish than very small electorates indeed. The view that the few (the best, the *aristoi*, the elite) are special is not in all circumstances inherently absurd. The wealthier and better-educated do have some opportunities denied to the poorer or wholly illiterate. Not all of them squander these advantages. But, in the form in which it is usually held by the few themselves, it is almost always palpably ludicrous.

The important critique of the rationality of electors rests not on their open snobbery or personal contempt, but on direct clashes of political judgment between critic and elector. In this clash the critics, naturally, presume their own judgment impartial: to stem from, and to be validated by, considerations independent of their personal interests. But in making that criticism they can scarcely hope to carry the objects of their criticism with them. Virtually no human beings regard their own judgment as corrupted just by its being their own: as *infected* by its very partiality. The status of academic analyst or political activist is no guarantee that its incumbents will have much insight into their own personal stake in the judgments they make. For the critic to be right, the elector must be not merely wrong but wrong by what are in some sense their own lights: wrong in terms of interests which are plainly and unconfusedly theirs (Geuss 1980).

What establishes the grounds for criticism in the critic's eyes is not a rich awareness of the realities of the life of any elector concerned (still less of all the electors concerned). It is an extremely confident theory of what their main interests must be (cf. Lukes 1974). On any reasonable view of human motivation (of what human beings are really like and what prompts them to act as they do) the chances of adopting such a theory for reasons unconnected with one's own personal judgment and experiences are not high. What I feel and experience personally is the main source of the partiality of my judgment. It can hardly be taken by anyone else as sufficient reason for sharing that judgment.

GOVERNMENT AND DOMINATION IN BRITAIN SINCE 1979

For eighteen years the governments of Thatcher and Major used the machinery of the British state to alter the economy and society of Britain in a wide variety of ways. Their main explicit objective was to refashion both economy and society to compete more effectively on the world market. There is every reason to believe that, insofar as they succeeded in doing this, that outcome would be decisively advantageous for a clear majority of the population. The promise to attempt something of the kind (and, less plausibly, the boast of partial success in having attained it) were the basis on which they won governmental power in the first place and retained it on three successive occasions. Thus far, the state, even in their hands, appears more as an instrument for the service of openly avowable ends, and their acquisition and retention of control over it appears as a due recognition that placing it in their hands was more likely to promote those ends than placing it in the hands of their immediate antagonists. But to serve those ends in the ways which they envisaged required them to struggle more or less brutally with many antagonists. It required that many groups and institutions which stood in the way should be crushed or brushed aside. It ensured that, even if the majority did indeed benefit, a great many (over and above their competitors for governmental power) would lose, not a few of them severely and permanently. As they set to work to serve the public interest as they saw it, the state in their hands was often unmistakably a structure (and indeed an instrument) of domination.

The government of a state is always in some measure a site of action, from which some set of human beings is attempting to bring about more or less elusive goals in the society over which they rule. The goals will differ dramatically from case to case: the Versailles of Louis XIV, President Mobutu's or President Kabila's Zaire, Pol Pot's Kampuchea, Mr Major's (or Mr Blair's) Britain. Other things being equal, the more ambitious the goals, the greater will be the prospective need for domination. But other things never are equal. What made the Thatcher governments so overbearing was less the formidable personality of their leader or any extremity in her avowed goals than her need, in some cases, to pursue them (and her preference in others for doing so) by direct confrontation with political opponents. In retrospect she was sometimes fortunate in her enemies (General Galtieri, Arthur Scargill). But it was not a matter of fortune that she encountered so many enemies: Argentinians, Irish nationalists, Europeans, trade unionists, universities. It was a matter of choice – of personal political style. From her point of view, this decade and more of conservative government was a single potentially decisive Just War in which ultimate victory was in the end jeopardized by the pusillanimity of her colleagues and of her (reluctantly) chosen successor.

Within this Just War, other states and international agencies were in the end essentially bystanders (even a close and powerful ally, like the United States, or a deeply cherished foe, like the Soviet Union at the end of its tether). Only Argentina, briefly and fortuitously, blurred this line. What obstructed the British state as a site of agency in these years, what stopped it from being an effective site from which to realize the goals which Mrs Thatcher set herself, was certainly not markets.

Markets, especially international markets in goods and services, set the canons for success and could be relied upon to enforce her desired outcomes, if only they could be brought fully into play.

They told her what she wanted to do and how, in general, she might hope to do it. What obstructed the agency of the British state in her hands was not something beside or above it, but something beneath it: its own subjects. Indeed it was the electors who had chosen her to govern in the first place, organized rather differently and for many other purposes. There is no reason to suppose that many of those who opposed her most tenaciously and effectively were among those who had selected her in the first place (though that could happen: Gilmour 1992(b)). But the society and economy which she sought to refashion were themselves the habitat (or even the substance) of the persons who, together, had chosen her party to form their government, and done so at a time when she was already its leader. If this sounds confused, the confusion in this case lay in the reality as much as in the description. Seen accurately, the political processes of a modern representative democratic state are almost certain to be confused (Hirschman 1991). To extricate oneself from the confusion, even temporarily, is a strenuous effort; and even where that effort is largely successful, it is unlikely to prove at all durable. On what basis (if any) can we hope to understand what was really happening to (and through, and in) the British state under Mrs Thatcher's premiership?

MAKING THE STATE AN AGENT (ONCE AGAIN)

Mrs Thatcher herself had a very definite answer to this question. The British state while she was Premier was (for once) a potential agent of immense beneficence. It was such because (and insofar as) it was a potential extension, and a very potent amplification, of herself as agent. It could implement (and was sometimes made to implement) purposes which were unmistakably hers, and do so with great energy. As a state, to be sure, even the British state was an ambiguous entity. In the wrong settings and the wrong hands, it had been, and was all too likely soon to prove again, an immense evil. But in the right setting, and in the right hands, it was both the supreme political prize and the most effective political instrument potentially to hand for achieving the outcomes which she had in mind. Even as Prime Minister, naturally, most of the British state remained irredeemably other, constituted not merely of other human agents but often also of agents who were both acutely distasteful to her and disinclined to assist her in realizing her goals. To be serviceable for her purposes, therefore, the state had in some measure to be made over. Above all, its personnel had to be purged ruthlessly, until at least those with whom she dealt at all directly could be trusted to act as she would wish. In the first place she had to purge her own Cabinet and the office-holders of the party which she led. Next, she had to purge the higher ranks of the civil service, the human site of the state's capacity for real agency. She had, too, to overcome the powers of resistance of a wide range of other sites of potentially opposed agency, notably the public sector trade unions, the main civilian professions which depended directly upon the public sector (above all medicine and education), and the institutions of local government which had fallen into the hands of her party's opponents and were effectively ensured, through the social composition of their electorates, of remaining in those hands indefinitely. In face of such widely distributed partiality of judgment, the judgment of the Prime Minister herself could hope to prevail only by clarity of mind and strength of will, and the unstinting use of the effectively sovereign powers which she enjoyed under what passes for the British constitution, as long as her party in Parliament could be trusted to do as she told them. From her own point of view Mrs Thatcher's protracted tenure of the highest political office was an object lesson in the force of Hobbes's central argument. It was a ceaseless and, by its own lights, for long a remarkably successful crusade against the tendency for every society's capacity for political agency to dissipate helplessly into endless factional squabbling and inanition.

This was a genuinely obsessive vision, secured by an incapacity (or a resolute refusal) to register much else which was also happening. But it was not simply delusory. The idea of carrying through a single programme of coherent and fully intended actions is intimately related to the very idea of a state. In some ways at its least implausible in the conduct of war (consider the Falklands expedition, but compare too Tolstoy on the battle of Borodino:

Tolstoy 1957, caps 27–38, pp. 928–73), such a vision can never be literally true. But the picture which it gives of what politics might on occasion be like has some attractions for almost anyone. To a career politician with real ambition, a far from unusual characteristic in the *métier*, it can be intensely seductive. Even so, it is likely that even Mrs Thatcher herself would always have conceded that it was a fuller representation of what was happening *through* the British state than of what was happening to or in it.

Academic writers are at least as politically impressionable as any other group of citizens. But they have less excuse for simply ignoring what is happening to or in a state with which they are concerned. They, of all citizens, should be especially suspicious of all pictures of politics at any place or time as consisting exclusively of small groups of actors attempting to get their own clearly defined ways. Such pictures are always more than a little credulous in their judgment of the precision and determinacy of such purposes. They greatly over-estimate the clarity of mind and singleness of purpose which any real political actor can afford for any length of time. They narrow the cast list of political agency recklessly to provide themselves with a manageable plot line. They mistake the rhetoric of coherence and steadiness of purpose for the reality of improvisation, trade-offs, confusion, discomfiture and sheer fatigue. They see much too much of the relevant causality as coming from the experiences and mental operations of a few individuals and much too little of it as coming from far outside this narrow space, and flooding constantly into it in ways which even the most dominant and alarming of political leaders cannot begin to prevent (cf. Getty 1985).

Mrs Thatcher, even in her own eyes, effectively identified the British state with herself (following broadly the precedent set by Louis XIV, if on somewhat different assumptions). This was a considerable political feat in itself. It drew on intuitions of unmistakable political importance. No state can afford for long simply to abandon the conception of itself as agent. A state's laws, for example, cannot be seen merely as systematic commands backed by consistently effective sanctions. They must always, also, be seen in part as the central expression of its publicly enunciated purposes: as what it most seriously means, and proposes to stand by and defend. Where states are wholly corrupt, and their laws are a travesty of the clear intentions of their present rulers, the image of the state as agent remains a powerful standard, by which their own subjects, and others elsewhere concerned at their doings, can seek to call them to account.

The preoccupation, for example, of Western aid donors and agencies in the 1990s with the 'governance' of relatively poor states, while always a manifest impertinence by the criteria of sovereignty, is also sometimes an effective normative pressure on practices which are patently indefensible even from the viewpoint of those who are perpetrating them. No sovereign state can be happy to accept instruction from other states or foreign busybodies on how it should govern itself. But, today at least, no state can still frankly offer for long an account of the purposes of its current rulers which fails to connect these intelligibly with the interests of most of its subjects over time. The privilege to misgovern may be all but universally enjoyed in practice. But it takes some nerve today to espouse it consistently in public.

STATE PURPOSES AND STATE CONSEQUENCES

Conceived as would-be or actual agent, a state has two very different aspects: a set of purposes which it more or less actively entertains, and a range of consequences which may be rather weakly related to these purposes, which it somehow brings about through the manner of its operations over time. Because the state is a feigned, not a real, person (Hobbes 1991, cap. xviii, pp. 111, 114, 120; caps xviii, xix, pp. 184, 187; Rousseau (*Contrat Social*, Bk I, cap. vii): Rousseau 1962, II, 35–6; and for the subsequent development of this line of thought see Runciman 1997) it cannot be literally an actor. (This much, almost any analyst of the state would have to agree.) But it is far harder to pin down the senses in which it may or may not be appropriately said to entertain purposes, implement or fail to implement these, and generate consequences which follow directly from its attempts.

It is hard to deny that the existence of states, and the ways in which they operate, have consequences. Whether or not they are thought of as agents at all, whether or not they are seen as having purposes of their own, and however far such purposes are seen to control their actual operations, it is hard to deny that in many instances they modify the world quite dramatically simply by virtue of being there. The Soviet Union, throughout its history, may always have been more of a malignant chaos than an integrated product of a single domineering will and intelligence. But that conspicuously failed to prevent it from poisoning Lake Baikal or drying up the Aral Sea. It is a primitive but powerful impulse to attribute massive devastation (or, for that matter, unusual blessings) to a single purposive agent, and still more to attribute them to a single agent who fully intended the outcome in question. (The Soviet Union, insofar as it was at any point a single agent, can scarcely be suspected of intending to poison Lake Baikal or dry up the Aral Sea.) But there is every reason to regard its actual consequences as a state's most important characteristic, to hold it responsible for these consequences (Dunn 1990), and to press upon it the standard of intentional agency as the only possible basis on which its subjects (or other states) can seek to hold it to account. As an analytical model of part of the human world, however, a conception of the state which depicts it as a potential actor with clear purposes, definite powers of action and readily attributable consequences to its actions is singularly implausible.

THE MODEL OF AGENCY AS IDEALIZATION

Even with individual human beings, models which portray them as bearers of clear purposes, possessed of definite powers of action, involve a great deal of idealization. (Think of yourself.) But the temptation to think of human beings as bearers of purposes, with real powers of action intimately connected with these purposes, is extremely strong (and may simply issue from already knowing that that is what most of them in a sense are: Davidson 1980; Nozick 1993). Once purposes and powers of action are at issue, too, the pressure to impose some degree of clarity and order upon these, and to edit out the more from the less unnerving among the purposes in question, becomes even stronger.

No human being is quite born an agent; but most, over time, in no way need to have agency thrust upon them. States are not born, though they certainly begin, and in due course come to an end. But they begin as a result of the actions of particular sets of human beings. Any state which is ever to approximate to the model of an agent needs to have agency thrust upon it, and thrust by the persistent and vigorous actions of particular sets of human beings (cf. Joliffe 1955, caps 3 and 4: *Vis et Voluntas*, *Ira et Malevolentia*). Mrs Thatcher's image of the British state, while it was in her charge, was scarcely selfless. But it was a distinctive and unusually urgent version of a perfectly honourable intention. If she is open to criticism, it is not because she tried, but because of what she attempted to do: for the content of her goals, not for the fact that she had goals and pursued them with gusto. Some of these goals were not merely consciously entertained but at least partly realized in practice. The massive shift in wealth and income from the somewhat poorer to the very much richer may not have been an outcome which she precisely envisaged or intended. (It is hard to be certain about this, since the evidence unsurprisingly is not on open display.) But it plainly caused her little chagrin, and was a wholly predictable consequence of actions which she very evidently did intend. What was happening through the British state during her premiership was often quite aptly identified with the Prime Minister herself as an agent. To at least this degree she succeeded at times in thrusting her own vehement will to agency on to an entity singularly resistant to the venture.

What happened to or in the British state under her premiership could not, in the same way, be an instance of agency on the state's own part. It could, of course, be – and presumably was – a consequence for the most part of the actions of human agents. But the agents in question, whether they happened to be located outside or employed inside the British state, could not reasonably be identified with that state, nor their actions with its actions. It was above all the actions of these sets of human agents, inside and outside the British state, and inside and outside British society, which determined the outcome of Mrs Thatcher's efforts, and doomed so many of them to failure even before she started. Mrs Thatcher's own purposes and energy are to be attributed in the end to her idiosyncratic endowments and her personal biography, and the impact of these purposes on the British state to its initial susceptibility to that combination of energy and purpose in the holder of her office. But how are the limits of its susceptibility or the recalcitrance of so much of the rest of the world to those purposes to be understood?

L'ENFER C'EST LES AUTRES

This is not a manifestly appropriate way in which to frame these questions. To Mrs Thatcher it was a continuing source of surprise (as well as displeasure) that so many should prove to be against her. But there is no particular reason why anyone else should share that surprise. (If anything, the puzzle, in comparison with most of her predecessors or her hapless successor, is how for so long she contrived to induce so many to remain with her.)

The initial difficulty in addressing such questions is that they are hopelessly open-ended. It always makes sense to ask why some particular political event occurred: the passing of a law, the sacking, or retention, of a Cabinet Minister or Police Commissioner, the placing of a huge public investment. At a minimum, there is always a valid narrative to be given of how such events have come about. More ambitiously, but also more hazardously, there are also always elements of political logic to the occurrence, and patterns of probable happening within which it plausibly falls. Political scientists with a strong conviction of the applicability of the methods of the natural sciences to their subject matter aspire to go much further: constructing models and applying statistical tests which they hope, between them, will establish clear causal relations between the phenomena in question. But even the most ambitious of political scientists or the most voracious of historians would scarcely hope to explain in its entirety what was virtually a political epoch in itself.

Professional students of politics (most political scientists and even many journalists) have strong explanatory tastes and habits: definite preferences in how to set about explaining, and convictions as to what can or cannot explain satisfactorily in practice. But even those who are extremely illuminating about politics do not necessarily understand very well just what it is that enables them to be so, and frequently mistake habits of mind or favoured rhetorical formulae for dependable sources of insight. On present evidence, there are no dependable sources of insight, and no methods which, clearly grasped and accurately applied, ensure even the haziest comprehension of what is really going on politically. But there are certainly more and less promising approaches to trying to find out. One of the least promising approaches is to presume that all states must always be something in particular and to draw substantial conclusions in given cases from whatever it is that they are deemed to be bound to be.

THE STATE AS FORM AND SUBSTANCE

It is reasonable to presume that states have some definite conceptual properties. Under international law, in processes of law-making and adjudication, in diplomatic relations with one another, it is perfectly appropriate to conceive them (and treat them) as agents, just as they publicly conceive of themselves. But these characteristics are formal; and the real substance behind them is always very largely opaque.

The United States has a constitution and a current president. It signs treaties, goes to war, still makes an immense number of individual payments to individual citizens, and maintains not merely a great many embassies but also a substantial public espionage operation. In all these ways, unmistakably and incessantly, it acts. But we cannot hope to find a general answer to the question why the United States as a state acts as it does, since for most purposes it is so far from being a single agent and hence cannot aptly be said to *act* at all (cf. Allison 1971). Does this line of argument support the judgment that there cannot be dependable methods for explaining why a state has acted as it has, or predicting how it must (and therefore will) act in the future? I suspect that it does. But I very much doubt whether it could possibly be clarified and strengthened sufficiently to demonstrate that there cannot. It is unwise here to try to convert a prudent scepticism into a claim (however negative) to epistemic authority.

In the United States House of Representatives, because of the importunities of biennial election or re-election, the legislative process itself cannot reasonably be thought of as an attempt on the part of a unified agent to decide what it should do. The relation between the two branches of Congress and the President's executive subordinates certainly separates and counterbalances powers, as it was intended to do. But it is more illuminating to see that relation as consisting of struggles between contending interests than of arguments as to what, from the point of view of public or even majority interests, it would be best to do. Some states (notably France under the Fifth Republic and Britain under Margaret Thatcher) take the rhetoric of unified agency very seriously: the majesty, authority and clarity of purpose of the state. But, even under the exigencies of the Cold War, the United States never fully succumbed to this rhetoric (Calleo in Dunn (ed.) 1995). It has effectively resisted the construction of a powerful and internally coherent state throughout its national history (Skowronek 1982), and remains unabashed by a diffuseness in legislative process (Mayhew 1974) and a discontinuity in executive power which would have appalled the rulers of France or Germany for at least the last century.

It is therefore natural for Americans to treat the view that states really are, or could be, unified agents as a palpable absurdity, and the view that they should be such as both offensive and ridiculous. This is important in the context of any attempt to interpret the vicissitudes of the British state under Margaret Thatcher, since some of the principal effects at which she aimed (and which she quite largely secured) were also aimed at (and at least as effectively secured) in the United States under the less formidably domineering figure of Ronald Reagan. In each case, too, the outcome plainly eventuated through the operations of the state itself. In each instance there is a rich narrative of partly collaborative and partly competitive activity to be given as to how the outcome came about. The collaboration was probably indispensable to anything even broadly so intended coming about, and the competition is pre-guaranteed by the self-selection of career politicians. All politicians need to know how to make, retain and deploy political friends. But almost any politician can happily envisage their own promotion, and often at almost anyone else's expense.

Each narrative involves a cast of many thousands. At the limit either cast list might prove incomplete if it omitted a single citizen of the country concerned. Since what happens through a state must plainly depend causally on what happens in it, the lack of definite human boundaries to the state itself, even within its own territories, strongly discourages any expectation of collectively coherent agency overall. If what happened in it happened essentially and exclusively within the upper echelons of its formal political leadership, its public bureaucracy and the high command of its armed forces, the range of co-operation required and the prospect of relative transparency in mutual understanding across this space might not seem impossibly demanding (but cf. Allison 1971). But, once agency is recognized to dissipate downwards and outwards from these select circles, any conception of an overall rationale structuring the way matters turn out may seem just credulous. Yet there remain quite decisive shifts in state commitment, and in the consequences of state performance, to be explained. The United States of Newt Gingrich in 1995 was not the United States of Lyndon Johnson in 1965. The Britain of Margaret Thatcher in 1990 was not the Britain of Clement Attlee in 1950. What does (or could) explain such huge shifts in the exercise of state power?

EXPLAINING SHIFTS IN STATE POLICY

The most cogent answer to such questions is not something internal to the machinery and personnel of the state at all narrowly conceived. Even if the state is conceived as broadly as it well could be (for example, as extending to the pertinent beliefs and attitudes of each of its potentially voting citizens), it is less than illuminating to present the explanation essentially in terms of the public status of its human constituents. Changes of this scale which evidently come about through the state, it is more reasonable to suppose, come about less from something which happens in it than from something which happens to it. Even if alterations in the beliefs and attitudes of its own citizens at large, or of its key political leaders or public officials, directly generate the outcome, what explains that outcome must in the end be what *prompts* these changes in belief and attitude, not the beliefs and attitudes themselves.

LOCAL INSTANCES OF A GLOBAL PROCESS

This at least gives us something to explain which is the right shape. But it casts no light whatever on the content of the explanation. In the case of the global neo-liberal agenda of the 1980s and 1990s (of which Reagan and Thatcher were prominent and consequential exponents), its public impact across large areas of the world, from some of the richest states to some of the poorest, depended both upon ideological impetus and upon drastic shifts in the international context in which national economies operated.

There were close and obtrusive links between these two factors throughout, since the agencies of international economic co-ordination were often potent vectors of the conceptions of sound policy, and the ways in which they operated, and the institutional changes which they brought about, themselves brusquely altered the incentives faced by governments and economic actors across the world.

The ideas themselves were in no important way novel (though their expression was naturally more up to the minute). What had always been less than engaging about them, and what had long proved ineffectual, remained just as unengaging, and very often every bit as ineffectual. But ideological infection and institutional change, both carefully planned and essentially inadvertent, reinforced each other massively. What was evidently going on was a single interconnected process, a vast tipping in the balance of advantage between one set of ways of organizing production, distribution and exchange, subordinated, at least in intention, to the pursuit of social welfare through public policy, and another set of ways of organizing production, distribution and exchange, which had far weaker connections with the goal of pursuing social welfare, more especially through public policy.

There is now an entire branch of contemporary social science, international political economy, which at least attempts to analyse and explain transitions of this kind as single interconnected processes. It is still imaginatively dominated by the policy preoccupations of America's state elites and has scarcely as yet discovered how to identify convincing explanations at this level of grossness (where they may, in any case, be simply unavailable). But it is already distinctly more useful when it comes to plotting the transitions themselves. Its products may be cast in terms either of structure or of agency. With the former, it begins from market structures (ideally from the image of a single global market economy, varyingly distorted in detail throughout), and presents state policy as the outcome of the (more or less reluctant) recognition of constraints imposed by these structures. With the latter, it begins from the beliefs of those who in the end endow state elites with their key beliefs (in this case, their conceptions of economic rationality and efficiency); and it presents state policy (including the embodiment of that policy in the entire apparatus of international economic co-ordination) as the following through of the implications of those ideas.

Because in this instance the two reinforced each other so emphatically, there is considerable plausibility in each line of analysis, and little ground for seeing either as a full alternative to the other. Even the most clairvoyant and fearless of economists (cf. Skidelsky 1992; Clarke 1988; Hall (ed.) 1989; Barber 1985) cannot hope to understand very much of what is going on in the global economy (and least of all when the structure and rhythms of that economy are changing rapidly, as they have been for several decades, and are likely long to continue to do). Consider, for example, the scale of the collapse of the Asian market economies in 1997–8 (M. Wolf, *Financial Times*, 15 June 1998). Even the most abjectly reactive of governments needs interpreters of what there is for it to react *to*, and what responses could or could not reasonably hope to prove appropriate to these pressures and opportunities.

What these two lines of thought have in common is a conviction of the explanatory priority of economic interpretation over political sentiment and professionalized political purpose. Is this a reasonable presumption?

The answer naturally depends on quite what you wish to understand. If this happens to be what motivates in detail the political machinations of individual political professionals, or what indeed explains the entry into, or persistence within, professional politics of these women or men, it certainly is far from reasonable.

Modern professional politics is a highly structured career which places severe (if inherently somewhat indeterminate) constraints on those who wish to pursue it. For those already in politics it is natural, and in many circumstances probably even rational (existential sunk costs), to wish to remain there and make headway in their distinctive career. To remain in politics in a modern democratic republic it is, for the great majority of those concerned, necessary to contest elections, and at least intermittently to win these. To win elections it is necessary for the most part to belong fairly convincingly to a political party which already enjoys some popular support and to look to those who manage the party as though you are reasonably likely to win an election. (For the background to all this see Ostrogorski 1964; Michels 1959; Schumpeter 1950; Duverger 1954; Sartori 1976, and for Britain Beer 1965; Mackenzie 1963; Whiteley, Seyd and Richardson 1994; Kavanagh 1998; Ramsden 1998.) To win elections it can prove helpful, perhaps even essential, to do all manner of things which might be otherwise wholly unwelcome. Hence the all but universal presumption across the world that a career in politics anywhere but very close to the top is a vaguely degrading occupation.

To choose a political career is, among other things, to choose a milieu and a way of life, one with its entertainments, exhilarations and even glories, but also with its singular indignities and its all but unimaginable tedium and interminability. Most ways of life of course, have their ennuis. But why should anyone with many other options open to them (anyone with enough talent, finesse, expressiveness and nerve to have much chance of political success) choose to offer themselves repeatedly for election (and hence also perforce always for potential rejection: these are not the ordeals of the late President Kim Il Sung)? In some settings the answer may simply be that only repeatedly offering themselves for election can keep open the opportunity for a cumulatively truly grand career (Meier 1995). Once that ceases to be so, the need to offer oneself for election can be gratefully cast aside.

But, in a society like Britain or the United States today, this is very obviously not the case. The importance of this issue was highlighted by the ordeals of President Clinton. Clinton, it is clear, had long been greatly excited by politics. By a number of simple technical criteria he was exceedingly good at it – clever, charming, fluent, alert, indefatigable, strong-stomached. He was also, however, on the record, at least equally excited by sex. In many societies a keen interest in sex is no disqualification for a politician. But in the United States of the late 1990s (unlike three or even six decades before) for its leading public official to pursue happiness in this way wherever it may lead had become singularly ill advised. What in France might seem merely a shade uncouth, and in Ghana or Nigeria just bizarrely and somewhat humiliatingly furtive, has proved in America politically reckless to a degree. Why should someone so keen on these two contextually ill-assorted activities choose a way of life in which the second carries such disproportionate costs?

The individual answer here is of no lasting importance: more an occasion for personal sympathy than for impersonal condescension. (He hoped to get away with it. He expected not to be found out. He barely took the trouble to consider the risks at the time. He derived some pleasure from the risks themselves.) But the significance for political explanation cuts deeper. Much of what is happening in politics everywhere all the time has no intrinsic political meaning and virtually any of it could in principle have quite dramatic political effects. Understanding politics could never be a matter of knowing all of it and grasping the full range of consequences which might conceivably issue from it. By these criteria politics simply could not and cannot be understood. (It never has been. It never will be.)

To understand what is happening in politics anywhere we must approach the task with altogether more humility. We need to accept a very great deal as given (much of it not readily discoverable in detail, and some of it in practice not discoverable at all). We need to learn to recognize its presence, to feel its weight and to do our best to measure its implications. But our best will always be pretty modest. Politics at any time is always the intersection of an immense number of (no doubt often very ill-considered) personal trajectories, an endless series of hasty exchanges of favours or punishments, a huge mass of more or less painful collisions between individual predicaments. To get where they would like to be the great majority of human beings who have not chosen to devote their lives to a political career would certainly not choose to start off from where virtually any career politician now is. But neither, plainly enough, would most career politicians.

As a medium of activity professional politics just takes clearly formed and fully avowable intentions of any durability very badly. Even for the unusually ingenious, vital and wilful (Thatcher, Blair), it is a taxing setting in which to keep trying to get one's own way. Only the terminally cynical (those who can barely remember what their own way is, or used to be: Andreotti, Mobutu) can hope to find themselves fully at home within it. But whether we like it, or even recognize it, politics is still there. These muddled and often unprepossessing trajectories, exchanges and collisions, between them, do a bewildering amount to determine the settings within which all of us live our lives. Not only do they do so at present (in a way in which they palpably did not in the days when peasants ploughed that knights might ride, or virtually everyone hunted or gathered). They are all too obviously going to continue to do so for a very long time to come: I would say, for as long as the human social or political imagination can stretch with any accuracy at all.

Interpreting political outcomes within the heavily professionalized political context of the modern democratic politics we need to take most of that context as historically given at any point, if we are to make any instructive sense of what is going on. Professionalized political purpose is unrelentingly competitive and most of the conditions for its competitive success depend upon the intimate detail of this context. Political sentiment for participants in the competition has a strong tendency to accommodate itself to the perceived requirements for success. But political parties of any longevity or popularity are not just support mechanisms for randomly composed teams of would-be competitors. For them to provide such support they require the financial resources to survive and organize and the projective capacity to reach out to the political sentiments of very many others.

In the modern democratic republic ordinary citizens (the voters) ensure at regular intervals, however clumsily, that contenders for governmental authority should reach out, and convince them that they are doing so, towards these sentiments. Altogether more irregularly, and far more obscurely, they (or their predecessors) have also by now succeeded in enforcing the establishment of this state form in most of the wealthier and more powerful societies in the world. Seen close up and contextually professionalized political purpose fills the screen and appears overwhelmingly potent. But seen from much further away it looks altogether less potent: more the provision of a reasonably well-sanctioned service. (Compare the assessment of the Abbé Sieyès before the profession had really come into existence: Pasquino 1994.) It may not be exactly menial and it is certainly far from reliable; but it clearly belongs well within the service sector, and for as long as there have been stewards it has always been easy to find oneself cheated by them.

The reason why economic interpretation has explanatory priority in the end over political sentiment and professionalized political purpose in modern politics is because in that politics in the end the political sentiment of the citizenry at large dominates the purposes of political professionals, and those sentiments increasingly centre on the perceived requirements for agreeable and dependable consumption.

Mrs Thatcher's presence at the head of her party was a demonstration of the continuing force of personal contingencies (in this case of courage, nerve and single-mindedness) in determining competitive success in any possible contest for governmental power and any form of political arena which was not dominated by random selection. But her political project was a response, and an acute response, to the perceived sentiments of an electoral majority of her fellow citizens, and those sentiments, in turn, a response on their part to the role which they quite reasonably supposed that governmental choice had played and could play in shaping the conditions for their own prosperity or penury over time.

5

The Centrality of Judgment

Necessity, Normative Rationality and Practical Judgment

Mrs Thatcher's political impact, then, was both an intensely personal interpretation of the political and economic needs of her fellow citizens and an effective communication of that interpretation to an ongoing electoral majority among them. It was a startling feat of personal projection, and an impersonal discernment of concerns and interests distributed among the electors to whom she sought to appeal. Because she held and exercised such remarkably personal authority through the structure of a state, it was also both an exploration and an experimental test of that state's responsiveness to the concerns and interests of its subjects. How should we see that state's response?

It is possible to consider the responses of states from at least three very different points of view. We may choose to view them in terms of the category of necessity (how they must act), of the category of normative rationality (how they should act, or have best reason to act), or of the category of probable judgment (how they are likely in practice to judge that they would be best advised to act).

Only the first and last of these are unequivocally causal viewpoints. Of the two, the latter is considerably more plausible in its causal presumptions. This greater plausibility is not simply a product of ideology, although it has a prominent ideological component. The state, as we have already seen, is an idea, not merely a lump of historical fact. At the core of that idea is the claim to be entitled in the last instance to judge on behalf of its subjects, a claim which gains its force from the conspicuous propensity of those subjects, in larger or smaller groupings, to judge firmly for themselves, and to attach considerable weight to the judgments which they make. Because the prominence and urgency of conflicts of judgment is so central to the state's self-conceived identity and point, the idea that only a single judgment is even open to it at any given point in time is likely to appear extravagantly superstitious, a relic of a very different vision of human history, at home only in a long-bygone epoch. But, since the first and last of these three viewpoints are firmly causal in intention, the ideologically discomfiting relation between causal model and self-understanding of what is to be modelled is not necessarily to the point. What matters, simply, is the extremity of the causal assumptions adopted in the first instance, and the relative parsimony of those required in the last. The view that the second of the three viewpoints, the viewpoint of normative rationality, is not a causal viewpoint at all does not imply that states never act as they should. It does not even mean that the fact that, in some sense, they should have acted as they did (where that is indeed a fact) had no causal bearing on their doing so: a morose and extravagant presumption. All it means is that it could never be literally true that a state acted in a particular way, because and simply because, that was the way in which it should have acted.

THE STATE AS A SITE OF PRACTICAL JUDGMENT

The key issue here is how to conceive the causal bearing of the exercise of political judgment. For the view that states always act as they must to come out true, judgment must be pre-guaranteed to be either perfect or inconsequential. Either the state cannot fail to judge as it does because it is incapable of error (of judging wrong), or it does not matter how it in fact judges because nothing answering to the description of judging has any detectable causal impact on how it proceeds to act. The view that the judgments of public authority are infallible was one of the most important premisses which the modern state discarded. Its rationale precisely combined a recognition of the need for the judgments of public authority to be unchallengeable at the point at which they are to be applied, with a recognition of the forlornness of any hope that they may prove to *be* infallible in practice (or to be so regarded by those to whom they apply). The simplest fit between structure and agency in the changing history of state policy and its implementation views the determination of state judgment on how best to act as the core of that history. Here, external shifts in the context in which states must formulate and seek to implement policy mesh directly with internal shifts in conceptions of what such policy should consist in: what it can reasonably hope, or aim, to bring about. Each drastically modifies the other over time; and neither, accordingly, could accurately indicate on its own why the other alters as it does.

In the massive deregulation and liberalization of global economic relations over the last two decades of the twentieth century, this is certainly what appears to have happened. State-concerted production and distribution have shrunk dramatically over huge areas of the world; and the residues of both are on the political defensive virtually everywhere. This may do little to illuminate the future; but it is hard to dispute as a verdict on the recent past. State-concerted trading is much less widespread than it was, and far looser in its modes of control than was common in the 1970s. Even state efforts to massage the terms of trade to the advantage of local economic agents at the expense of foreigners, by manipulating tariff and non-tariff barriers to trade, while still both vigorous and ingenious in most parts of the world, are far shiftier and more surreptitious than they used to be. Rather more erratically, states themselves have altered appreciably over the same span of time, not always in the same direction, but on balance in ways intended to accommodate better (more comfortably, more securely, more prepossessingly) to this great movement.

Why did they so alter? In some cases and at particular points in time, no doubt, because they simply could no longer go on in the old way. But, in most cases and over most of the time, more because it had become steadily harder to sustain the judgment that they would be well advised to remain as they were. Much of the shift in judgment was very much a matter of particular causal beliefs. But some of it also, whether or not in consequence of such changes in causal belief, also became a shift in the assessment of normative plausibility; or at the very least of what it was now reasonable to suppose that others could be induced to regard as normatively plausible, and of what therefore might prove politically defensible in practice.

UNDERSTANDING JUDGMENT: EPISTEMOLOGY AND SOCIOLOGY

If it is right to see shifts in judgment as being so central to political understanding, how should we try to understand the process of judgment itself? Which aspects of it do we really need to concentrate on? Which can we safely ignore? This is a very old question in the Western attempt to understand politics, but it has lost none of its sting with the passing of the millennia. The upshot of two and half thousand years of effort to answer it is relatively clear in outline.

We need to understand the process of judgment both epistemologically and sociologically. We need to ask how far, throughout, the judgments are well or ill founded; and we need to ask why exactly they come to be made as they are by those who make them. Epistemologically, judgment is always personal and immediate, and virtually always potentially vulnerable. No one can be guaranteed to judge right about anything of the slightest importance (or perhaps about anything at all). Seen sociologically, judgment could hardly be more different. Most judgment is both habitual and heavily conventional. Virtually none is genuinely idiosyncratic or of the moment. The judgments which most of us make about most things are incurred more or less inadvertently, and almost in their entirety, from others. Politicians, journalists and civil servants (even economists) are as limply conventional in their judgments as any other occupational group. Most judgment is overwhelmingly dependent and, at least in its most important elements, formidably inattentive and potentially obtuse. Why is this contrast so extreme?

In essence, because the epistemological view is acidly normative (utterly unreconciled to human weakness), while the sociological view is conscientiously attuned to accept human beings as no whit wiser or more adventurous than they actually are.

Put like this, it sounds as though only the sociological perspective on judgment can possibly be pertinent to understanding political causality. It, at least, is consistently concerned with causality, while the epistemological view is essentially indifferent to how human beings obtain their beliefs. (It might, to be sure, be *contingently* concerned with this, if it saw some sources as epistemologically dependable and others as especially epistemologically treacherous.) But radical indifference to the sources of belief, in any case, would certainly be an indiscretion, since human belief is not a single sealed circuit, but an extremely porous membrane. Many of the determinants of everyone's beliefs are other beliefs of their own, or beliefs of other people. But no human being can have only beliefs which are unaffected by the impact of anything but other human belief. This claim can be made to look like an arresting, or ludicrously ingenuous, philosophical hypothesis. But it is probably the single dominating truth of human experience.

Over time, the truth of true beliefs and the falsity of false beliefs can, and often do, make themselves felt. This is seldom a tidy process; but it is sometimes a very pronounced effect. In practice, if usually somewhat inexplicitly, the recognition that this is so is almost certain to be incorporated into the most sociological conception of judgment or belief about any particular issue of consequence in any society over time. In the case of the massive impetus towards economic liberalization of the last two decades of the twentieth century, the main shift in question was in the ways in which it was credible to view a range of economic processes.

Viewed sociologically, it is natural to see this shift as drawn towards its apparent destination by the pull of true belief, the discovery of ever clearer and more reliable techniques for fostering economic efficiency and promoting economic flourishing. This is very much the way in which a whole generation of economists actively engaged in public service have come to view it, just as their Keynesian predecessors a generation or so earlier saw the previous move in a roughly opposite direction. Viewed epistemologically, however, the sequence looks strikingly different. Certainly the truth and falsity of belief have had an unmistakably causal impact within it. But it was the increasingly evident falsity of one set of false beliefs (Dunn 1984(a); Nove 1983; Brus and Laski 1989; cf. Gamble 1996, or, from a very different angle, Brenner 1998), not the steadily growing epistemic authority of their replacements, which did most of the work. Some countries have seen striking economic success over this period – consistently high growth rates, and considerable advances in the welfare of a clear majority of their population. All of these countries now permit (or in many cases enforce) a wider scope for markets and a narrower scope for direct governmental control of economic processes than they did fifteen years earlier. Many other countries, which for long failed to move in the same direction or which still refuse to do so, have seen their state virtually dismantled, or the welfare of the great majority of their people comprehensively devastated, and seen these, plainly, as a direct result of the refusal so to move. But so too, unfortunately, have a good many countries in which the state, under the tutelage of the international agencies of economic co-ordination (especially the World Bank and the International Monetary Fund), has also attempted with some vigour to move in just the same direction.

Viewed epistemologically, one old and loose hypothesis has become almost impossible to defend, while another (as it happens, in essence even older) hypothesis, which is certainly at least as loose, has turned out to be relatively compelling over a considerable range of cases (cf. Dunn (ed.) 1990; Lal and Myint 1996), if excessively hard to formulate at all tightly, and far less positively directive than its exponents usually suggest. The clear result is the negative result. Above a certain level of economic complexity, the central concerting of what is to be produced for an entire economy and of how this is to be distributed is not readily feasible, and not compatible with much personal freedom on the part of the population (Nove 1983; Brus and Laski 1989). Both establishing it and sustaining it require high levels of coercion. As production becomes more complicated, the eliciting and control of information, which is needed to enable it to work effectively, become ever more impracticable; and the design and installation of structures of incentive which prompt economic agents to act as vigorously, deftly and broadly as their planners have in mind become more and more patently impossible. The entire conception, never very clearly thought through in the first place, can be seen ever more plainly just not to make sense. The result is not a radical collapse in the plausibility of socialism (the very idea of organizing on any basis but that of private ownership and control of the means of production). But it effectively is an end to any widely shared conviction of the feasibility and efficacy of particular ways of doing so, and an increasingly clear consensus that none of the ways that has ever been implemented for any length of time and on any scale can be confidently expected to prove successful in practice.

As this becomes ever more apparent, the practical defence of socialist residues becomes increasingly furtive and inexplicit; and the political charms of commending any clearly characterized interpretation of socialism in practice become increasingly threadbare. This does not tell us what the future will be like. But it does bring out how different the present is from even the relatively recent past. The main causality here, I would claim, unmistakably comes not from a social and political process of diffusion of free-floating belief, in no way effectively responsible to external realities, but from the increasingly evident objective properties of particular human practices: not from what different human agents can be induced to believe, but from what palpably is the case.

THE EXPLANATORY IMPLAUSIBILITY OF THE INTEREST MODEL

How then is it appropriate to see such huge shifts in political (and economic) judgment? There are ways of seeing them which are admirably clear but singularly unconvincing; and other ways which are comparatively nebulous but far less heroic in their assumptions. The key difference between the two lies in how sanguinely they view human proficiency. On the clear but implausible view, all human beings have distinct and definite interests. All know just what their particular interests are, and all act effectively and with some degree of self-discipline (just enough to get the best returns on the degree of effort they expend) in order to promote these interests. These are not the human beings with whom you will be familiar. (Most unmistakably, they are transparently not yourself.) If human beings were indeed like that, it would be relatively easy to tell how they would act, and even easier to explain why they had acted as they did.

Politics would be a most unmysterious activity; and it would always go about as well as it could. In this condition, we would be very close to the best of all possible worlds. But, if this is indeed the best of all possible worlds, it is natural to ask, as Voltaire challenged Leibniz in *Candide*, what then can the others be like (Voltaire 1968, 69)?

In such a world, in any case, there would be little, if any, room for judgment, seen as a consequential and effortful endeavour. All judgment would be both compulsive and felicitous. Unsurprisingly, therefore, this conception is at its least plausible in relation to intellectual effort itself. If we considered, for example, the question of why the history of economic thinking develops as it does, it might be easy enough to explain the shifting foci of analytical attention, or the choice of problems on which to work or of conclusions to seek to defend. But it would be appreciably harder to explain why any economist ever makes an identifiable mistake. For the account to come out coherent at all, it would probably in the end be necessary to concede that economists have a plain interest not merely in not being seen by others to be confused or evasive, but also in avoiding being so seen by themselves. It is also likely in the end to be necessary to concede that the feature of the external world which it will prove most damaging to most economists to be plainly seen to evade is the regular consequences of applying particular policies in the world.

Because such models exclude variations in skill and imagination on the part of the agents, they are at their least illuminating when applied to processes in which variations in skill and imagination play a prominent causal role. It is not self-evident that the choice and implementation of governmental economic policy is such a process. But it is definitely a reasonable belief that it might be and even that it sometimes has been. Alfred Marshall was no doubt a trifle ingenuous when he claimed that the ambition to put mankind in the saddle is the ambition behind all serious economic work (Skidelsky 1992, 170). But it is hard to see how anyone could combine a consistent fatalism with an active interest in economic causality. Whatever else it may have been as well, the great shift in political and economic judgment of the last twenty years has been an episode in political and economic thinking. That thinking, moreover, however little of it may have been either intellectually very impressive or particularly original, was also rather evidently consequential. To judge how far the outcome has been felicitous, we need to rethink that history, at least in outline, and try to pin down how it led to the consequences which have followed from it.

Some political processes depend upon the judgments and actions of small, well-defined groups, with relatively definite and substantial powers of action. But this great shift could scarcely have been further from a process of that kind. It is far from clear how to distinguish it at all sharply from the entire history of the world over the same timespan. It involved immense numbers of people in a huge variety of roles and settings, few, if any, of whom can have had a coherent and well-informed conception of what it consisted in or meant as a whole. Because of the scale and impact of the shift, it is even less likely than usual that most of its human participants could judge with much precision quite how the shift itself was likely to affect even their own interests over time.

REFINING (OR BLURRING) THE INTEREST MODEL

To understand such a process, we can be sure, we need to understand why very many human beings chose to act as they did.

What sorts of conception of human interest might help to understand that choice, and what sorts might impede us in doing so? I would argue that an active and exploratory conception of the nature of human interests can help us, and a closed and determinate conception can only hinder us. One way of describing the shift as a whole would be to characterize it precisely as a mass shift in the assessment of what is in the interest of the majority within a modern population: above all, a flight backwards from a newer to an older economics. (For a modest and lucid sketch of one aspect see Gamble 1996.)

In this shift, little of the specification of interest within the newer economics simply lost force. Everywhere where it has occurred, a great many have lost from this shift. Few of them, probably, can have been surprised on balance to have done so. Their political representatives, in parties or trade unions, saw the loss coming throughout, and fought against it as best they could. But virtually everywhere their struggle was essentially an effort to limit the damage, not a battle to reach a freshly identified objective which they confidently expected to secure and firmly believed would advance the interests under threat.

What effected the shift – carried it through so irresistibly – was a sharp gain in force from the specification of interest within the older economics. That specification was general and simple, in contrast with a specification in the newer economics which was from the outset detailed and relatively complicated (cf. Skidelsky 1992). It is scarcely surprising that detail and complexity in understanding should retain some force. The main case against the older economics, throughout its history (Hont in Hont and Ignatieff (eds) 1983 and in Dunn (ed.) 1990; Berg 1980), has been that it is absurdly selective in what it does attend to, and correspondingly undependable in what it contrives to register. The simple formal case for markets as generators of the natural progress of opulence was always balanced by their erratic impact in practice on the lives of individuals or groups, their drastic instabilities, their inevitable obtuseness to considerations of distributive justice, and their robust indifference to the existential ease and security of their participants. What shifted the imaginative and political balance between the two versions of economics was less a purely internal intellectual history of professional squabbling among economists themselves than a set of changes in the world at large which increased the potential rewards of extending and deepening market processes and weakened the opportunities for a government to handle effectively the detailed intricacies of its own national economy.

The most important of these changes was the sheer scale of the increase in world trade, the vigour with which the international agencies and the richer states pressed home the choice between full access to this dramatically expanding market (along with opening one's own domestic economy to foreign capital and technology, and at the cost of opening one's own domestic market to foreign goods and services) and effective exclusion from it. Those states which opted at all protractedly for exclusion found the price which they (and their subjects) had to pay increasingly prohibitive. Over two decades, this shift in the balance of advantages was strongly reinforced by governmental policy in many individual states, and by the policies of international agencies. By the close of the Uruguay Round of the GATT negotiations in 1994 and the foundation of the new World Trade Organization, the cumulative shift had rendered it very hard even for some of the most effective state co-ordinators of national economic construction in the preceding decades (Japan, South Korea) to stand out against it. But it was the initial structure of opportunity which made the shift possible in the first place, and the recognition of that structure of opportunity which prompted the policies which came to be adopted.

POLICY CHOICE AND POLITICAL CONTEXT: EXPLANATORY CLARITY AS POLITICAL ILLUSION

The circumstances of political competition between policy models differed from state to state, as well as altering over time. In some states the competition was effectively confined inside the formal apparatus of the state itself, and there was no pressing need to convince a majority of the citizens of anything at all about the altered conditions for economic flourishing. In other states access to the power of the state depended, more than any other single factor, on the capacity to convince an electoral majority of the enfranchised citizenry that one line of governmental action (or inaction) rather than another was the most likely to foster national prosperity (cf. Amiagada Herrera and Graham 1994).

All such proposals in the end, whatever their felicity as assessments of how best to enhance the productivity or international competitive advantage of the economy, were always also proposals to distribute the costs of attempting to do so in this way, along with the benefits of having done so, should the change prove successful, to some and at the expense of others. The political goal in each case (over and above the economic advantages aimed at) was to identify and consolidate a winning coalition of potentially interested groups, and forestall, if possible, effectively collaborative opposition on the part of prospective losers. To see exactly how this was done in any particular state would be a formidable research task in itself; and it has scarcely even been attempted across the world as a whole. But the political process in question was not elusive.

Even after two decades that process remains severely incomplete. Some clear prospective losers who were fortunate enough to occupy strong defensive positions may still have lost very little in some of the countries which were more fortunate at the outset: the powerful trade unions of West Germany's leading industries, Norwegian or Swiss citizens at large, even, after their fashion, most of the populations of Italy or Spain. Those who have lost virtually everywhere (not least in Japan) are the protractedly unemployed: the category which Keynes and the post-war European welfare states set out to eliminate. What has proved decisive in this increasingly global political and economic process is the fact that the protractedly unemployed are nowhere likely to be in a majority, even in the relevant age cohorts, and that it is relatively easy to form and sustain a winning political coalition against them. So easy, in fact, that in many countries with old and powerful labour movements, the leading representative agency of the labour movement – in Sweden the Social Democrats, in Britain the Labour Party – becomes effectively, if somewhat sheepishly, incorporated into that coalition. These coalitions do not always come out as they were meant to. In particular, the fiscal drain of very high long-term unemployment can cancel out much of the promised increment in welfare for those still in employment, leaving the state in question with a disagreeable choice between increasingly flagrant fiscal irresponsibility or tax levels which effectively eliminate the benefits already promised to most of the electorate.

If the politics of this shift everywhere and throughout was murky, complex and usually exceedingly muddled, the shift itself was simple, brusque and overwhelmingly important. For a large majority of the world's population in the last decade and a half of the twentieth century, nothing which has happened politically can have mattered more. This would not be true, for example, of countries in which something close to genocide has taken place within this timespan: Ruanda, Bosnia, parts of Iraq. But even the single most dramatic political happening of the epoch, the collapse of the Soviet empire and the disintegration of the Soviet Union itself, is best seen not in contrast with the intensification and liberalization of global economic relations, but as in large measure an aspect and consequence of that shift. To understand the politics of the shift with any precision plainly requires considering it historically and in detail everywhere where it has occurred. Because the shift in fact occurred through a huge accumulation of changes in belief, seeing it as a whole requires an intimately sociological vision of how the immense amorphous mass of pertinent belief did alter over time. But although to see it this way would be a real and valid understanding as far as it went, and although forging it would be an astonishing collaborative intellectual achievement the like of which has never been seen in human efforts to comprehend our political fate, it would also inevitably be acutely disappointing.

The picture it would offer of what politics really is would be that of a ceaseless and overwhelmingly muddled struggle: not a single well-defined tug-of-war between two distinct teams of consciously opposed contenders, but a seething *mêlée* of superimposed teams, of constantly changing membership, profoundly undependable commitment and often blatantly faltering grasp of what is going on.

This, certainly, is what politics is like. (It is, alas, no mirage.) But can it really be said to amount to political understanding? Would it offer us any real intellectual grip on what has been going on? There are two very different ways of responding to this challenge. The first, which is on the whole the natural response for anyone whose thinking has been formed by awareness of the last few centuries of Western intellectual history, is modest and despondent. What it would offer us, this response implies, is all the real intellectual grip we can ever hope to have: a limited but real control over something which, in all its manifest disarray, was nevertheless really there. Any genuinely different sort of grip would either be essentially illusory (a mere fantasy of intellectual control), or would be a clear and steady conception (an internally well-controlled vision) of something which was never in fact really there: a confidently and stylishly false presentation of the very different phenomena which have been taking place in the real world.

The Platonic Riposte

The second response is well over two thousand years old. By far its greatest exponent was the Greek philosopher Plato. (In the modern epoch its most impressive defender has been Plato's most surprising admirer, Thomas Hobbes.) What marks this out from most modern viewpoints is its fierce focus on the idea of understanding itself, and its relative indifference to promiscuously available information about the world. To understand, it insists, is to see perfectly. Imperfect or hazy vision is simply incompatible with understanding. (Vision, of course, here is a metaphor, not a specific biological or physical process.) In the ruck of politics, the sheer directly encountered chaos of political struggle, above all in the reflection of that chaos in the minds of its human participants, and the contribution to creating and recreating it which follows directly from what passes through their minds, nothing at all can be seen perfectly. Those who are convinced of the possibility and uniqueness of understanding so conceived can only view politics with an appalled fastidiousness, as a largely meaningless and remorselessly malign disorder. But that does not mean that nothing which satisfies their criteria of understanding can ever bear upon politics. It is hard for thinkers who set such store by clear understanding not just to settle for thinking politics away: for rejecting its claim to justifiable presence in the world, and spurning it for other and more rewarding objects of attention (usually mathematical). No contemporary political thinker, unsurprisingly, can match the *éclat* of Plato or Hobbes. But there are many professional students of politics (many persons employed to teach others how to understand politics) who share the taste for precision and intellectual control, and the consequent impatience with the muddle of political reality (to say nothing of those of their colleagues who choose to live on at all intimate terms with that muddle).

Those who set such store by clarity of understanding – the Platonists – are in constant danger of fetishizing clarity, of treating it as an intellectual good in itself. They can have little to say about the ruck of politics (the peacetime equivalent in politics of what the great German strategist Karl von Clausewitz christened the *Schlacht* – the apparently mindless mass slaughter that lies at the heart of modern war, and perhaps of all war: Clausewitz 1976, 259). What, if anything, might they reasonably hope to offer instead? There are at least two very different things which we might wish to know about this huge shift: how exactly has it happened, and what exactly does it mean? If we wish to know the former, the Platonists will be of very little help. The ruck is where it did happen; and they view the ruck too cursorily and from too far away to see, even for themselves, just how it in fact did. The meaning of the shift, however, is scarcely visible from within the ruck. The view there is almost all foreground, the time horizon inescapably narrow. To see that meaning with any clarity, we need to see it from much further away: in steadier perspective and in far better light. In the end, any such understanding will still need to be brought back to the ruck – applied to or in it, or at least aimed at it, if it is to be understanding of what actually occurs. When it is brought back, however, the Platonists assume, it carries something back with it, something which could not in principle have been wrung from the ruck itself but which is indispensable if we wish to take the measure of what has indeed happened within this. This is an elusive conception. But it is far from obvious that it is merely fatuous.

EXPLAINING POLITICAL TRANSFORMATION BY INTERESTS

What exactly does the shift mean? What is the human significance of its having occurred? To answer that question fully and compellingly, we would need to know much which no one at present really knows, perhaps much that no human being will ever know. But the idea of a conclusive answer (God's answer, as it might be) is too ambitious to capture the force of Platonic ambitions. Most of that force comes from something far less extreme and humanly much more serviceable – the recognition of the priority of clear and well-conceived questions over potentially instructive answers. To see what this great shift has already meant or is likely to mean in the reasonably near future, we need to start off not from the shift itself, but from the stakes which human beings have in what history does to them: from what is good or bad for them, in or against their interest. We need to ask if it is indeed true that humans have definite interests, if all of them know what their interests are, and if all are well equipped to judge how, or genuinely capable of acting as, these interests give them good reason to act. Each of these three presumptions is bold enough in itself; and the conjunction of the three flies in the face of almost all human experience (cf. Barry 1965, cap. 10; Geuss 1980).

If humans do have definite interests, what could be more evident than that most of them have little grasp of just what their own interests are? Even where they do have clear conceptions of what their own interests are, what could be more apparent than that they frequently find themselves incapable of acting as these conceptions make appropriate (Aristotle 1926)? What is or is not good for human beings, and what human beings are really like, are extraordinarily complicated questions, formulated and answered extravagantly differently across space and time. The range of variation in both question and answer is so awesome that almost anyone is likely to lose their intellectual nerve in face of it. Those who are most confident that there are real human goods and bads are seldom vividly aware of a wide cultural and historical range (but cf. Cohen 1997; Dworkin 1996). Those who are most keenly aware of this range of variation are seldom confident that we can pin down what humans are really like, or what leads them to act precisely as they do. The cumulative impact of all this scepticism, in the twentieth century more particularly, has prompted many to claim not merely that there are no clear human goods or bads (or that we can never hope to tell one dependably from the other), but even that there is nothing at all that humans are really like: no biologically or physically determinate human nature, or even no determinate nature at all, in the first place. This is not the sort of quarrel in which to intervene casually (but cf. Dworkin 1996). Nor, at this level, is it of the least importance. What matters is not how authoritatively we can validate the answers we ourselves are tempted to give (no doubt far from authoritatively), but how clearly we can pose our questions, and how instructive we can hope their answers to prove. This is a matter to be discovered in practice, not one which can be foreclosed dogmatically in advance.

CUI BONO?

It is not overwhelmingly difficult to judge, country by country, which groups of human beings have benefited directly from the global impetus towards economic liberalization, and which have lost directly. Historical studies of the movements of real incomes over time, and of the changing distribution of these incomes between different social groups, are a well-established genre of applied economic research.[5] From the viewpoint of any particular country, the overall movement of real incomes is likely to prove more important over time than their distribution at any particular point. Thus far in human history it has been hard for high growth rates over long periods of time not to transform the life chances of most of a population for the better (as in many East or South-East Asian countries over this period, however uncomfortable conditions may be at present). By the same token, and for as long as it continues, a combination of falling production and rising or constant population can scarcely fail to inflict misery on a great many (as in numerous African countries over the same period, and in the former USSR somewhat more recently). But the aggregate movements of whole economies are statistical artefacts, not particular human experiences. From the viewpoint of individuals, or even of entire social groups, distribution is just as important as overall directional movement.

The central political disagreement about the significance of the shift concerns the relative weight of these two elements. Those who dislike the shift focus especially on the degree to which many of the winners have manifestly not deserved to win, and most of the losers in no obvious way deserved to lose. The absence of any convincing relation between desert and advantage has always been capitalism's Achilles' heel. Since the shift itself directly involved an intensification of capitalist production and exchange, and in some measure a rescuing of capitalism from a variety of political and social inhibitions placed upon it over the preceding three-quarters of a century, the disjunction between desert and reward was bound to come out far more starkly in these conditions. It is natural to take undeserved losses personally, and undeserved losses directly inflicted by political choice more personally still. Since the juxtaposition of undeserved misfortune and suffering and equally unmerited affluence is not in itself attractive, advocates and defenders of the shift have usually stressed other consequences: above all, the long-term benefits to all, *ceteris paribus*, of large aggregate rises in production of goods for which there is profitable effective demand.

This emphasis is more compelling where substantial aggregate rises did in fact occur than where (as in Britain or Mexico over protracted periods) they largely did not. (It is surprisingly difficult, outside China, to find instances where liberalized economies have in fact shown substantial and sustained gains in economic dynamism.) But, even where it is relatively compelling, distributive doubts remain; and the human pertinence of the long term is often open to question.

LONG TERM AND SHORT TERM

Economic liberalization may well be the only coherent long-term strategy for living within a dynamic global economy. But its consequences are clearest and most discouraging in the very short term. Those who lose worst in the short run are far from guaranteed ever to benefit at all, and sometimes unlikely to benefit personally or at all directly over any time horizon which it could make sense for them to consider. Keynes's famous objection to disregarding the importance of the short term – that in the long run we are all dead (Skidelsky 1992, 156) – was not just a *bon mot*. It highlights a permanently important dimension of political choice. We can think accurately about the short-term future, and act relatively effectively in relation to it. There is no way of thinking accurately about most aspects of the longer-term future, and no possibility whatever of ensuring most consequences we might reasonably hope for from the actions we aim towards it. The difficulties we face here are difficulties of comprehension; but they are also very much difficulties of implementation. It is hard for us to bind even ourselves as agents effectively forward, still harder to bind each other (think of the acts of marriage and divorce), and effectively impossible for most purposes to bind our successors. (The key difference in this respect between us and our distant ancestors is  that we *know* we have extremely little idea what the human future even a few decades ahead will be like, while they reasonably supposed that for most pertinent purposes it was bound to be exceedingly like their present.) This has dramatic implications for how we can sensibly envisage political action. We cannot view our practical future as Edmund Burke did, not only because we live in a more licentious age and are shaped by a more feckless culture, but also because we cannot sanely view the cumulative experience of our ancestors as an adequate source of guidance on how to handle our own future as that develops (Burke 1989).

Their experience, intelligently interpreted, may still be the best guidance we can have. But we have no guarantee whatever that it will prove to be adequate, nor that we shall contrive to interpret it intelligently. Neither, of course, in the event, had Burke.

PLATONISM AND THE MARKET

One way of looking at the shift, as we have seen, is to view it as a blind struggle. But another, and at least equally illuminating, way to see it (not an alternative, but an indispensable complement) is to see it as an immense argument, within particular societies and across the globe, over what is or is not a reasonable way for a society to choose to organize its economic affairs. Politics is the site of choice: how and where the members of a society do now choose over such matters. But economics today is overwhelmingly the most important domain over which their choice is exercised. Consciously at stake in the argument is the issue of whether or not, and, if at all, to what degree, it is possible to act rationally in relation to anything but the short-term future. On the most despondent conception of human rationality, individual agents ought certainly to be able to act rationally in the very short term, following the axiom, if nothing else, of *sauve qui peut*. But, insofar as they do just this, you need a very strong theory (or a robust confidence in Providence) to be sanguine about the prospective overall outcome of their actions. A Platonist, looking at this great argument, would see the worst threat facing this generation as being trapped in the very short term, acting in narrow and poorly lit contexts, and in a permanently hasty and under-considered way. The key Platonic challenge is how to escape from this trap: to see and feel time and the context of agency in a steadier and more temperate fashion. But to identify a challenge is not to see how it can be met. Indeed, it may well on occasion be to see that it simply cannot be met. To see what could count as a solution may be to see that no solution is or can be available. The struggle between the old and the new economics, and between the policies with which each has its own elective affinity, has Platonists on both sides. The Platonists of the market stress the limits on human knowledge, the short-term and short-range ingenuity of human agents, and the logical obstacles to their rational co-operation with one another.

Even today, however, the market probably has more Platonic critics than it has devotees. These critics are less impressed by the ingenuity of human agency than they are by its intemperance and practical folly. They see most human action as deformed by passion and bad judgment, and the victory of the very short term over the long term as the emblematic mode of human moral and spiritual defeat. It is no surprise to them if, in pressing over-eager conceptions of short-term interests, human beings at large prove to be wrecking the world which is their only home. They have never felt at ease with a mechanism (or process) the advertised *modus operandi* of which is to leave human agents to pursue their own conceptions of their interests under the lightest of regulatory constraints. They have always seen this process as culturally corrupting and wholly untrustworthy in its ultimate human impact. What could be less remarkable than the discovery (supposed or real enough) that its capacity for destruction now reaches well beyond human beings themselves to take in the entire ecology within which they live.

Platonists have seldom been at their most politically compelling in their assessments of what to do to implement their political tastes. But in this particular encounter the Platonists of the market are more comfortably positioned than their equally Platonic adversaries among the ecologists. The former at least know exactly what is to be done, while the latter vacillate unprepossessingly between ineffectual preaching, aimed at the wholesale transformation of souls, and not especially noble lies, designed to fit more comfortably into the political struggle as this is already being waged.

It is easy enough to see why a Platonic vision of contemporary politics, shaped by more or less acute ecological anxiety, should have had limited political impact. What is odder, and overwhelmingly politically important, is the remarkable impact made over the last two decades of the twentieth century by the Platonists of the market. One possible explanation of that impact, of course, might simply be that the key figures in this intellectual movement had not merely a powerful internal comprehension of their own ideas (a near-perfect vision of the Form of the Market), but also a proven record of modifying the real economic world successfully by applying these ideas. Yet the case for supposing this could scarcely be weaker. For every clear success in applying these ideas over this period, there are very many more far clearer failures. If the hypothesis is to be rescued from the phenomena, each such failure must be explained away – shown, ideally, to have resulted from the ideas not having been genuinely applied, or applied with insufficient zeal, excessive delicacy or readily avoidable clumsiness. But this structure of explaining away (and especially the frequency with which it proves to be needed) was precisely what had made the Keynesian approach politically vulnerable. If the Platonic market is as hard to implement at all, or as impossible to implement accurately, as this suggests, its comparative advantage over against Keynesian demand management becomes distinctly less obvious. Certainly, it cannot have been its continuously proven success as a technique for controlling real economies – its proven practical superiority in economic statecraft – which explains the sustained momentum towards economic liberalization in such a variety of settings and over such a long time. There just has been no such proven success.

AN ARISTOTELIAN RIPOSTE

It was not the countries which adopted anything resembling a Platonism of the market which prospered most in this period. (When their advantage really showed, with the Asian financial crisis of 1997–8, was at the end rather than the beginning of the episode.) If a single determinate set of countries did so, it was one which treated the market in a far more detached and carefully controlled manner (Amsden 1989; Okimoto 1989; Wade 1990). Insofar as a vision of the market contributed to this great shift in opinion and practice, it did so not by the precise instrumental control over economic causality which it provided, but by the imaginative force within the political struggle of a single simple and potent image: less as a repertoire of techniques than as a compelling myth.

While this may be an accurate diagnosis, however, it is no answer to the question from which we began. To counter the potency of one myth (the myth of skilled, detached and benevolent modulation of economic activity by a set of public-spirited technicians), only an alternative (and older) myth could hope to suffice. But why should the myth of the market's dependable dexterity have proved easier to believe over this period of time than its immediate predecessor? Why were market dynamics in this period, at least for journalists and voters, easier to trust than Keynesian economists? The puzzle appears to be intact.

UNFATHOMABLE CHOICES

Much of the answer here is simply a matter of sequence. In the real world, the actions both of Keynesian economists and of market Platonists have many unintended and deeply unwelcome consequences. Wherever one or other set of interpreters of the dynamics of modern economies prevails politically for any length of time, it is overwhelmingly likely for the perceived balance between intended and desired consequences and unintended and unwelcome ones to come out extremely unfavourably in the judgment of many (often not very observant) observers. Those outcomes which have been both intended and desired come increasingly to be taken for granted, and many cease to notice that their continuation still depends quite directly on further intended actions. The institutional setting in which the outcomes have been pursued hardens and becomes less flexible (Olson 1982): less good at incorporating the pursuit of new objectives. The unintended and undesired consequences become far clearer, their connection with the policies in question more blatant, and their human demerits more prominent and more resented. The experience comes increasingly to be seen *en bloc* (as a single internally related option), and the attractions of pursuing a decisively different option become correspondingly salient.

No one in fact knows what the consequences of pursuing the

new option will turn out to be. Even if it has been adopted quite extensively in the past, few will now remember or be aware of what then resulted from its adoption, and the adoption itself will have occurred in a context in many respects so different from the present that confident conclusions for the latter from the former are bound to be hazardous. The choice between organizing a country's economic affairs in one way rather than another is a very gross choice. To see exactly what such a choice means is never humanly possible. It involves too many intricate and largely opaque causal judgments, too many comparisons between always patchily known and poorly understood actuality and an endless array of possibilities, none of which can in principle be known in the same sense, and any of which may readily be surmised without the slightest trace of imaginative responsibility. The cumulative political revulsion from organizing an economy one way is by definition deeply grounded in experience. But it is always, and by necessity, quite hazardously related to the future. The effort to escape from a misliked past (always a selective interpretation of the actual past) is no guarantee of reaching a more welcome future (cf. Dunn 1989(a)).

As they arise in political practice, choices of this grossness are always unfathomable: beyond the reach of human cognitive powers. In the summer of 1789, as events proved, the French nation had to choose between the *ancien régime* and something very different. It was, of course, as Burke underlined (Burke 1989), distinctly more familiar with the former than with the latter. But no one in France at the time can have understood either very well; and there is overwhelming historical evidence that no one at all understood the nature of the choice between the two. (Over two hundred years later, it is far from clear how much headway in doing so we have made since.) It is not analytically wrong (not a clear intellectual mistake) to see the taking of such choices as a combat between myths. But it is unwisely abrupt to leave the issue at that.

Explaining Unfathomable Choices: Sociology versus Epistemology

A purely sociological study of the movement of political judgment must stick very close to the political process and may find it evocative to present its findings as an encounter between myths. But political understanding requires another dimension too: an explicitly epistemic dimension which tries to capture, with such analytic distance as it can muster, the clearest and most accurate practicable conception of what really is at stake in the choice, of the ways in which the human agents concerned have good reason to envisage it, and of the impact of the context in which they must make it on how it is appropriate for them to see it.

What is baffling about these last three components is the sharply different directions in which they seek to focus attention, and the brutal intellectual demands of any attempt to relate the products of all three. Each of these four varieties of interpretation, naturally, has its own corps of practitioners: persons trained to carry through the line of inquiry to a definite conclusion, and strongly inclined to attach weight to the forms of understanding which it habitually generates.

Most have obvious exponents within the present academic division of labour: in the case of the sociological study of the movement of political judgment, political science; in the second, much of contemporary economics. What is more elusive is whose task it is at present to provide and relate together the last two forms of understanding. In them the epistemic and the sociological plainly intersect, and it is far from clear on whose terms that intersection should take place. Does the ideal (or best available) modelling of economic causality define how a particular historical agent has best reason to envisage their choices? Or should it be the beliefs which they already happen to have, and the salience (for them) of different hazards and opportunities within the context in which they must choose to act which defines how they should see these choices? Just how personal, individuated and context-dependent is epistemic rationality in such contexts (Nozick 1993)? These are questions for philosophers (or all of us), as much as for economists or political theorists. They have been pressed harder in the last few years, especially by students of the logic of collective action, than they have ever been before except by brilliant individual intuition. But the collective effort has produced few conclusions which are both confident and immediately serviceable in face of the question itself. The matter, it seems increasingly clear, can reasonably be viewed either way round. Each viewpoint illuminates much. Neither can substitute for the other. What is decisively important for our present purposes is the image of politics which arises from adopting one or the other.

On the more sociological perspective, in which epistemic rationality is submerged in the largely false belief in which all of us inevitably participate, politics is confusion all the way down. There may be a way to see it – an ideal epistemic standpoint – in which the view itself is immune to confusion. At least the idea of such a standpoint does not obviously fail to make sense. But any such way is a view from outside politics, and probably from outside the real historical life of human beings; and any coherence and intellectual respectability which it can hope to muster will dissipate at once as soon as it is brought to bear in any way within politics. The choice, put like this, is one between an inevitably confused acceptance and embrace of confusion, and a resolutely unconfused rejection of an irretrievably confused reality: a choice between succumbing to politics and simply refusing to acknowledge its presence. This is why the Platonic element is so hard to eliminate from human efforts to understand politics. It is constantly being expelled with instruments as sharp as academic enemies can find to hand. But, like nature, it keeps creeping back.

If the choice is between trying to understand and just not trying, the case for not trying is bound to appear weak. But once you begin to try to understand, there have to be criteria for what understanding consists in. These criteria are always open to question, and to unfavourable (and carefully selected) comparisons with other possible criteria. The interrogation of criteria has an insistently epistemological momentum and a very evident political point. Once one has begun to move, why not go as far as one can get?

There could not be a way of understanding how human beings make their political choices which was both completely causally convincing and effectively sealed against epistemological pressure. If the most economical explanation of why we act (or fail to act) as we do in politics is that we follow our sense of what appears to us politically obvious, the impulse to sharpen the judgment of whether it should so appear is bound to be insistent. The better we understand politics, the stronger reasons we will have, other things being equal, to wish it less confused or maladroit, less practically inane. Only those comprehensively indifferent to the human future – who simply do not care how it comes out – are effectively buffered against this impulse.

This epistemological impulse can carry students and observers of politics in very different directions: towards a faithful recapitulation of its full confusion and disorder, a starkly contrasting depiction of a clear alternative order (as yet actualized only in the moral or analytical imagination of the student in question), or a simple and precise structure of understanding (like the theory of games) which, however it bears on what human beings actually do, at least in itself offers the possibility of precise and internally complete understanding. All these responses have their own point and can be illuminating as far as they go. But they do not sum up into a single coherent strategy of understanding. Indeed, unless their practitioners are exceptionally clear-headed, each of them tends more or less immediately to collide with both the others. Once the collisions have occurred, moreover, it is natural for bruised victims to respond with some impatience. Even where they do not feel inclined to question one another's motives for taking such different views, it requires great goodness of disposition for them not to sneer at each other's clarity of mind, or at the naivety of one another's assumptions about what human beings and the world are like, or about what it is to understand or fail to understand.

In the practical effort to understand politics it is imperative to try to avoid this outcome. Each approach, carefully deployed by an intelligent and patient analyst, is a real potential resource in understanding. A firm grasp of the internal properties of each approach is an effective safeguard against the temptation to identify it with the way the world just is; and a firm grasp of the properties of all three is a constant reminder that there are very many quite distinct questions we may well need to consider about politics, and we have no reason whatever to suppose that the best available answers to all will add up to a neat and internally stable whole, which furnishes the correct answer to every further question which can arise about politics. The idea of a collective intellectual instrument of comprehensive understanding, whatever its merits in relation to natural science, is utterly misguided when applied to politics. There just is no good way of understanding politics, independently of what you wish to understand it *for*, and when and where you need to understand it.

But how can it be *true* in this blunt way that political understanding should depend on the purposes and predicaments of those who seek it? Isn't politics just there? Doesn't it take the forms which it does and have the consequences which it has quite irrespective of what anyone not directly contributing to it happens to feel or believe about it?

The purpose-relativity of political understanding is more a point about how to act (and what it is to live) than a point about what it is to know. It does not alter the validity of political explanation and in no way modifies past physical or chemical events. But it plays a very prominent (usually a causally decisive) role in determining what is occurring politically in the present; and hence also determines what the political future can be and what politics there will be to explain in the future.

Both of these assessments are intuitively obvious as soon as you think about the matter with any care. Our purposes and predicaments define the content of politics not by brushing aside pre-existing causalities but by defining for each of us what these causalities mean for us, what is pertinent about them from our point of view, how they bear on the lives that we (and those we care about) can hope to go on living. For each of us, political understanding defines a key part of our fate, many of the main limits on our real freedom of action, and virtually all the principal opportunities open to us once we try to act on a scale larger than our own domestic setting. Insofar as we lack it, we can hope to comprehend only the most local and obtrusive features of our lives. And even these perhaps not very well.

I have tried to show that the single most prominent question in Britain's domestic politics in the two final decades of the twentieth century is best understood not as a purely domestic question but as one about what has determined the development of most of the more advanced capitalist states over this period. (For the background history of the world economy which in the end did most to determine it see Brenner 1998.) I have also tried to show that, so formulated, it is neither a question which modern professional students of politics know how to answer nor one which proves, by that inability, their professional techniques for explaining politics to be ill considered, let alone worthless. Above all, I have tried to show that any such suspicion is peculiarly misplaced where their reasons for attempting to understand it in the first place are practical and humanly responsible. The more the question of why what has happened has done so is fuelled by concern over how it would be best to act in the future, the less tractable it is bound to prove, and the more forlorn the enterprise of seeking to professionalize the study of politics in order to furnish it with a certified and trustworthy answer.

6

The Modern Representative Democratic Republic

An Hegemonic State Form?

THE DISTINCTIVENESS OF THE MODERN REPRESENTATIVE DEMOCRATIC REPUBLIC

We do not at present, as I hope I have made clear by considering the example of Mrs Thatcher's impact, really understand quite why our own countries make the more drastic and consequential political choices which they prove in retrospect to have made (why the Germans succumbed to Adolf Hitler in 1933, or the British succumbed to Margaret Thatcher in 1979 and afterwards, or, for that matter, at long last to Tony Blair and Peter Mandelson). We can certainly hope to understand any particular choice better by worrying protractedly over its narrative outline, and the history which leads up to it. But, if we are to develop a political judgment which is of any practical use, we need to start elsewhere, with questions of much greater generality, and ones which give us at least a chance of compiling a basic inventory of considerations which we shall need to continue to bear in mind. The most plausible place at which to start at present is not with local idiosyncrasies or particular historical contingencies, but with the attempt to locate the basis of the prevalence of a single hegemonic political conception.

Today, however briefly, for the first time in human history, there is a single clearly dominant state form, the modern constitutional representative democratic republic, distributed across the globe. There is no reason for confidence that its dominance will last, and there are no grounds whatever for assuming that it is bound to prove effective in face of the very many practical tasks placed upon it by continuing human needs and the cumulative consequences of human actions. Since it also happens to be, despite many and vulnerable idiosyncrasies, the state form which prevails in Britain today, it is natural for a British citizen attempting to understand politics today to set it at the centre of their efforts. (The idiosyncrasies are far from trivial. Britain is in many respects not excessively modern. Only in the vaguest of senses can it be said to have a constitution. Its system of representation is in several ways notably distorting. It has always had pronounced reservations about the merits of democracy. It is not at present a republic, and has been one, even in the past, only for a very short time. But, in contrast with any state at all in the world four centuries ago, the Britain of today very clearly is an example of this now so widely conventional modern state form.)

The practical case in favour of this regime has been expressed in terms both of its serviceability for meeting human needs and of its adaptation to the cumulative consequences of human actions. These are very different sorts of cases; and the first is simpler, more stable and easier to assess than the second. If a regime is to be dependably serviceable for meeting continuing human needs, it must have some grasp of what these needs are and address them directly and with some energy. The case in favour of the modern regime, on this score, is that it is a better general solution to the problem of security than any other so far envisaged and tried out in practice.

It is better than genuine monarchy or open oligarchy, because its explicit goal is equality of protection, and because it builds this goal as deftly and thoroughly as it can into its core system of authority. None of the techniques for doing this are beyond criticism. Formal equality of power for adult individuals in the suffrage (one adult person, one vote) is easy to mistake for an equality of impotence. Constitutions specify clear and dependable relations between governmental powers and civic rights. But no constitution can ever enforce or secure itself; and no constitution's protection of the rights which it does effectively protect can guarantee that those rights are specified justly, or even clearly. All constitutions separate some powers from others; and the majority, since 1787, have at least suggested that some of these powers always may, and sometimes should, inhibit the action of others: in particular that conscientious judicial judgment should obstruct unedified executive will. (And what then about the converse: unedified judicial will obstructing conscientious executive judgment?)

The most rigorously constitutional of states is always staffed by human agents. Much of what these agents do is always in some tension with the goals intended by those who initially established the constitution. It is a very interesting question how one should conceive what a constitution really is. Is it a relatively determinate mechanism with relatively determinate causal properties? Is it an ambitious, but necessarily somewhat hazy, system of intentions, continuously modified over time, as the intentions of succeeding generations of interpreters feed into it and are evacuated from it? Is it a firm structure of rights, which can be modified only on its own terms, and must lose its identity once and for all as soon as it is altered in any way which conflicts with these terms? Constitutions can only allocate the power to carry out the tasks for which they exist by allocating powers which in practice enable different sets of agents to do a great deal else. There can never be adequate public power for any type of purpose without there being on many occasions a clear excess of it. All constitutions which have a real political presence (which are not pure imposture) oscillate permanently (though not, of course, in equal proportions) between insufficiently constrained governmental vigour and all too effectively constrained governmental paralysis (cf. Manin 1994). Specifications of citizen rights in face of the state are either a part of the constitution itself (Bills or Declarations of Rights), or they are at the mercy of an ongoing process of sovereign decision-making which itself is always heavily influenced by governmental power.

THE ROLE OF THE POUVOIR JUDICIAIRE

Thus far, however, we have no reason to suppose that there is any better general solution to the problem of security, and little, if any, reason to regard any other possible countervailing value as a serious rival to security as the dominant continuing human need. If we cannot dependably preserve ourselves and those we care about, there will not be much else we can reasonably devote ourselves to promoting. We may sometimes choose to sacrifice ourselves; but we will need something to sacrifice ourselves for.

For this solution to the problem of security to work, it does, of course, have to be intended; and the intention must be sustained over time, and across the full range of human participants and the vagaries of their subsequent interpretations of it. It must never collapse into pure fraud. Considered as a relatively determinate mechanism with relatively determinate causal properties, there is no reason whatever to think of it as self-guaranteeing in these terms (Vile 1967; Gwyn 1965; Montesquieu 1989; Manin 1997). But there is also no reason to presume that there is any better mechanism which could stand in for it more dependably across the board. What can perhaps be said in criticism, even two hundred years and more after it was first seriously pioneered, is that two elements of it remain very vague indeed. One is the social or political antecedents of those who exercise the key power of restraint upon potential misgovernment: the constitution's privileged interpreters, the judges or magistrates. In this respect, there is still something archaic and purposefully inexplicit about the modern constitutional democratic republic: the special characteristics of those who are to judge whether it is or is not cleaving to its own rules that palpably fit them for this awesome responsibility, and the social and political mechanisms which ensure (or even render particularly likely) their possession of these characteristics. It is an important fact about the greatest interpreter of the political significance of the separation of powers, the eighteenth-century French nobleman Montesquieu, that he was an hereditary constitutional magistrate under the French *ancien régime* (Shackleton 1961; Ford 1953; Kingston 1996), whose own public legal status in the

Parlement of Bordeaux had come to him through no merit of his own, and in common with fellow magistrates who probably did not strike even themselves as dedicated or prospectively dependable protectors of the legal rights of every French subject (but cf. Van Kley 1996; Kingston 1996). Montesquieu, to see the matter at its crassest (Althusser 1959), put a forceful case for the public utility of his own class or occupational group. But he scarcely contrived to pin down how any society can hope dependably to obtain the devoted and punctiliously professional adjudications on which it must ultimately rely.

THE ROLE OF VOTERS

A second unclarity in the model of the modern republic lies in the mode in which the sole element of equality in ultimate authority over the government is exercised: the individual vote. Electoral systems are complicated. They can be designed in outline, and manipulated in detail, to produce an endless variety of effects. Any electoral system there could possibly be would be subject to politically damaging criticism on some ground or other (most on a great many different sorts of grounds). In particular, no electoral system by itself could ensure clarity, good judgment or mutual amity in the range of active political purposes entertained by a given body of citizens (cf. Dunn 1996(d)). Even such fundamental desiderata as decisiveness of outcome, accuracy in the registration of opinion and will or fairness to all citizens must often pull sharply against one another.

This matters greatly, since it may in the end always force a choice between two distinct ways of seeing the regime as a whole: as a radically alienated mechanism (a black box) for maximizing the security of the members of a given population, or as an utterly direct structure of action through which (and through which alone) individual citizens confer the authority which only they can confer upon their temporary (and in themselves utterly unauthoritative) rulers. The relation between these two conceptions remains highly unstable; and most analysts of modern representative democratic states are still exceedingly reluctant to confront it (cf. Dunn 1994).

GUARANTEEING SECURITY: EFFICIENCY AND AVAILABILITY

Some states today are fairly thorough failures at meeting even the most elementary of continuing human needs: Liberia, Somalia, Rwanda, perhaps, alas, the Russian Republic. Nothing about the model of a constitutional representative democratic republic ensures that such a state will hold together, or that its coercive powers will not be turned protractedly and brutally against large segments of its own population. But it is unusual for the model to survive, even as a façade, in conditions of long-drawn-out civil war, let alone in face of state disintegration. (The travails of Northern Ireland, from this point of view, whatever else they reveal about the Six Counties, are also testimony to the strength and resilience of the British state.) In conditions in which the model has indeed survived for long periods of time, the judgment that it is an effective solution to the problem of security has worn rather well. Not for everyone. Not always. But for most people and very much of the time, and in contrast with all other recipes of comparable generality and abstraction.

ECONOMIC SECURITY

Where modern constitutional democracies fail to meet the elementary continuing needs of many of their population, that failure in most instances is obtrusively a failure in their economy: in the ways in which goods or services are produced and distributed within them. Producing and distributing goods has never been a task which fitted comfortably with either the core goal or even the main powers of agency of the state as an institution. States protect their citizens against each other, and all of them against threats from elsewhere. They profess to provide security by preventing other agents from acting in particular ways. This is a negative and limited, if permanently challenging, assignment. Some states, throughout history, have shouldered the responsibility for causing their economy to flourish, until recently more at the level of fantasy than of practical intervention. The great twentieth-century project of assuming full responsibility for an economy's flourishing – above all the model forged by the Bolshevik Revolution and Stalin's industrialization drive – has by now broken all the states which espoused it and have not since chosen to repudiate it in practice. Even the far more tentative endeavours of the post-war Western welfare states have wilted extensively.

The view that the state as such can ensure subsistence (by redistributing the minimal requirements for this from those citizens who have far more than they need to those who do not even have that) has always been a trifle uncomfortable. It could only reliably apply where the numbers of those whose subsistence needs would be otherwise unmet was not too vast, the range of resources at the disposal of the more fortunate was fully adequate to make up the deficit, and the state itself was able to effect the transfer from one to the other. This last proviso is as important as the first two, since the state has no intrinsic need to presume itself capable of closing a gap between insufficient supply and excess demand, but cannot readily accept an incapacity to compel its subjects to act as it deems essential or fundamentally important. A discovery of what a state cannot do through its tax system is more intimate and ideologically discomfiting than one about the limits of its capacity to improve the operating efficiency of an entire economy. Either a state has the power to judge on behalf of its subjects and enforce its judgment upon them, whether or not they share this, or it does not. A state which manifestly lacks this power fails by its own core criterion. Its surrender of power to another human grouping, or its tacit acceptance of a right of judgment on their part over against its own, conflicts with its central self-definition. States do not have to believe that they can make any of their subjects healthy, wealthy or wise. For them to believe this, indeed, may be profoundly superstitious. But no state can simply accept on the part of groups of subjects an equal right to believe, and act on their beliefs, against its express will about matters on which it has publicly made up its mind and firmly announced what that mind is (cf. Weber 1968, 56).

States can neglect the subsistence needs of their subjects quite deliberately. Indeed they can choose to starve the latter to death by whole communities. But where they simply prove unable to secure the subsistence needs of significant numbers of their subjects, where the unintended starvation of the latter is more than a dramatic individual calamity, which could scarcely have been averted by coherent public action, the state itself must either misconceive its core responsibilities or preside ineffectually over an economy in ruins. Unintended starvation of its own subjects must result either from a failure to define their effective entitlements to subsistence goods in a way which guarantees that subsistence, or from a drastically destructive governmental economic policy. In either of these cases, by the late twentieth century, the outcome must stem less from the state's inherent inadequacy as a solution to the problem of security than from its failure in adaptation to the cumulative consequences of human actions. As a solution to the problem of security, the state is not, of course, literally outside history. As an idea, as we have seen, it was first entertained at a particular time and has been modified in interpretation ever since. But it was as a solution to the problem of security that it has always been most emphatically and incisively identified, and can make the strongest case on its own behalf. That case, too, has been modified over time and as a consequence of institutional innovation. But the case itself does not depend for its main force on historical development; and it is easy to exaggerate the degree to which its weight has really altered with historical change. As an adaptation to the cumulative consequences of human actions, by contrast, states are historical through and through. One sort of state might serve well enough at one epoch, and only a very different sort of state serve at all at another. Mutual human menace and vulnerability may well lie at the core of the human condition (along with need and a range of more agreeable characteristics). But the cumulative consequences of human actions change all the time. Nothing could guarantee that a device which was well shaped to handle the former would also prove reliable in handling the latter, and do so indefinitely and whatever the latter turn out to be.

OPTIMAL SOLUTION TO THE PROBLEM OF SECURITY?

The modern constitutional representative democratic republic as a conception has been thought through systematically, in both theory and practice, as a would-be optimal solution to the problem of security. There is a set of cases against the state in this first guise – essentially the range of versions of anarchism, from the most elegantly philosophical to the most grubbily practical. Some of these cases are undeniably instructive. But none of them in the end is wholly convincing, since none does anything to support the judgment that most human beings in the epoch since the idea of the state first drastically entered into the lives of whole communities would on balance have benefited from a permanent collapse even in the state power to which they were immediately subjected, unless it had been promptly replaced by another. The comparisons are hard to make clearly, and always potentially misleading. But the more carefully they are carried through, the less plausible the judgment that, other things being taken as they could readily have been, most human beings would on balance have benefited from the permanent disappearance of state power. (For a thoughtful caveat, however, see Scott 1998.)

Besides its self-conception as optimal solution to the problem of security, the modern constitutional republic has also been compellingly identified with an historical epoch and a set of public responsibilities distinctive of that epoch. These responsibilities include the protection of a particularly effective and counter-intuitive system of property rights, on which the development of human productive powers has for long directly depended. As the capitalist economies built by these developing powers grew and changed, their political requirements and vulnerabilities changed with them. The modern constitutional representative democratic republic was consciously devised to meet these new requirements and protect these new vulnerabilities. But it was also devised with other tasks in mind and under conditions of continuous (and usually extremely confused) political struggle and continuous (and often equally confused) attempts to understand the causal dynamics of these economies. Very strenuous (if intermittent) efforts have been made ever since the 1780s to show just how one set of characteristics meshed or clashed with the other. Confident theses have been advanced and defended, some suggesting an exquisite and endlessly flexible adjustment of the political form to the ongoing social, economic and political task, and others that only a complete transformation of the state structure, or an effective eviction of state will and choice from the entire domain of economic causality, could offer any reasonable hope for the future. Some thinkers (Hayek, for example) have argued that the representative and democratic features of the state conclusively unfit it for any direct role in economic regulation, insisting on the need for a new (and presumably politically created and enforced) constitution defining the space of economic agency, and placed beyond the corruptions and vagaries of political choice (Gamble 1996, esp. 91–9). Others have insisted that the representative elements simply cancel the democratic, and thus remove any claim on the state's part to be authorized to regulate anything. Others, again, see the very existence of private property rights in the means of production as radically at odds with the compelling claims of personal self-rule (of which they see democracy as simply a generalized form).

Representative Democracy and Economic Policy

VINDICATING THE MODERN REPUBLIC AS JUDGE OF ECONOMIC POLICY?

For most of the last two hundred years, it has been natural (and perhaps reasonable) to suppose that the root of these disagreements lies in a conflict of intuition about the imaginative and material basis of political authorization, on what (if anything) could rationally entitle some humans to command others so decisively, and what might imaginatively impel the latter to concede that this was reasonable. No state, it was easy to believe, could be entitled to be obeyed if it gratuitously failed to furnish its subjects with their subsistence needs or deliberately chose not to recognize and guarantee these as effective entitlements. It could not, because gratuitous failure or choice in these instances would infect any defensible claim to be entitled to their obedience.

Since 1973, however, a second and very different way of seeing the sources of these disagreements has loomed much larger. It views them as coming not from deep conflicts in intuitions about human value, but from an increasingly widespread (if patently shallow) commonality of intuition about human value (that material prosperity is plainly to the advantage of all who are fortunate enough to have the opportunity to enjoy it), along with a distressing breadth of conflict in judgment as to how such prosperity can reliably be engineered. Here we return, plainly, to the political and economic determinants of Mrs Thatcher's impact on British politics, and of the effects of the global wave of economic liberalization on the politics of very many other countries.

Here too attempts have naturally been made to vindicate the claims of the modern constitutional democratic republic to be equipped to judge well and act effectively in this task. But these attempts have been altogether less successful, and for very good reasons. For one thing, they must contend throughout with direct experience of just how successfully these states have discharged and are discharging the task. The view that they are admirably equipped to do so was distinctly more plausible in the protracted post-war boom than it has become in the more erratic conditions since this ended (Brenner 1998). Since no advanced capitalist economy within a state of this character has been consistently dynamic even throughout the 1990s, it is hard to defend the judgment that the state form itself is sufficient to guarantee their enduring prosperity. Almost as discomfitingly, its claim to peculiar suitability for ensuring material prosperity for given populations within a still notably dynamic world economy has had to contend with the fact that many of the most dynamic capitalist economies over this period have been located in states which deviated sharply from the model.

AN ENDANGERED CIVILIZATION?

How far, then, is it still reasonable to believe (or even hope) that this state model is well adapted to the economic present and near future of the world in which we live? We should note, first, that the main grounds for doubt about its adaptation to securing human flourishing in the more distant future are probably best seen not as doubts about the properties of different varieties of states as sites of political agency (cf. Dunn 1996(d)), but as doubts about the sustainability of an entire human way of using the world. If these last doubts in the end prove well founded, it is scarcely likely that any format of political agency will prove capable of responding to them wisely and effectively (Dunn 1996(a), caps 10, 12 and 13).

THE CONTINGENCY OF GOVERNMENTAL ECONOMIC POLICY

One may doubt the suitability of the modern democratic republic for handling the ongoing local consequences of a global economic process for several different sorts of reason. Each may carry some real weight. But they offer very different diagnoses of the political vulnerability of modern economic existence; and the varieties of remedy which they strongly suggest are largely incompatible with one another.

If we take the choice and implementation of governmental economic policy as the key site on which this suitability must be demonstrated, the doubts may focus either on the choice or on the implementation. But, on this front at least, doubts over the implementation cannot reasonably be levelled at the modern democratic republic in particular (in contrast to any other comparably determinate type of existing regime). It cannot, because the contrast, however it is drawn, is certain not to come out clearly in the right direction. For one thing, the modern democratic republic is too capacious a category. The still highly bureaucratized constitutional empire of Japan clearly belongs within it, but shares, too, many of the structural and economic characteristics of other Asian states like Indonesia, or Singapore, or, until very recently, South Korea, which clearly belong outside. For another, it is all too clear that many of the most administratively ineffectual of states are firmly outside it and most of the more administratively deft ones very much inside it. Germany and Sweden, for example, are distinctly better administered than Zaire, and Australia and Canada scarcely less well so than Indonesia.

No state can make its subjects do whatever it happens to choose. None ever has been able to and none ever will. All subjects have many other purposes besides doing what their state tells them. Many of them are sly, ingenious, determined, vigorous and strongly committed to their own discrete purposes. States can muster a formidable surplus of repressive force, and unleash this from time to time on groups of their subjects. They can also, if they so choose, put a large proportion of the resources available to them into systematic surveillance of their subjects. But states which do the latter (North Korea, Myanmar) can scarcely hope to expedite the overall workings of their domestic economy by doing so (compare China before Deng). If there are special grounds for doubt over the suitability of modern constitutional democracy for operating a domestic economy efficiently, they turn less on its capacity to carry through the public actions on which it decides than on its selection of those actions in the first place.

STRENGTHS AND WEAKNESSES OF DEMOCRATIC DECISION-MAKING

The case against the choices made by modern constitutional democracies often focuses on the inherent confusion of the decision-making process itself – the impossibility of seeing clear relations across it, and the degree to which it is dominated by the judgments of the many, ignorant and all too erratically motivated at the expense of the few, learned and steadily concerned. The fundamental contrast here is between choice by experts, who know what they are doing, and choice by amateurs, who don't. So expressed, this is a tendentious, but not an inane contrast. What it highlights, it genuinely does illuminate. Who could prefer important choices which affect them deeply to be made, other things being equal, by those who do not understand what is at stake, or what will lead to what, rather than by those who do?

But, of course, besides highlighting these pressing considerations, it also, as Aristotle long ago pointed out (Aristotle 1932), occludes others: notably the considerable gap between the preoccupations of most of the citizenry and the preoccupations of the stratum of experts in question. What makes the citizenry's choices confused is more the bewildering range and elusive relevance of their preoccupations than the limits of their individual factual knowledge or analytical insight. How to use experts wisely is not a special problem for modern democracies, but a general problem for non-expert holders of authority in any possible state form. Only the most ingenuous could suppose it not also to be a problem for experts themselves (however narrowly conceived), since these are seldom united in their conceptions of the nature of issues which strongly divide many of their fellow citizens. (An example sufficiently culturally distant to permit some detachment would be the Shi'ite *ulama* of Iran in the epoch of Khomeini and after: Abrahamian 1995.)

The view that the extreme technical complexity of modern civilization requires that it be run by those who understand the key types of technique loose within it has obvious elements of common sense to it. But it is far less directive than it sounds. The presumption that what it dictates in practice is technocratic government (a regime in which technique as such rules) suggests to some (not least to themselves) that scientists and engineers, or graduates of the French École Nationale d'Administration or great international business schools, must be the ideal state cadres for the regime of today. But a more reasonable view of the matter is simply that any set of state cadres today will need to draw promptly and attentively on the full range of causal understanding of the major techniques of production in use within the space for which they are responsible, to say nothing of their cumulative ecological consequences. No one has yet shown the modern democratic republic to be any worse equipped to do this than any other type of state in existence today. (It would be hard, however, to argue that anyone has shown it to be dependably better than any other in this respect either: cf. for example Dryzek 1990; Wade 1990.) It is reasonable, therefore, to presume that political choice today must reckon with a very much wider range of techniques than the citizens of Athens had good reason to worry about. But it is far from clear that this alone compels them to abandon their claim to judge and decide what is politically acceptable over a range wider than their predecessors. Still less is it clear that this alone could make it any wiser for them to surrender that ultimate freedom. Alienating power and judgment in detail and by choice is very different from doing so wholesale and in a way which cannot readily be reversed at will, however unwelcome the consequences prove to be. A process of decision can be defective from a number of different angles: among others, in the outcomes which it is likely to engender, in the components which enter into it, in its structure or absence of structure, in the incentives faced by those who choose whether or not to take part in it. Probable or actual decisions within a particular decision process contrast with fully appropriate decisions in an ideal decision process. A fully appropriate decision, again, might be so in virtue either of its outcome or of the mode through which it has been reached (cf. Rawls 1972; Barry 1989). The central case for the modern democratic republic is that it represents a mode of decision-making fair to all entitled to take part in it (its adult citizens) and likely to produce outcomes which are on balance to the benefit of all (or where not of all, at least of as many as possible). More optimistic glosses upon it seek to coax these outcomes into a pattern in which they are not merely on balance (and somewhat equivocally) to the benefit of all taken together, but also throughout and systematically fair to each taken apart. By the time these provisos have been formulated with ideal clarity, however, the decision processes in question no longer display the faintest resemblance to those of any actual state (Rawls 1972; Barry 1989 and 1993; cf. Rawls 1993). Even in this respect it is hard to justify the judgment that these decision processes can be trusted to prove fair to those not entitled (or simply unable) to take part in them: existing minors, resident aliens or helpless denizens of other lands, generations yet unborn. The case that they should be so trusted has to work through the supposedly natural motivations, and hence the dependable agency, of those who are entitled and able to take part in them. In the case of existing minors this may have a modicum of initial plausibility; but it is important to note that this is exactly the presumption which used to be offered in favour of entrusting the interests of women to men, and of the poorer and less educated to the wealthier and better educated. In the other instances, it is hard to see why anyone should be tempted for a moment to accept it.

PARTICIPATION

A mode of decision-making which would be fair to all those entitled to take part in it, if they did indeed do so, cannot reasonably be expected to prove fair (for this reason alone) to those who, while formally so entitled, do not dare to do so, or cannot in practice afford to do so because of the costs which this will impose upon them, or choose not to do so from rational pessimism over their own limited practical insight or competitive eloquence (cf. Hobbes 1983), or the sheer odds against them. The judgment that the political odds are stacked against one may not be a noble reason for giving up. But it is always a potentially good reason for doing so, and, where the judgment itself accurately captures the main facts, it is as decisive an instrumental reason for inaction as a potential agent can well have.

All decision processes in which participation is allocated by entitlement can be seen both as systems of rights and as systems of power. The modern democratic republic is, on the surface, a relatively prepossessing system of rights; but only the most intimate and detailed exploration of its penetralia in any given instance will reveal quite how it comes out when viewed as a structure of power. It would take a very optimistic interpreter of its properties today to suppose it provenly sound, either in the outcomes which it is likely to engender, or in the components which enter into it, or in the incentives which it offers to those who choose whether or not to take an active part in it. The case in its favour rests more on scepticism towards any alternative, actual or possible, than on experience of its past achievements or conviction of its inherent justice or rationality. All the more striking, then, its increasing ideological domination of the modern world; and all the more urgent, accordingly, the need to explain this.

THE NEGATIVE CONSEQUENCES OF DEMOCRATIC DECISION-MAKING

The case against this state form, however, may rest more directly on experience. The core of that case is simple. The modern democratic republic sounds like, and can be readily described as though it were, a fair system of rights, embodied in an actual process of decision-making. But, directly encountered, it is quite obviously (and, in all probability, irreversibly) corrupt and feckless. Its outcomes are deeply pernicious and destructive. Its actual mode of decision-making is a travesty of the system of rights which it continues to profess, and systematically distorts these rights in practice. The most drastic version of this verdict is constructed backwards from the perception that many of the outcomes of the state today are plainly unwelcome and likely in the long run (unless effectively redressed) to subvert its own conditions of existence. The consequences of an institution provide a basis on which to judge it which is conceptually independent of its explicit goals and of the formal (and perhaps even the informal) system of rules of which it is composed. If its consequences are blatantly deplorable, who cares if its overt goals are edifying and its system of rules appears on the face of it to be fair?

To assess its consequences is to view the modern democratic republic, as a system of rights, firmly from the outside. In this perspective, the modern democratic republic merely masquerades as a modest solution to the problem of mutual human security. What it really is is the local political form of a global civilization of high and capriciously distributed mass consumption, based on energy-intensive industrial production and the relentless exploitation of a natural world increasingly defenceless in face of its human predators. This is a vast wrong in itself for anyone who sides with the natural world as a whole (or other species within it) against their human fellow plunderers. In this respect the rights and duties of the citizens of a modern democratic republic are a form of systematic complicity in an immense spiritual and natural crime. But, even for those who take a lower and more humanly egoistic view of the outcomes (who see them simply from the point of view of humans themselves), the outcomes alone may be worse than a crime; they may be a blunder (cf. Passmore 1974) – at worst, indeed, an irretrievable and terminal blunder. The phenomenon of global warming, the relatively rapid rise in the overall temperature of the earth's surface, may prove sufficient in itself to show this entire way of life to be a blunder: an unsustainable system of action, with an increasingly hectic momentum and extremely powerful mechanisms inhibiting its own reversal. Even if it is a blunder, however, what has brought it into existence, and what continues to sustain it, are the ways in which it seemed or seems to vast numbers of human beings to be best for them to act. Even if (to take the worst possible case), this way of life as a whole proves a single extravagantly powerful mechanism for the inadvertent collective suicide of an entire species, it would be hard to convert that insight back into a set of reasons for action sufficient to move generations of human actors steadily away from the brink.

THE MODERN REPUBLIC AS BEARER OF ECOLOGICAL DEGRADATION

Viewed as a system of rights, the modern democratic republic is an empty political form, designed by humans for humans for quite modest purposes (Fontana (ed.) 1994). But, when encountered in the historical world, the economic, social and ecological content which inevitably fills it reveals it instead to be as deadly as it is arrogant, an irresistible machine for destroying the human world. What follows from this, naturally, is that virtually everything now human needs to be different: the goals which women and men find it natural to pursue, the considerations which they are apt to see as practically pertinent, the institutional settings in which they have become accustomed to act. But this is inevitably an extra-political, as well as a supra-political, point of view: too gross and comprehensive to give any particular set of human beings useful guidance on what they should do next, or perhaps on what they should do at all. To turn it back into a political point of view, to reintroduce it to (and into) politics, it must be transformed from a single dominating image of what is to be avoided and what must stop (a historical Form of the Human Bad) into an endless variety of humanly more manageable apprehensions of what might with luck in the long run prove a less hectically indiscreet way to behave. Too comprehensive a disapproval of the ways in which human beings have come to behave cannot hope to be politically directive. It confuses an attack on what we are (or have become) with a proposal for what we might now profitably do. It is imaginatively exhausted in the moment of rejection. It too is therefore bound to prove every bit as feckless as the nineteenth-century French revolutionary Auguste Blanqui: 'I am not a professor of politics or socialism. What exists is bad. Something else must take its place' (Spitzer 1957, 135. Note what has subsequently happened to socialism: cf. Dunn 1984(a)).

THE CASE AGAINST CAPITALISM

The view that there is something systematically depraved about capitalism is not novel. To organize what is made and used in a human society largely through what others are prepared to exchange for it has proved extremely dynamic. But it was never a deliberate choice at a particular point in time. (One choice led to another.) To present it as a single coherent choice overstates the force of the case for rejecting it and resolutely ignores the penalties for doing so. It constructs the alternative social, economic and political world which is to replace it by pure sentimentality: as an exercise in unimpeded wish-fulfilment.

There are three principal cases against capitalism. The first is that it is obtrusively and offensively unjust: a systematic affront to the moral sentiments. It is so because of the central role which it gives to personally unmerited (and often far from needed) private property. The force of this case was essentially conceded even by David Hume and Adam Smith in the eighteenth century, though they firmly repudiated this way of expressing it (Hont and Ignatieff (eds) 1983, Introduction). The best defence to this case – that capitalism is less offensive, and probably on balance less inimical to human rights, than any practicable alternative – is less an answer to the charge itself than a tactful deflection of attention on to other at least equally pressing matters. The second case against it is that it is ineliminably wasteful and destructive. Here, too, the best defence has proved to be a counter-attack: the taunt that no other way of determining what is made and used in a human society in such a populous and crowded world has proved less wasteful and destructive, and none which is equally clearly characterized provides any reasonable grounds for hoping that it will prove so in future. Since it has a better track record than its extant rivals, and (perhaps more charitably) since it has also learnt to reflect on its own workings with more care and precision and to describe them with greater frankness than any of these, the wiser course is plainly to try to emend it rather than replace it.

For this response to prove adequate in face of global warming would be a more impressive political feat than any of its earlier victories, since the latter have been won against inherently vulnerable human antagonists, and the former will need to be won against a humanly indifferent nature. But in neither case are there grounds for supposing that a better response is readily available (and only weak grounds for supposing that one must be available at all).

Only the third case reaches determinedly beyond politics. Its burden is not that capitalism involves unjust relations among human beings and ugly and imprudent relations between humans and the rest of the natural world, but that capitalism maims human beings themselves, and does so in the most intimate manner possible – by defiling and deforming their souls. Capitalism takes humans who are capable of something altogether finer and bends them to its own ignominious purposes, turning their lives into endless quests for the basest of rewards. Seen as a whole (which is what it really is), it is obsessive, profoundly unreasonable and wholly uncontrolled by the nobler ends which should control and shape human lives (the good, the true, the beautiful, the brave, the noble).

This is a much harder charge to meet politically, partly because it is less clearly expressed, and partly because there is much truth in it. The sting of this truth is scarcely drawn merely by pointing out that there are many other ugly ways for humans to live, and little probability of their collectively hitting upon a less ugly one merely by losing their nerve over the defensibility of capitalism. All human lives acquire some goals of their own, however short term and defensive. In all societies which have seen a deepening and intensification of capitalist relations (which means by now virtually all societies of any scale in the world today) many have noticed with dismay a shift in attention and commitment from other older (and often apparently more edifying) foci of concern to the increase of personal income. The experience of the intrusion of capitalist relations into pre-capitalist societies has always been quite prominently one of degradation in the avowed goals of the lives of many of their inhabitants. This may be applauded as a gain in self-understanding, public frankness and practical rationality (Hundert 1993; Hirschman 1977). But it can scarcely in itself be seen as a spiritual enhancement.

The third charge is, in this way, either above or beneath politics. It challenges humans to do better than they have chosen, and would in all probability choose again, and holds this possibility sternly against the setting in which their choices must now be made. The charge gains greatly in political force if the conduct in question can also be seen to menace in the longer run even the opportunity to pursue the less elevated goals on to which it deflects such urgent attention. (It is easy, of course to exaggerate the urgency of attention. Many denizens of capitalist societies have always made considerable and often rather successful efforts to ignore the fact that these provided the setting in which they were compelled to live.) The allegation that capitalism will in the end prove self-cancelling (a far from novel charge) is less perturbing while that end seems some distance away. Even the belief that when it does end it will long have richly deserved to do so is more imaginatively gratifying than practically motivating.

The charge that capitalism is culturally and imaginatively corrupting remains dismayingly plausible. (So little isn't.) But it draws whatever practical weight it holds from perfunctory, highly selective and almost certainly in the end unsustainable contrasts between the spiritual consequences of participating in a capitalist economy and those of participating in some other feasible and accessible way of organizing human use of the world and each other. In a world which capitalism has already altered so comprehensively, the modes of human life where the contrast is least flagrantly absurd (the Elysian simplicities of hunting and gathering) can barely survive on the outer margins of encroaching settlement and are simply out of the question for the vast bulk of the world's present population, let alone its future population.

It is an ancient and well-founded suspicion that no system of human authority can hope to prove nobler or more trustworthy than the human beings who exercise it. Plato's rejection of democracy as a political form rested firmly on the judgment that most Greek citizens were not especially noble or trustworthy (Plato 1930–5) – then, as now, a perfectly reasonable assessment. But even Plato had some difficulty in explaining how his contemporaries could hope to institutionalize in practice a system whose holders of authority were dependably noble and trustworthy. It is a more decisive limitation of his argument that he failed to suggest a compelling remedy for the pathologies which he diagnosed than that he may have been personally predisposed to confuse social rank with spiritual excellence. In itself no one could mistake the modern representative democracy for a remedy for whatever spiritual damage capitalism in fact inflicts. It was initially devised, and has been developed ever since, in a world already strongly marked by capitalist dynamics. Its critics have always been at pains to insist that it is all too neatly adjusted to these dynamics: that it predictably reinforces, rather than mitigates, the harm which they do. This may be a trifle brisk, since the critics who see it as over-adjusted to the spiritual destructiveness of capitalism must be set against their increasingly vociferous counterparts who see it as very poorly adjusted to the requirements of an efficient capitalism, and as showing depressing indifference to these requirements in practice. But the modern representative republic is even less eager to portray itself as a remedy for the spiritual inadequacies of its citizens than was the democracy of ancient Athens (for a foretaste see Wood 1991). Both take their stand on their capacity to sustain the freedom of their citizens, the latter's right to choose ultimately for themselves how their state is governed, and, just as importantly, how to live their own lives. The range of this freedom is necessarily interpreted in practice through the mutual impact of citizens on one another. But it is open to such interpretation only insofar as the ultimate judgment of how that impact comes out is left fully in the hands of the citizens themselves, and thus fully subject to whatever spiritual infirmities they collectively exhibit. It is not a damaging contingent discovery about the modern democratic republic that its decisions are apt to be contaminated by the spiritual qualities of these citizens. Rather, it is the principal intended point of this state form that they always should be. Plato's *Republic* was an integral device for minimizing the damage done by spiritual weakness. The modern democratic republic has more modest aspirations. The risks which it seeks to minimize are not to anyone's soul; and the means which it adopts for minimizing them do not for the most part aim at souls at all.

If the case against the modern democratic republic is that it is structurally committed to pursuing the wrong goals (whatever the majority of its citizens happen to wish to pursue at the time), then that case presupposes a compelling account of what the right goals are, and a feasible means for ensuring that an alternative state form will pursue them more dependably. There have been many attempts to provide such an account over the last two and a half millennia. But none of them has much residual intellectual cogency. Certainly many contemporary states do pursue goals very different from any which a majority of their subjects can possibly be presumed to desire: the personal wealth and power, for example, of the higher ranks of the Burmese or Nigerian armies. Some even avow their pursuit of very different goals: the preferred interpretation of Allah's requirements of the people of Iran (Abrahamian 1995) or Saudi Arabia. (Allah's will, plainly, needs no sanction from the sometimes all too faithless people of Iran.) But even those which claim a genuinely oecumenical legitimacy (as the rulers of Iran or Saudi Arabia quite explicitly do) take care to rest their claim less on the formal properties of the state itself than on the mode of interpretation of the transmission of their own legitimacy. What they claim is that they in particular are entitled to rule, not that a state form which they happen to embody and which could be equally well instantiated in any other set of human beings in any other territories can readily be seen to be entitled to do so. To reject the modern constitutional democratic republic because its avowed goal is the pursuit of the contingent objects of popular desire is a perfectly coherent choice. It shows a certain tasteful fastidiousness. But for the present it is hard to combine such rejection with an open endorsement of any other choice which does not immediately sanction the coercion of a popular majority. Only where the defence of the modern democratic republic collides, as for example in Algeria for much of the 1990s, with the clear preferences of a majority of the citizens does the rational case for defending it collapse into incoherence, and leave the ground free for state rationales of an altogether more cursory and peremptory character.

There is thus a deep and intrinsic case against the modern democratic republic: that it is the appropriate state form of a profoundly corrupt civilization and does not either hesitate to make explicit this appropriateness or attempt to deny the plain facts of that civilization's utter corruption. This case is at its most evocative when the state form under attack is identified with overweening foreign power and wealth, and the corruption is seen at its most odious, as in Iran or Algeria, in the intrusion of the culture of that foreign power into the culture of one's own nation and civilization (cf. Mottahedeh 1987). To defend the modern democratic republic against that case, it is necessary in the end to defend the civilization itself: to challenge the judgment that it is utterly corrupt, or, for that matter, any more corrupt than any other known form of civilization which is more furtive in style or more bashful in acknowledging the range of values which it enables (or even prompts) its inhabitants to pursue (cf., less drily, Huntington 1997).

Here, too, there has been dense, vehement and tangled argument for at least three and a half centuries about the merits of the case. In that argument, the modern republic (or its more shadowy intellectual prototypes) has taken a lot of punishment. But at no point along the way (as history has so far turned out) has it had to confront a challenge which could win, and keep on winning, through the relatively unmolested and open choices of its subjects. In the end, that comparative advantage has proved extremely strong. It could (and of course still may) be overridden by a more imaginatively conceived and deftly engineered alternative. But for the present we have no real conception of what such an alternative might be, and hence no reason for confidence that any such alternative exists. If it proves true, therefore, as some Western political scientists and political theorists now argue (Huntington 1993 and 1997; Gray 1995), that the viability of this state form depends decisively on the distinctive cultural history of Western Europe, and that it therefore cannot hope to strike deep roots in societies with very different cultures of at least equal antiquity in other areas of the world, that will, for the present, be worse news for those areas of the world than it will for those fortunate enough to live under its authority and within its own cultural heartlands.

THE ECOLOGICAL HAZARD

There is, however, a further deep but more contingent case against it: that the civilization of which it is the (all too) appropriate state form is itself jeopardizing the conditions of its own existence by its internal dynamics. Here, what is diagnosed as pathological is not the explicit purpose of permitting its citizens to live essentially as they choose, but the cumulative overall costs of the economic practices which are fuelled by that purpose, and by the choices which it sanctions and protects. If that judgment is indeed valid, the pathology itself can hardly be denied. It consists in a cycle in which in the long run the unintended collective consequences of individual agency will overwhelm the opportunity for any future individuals to continue to act at all. But, to bring the case against the state form itself, one or other of two further claims needs to be established clearly. Either there must exist some other clearly describable and plainly feasible state form which would predictably avoid this malign outcome, or, at least, the modern democratic republic itself must be knowably incapable of responding effectively to the increasingly blatant and unwelcome consequences of actions which it has hitherto encouraged or sanctioned. The first of these claims may well be valid; but no one has yet provided a convincing account of the state form in question. The second might be wholly convincing (and indeed may simply be true) in a particular country at a particular time: in Italy, for example, in 1994 or 1995. But in this case it would be so because of the particular human beings and the contingent purposes of which the regime itself was then composed: because of its human content at that time, not because of its political form. It would be a local and historical human response to the ongoing threat of collective catastrophe, not a general and theoretically reasoned (let alone structurally necessitated) response to the same threat. Hence it could not tell in general either against the modern constitutional republic or in favour of any alternative to it.

To show that the claim holds true of this state form quite generally would require an entirely new level of understanding of the properties of the state form itself. We would need to see not merely that its citizens were sure to be tempted to act with greedy fecklessness, and all too likely to succumb to this temptation, but also that they could not in principle choose more temperately and live out that choice in face of temptation. It is hard to see how such a demonstration could be effected, and quite certain that thus far it never has been. So the deep and more contingent case that the modern democratic republic is the local political gravedigger for global ecological and economic catastrophe is still very much moot.

Both these deep cases construe the alleged (or proven) historical limitations of the modern democratic republic as irremediable: as consequences of a fundamentally corrupt structure, which can be eluded only by subverting that structure in its entirety. They are an immensely intellectually ambitious (and confident) diagnosis of the political sources of a potentially irretrievable human disaster.

They may just be right. But they are certainly not as yet *known* to be right. They have extremely discouraging implications for the rest of human life; and, even as a dramatic device for attracting imaginative attention, it is easier so far to imagine them affecting collective judgment and action drastically for the worse than stimulating a more imaginative and creative collective response. Defter solutions and less feckless ways of life are definitely going to be required. But at present there is little reason to suppose that we can usefully look to the history of political thinking to discern what these might be.

Reorientating

It will by now, I trust, be clear that this is not because the history of political thinking has nothing of value to tell us about politics today or in the future. It is simply because its more concrete lessons on the effectiveness of different forms of institution and practice are drawn from a historical world very unlike that in which our descendants will have to live, and were in no sense aimed at dealing with some of the main problems which they will certainly face.

The young Karl Marx in mid-nineteenth-century Europe once described communism jauntily as 'the Riddle of History solved, and knowing itself to be the solution' (Marx, *Economic and Philosophical Manuscripts* (1844): Marx and Engels 1975 (a), III, 297). What he meant by 'History', as a mutinous disciple of the German philosopher Hegel, is a complicated matter which need not concern us here. For us, what matters, if we think of History as a loose name for the main shape of the human past and future, is that in our epoch we no longer have the slightest reason (*pace* Francis Fukuyama: Fukuyama 1992) to suppose that History is a single Riddle, or that, even if it is, that Riddle has a solution. More definitely, we have overwhelming reason to concede that if it is indeed a single Riddle, and that Riddle does have a solution, we at least, at present, have no idea whatever just what the Riddle is, let alone where its solution might lie (cf. Dunn 1993, Conclusion).

7

Crisis, Routine and Political Intelligibility

Focusing the Problem

What we are trying to understand is what is really going on in politics today. Most political scientists or political journalists, very sanely, try to understand this very much from the ground up: from particular patterns of behaviour and interaction which are conventionally understood as political. Much is unmistakably going on in politics today. Governments rise and fall. Armies drill and feed, obey or disobey their orders, and sometimes kill people in substantial numbers. Taxes are levied and spent. Political parties are created and dissolve. Laws are proposed, debated, passed, interpreted and at least sporadically enforced. Citizens vote (or decide not to bother to), starve or guzzle, worry about their health or solvency in later years, and dream about happier lives for their children (or about how much wealthier they might have been if only they had avoided having their children). All of this behaviour can be investigated, described and listed. Many questions can be asked about how exactly it fits together, and which aspects of it cause, or depend on, which others. It is easy enough to study politics directly encountered; and, as long as the study itself is careful and honest and the questions which prompt it are formulated clearly, it is not difficult to make some headway in understanding it.

In the end, though, this kind of study is bound to prove unsatisfying. It can certainly contribute to political understanding;

and there could scarcely be political understanding which was not grounded in a very great deal of it. But it is not in itself quite what most of us mean when we think of understanding politics. Knowing a great deal about politics, being comfortably in command of a wide range of political information, is quite compatible with having no understanding of politics at all: not the haziest comprehension of what it really means, or what is really going on in it, or at stake because of this. If we view the matter less pusillanimously, if we set less abject standards for what it is to understand, it is altogether less obvious how to proceed.

CRISIS, ROUTINE AND POLITICAL INTELLIGIBILITY

Supposing we had wished to know what was really going on in France in 1788, the year before the French Revolution unmistakably broke out, or in the USSR in 1988, the year before the Soviet hegemony over Eastern and Central Europe came to an abrupt end, or more challengingly still what was really happening in Germany early in 1933, it is clear at once that at the time it was inordinately hard to tell. Indeed, it is not difficult to defend the verdict that it was simply impossible to tell – not merely impossible to know, because the decisive outcomes still lay in the future, and had not yet *come* out, but impossible even to surmise for good reason because there was no obvious way of interrogating the then present which could have shown the most prominent aspects of the pertinent future to be in question – let alone likely.

Certainly no specifiable method or process of inquiry, however meticulously applied, could have shown the imminence of much which in fact lay ahead, in France in 1793–4, in Germany and Poland in 1944, even in Russia in 1998. Even now, the accumulated energy and intelligence of professional historians, over more than two centuries in the first place and a full half-century in the second, have made only the most faltering progress in showing anything of the kind, despite the capacious (and unique) advantages of hindsight.

THE VISIBLE AND THE REAL

I have deliberately chosen examples of spectacular disruptions and discontinuities in routine politics which had unmistakably momentous consequences. But the point which these examples highlight does not bear solely (or even especially) on such disruptions. It is just as true of routine politics as of the politics of extreme crisis: a point not about the rhythms of political experience but about its formidable opacity.

Good clear methods for studying politics are likely to privilege what can be seen clearly, dependably and accurately. But it is intrinsic to politics that its most important features cannot be seen in this way. They do not lie at the visual level (or anywhere near it). Many of them effectively preclude an understanding which is particularly dependable. With some, even the idea of accuracy in understanding has no obvious application. Energetic academic entrepreneurs often claim to have at their disposal techniques of understanding which do not deal with the visual level, but are nevertheless clear, dependable and accurate. The claims to accuracy in these cases, however, are transparently evasive, and the claims to dependability more expressions of bravado than grounds for others to accept that the claims are valid. Clarity on its own is a necessary, rather than a sufficient, condition for understanding. Those who are incapable of clarity cannot really understand even for themselves, and certainly cannot hope to convey understanding to others. But pure dogmas are every bit as easy to express clearly as true beliefs about the world. Indeed, in one obvious respect they are appreciably easier to express. Clarity is an internal property of thoughts, perceptions, beliefs, judgments or assertions, not a relation between any of these and the aspect of the world which it seeks to capture.

Judging what is really going on in politics is not merely vastly more ambitious (an attempt to see in clear and accurate relation immensely more types of phenomena or considerations), it is also far more distant in imaginative standpoint. It conceives politics, not from the ground up, but more from the sky down. A view of politics from the sky down (the perspective of Icarus, if not of

God) may be a gratifying prospect for some, but it is not on initial consideration in any way a practical need. Not only is the idea itself at best elusive; the quest for it in practice may also seem more than a little frivolous. There is vastly less effective demand for such a view (even in the blowsy world of today's universities), and still more drastically less effective supply. (Since the very idea of effective supply in this case may well be incoherent in the first place, the latter is scarcely a matter for surprise.) Almost anyone today may well need a modicum of understanding of politics viewed from the ground up. At the least consequential, citizens in the polling booth, and, perhaps even more, citizens deciding whether or not to bother to get as far as the polling booth, need one at least tepidly. Lobbyists, and those on whose behalf they lobby, evidently need it more urgently. Potential victims (or agents) of political assassination need it more starkly still.

What is important about the spectacular disruptions and discontinuities in routine politics is that they show that the practical need for such understanding cannot be dependably read off the current awareness of historical actors of their need for anything of the kind, nor off the political structures and processes which determine how far they do in fact need this. The urgency of the need depends unmistakably on what is actually going to happen. But, more reflectively and less tendentiously, it also depends on what might or may be going to happen.

Here we must return once more to the question of how the political significance of the modern democratic republic is best understood. If it is indeed true that this will prove to be the key political format within which the world is ruined irretrievably as a human habitat, that certainly will not show that all humans now alive (or perhaps even most humans now alive) need to perceive it as such, and grasp why it is such. Most of us (if this is true) will be able to do virtually nothing about it. All of us together may well prove unable to do anything about it. But, unless the ruin is certainly irretrievable already (which no one at present could possibly know), the possibility that it *may* prove so is quite enough to show that a great many of our contemporaries have a pressing

interest in understanding just how and why this is the case, and in seeing more clearly what, if anything, might be done to avert or delay the outcome. To accept reality because one can see that that is what it is is very different from simply failing to recognize a schedule of dangers. It may sometimes be right to be a fatalist. But, if so, this is a practical discovery about a particular historical situation, not an *a priori* truth about the human condition in its entirety.

LOCATING POLITICAL UNDERSTANDING

Somewhere between the ground and the sky, the virtually inescapable and the loftily and hazily speculative, there lies a continuum of causality in which understanding of politics can for the present most promisingly be sought. One reasonable guess for the moment is that this continuum for the present consists principally of a single political form, the modern constitutional democratic republic (however travestied in practice), and of a global system of weakly politically circumscribed economic transactions. Considered with any care, each of these two elements is surprisingly elusive; and the interaction between the two, therefore, extraordinarily hard to pin down. If the cumulative consequences of modern economics and politics have in some ways proved astonishingly injudicious (two world wars, the thermonuclear arms race, widespread ecological degradation, global warming), what we collectively most need to be able to judge today is how far these consequences have emerged from a single rigid and effectively uncontrollable mechanism or logic, and how far they have been merely the unintended consequences of intended actions, which could readily have produced more benign consequences if the agents in question had understood their own powers, or the risks which they faced, just a little better.

In judging this, there are three very different issues we need to bear in mind, all of great antiquity, but all also potentially changing profoundly in form and practical significance as human societies alter over time. Two are concerned with the availability and tractability of information for the human mind. The third turns on the human capacity for self-control and self-restraint. All three are questions about the nature and effectiveness of humans as agents. All three are variants on the question of how far human beings do or can know what they are doing.

LIMITS TO HUMAN INTELLIGIBILITY

The first issue turns on the murkiness or potential transparency of human intentions, on any scale from the single individual in the present to the human population of the globe acting over time. The second issue turns on the extent to which, and the means through which, humans are ever in a position to apprehend the prospective consequences of their own actions. The third turns on the degree to which humans can in principle control and mould their own passions so that these will either maximize their power to realize their own will in future, or turn that will most steadily to purposes of which they can in the end expect to be appropriately proud. (Compare Leo Tolstoy, *The Death of Ivan Ilyich*: Tolstoy 1960, 99–161.)

Professional students of politics tend to concentrate principally on the second of these, investigating just how unintended consequences of individual or group actions inevitably depart from or frustrate the purposes of the actors, and reflecting with varying energy on the significance of these disappointments for some or all concerned. These preoccupations are real enough, and unmistakably political. But it is always possible for their significance to be swamped in practice by either or both of the other two issues.

On a very grand view, the first and third issues are in the end indistinguishable from one another. Human beings lack power (they are feeble) because they attend too fitfully to their own long-term good. Because (or insofar as) they lack power, their interests, their intentions and their actions (and indeed their lives) are inherently vague and muddled. Because they cannot control themselves, they cannot hope to pull themselves together as agents (what is to do the pulling?), and hence cannot hope to live effectively over time. A creature (or set of creatures) of this kind is in no condition to view the causal arena within which its purposes must be effected clearly and realistically. It is already so deeply contaminated by fantasy, and so weakened by evasion, that the causal refractoriness of the external world and the bemusing logical challenges of rational co-operation are bound to prove hopelessly beyond it. How should such a creature accommodate itself to the grim truths about its own nature and condition? If this is the sort of creature that we are, how should we (how had we better) try to live? It is important not to misunderstand these questions. It is not that humans palpably have one set of definite characteristics, and face some given and unmistakable factual predicament. Their characteristics differ dramatically from one to another, and the concrete predicaments which they face over time and space are extravagantly various. Yet all humans who are not completely paralysed and incapable of expressing themselves remain nevertheless *agents*. In virtue of their common membership of a single species, they must share some common range of biological properties; and the question of how to act faces each of them, and faces them as a question. Insofar as humans share a nature and a condition, they do so in the end not because of some undeniable external matter of fact, but as the setting of an always common puzzle: the puzzle of how to live, of what they had better do.

The attempt to understand politics characteristically begins (and perhaps should begin) with the issue of the degree to which human beings at the time are or are not, on a relatively large scale, in control of the consequences of their actions, and hence, more grandly, in control of their own destiny. But that issue leads inexorably on (and back) to each of the other two. It is the cumulative power of human beings to transform the world in which they live, and the conditions in which they inhabit that world, which have generated the way we live now, and the circumstances in which we can hope to live in the future. In that vast movement of reshaping, the balance between intended and unintended consequences of human action is always hard to identify. Even with the most purposeful and carefully considered actions which you can perform (where the intention at least is as clear as it well could be), to identify the spreading consequences of what you have done is never simple, and often quite palpably impossible. With most actions, on any plausible understanding, the governing intention is far less clear in the first place. Where many individual agents or groups of agents interact with one another, struggling to aid or frustrate each other, or simply colliding inadvertently, the idea of capturing the consequences of their actions is quite unreal. We can think about what is happening in those terms, and speak about it as though we could capture (or even have captured) the consequences. But we cannot do so in practice. To do so is simply beyond our powers. The habit of speaking as though we could do so, or even have done so, is not merely widespread in modern politics. (It fills the speeches of our politicians and the columns of our newspapers.) It is also probably ineliminable from modern politics. It is how we think politically, and in part even how we believe that we are acting (and must act) in politics. But, when we speak and think in these terms, we can very seldom (perhaps never) be doing more than guessing what we are doing. We act in hope and fear, in speculation driven by varyingly pressing motives. We cannot act on knowledge, or, indeed, in large measure, even on comprehension. What exactly did the late Nigerian President General Abacha believe he was doing when he executed the Ogoni writer Ken Saro-Wiwa? He certainly meant to kill a man (an archaic enough political act). But, beyond that core intention, can we be sure that even he really knew? What does the Prime Minister of Britain or the President of France suppose that each has been doing even for the last six months?

ADJUSTING AGENCY TO CAPABILITY

The last three centuries of political thinking have faced, however feebly or inattentively, one dominating question. How can we adjust the intentions which govern our agency so that they fit less disastrously with our powers as agents? That question has been asked and answered with varying insight and energy in a setting in which the scale of the consequences of human action has become steadily more awesome. The sense of the question has altered strikingly along the way. From bearing most pressingly on the spiritual susceptibility of individuals, it has come to bear ever more painfully on the biological destiny of our own and immensely many other species.

The old sense, of course, has not dropped away, or even ceased to be of great cumulative political importance. But taken on its own and in the new setting, it now looks damagingly narcissistic. The history of politics in the West, in its most generous understanding, has centred on the hope and purpose of producing effects which are intended and beneficial, on the attempt to define and secure a public good. In the period since the seventeenth century, the principal surviving agency picked out and espoused to realize this grand purpose has been the modern state.

On balance what has caused it to be singled out to this degree is less its inherent dependability for the purpose than its prospective efficacy in general for whatever purposes it happens to espouse. Where other agencies have been strongly preferred to it, as many have over this period, the ground for preference has almost always been their superior dependability from the point of view of most humans whom they affect, not their superior efficacy. It has rested on the presumed trustworthiness of their intentions, rather than on their greater capacity to realize these intentions. The state (like the Church) can never be a wholly dependable vehicle for the intentions of individual citizens or subjects, since it distinguishes itself so sharply from them in the first instance, and insists so tenaciously on the primacy of its own will and judgment over theirs, and on the priority of the purposes which it has the duty to serve. But the service which it promises in return for this determined distancing is a special capacity for agency which the individuals who make up a particular population can never hope to muster for themselves, just as they happen to be (in their full heterogeneity of opinion, judgment and sentiment, and their severely limited sympathy with one another). Unlike them, at least in its own eyes, the state wills and judges as a single well-ordered agent. It really can *act*, while its individual constituents can only act collectively as a single agent by the purest of flukes. They, it claims, cannot in the full sense be a single agent. It, it claims, simply *is* one. The gap between intention and consequence is therefore especially damaging to states. It wounds them in the core of their self-esteem and public pretensions. It calls their bluff.

CORRUPTION OVERT AND COVERT

Much of the politics of the wealthier parts of the world over the last decades has, as we have seen, turned on exactly this permanent vulnerability of the state as putative agent. The gap between intention and consequence has been pressed relentlessly on both its open friends and its more or less helpless dependants and clients. To be a friend of the state has been made to seem an index either of stupidity or of corrupt purpose. To be a dependant or client of the state has been made to seem odious and degrading. By contrast, the state's enemies have vindicated their enmity as a direct expression of their own practical insight and purity of intention. They (unlike their own enemies) wish to use its coercive powers only to prevent the oppression of their fellow citizens (in nation or cosmopolis). They are willing to abandon any pretence to be able to control most of the circumstances of most of the lives of these citizens. They abhor the creation and maintenance of dependence (cf. Hume and Adam Smith: Dunn 1985, cap. 1). They have no need for clients, and are proud to be able to pay their own way. All this, however, is not merely heavily selective and questionably honest. It has also been pressed home, and enforced upon their enemies, with some gusto through the machinery of the state.

This is a precarious line of conduct, insofar as it requires the state's power to be effective, but views the state in a way, and describes it in terms, which can scarcely fail over time to impair that power. The description itself, moreover, is open to the suspicion of being simply inconsistent. The charge that a state is corrupt is not incompatible with the complaint that it is ineffectual (consider Zaire); but the two claims need to be related to one another with some delicacy. A corrupt state may be even less able to achieve some sets of consequences than one which adheres more closely to its own avowed purposes. It may well have a less internally coherent structure of authority and decision-making, and enjoy a still lower level of popular esteem. But it must at least serve as a means of transferring much which should by right belong to some of its subjects to others who have no just claim to this. It must be at least redistributively effective. This is more obvious, and perhaps more important, where the distribution is public, acknowledged and to very large numbers of its subjects, than when it is private, furtive and to comparatively few.

The neo-liberal complaint, that the redistributive welfare state is corrupt because it draws its political supporters through open bribery with the assets of the more productive and deserving of their fellow citizens, depends for any moral force which it can hope to muster on a very literal-minded conception of the rights to property. It is a complaint addressed principally to those who already share this conception of property right, and thus a basis for party solidarity, rather than external political persuasion. It has little politically or analytically in common with the charge that the redistributive welfare state is a tax on economic efficiency so brutal as to jeopardize any long-term prospect of competitive success in face of less handicapped producers in other parts of the world.

The former complaint is one which the friends or beneficiaries of the welfare state can hardly take seriously: to do so is precisely the welfare state's point. But the latter complaint is one which they can only avoid taking very seriously indeed (cf. Wood 1994) because they believe the causal claim to be false, or because they are stupidly short-sighted, or because they have indeed become irredeemably corrupt. What makes the neo-liberal assault on the welfare state politically suggestive is not the specious conception of property right on which it trades so heavily, but the plausibility of the claim that their immediate enemies continue to befriend it because they do not take its efficiency costs seriously, and do not do so because they are too stupid to understand these, or too hardened in dishonesty to care. Even those who regard the conception of property right itself as entirely fraudulent have been hard put to it to deny that there has often been something to this hugely damaging charge.

The neo-liberal critique of the state, thus, is far from denying that those who exercise state power (including, of course, themselves) can be well placed to realize some types of intention: to pay, or refuse to pay, revenues from the public treasury largely to those to whom they intend to pay them, or to raise such revenues in the first place preponderantly from those whom they intend to provide them. What such critics wish to deny is that the redistributive patterns of the welfare state over extended periods of time enhance the welfare even of the categories to whom they flow. They also deny the state's capacity to enhance wealth effectively over time through its own directive and coercive agency. They see the welfare state not merely as a system of self-righteous routinized theft, but also as an increasingly relentless privileging of the present over the future, an ever more reckless bet on the very short term. (The funding of public sector pensions arrangements in virtually all advanced industrial societies is a conspicuous example: cf. Shaviro 1997.) The key consequence over which they see the state as incapable in principle of achieving intentional control is the overall productiveness and efficiency of its own economy in comparison with other economies. But here they are in obvious danger of going too far. To be frankly incapable of achieving any intended effect on this would scarcely impress their own subjects. It would erode the state's authority, destroy any claim on their part to be entitled to exercise that authority, and evoke open contempt rather than docile obedience. What the political exponents of neo-liberalism require is an account of the state as agent, and a range of forms of action which it is capable of undertaking, which will affect the competitivity of local producers predictably to their long-term advantage. This is a good deal to ask for; but the neo-liberals have naturally done their best to supply it.

STATES AND MARKETS

The space of modern politics is still principally defined by two structures: the modern constitutional democratic republic and the global market economy (Dunn (ed.) 1990). Neither of these, even now, is an instance of inflexible destiny. In many settings the modern democratic republic is not even in place. Even where it has been firmly in place for some time, it has often been surpassed, either militarily, or in ideological *éclat*, or in economic dynamism (Dunn 1980, cap. 9; Dunn 1996 (d)), in many settings by very different models, and will no doubt long continue to be so. The global market economy may still be unravelled to some degree in the short (or longer) term by the political response to long-term slumps, or by retaliatory protectionism between individual states or trading blocs. It might also be eliminated in the longer run by cumulatively uncontrollable ecological disaster, or, of course, by large-scale warfare.

For the moment at least, nevertheless, these two structures largely set the terms for participation in the public life of the modern world – not by ideological fiat or exclusion, but by readily apparent practical primacy (Dunn 1996(a), cap. 10). Each can be viewed abstractly, in generosity or optimism, as a device for remedying the inherent limitations of humans as agents. The state imposes a clarity of structure on the intentions of its citizens which they find it hard to reach as individuals and impossible to generate together in confrontation with one another. In place of real confusion (and concomitant danger) it puts artificial order (and potential security). By drawing together and aiming the coercive powers of its subjects, it makes that intention effectively irresistible within its own domains, and maximizes its power beyond these. It assumes the right to be effective for whatever purposes it deems fit. Because it assumes that it should be effective, it tends also to presume that it will prove so in practice: that the consequences of its actions will be largely and on balance those which it intends.

This is more a consequence of its espousing the paradigm of agency than a symptom of delusions of omnipotence. Even agents who are deeply despondent about the scope of their own causal powers still conceive their actions through the idea of intended effects. To abandon this perspective is to abandon the conception of the self as agent – and abandon it, in either case, for exactly what? Individuals can be inured to their own ineffectuality, can even embrace an essentially private humiliation. But it is hard for states, with their explicitly public pretensions and commitments, to acknowledge frankly that there is very little which they can both intend, and also reasonably hope, to bring about. The model of rational (and prospectively causally efficacious) actor may be largely a fantasy when applied to a particular state. But it is a necessary fantasy for every modern state: even a constitutive fantasy.

Markets could hardly be more different. They are not agents at all. They decentralize intention radically. (A monopoly is the opposite of a market: a setting in which a single seller can, over a very considerable range, impose whatever price it chooses.) By decentralizing intention radically, they also decentralize both the need for information and the need for commitment, energy and practical intelligence. They leave individuals to do what they can for themselves, secure in the knowledge that each of them can be trusted to wish to act as effectively as possible, and confident that they will use their intelligence, knowledge and vigour as deftly as they can to get what they want.

Markets in this sense, however, are just a very abstract idea (Dunn 1999; as the idea of the modern state also began by being: Skinner 1989). It is a very nice point, as with the modern state, just how the general conception relates to any actual instance. There was nothing about the idea of the modern state itself which made it unattractive or implausible to envisage it controlling the productive activities of its subjects in detail for their own presumed good. But it did not take long for interpreters of the modern state's predicament and destiny to begin to recognize that markets in general, and especially the growing global market, placed many constraints on what states could hope to bring about (Hont 1990).

Between the state's intentions and the consequences of its

actions, a new and increasingly dense and intractable space intruded, a space in which the state's custodians had to decide how far to modify, discipline or truncate their public intentions, and how far instead to seek to expel markets of any kind from their own sovereign domain. The second response has always had keen attractions for custodians of state power. (Note, for example, the travails of President Mahathir in the Asian financial crisis of the late 1990s.) It preserves their self-image intact; and insofar as they can hope to implement it, it offers a more engaging interpretation of the grounds for their authority than open licence of the market's vagaries could possibly supply. States, as Adam Smith explained more than two centuries ago (Smith 1978; Hont 1994; Dunn 1985, cap. 3), depend upon authority. Markets depend upon, and foster, utility. To seek to ground authority on utility is in no way discreditable. But it sets the state a Sisyphean task, a task in which it can never decisively succeed, but may always at any moment definitively fail.

The main lesson of the late twentieth century, however temporary it proves in retrospect, is how little states can reasonably hope to exclude market dynamics from their own sovereign domain, and what overwhelming costs they must accept should they nevertheless attempt to do so. It is a lesson of political impotence and market potency. Behind the lesson, above all, is a growing, if reluctant, awareness of the awesome scale and heterogeneity of the information which needs to be handled for a modern society and economy to operate effectively. Markets, Hayek in particular argued (Gamble 1996; Gray 1986), are exquisitely sensitive to information of a high quality, and can handle it, and respond to it deftly, on any possible scale. States, in comparison, are irretrievably clumsy and myopic, and virtually certain to deform most of the information which they require in the very process of eliciting it. States may plan; but markets in the end dispose. The more states plan, the more brutally markets will in the end dispose. A state can certainly set itself to plan an entire economy, but over time its subjects cannot reasonably hope to enjoy the economy which will result from its efforts to do so. In the end they will hold their lack of enjoyment against the state that claims their obedience. And why should they not?

But, although any state can readily abandon the attempt to plan an entire economy (and many have never been tempted to try anything of the kind), they cannot in the same way comfortably abandon the attempt to plan anything over and above their own survival. States which confine their ambitions to that degree no longer have any publicly avowable intentions. In the world of today, their chances of even surviving are increasingly poor. The best strategy for particular rulers or ruling groups may still be to hang on to power for dear life, since relinquishing it will put them at mortal risk. But what is best for them is likely to be worst in due course for their successors, and worst too for the state itself. For modern democratic republics the open abandonment of any intention to plan is scarcely even an option, since no one could hope to be chosen to exercise coercive power without some belief in their capacity to exercise it on balance for the better rather than for the worse.

Any modern democratic republic must residually plan two aspects of the terms on which markets are to operate within its domains: the property rights which markets must take as given, and the limits on the range of consequences which it is acceptable for markets to generate. There is much else which they may choose to plan (some of it very obviously beneficial to market functioning: laws enforcing free competition, schools and universities successfully skilling a workforce, cheap and effective prophylactic public medicine). But there is a much larger, more technically economic and appreciably more refractory set of factors for which they will certainly be held responsible sooner or later, and which plainly affect market dynamics quite profoundly.

No modern government can comfortably dispense with an economic policy – a view of how its own actions are likely to affect the operation of its own domestic economy, and how that economy meshes with the wider system of world trade. (While it is still politically natural to think of a domestic economy, since this is the site of governmental responsibility and the natural focus of civic concern, the view that there really is any such thing as a reasonably effective domestic economy, which might be causally isolated from the world trading system for any but analytical purposes, is now practically absurd. Over fifty years ago, and very temporarily, this had a measure of realism about it in the case of the United States (Gilpin 1987; Keohane 1984; Brenner 1998). But, as the aftermath of the Asian economic crisis has now shown, even in economics that was very long ago.)

Two Perspectives on the Modern Democratic Republic

At present there are two main views of how to tell how far the modern democratic republic provides an adequate political format in which modern populations may face the future. One, usually markedly despondent, concentrates, as we have seen, on its effective subjection to a global economic and ecological dynamic of ever more frenzied destruction of nature. The modern republic is a passive local implementation device of a global and utterly humanly uncontrollable collective madness. It sustains a façade of local (and human) control, and by doing so facilitates and reinforces the profound corruption of human purpose which has always lent such force to the market, and which by now has fashioned a world in which almost anything is openly for sale. This picture was vividly foreshadowed in Thomas Hobbes's brutal summary of the human condition: 'a perpetuall and restlesse desire of Power after power, that ceaseth onely in Death' (Hobbes 1991, cap. XI, p. 70). In this vision, the decisive site of damage is the psyches of the citizens at large: above all the structure of control over their passions which is established and reinforced within these, and the purposes and lives which that structure opens up or closes off.

The most impressive contemporary philosophical protagonists of the modern constitutional democratic republic, American liberal philosophers like John Rawls or Ronald Dworkin (Rawls 1972 and 1993; Dworkin 1986), see the mission of this state form, and the achievement which it is already within sight of reaching, as the opening up to all its citizens of the opportunity to conceive, and live out within the limits of historical possibility, the lives which they would freely choose. This may well not be all that human beings (and perhaps women more particularly) should ask or hope for. But it would, if reached, be unmistakably a pinnacle of civilization in comparison with most past human public goals. It is a mark of the radicalism of the modern republic's ecological critics that they should see this structure virtually in reverse. The lives which such citizens would freely choose, the states which might (by extraordinary feats of social and economic skill, and political dexterity and determination) place these lives within their reach and the economies which would enable those states to do so form a single great system of wrong choice. Many particular choices within this might no doubt be impeccable in themselves, but on these terms even the best of lives within it, the simplest, noblest, most generous, most self-sacrificing of lives there could be, would find itself in inadvertent complicity with the great overarching historical wrong (or insanity) of the human world within which it must be lived. To elude that complicity, only one course in the end could be sufficient: to see the system as a whole, see it as the profound error (and even crime) which it is, make oneself its open enemy, and devote one's whole life to the (in practice, comically unavailing) struggle against it.

This sounds pretty inane. But I very much doubt that it is. At worst, it is a natural contemporary expression of a perspective on what it is to be human which has great spiritual force and which remains all too illuminating about what it is to be human. It may not pick out convincingly the life for you or for me. (It certainly does not for me: cf. Williams 1981, cap. 8. I have lived within this great interconnected system all my life, and am more at home in it than I could any longer hope to be in any other setting. And how can there still *be* any other setting, since this is the way the human world so comprehensively now is?)

What this perspective does do, however, is to show, with unflattering clarity, some of the more important implications of the lives we have all been choosing, however blearily, to live, and which we will no doubt continue to choose. If the human world proves to end relatively soon (within the next few thousand years), and if it ends much as this vision or prophecy suggests, then it simply must be the case that those who hold this vision are essentially right, and the rest of us, the immense majority, are largely wrong, and wrong most decisively of all where it must most matter to us, in the lives we are choosing to live, and the examples of how to live which we are passing on to our descendants. What we most need to see in this context, however, is that even if we all do prove wrong (and would have been altogether wiser to have lived quite differently: looking around, it is hard not to suspect that), this will scarcely yield a coherent charge against the modern democratic republic as a state form, still less against state forms in general.

The case for modern states in general, and still more the case for the modern constitutional democratic republic, has never rested on their prowess at mass spiritual edification or the transformation of souls. It rests, as we have seen, on their capacity to minimize the immediate and lethal threats which human beings, individually and in groups, pose to one another. That task will only be superannuated when humans cease to pose such threats; and they will cease to do so only if (and where) they cease to be agents at all, or cease to act for purposes which are likely to harm one another. There is nothing which a modern democratic republic is equipped to do which is likely to move them briskly or reliably in this direction, and nothing which, on its own terms, it might permissibly attempt to do to erase their character as agents. In the modern democratic republic, it is the citizens who must change themselves. They cannot hope for their state to do this for them. If the purposes which govern state power within these polities are to become wiser, less myopic or more austere, it is we who must change, not the states to which we belong (Dunn 1990, cap. 12).

The charges which may indeed go home against the modern democratic republic are not charges of spiritual defilement. They do not turn on an assumed superiority of ancient over modern liberty, or of one or another brand of tasteful self-subjugation over any form of liberty at all. They cannot rest in the end on the claim that it is this state form itself which weakens or destroys our capacity to discipline or control ourselves. They cannot, since that form so explicitly leaves each of us largely to work out for ourselves just how far we choose to do anything of the kind. The charges which may indeed go home are far less elevated or evocative. They are charges essentially of practical confusion and inefficacy in relation to whatever purposes the citizens of these states happen to hit upon. They offer not a comprehensive normative attack on the state form from the outside, but a relatively specific diagnosis of its internal contradictions, judged from the inside and by its own chosen criteria.

FORMING AND SUSTAINING COHERENT COLLECTIVE INTENTIONS

In essence the charge is that these states, for one reason or another, prevent the formation and steady pursuit of clear and internally reasonable collective intentions, and that they fail at least equally decisively to inject into such collective intentions as they do pursue a reasonable degree of foresight about the prospective consequences of acting in one way rather than another. The politics of these states, the complaint runs, are overwhelmingly confused; and the public policies which emerge from, and which are implemented as a result of, these politics are all too obviously feckless. But these sad failings follow not directly from the individual confusions and imprudences of the citizens at large (no doubt, none too clear-headed and practically reasonable in the first place), but from the structure of decision-making and the allocation of power within the state itself.

It is unlikely that anyone who has spent the last few years reading carefully through a serious newspaper, or trying to run a government department or even a university, would be inclined to doubt that there is something in this complaint. There is, too, a great deal of accumulated evidence that that judgment, in a less focused and attentive form, would be echoed by most citizens of these states today. More interestingly, perhaps, there is also some evidence that these citizens would make the judgment more emphatically and comprehensively today in many settings than they were inclined to make it even in the late 1980s (Nye 1997; Dogan (ed.) 1997; but cf. Klingemann and Fuchs (eds) 1995). Something about these states is manifestly not working. Whether it can be caused to work again is not evident. Much contemporary political dispute turns on the allocation of responsibility for the degree to which they are not at present working, and on a miscellany of proposals for how they can be caused to work better in the future. To see whose fault the present débâcle really is, and what prospect there is of things going better again in the future, it is necessary to pin down just why these states now appear both so confused and so ineffectual.

One jaded but not wholly unreasonable view is that the confusion and ineffectuality are hopeless but not serious: ineradicable from the state form, but readily endurable by its citizens, or at least by those among them who appear currently to be reasonably prosperous. But even for the latter the calm of this verdict depends heavily on how far they (or their children) can reasonably expect to remain prosperous. (For the less than exhilarating prospects for most American citizens, see, for example, Nancy Dunne, 'Wage Squeeze Set to Continue, Says Report', *Financial Times*, 13 September 1996, citing US Competitiveness Policy Council Report; or, on a larger historical scale, Brenner 1998.)

In this respect, the judgment that the confusion and ineffectuality are hopeless has probably gained somewhat in analytical cogency since 1979 (though there has been little convergence in judgment on precisely what makes them so). In the viewpoint of professional students of these questions, the confusion and ineffectuality now tend to seem heavily over-determined. Several quite distinct structures have been isolated which might be more than sufficient to explain this outcome. All have at least some plausibility; and none has been in any sense vindicated as causally decisive. But, taken together (or at least considered in sequence), they are more than sufficient to remove any element of surprise from the array of confusion and ineffectuality duly encountered (the Major or Chirac governments, Tokyo throughout the 1990s, Washington during Bill Clinton's Presidency).

A CHANGED HORIZON OF EXPECTATIONS

What is distinctly less convincing today is the judgment that the confusion and ineffectuality are not really serious. Since the mid-1980s, for the first time since the Second World War, it has become far less clear for very large proportions of the citizens of these states (in some instances for clear majorities) that they – or still more most of their children – can be reasonably confident of remaining as prosperous as they now are, let alone becoming more so. Some, of course, who are far from prosperous today can reasonably expect to become so; but most who are not at present prosperous are relatively unlikely to become so. And many who, in the mid-1980s, were in fact extremely prosperous in comparison with their parents or grandparents have already become much less so. For a number of different reasons, too, even those who still remain prosperous cannot reasonably be confident that the same will prove true for their children or grandchildren.

All human beings live their lives within a horizon of expectations. It would be quite wrong to suggest, across time and space and class membership, that the horizon of expectations of the populations of the wealthier capitalist states over the last two centuries has been set by a vision of a natural and dependable progress of opulence. That is not at all what it was like for most citizens to live through either of the two world wars, or the Great Depression. It has never been what it is like for most of the black population of the United States (or indeed Great Britain). But, for almost three decades after the end of the Second World War, this did indeed become a relatively obvious horizon of expectations for clear majorities of the populations of the states of Western Europe, North America and Australasia, as it did more recently for those of a number of countries in East, and for a time, even South-East, Asia. Establishing such a horizon is a slow and uneven process. Blotting it out could scarcely be instantaneous or uniform. But, however elusive or diffuse the phenomena in question, we can be confident that they are of immense political importance.

Within a relatively confident horizon of expectations, it is easy for political actors to feel that they know where they are, and what they can afford to risk. It is easy, too, for them to act with relative calm. Within a horizon of acutely despondent expectations, it may also be relatively easy for them to judge their situation and their most urgent interests, and all too apparent that they can afford, of their own free will, to risk virtually nothing. (It is likely, too, to be harder for them to act at all calmly.) In between these two conditions, and more markedly as they move from a confident to a despondent horizon, it is far more difficult for them, both psychologically and cognitively, to know where they are, or to judge how they would be well advised to act.

What has changed this horizon of expectations? As we have seen, there are really two classes of answer to that question: political action or economic experience. The change in horizons has been a product of energetic and purposeful political action through the state apparatuses of the most advanced states in the world, and under the leadership of a global political and ideological movement. Or, rather, it has resulted directly, and all too reasonably, from a massive shift in the economic experiences of the populations of these same states, along with all too many other parts of the world. These two answers are not in fact alternatives. Since a horizon of expectations is itself a dimension of experience, and since the expectations in question are in this case predominantly economic, it is a truism that what has caused the change in economic horizon must have been at least in part the economic experiences of those whose horizon it is. The key question is what has caused these economic experiences.

Here, the dramatic impact of political victory and defeat, the haemorrhaging of trust and support from parties of government across the advanced societies, the crushing (at least temporarily) of social democratic parties in many settings and the rise of neo-liberalism are less illuminating than the spreading burden of disillusion with political action itself: the decaying plausibility of the political party as an instrument of collective action, or the nation state as a focus of loyalty. (Note, for example, the more recent, if perhaps equally temporary, resuscitation of social democratic governments in just as many settings.) Within this shrinking horizon of expectations, none of Albert Hirschman's triad of options (exit, voice or loyalty) has come to seem especially promising (Hirschman 1970). Exit is difficult and costly. (Where is there left to go?) Voice appears increasingly ineffectual. Loyalty seems essentially misplaced, neither an appropriate sentiment (to go beyond Hirschman's categories), nor at all a compelling line of conduct. Activity therefore gives way to passivity, if not necessarily to apathy. The people come to view their state and its temporary custodians with sullen mistrust, if not with active animosity (cf. Nye 1997; Dogan 1997 and Dogan (ed.) 1997; but for more cheerful assessments see, for example, Kaase and Newton (eds) 1995, Klingemann and Fuchs (eds) 1995, van Deth and Scarborough (eds) 1995, Miller, Timpson and Lessnoff 1996).

This last contrast remains decisive. Opinion surveys certainly show that British citizens now think little of their career politicians. But it is not necessary to rely on opinion surveys to judge what many Algerian citizens think of their state and its current custodians.

Political victory and defeat have contributed strongly (and in the former case quite deliberately) to distributing the costs of relative economic torpor among the populations of the wealthier countries. In the great majority of wealthy countries today the very rich are drastically richer than they were in 1979, and very many of their fellow citizens are drastically poorer; and each of these shifts can be traced directly to quite conscious changes in the tax structure, and in the scale and allocation of state expenditures (for Britain see, for example, Gilmour 1992(b)). But it is far from apparent that it was these policies which caused the relative torpor in the first place. To concede this is not to take the policies at their own face value. The political case in their favour, as we have seen, was precisely that they would revive these economies and lend them new dynamism by increasing their operating efficiency, intensifying their trade flows and thus sharply raising their overall rate of growth. They have been less unsuccessful in some of these endeavours than in others. (Trade flows, in particular, have grown strikingly.) But the rates of growth in almost all of them have remained stubbornly low over these twenty years. Allied with the purposeful redistribution from the poor to the rich, this has had a notably malign effect. One point to notice is that this outcome cannot be attributable to the state form itself. These same states, for a good quarter of a century earlier, had moved steadily in exactly the opposite direction. It was the patterns of redistribution through the state budgets in this period, and the levels of taxation required to fund these, which set up the political target which the neo-liberals assailed with such gusto and such notable political success. If the essential lack of dynamism of their economies altered very little under either dispensation for nearly quarter of a century, it is hard to believe that it is the patterns of distribution which principally determine it (cf., again, Brenner 1998).

DEMOCRATIC CORRUPTION AND POLITICAL BUSINESS CYCLES

This is extremely important, since most of the attempts to diagnose the defects of the state form (and thus explain the more disappointing features of its performance in practice) have also been intended to show how it might be emended to perform better. A number of different features have been picked out: a propensity to inflate the currency by printing money, a propensity to bribe the electorate profligately with their own (or each other's) money as the time for re-election nears, a tendency to bribe the present generation of electors by mortgaging the incomes of future generations, a tendency to expand the welfare clienteles of the state, even when those in office view these with open distaste or animosity. The evidence presented for these diagnoses is often simple and sometimes beyond dispute, though its bearing on the diagnosis itself is never conclusive.

The tendency to inflate the currency by printing money can be read, in due course, off the rate of inflation. But, when it is so read, the view that what is in question is a structural property of the state becomes extremely hard to defend. Once a relatively high level of inflation is established, it is hard for any form of state to deflate rapidly, and as its custodians intend. But states which suffer protractedly from high inflation differ from those which do not, not in their form, but in the policies which their rulers, over time, have elected to pursue, and in the political alliances and feuds which permit them to pursue, or preclude them from pursuing, these policies with steadiness and precision. States which are subject to short bursts of relatively high inflation are even less likely to differ from those which do not in structural aspects of the state itself (though they may well differ in the role which they give to their central bank in determining and implementing monetary policy). In their case, as in the initial shifts which establish protracted high inflation, it is hard to deny the element of sheer miscalculation in creating conditions which inevitably damage very many citizens, and redistribute from some to others in ways which are bound to prove politically provocative. It is extremely unlikely, for example, that any of the Conservative Chancellors of the Exchequer in post-war Britain whose policies at some point sharply raised the rate of inflation (Barber, Howe, Lawson and others) fully intended the effects which they generated (Dow 1998). Where the inflation rates were subsequently lowered sharply and for lengthy periods of time in the same setting, by contrast, it is clear that they were so on the basis of deliberate political choice, and in many instances relatively steady political determination. It would, of course, be possible to alter the form of the state in such a way as to impede inflation extremely effectively: for example, by setting up a wider framework of monetary and fiscal co-ordination which binds national governments (as has in part occurred with the establishment of European Monetary Union). But there the relation itself and the way in which it must operate if it is to be effective are both entirely explicit. The causal relation between state form and inflationary potentiality in the meantime can scarcely be either that of a necessary or that of a sufficient condition. Because the governments of sovereign states can act in such matters as they choose, they may always choose to inflate, rather than face other, and even less welcome, outcomes.

This could be a valid charge against the state form itself only if there were no other possible outcomes which would be less welcome than a substantial increase in the rate of inflation (Dow 1998). This is an extremely odd view, even if some economists and politicians now affect to hold it.

The propensity to bribe the electorate with its own (or each other's) money as the time for re-election nears is better established. In the United States House of Representatives, for example, the time for re-election is always near (Mayhew 1974); and the process of quite open bribery, in effect by individual Congressmen of their own constituents, never ceases. Seen in relation to the national budget as a whole, this may be more a matter of the petty cash than of grand larceny. But it is not necessary to be an impressionable reader of Plato to feel that this is scarcely a rational way in which to organize anything, and that its cumulative consequences can hardly be benign. The priorities which it espouses could not readily emerge from any other specifiable decision procedure; and the whimsical relation between need and disbursement is singularly unprepossessing.

There are two very different ways to see this kind of pattern: in terms of the quality of will which it discloses in its participants, and in terms of the structure of essentially non-moral (though not necessarily in any sense immoral) incentives which they face, and to which it is always hard (and in the end sometimes simply impossible) for them to fail to respond.

These two perspectives correspond, very crudely, to the viewpoints of ancient and modern political theory. Each is on to something important; and neither is much of a surrogate for the other. The first yields a diagnosis of habitual electoral bribery essentially in terms of the corruption of the political class (or at least of that portion of the political class which is compelled to offer itself for popular election, if it hopes to take part in ruling: Manin 1997). The political class is viewed as the agent; and the electors are viewed as succumbing to its bribery as passive recipients, not as being in a position actively to exact this.

The second perspective offers a diagnosis in terms of the formal structure of political competition. It accepts the corruption of the political class as a given, assumes that, for one reason or another, politicians will on balance act for their own personal political advantage, and that the institutions through which they do so should be designed (and nowadays have been designed) so as to work adequately, even when those who operate them care nothing intrinsically for any outcome but their own self-advancement. Much of modern political theory, from Hobbes, through Jeremy Bentham and James Mill (Mill 1992), to Joseph Schumpeter (Schumpeter 1950) and the young Robert Dahl (Dahl 1953), has attempted to specify (or has claimed to identify in operation) institutions which are in this way robustly benign, even in face of the worst suspicions one can reasonably have of those who operate them. But in the last half-century political theorists have become far more despondent on this score, as the study of rational choice and the theory of games have shown ever more clearly that it is inordinately hard (or perhaps simply impossible) to devise institutions which will be robust in this way. What comes out of this sequence of increasingly sophisticated analytic thought is that the very conception of the form of a state is ingenuous in the first place. There can certainly still, on this analysis, be predictably bad forms of state: structures which allocate power in ways which are extraordinarily unlikely to prove benign over any length of time. In the end, in this century, military governments and communist states, where at all protracted, have each proved notably unpromising in just this way.

What there probably cannot be is predictably good forms of state: forms which give to their political participants clear and reliably structured incentives to act on balance for the collective better, rather than for the worse. The well-devised state may be a relatively effective expedient for restraining human malignity (Manin 1994). But even the best devised of states can scarcely hope to prove impervious to human indiscretion.

This is a setback for modern political theory, and in some measure for modern political life. But we may just have to learn to live with it as best we can. It is important to recognize, too, that it may also be a setback for one branch of modern political theory, to the benefit of another. The idea of dependable and self-enforcing mechanisms with predictably benign consequences has obvious attractions. But the more dependable and more self-enforcing the mechanism, the less imaginative or causal room for human agency, in the free and disorderly manner to which we are now accustomed to this in our own lives, or those of others whom we know well. States which must in general act in one way rather than another are states which are in at least that respect unfree: states whose powers as agents are blocked or precluded at just that point. Such constraint is deeply at odds with the central motif of the state's self-conception: that it is above all a free agent (*princeps legibus solutus*; *rex in regno suo*), with the power and entitlement to judge and act for itself, just as it deems best. The more the actions of a state (or of the set of persons who in effect govern it at a particular time) are determined by its own judgment and choice, the freer the state in question, and the less room for it to turn out paralysed (incapable of acting at all), or enslaved to some domestic faction or foreign patron (compelled to act at the will, and on the judgment, of others who have no plausible claim to usurp its authority). By the same token, the more those who govern it are chosen by, and effectively accountable to, its citizens at large, the less room for the freedom of either to be set aside in favour of a controlling structure of effectively entrenched alien purpose.

INSTITUTIONALIZED PRUDENCE AND FREE AGENCY

Modern political theory (and the theory of the modern constitutional democratic republic, which is its favoured state form) is both a theory of institutionalized instrumental prudence and a theory of free agency. These two elements are permanently in tension. If it were palpably true that the modern democratic republic is now compelled to act in one way rather than another, and that way was evidently harmful, this would naturally be dismaying for either element. But if what is clear is that this state form is neither precluded from so acting, nor, on present evidence, even especially likely to avoid doing so, this is more of a setback for the state as an articulation of instrumental prudence than for the state as a system of free agency.

If We the People freely choose to be greedy and short-sighted, even if we choose to be so over and over again and to our immense and crippling cumulative harm, it is the boast, not the shame, of this state form that it will faithfully enable us to do so. In itself, democracy is not compatible with paternalism. Where the one starts, the other must stop. You cannot give to anyone both a maximum of freedom and a maximum of security. You cannot comprehensively protect a free person against the readily foreseeable consequences of their own free actions.

ELECTORAL CORRUPTION

The affinity between elections and bribery is deep, intimate and of great antiquity. There is a clear distinction to be drawn between bribery within and through the categories of the law, and bribery outside and in open contravention of those categories. But critics of the modern republic view this distinction as essentially specious. What the two have in common is more important, and politically more illuminating, than what distinguishes them. What they have in common is the exchange of money to which the recipient is not otherwise entitled for forms of consent which he or she would not otherwise consider giving, and with consequences which they cannot reasonably favour and will not in fact welcome. What distinguishes the two is merely the terms of the law. That distinction may (and often does) carry little significance for most of the citizens themselves, while the outcome in either case is bound in the end to matter greatly to virtually all of them.

Viewed sympathetically, electoral competition within this state form is a struggle on two levels. On the first, it is a struggle between groups of citizens to bend state policy and its implementation to their interests by securing political representatives dedicated to this task, and well equipped to carry it through. On the second, it is a struggle between groups of claimants to display such dedication and efficacy on behalf of reassuringly large proportions of the electors. In each struggle the key participants take part and act for their own perceived good (compare J. S. Mill on voting: Mill 1910, cap. X, 299).[6]

But the critics of the modern republic exhibit no such sympathy. For them, each type of participant acts for their own perceived good; but in neither case is the good in question fully legitimate; and, insofar as it is viewed as legitimate at all, the undesirability of the outcomes to which it leads is held decisively against the mode in which it is pursued.

As these critics portray the matter, both electors and candidates for election are either corrupt or stupid. Either their intentions are patently improper, or their comprehension of the consequences of their actions is lamentably inadequate. The candidates offer large (and essentially gratuitous) short-term pay-offs, blandly ignoring the negative impact which these are likely to have on the future welfare of most citizens (and perhaps even of the recipients themselves). The electors respond with naive alacrity, opting greedily to spend (or bank) the proffered gains while the going is good, and without thought for any negative longer-term consequences which may follow in their wake. This is not an elevated exchange. But in this model neither party is evidently irrational, even if both perhaps overweight short-term benefits against longer-term costs. Both, however, certainly deviate quite sharply from any vision of their roles which sees these as morally defining or constraining, and linked together into a single system of peremptory mutual obligations. A state which really was exactly and exclusively as this model conceives it could scarcely be a state to die for, and would be hard put to it to motivate any deliberate sacrifice at all on its behalf from any of its subjects. But the idea that it can, should and will impose on its subjects whatever sacrifices it deems necessary is one of the main defining components of the modern state (Levi 1997). It is neither a claim which the latter might conceivably abandon nor a task which it may excusably shirk.

The critics of the state form as it has operated in the twentieth century distribute the blame for its perceived failings in a number of different ways; but the main weight of their rejection has come to fall on the cynicism, and deliberately corrupt agency, of competitors for electoral office, and on the cognitive limitations of those with the folly to elect them. Elected governments in the wealthier capitalist states choose policies to maximize the chances of being re-elected (this is hardly a complaint in itself), and with a subsidiary concern for the resources at their disposal while they hold office. In poorer states, as in post-colonial Africa, this pattern of attention is firmly inverted (Bayart 1993); and the inconveniences for governments of maintaining electoral politics thus frequently outweigh its advantages. Electoral politics, accordingly, is suspended in most of these states most of the time.

As has become notorious, well-institutionalized and relatively open corruption has at times characterized a number of even the more prosperous of contemporary states (post-war Italy, Belgium, France, perhaps even Britain after more than fifteen years of uninterrupted Tory rule: note the conception of Political Services indicated in Mr Major's final Honours List: *Financial Times*, 21 August 1996). Thus far this has never been to a degree which has seriously jeopardized the continuity of electoral politics. More interestingly perhaps, very recent experience of a number of the most economically dynamic East Asian states has revealed even more pervasive public corruption. Under autocratic rule (as in South Korea), in open electoral competition (as in Japan) and in intermediate cases (as in Indonesia), it is now clear, the need to bribe electors is by no means necessarily the most potent incentive, or the readiest facility, for using state power to channel resources into private hands which are in no way entitled to them.

In classical political theory, the sole force which can keep a polity in good order is the selection as rulers of those with the intelligence, moral commitment and strength of character to rule as they should. Institutional expedients rendered this outcome more or less likely; but the only process which could secure it in practice was the moral shaping and self-maintenance of a trustworthy ruling elite. Modern political theory has largely abandoned these preoccupations (though they linger fitfully in discussion of the educational prerequisites for democratic citizenship). But the experience of systematic corruption in modern states, democratic and otherwise, suggests that ancient political theory may well be closer to the mark. Designing institutions which preclude corruption may simply be a causally incoherent project in the first instance; and the view that pervasive corruption settles most decisively in the imaginations of the citizens and their rulers – in their habits of mind and unreflective complicity – seems largely vindicated by experience. (For the conceptual difficulty in distinguishing corruption from conventional political behaviour see helpfully Philp 1997.)

The modern republic, from its inception, was designed to economize on trust. But only a structure that offers incentives which are both evident in their force and conclusive in their direction can simply dispense with trust. Can such a structure of incentives in principle be incorporated into the structure of a state? Let us consider in turn the principal forms of bribery indicted by critics of the modern republic. (Well-institutionalized and relatively open corruption as defined by its public law is hardly something which can be held against the modern republic's intention or purpose. To restrain or eliminate it, what is required is effective defence of this state form, not its subversion or desertion for something else.) One main form of bribery, these critics insist, can be seen in the tax system. This system redistributes property. It confiscates from some and gives to others. In doing so, it weakens incentives to acquire property in the first place by honest (or, presumably, by dishonest) economic exertion, shifts resources from potential investment into consumption, impairs the operating efficiency of the economy, and thus lowers its overall product and the aggregate welfare of its population. In a fiercely competitive international market, the short-term loss in welfare is dwarfed over time by the drastic weakening in the price competitivity of domestic production and the far greater long-term losses in welfare for the domestic population.

This line of thought makes many strong assumptions about economic causality, and requires that virtually all of these hold good for the final complaint (the weakening in international price competitivity, which genuinely is likely in the end to harm virtually all) to follow at all certainly or directly from the initial charge against the tax system. The view that taxation for anything other than public goods (goods which can only be jointly supplied and which do benefit all: Olson 1965) is equivalent to theft or forced labour is quite independent, both in appeal and in vulnerability, of this line of economic reasoning. It might be true that redistributive taxation necessarily lowered general welfare (though this is scarcely intuitively plausible in a markedly inegalitarian society, with many in acute poverty). It is even plausible that shifting resources deliberately from investment to consumption will under many circumstances impair the international price competitivity of some of a country's products. But these are judgments of consequential damage, not of *a priori* illegitimacy. For the view that taxation is theft or forced labour to go through, the key assumption has to be that those who are taxed are entitled to what they initially hold, in a way and with a clarity which no one to whom their property is coercively transferred can hope to be (cf. Nozick 1975). This involves either a distinctly feudal attitude to inheritance or a very literal-minded attitude towards legally valid acquisition within a given economic system. Neither of these orientations fits at all comfortably with any detached conception of economic, social or political causality in operation. They may appear prominently within modern political theory. But, when they do so, they are far from in their element. (Compare Brian Barry's review of G. A. Cohen, *Freedom and Self-Ownership*, *Times Literary Supplement*, 25 October 1996.)

It is therefore worth distinguishing two very different conceptions of how such bribery might (and perhaps sometimes does) operate through the tax systems of these states today. In one, elected representatives of the poor transfer a portion of the property of the rich to those whom they represent, and do so with some self-righteousness, because they deem the poor to need these resources more, and to be every bit as entitled to enjoy them. In the other, elected rulers tax the wealthy and transfer to the poor through public welfare provision (health, pensions, social security, education), in order to buy the votes or cement the political allegiance of the poor, since the latter have more votes than wealth and are duly grateful for what they can get for them, and the wealthy have fewer votes than financial resources, and hence cannot defend themselves through the ballot box (but compare, once again, Mr Major's final Honours List). Seen simply as a single system of economic exchange, poor electors act with impeccable (and relatively serene) rationality, career politicians act equally rationally (but under considerable duress), and rich electors are too impotent for it to matter how they act. (More realistic accounts of what is going on, unsurprisingly, credit the rich with many other ways of exerting influence besides the ballot box, thus sharply reinforcing the rationality of the ways in which the poor behave when they at last get the chance to vote.)

On this analysis, it is only if the rich are (in a slightly subterranean manner) a public good in themselves, and one which will be impaired by any incursions on their capital or incomes, that poor voters can reasonably be criticized for how they choose to vote, or politicians criticized for offering them these incentives to do so. And even if this generous view of the rich were analytically correct, the choice facing the impoverished voter may lie only between relatively dependable short-term rewards and altogether more speculative medium- or long-term gambles. What makes the latter speculative, moreover, is not merely that their being available at all requires the validity of some fairly ambitious judgments about economic causality. It also requires that the aggregate benefits which they promise will accrue to the impoverished voters (or those they hold dear) on at least the scale of the shorter-term benefits which they have forgone, and the advantages which would subsequently have followed from these. If the rich (luxuriantly) consume their unmolested incomes, or if they invest injudiciously or unluckily, the first of these provisos will not hold. If anything much happens politically (or even economically) in the succeeding decade, there is little, if any, reason to expect the second to hold. In terms of economic causality, what is decisive for this charge is not whose money the taxes in question should be taken to be, but how the consequences of their being levied and spent turn out: not their distributive, but their aggregative, impact. This is principally a matter of well- or ill-conceived governmental economic policy, or of the skill and vitality of private economic agents in response to this. It is hard to see what it has to do with the form of the state.

What obviously has everything to do with the form of the state is the extent to which the property order on the basis of which the economy operates, and the electoral system which selects and motivates governments, form a single system of economic exchange, in which all participants seek to secure as much for themselves as they can and at minimum cost to themselves. This is a notably disabused conception of what the state really is in the first place (a series of amoral power relations, an endless no-holds-barred bargaining game). It is far from clear how it can be combined with a comparatively sentimental conception of the moral standing of the property order which it incorporates and sustains. Either that property order must be vindicated as a site of value in itself, or it, like the rest of social and economic relations, must reasonably be taken as wholly plastic within the operating causality of the polity as a whole. It cannot reasonably be viewed as outside or above politics. The view that redistributive taxation is an instance of bribery requires that property be normatively (and perhaps chronologically) prior to politics: determined independently, and before the latter begins. Widely though it continues to be held and expressed, this is not a defensible view.

FISCAL INDISCRETION AND FISCAL DEPRAVITY

The serious case against the fiscal redistributions of the modern republic, therefore, cannot be that it makes any. It must be that those which it does make on balance do more harm than good, and that their propensity to do so follows directly from the form of the state itself. But it seems clear that where they do more harm than good (a very difficult judgment in the first place), they do so through the pursuit of economic policies which prove to do more harm than good. No one has yet shown that the harm which these policies sometimes indubitably inflict ever follows from the conditions in which they must be adopted and thought through. It is an entirely reasonable suspicion that they always may; but it is at least equally reasonable to assume that they never must.

Redistributive taxation might be a violation of right; and it might be an indiscretion. (It might also, until proved otherwise, be a requirement of right and an optimal economic policy from the viewpoint of the welfare of most of the population.) The case for supposing that it must be a violation of right has no direct bearing on the assessment of its discretion. While, like any other pattern of judgment-dependent choice (any instance of *policy*), it plainly always *may* be indiscreet, it is far from clear that there is any case whatever for supposing that it always *must* be so.

The serious charge against redistributive taxation in the modern republic, therefore, rests on a diagnosis of its indiscretion in particular instances, not of its impropriety or folly in general. If that case is to go home against the form of the state itself, it must be shown to be (in some way) *forced* upon those who exercise state power by the conditions in which they do so. In those conditions they must be shown to face what are, in effect, perverse incentives: incentives which strongly prompt them to act in ways which will do real harm to interests which they genuinely value, and in return for rewards which are predictably insufficient to compensate that harm.

This is a relatively intricate hypothesis, which can lose plausibility at a number of different points. It need not attribute to the elected leaders (or groups among these) any clear understanding of what is really going on. But, if the case that the perverse incentives genuinely exist and that they motivate so peremptorily is to be compelling, the structure of the situation must be unmistakably clear. If it can be made that clear to analysts and those whom they take into their confidence, it is difficult to believe that professional politicians with higher stakes in the matter (and not always notably less practical intelligence) could fail to notice it too. If the perversity of the incentives is that clear to professional politicians, it is difficult to see why it cannot (and will not) be made clear also to those who elect them. It is easy to view politics in a binary manner, in which highly motivated professionals with much to gain or lose, and clear comprehensions of what is going on, act vigorously upon the attention, imaginations and desires of altogether less motivated amateurs, with far lower stakes and little, if any, comprehension of what is occurring, and induce the latter to respond passively to some consequent overall balance of their own desire and aversion. But, even in this view, the professionals seem too much in command of themselves and of the domain within which they must act to be readily hemmed in in conduct which will certainly damage their own interests over time. Only if those who elect or fail to elect them are altogether more recalcitrant and less passive, if they judge and act very much for themselves, could the professionals be effectively confined in this way. But if the electors are interested enough and intelligent enough to judge for themselves, and concerned enough to act firmly, it is hard to see why the politicians in turn cannot transfer to their potential electors whatever understanding of the situations in which they must act they happen to have achieved for themselves.

A fatalist model of the modern republic as necessarily fiscally self-wounding over time must either be resolutely politically unimaginative (simply envisage very few forms of political agency or conviction), or it must either credit its career politicians with inordinately simple goals or its ordinary citizens with very little practical intelligence. At particular points in time any or all of these assumptions may fit the facts perfectly. But it is hard to see how anyone could defend the thesis that they all always must. What could they defend this thesis *with*?

A less structural version of this line of thought is altogether more convincing. It simply is not true that the fundamental form of the modern republic dictates fiscal folly over time. (Compare the eighteenth-century debate in Britain and France over the structural relations between monarchy and republic as state forms and the handling of the public debt: Hont 1993; Sonenscher 1997.) But what probably is true is that in particular epochs the propensity to raise the overall level of taxation can be remarkably insistent, and that different internal institutional realizations of this state form can and do provide their denizens with quite sharply contrasting contexts of agency and schedules of incentives. It is hard to distinguish the epochs accurately from one another without the privilege of hindsight. But it is easy enough to see that what determines them is principally the dynamics of the world economy and the international economic regimes which are shaped politically by the major world powers in response to these dynamics (Keohane 1984; Gilpin 1987; Kennedy 1988; Dunn (ed.) 1990). Within such regimes, national growth rates and changes in the volume of international trade furnish very different distributive possibilities at different points in time, and correspondingly different consequences of adopting one pattern of distribution over another. These opportunities and potential consequences, in turn, confront both voters and would-be political representatives with markedly different patterns of reward and penalty for implementing one tax level and distribution rather than another.

It is easy to see that these structures of opportunity and jeopardy are constraining: that they limit the options for political agency on the part of representers and represented. But it is also easy to see that shifts of this kind could scarcely in principle eliminate the opportunity to choose, and enforce instead a single mandatory line of conduct. When career politicians deplore the constraints under which they must work, they do so, on the whole, not because they lack options – because there literally is no alternative to the line of conduct which they select – but because they have (often well-justified) misgivings over that line of conduct, yet also believe that it will cost them more politically to deviate from it in a more reputable direction than they hope to gain from pursuing it. (For the fundamental political importance of this pattern of political choice in modern democracies, see Thompson 1998.)

Where this is how matters stand, the complaint can hardly lie against the modern republic as a state form, and must go through instead to the at least mildly corrupted purposes of those who choose to pursue their careers in this spirit. In this form, moreover, it may well be more compelling as a complaint about their failure of political imagination, nerve and force of will than as a lament for the discomfort of their predicament. Politicians who see (and feel) themselves constrained in this way may be succumbing to habit and resignation rather than accurately registering degrees of external constraint to which they are objectively exposed. The fault may lie less in their stars than in themselves. (Here, the career of Mrs Thatcher, whatever else one may think of her, genuinely is instructive: cf. Chapter 4 above.)

Experience, in politics as in life, is an unsteady teacher. To learn its lessons accurately, as Niccolò Machiavelli explained almost five centuries ago to his Florentine fellow citizens, may require courage just as much as analytical skill. Within a particular epoch and a given sequence of political experience, an existing fiscal structure can appear politically mandatory: simply not open to question or serious modification. Career politicians and electors can be as one in so treating it. Individual politicians may face prohibitive political costs for challenging it; and they, and still more particular groups of electors, may prove impotent if and when they do so. But what is in question is still a matter of semblance, not one of objective necessity. What holds the structure in place is the perceptions and choices of very many actual or potential agents, all of whom always could see, and choose, differently. Habit and resignation, and the calculations which we all make on the basis of each, often feel like fate; but it is right in the end to think of them distributively not as something done to us, but as something done by us: the lives we choose to live, and the vision with which we content ourselves. At its core the fatalist critique of the modern republic as irretrievably fiscally profligate locates the latter's fate in misapprehension and miscalculation. However accurately that identification may capture even whole epochs of the modern republic's political experience in particular settings, the terms in which it is cast (the terms of deeply entrenched cognitive error) must in the end subvert the diagnosis it offers.

The most important structural charge against the modern republic – that it compels its rulers to impair its economic performance over time by forcing them to transfer resources from rich to poor, and so, allegedly, from investment to consumption – would be valid only under very restrictive conditions. In the first place, the poor must be able to perceive their advantage in the transfer, and either be convinced that they will not themselves pay for this in the longer run or fail to notice (or care) that they will. In the second place, there must be enough of them to enable them to enforce their advantage, and they must act with sufficient solidarity and efficacy to do so in practice. (In virtually every country in the world where the matter has been studied, the poor vote less, and know less about politics, than the more prosperous.) In the third place they must be sufficiently politically autonomous (impervious to the persuasive efforts and facilities of the rich) to be able to resist the latter's attempts to prevent their identifying their interests accurately.

Only a confident, steady majority coalition, united in pursuit of this outcome, is plainly in a position to enforce it. There is no convincing evidence of such a coalition being formed and sustained for any great length of time in the vast majority of modern republics. The most plausible candidate is Sweden under uninterrupted Social Democrat rule for nearly fifty years; but even there, where cumulative habit and resignation must have been at their weightiest, it proved perfectly possible in the 1990s for the electorate to choose differently for a time.

In addition to the charge that it favours building political clientages by redistributing the wealth of others through the state budget, several further charges of economic profligacy have been pressed against this state form. One, as we have seen, is that it inflates the currency, since this is an option permanently in the rulers' own hands, and one which costs them little, if anything, and reliably augments their capacity to bribe. A second is that it massively over-borrows, running a deliberate fiscal deficit, steadily deepening the public debt and imposing ever more crippling funding costs on future generations, costs which in the end can be borne only by defaulting on the debts themselves. (This charge can readily overlap with the first.) A third is that it distorts its handling of the economy over time to increase its electoral appeal as the occasion for voting looms up, abandoning all concern for fiscal prudence and monetary rectitude before the spectre of the ballot box, and spending recklessly to cajole the electors into a wholly inappropriate gratitude. There is ample evidence of one or more of these charges holding good of particular modern republics over particular spans of time. The charge that the state form conspicuously fails to preclude economic indiscretion on the part of rulers or ruled can scarcely be denied. But this will seem surprising (or even deplorable) only to those who seriously presume that political institutions might in principle be designed which precluded economic indiscretion, and that, if they could, they would be likely to prove humanly attractive in the round. (There is more to life for any individual or group than avoiding economic indiscretion.)

For anyone who presumes nothing of the kind, and would not expect to welcome finding themselves subjected to rulers who protected them against every indiscretion which they might choose to commit, the key point about rising public debt, persistent inflation and political business cycles is that each requires extensive misjudgment or practical error on the part of either career politicians or ordinary citizens (and in most cases on the part of both). So viewed, even a massive accumulation of discouraging political experience is less a demonstration of subjection to external contingency than a challenge to collective capacities for self-enlightenment and self-discipline. One of the most austere and emotionally rebarbative truths about politics is that, at least in democratic republics, we all in the end, collectively, get the politicians we deserve.

THE MODERN REPUBLIC AND THE CONSEQUENCES OF FREEDOM

If there is something remediably amiss about the modern republic as a framework today for political choice and its implementation, it cannot be that it *permits* political choice, still less that it implements this, once it has been made. It cannot be that it exposes career politicians or mass electorates to temptation, and that the latter sometimes, or even often, succumb. (How can there be political choice without temptation? How can there be free agency without regular, if varyingly drastic, succumbing to temptation? In the modern republic, we may indeed show ourselves fools, but at least our follies will be our own.) The modern republic is scarcely a full remedy for original sin. But then it neither accepts the validity of the hypothesis of original sin, nor volunteers to remedy anything of the kind. (And for orginal sin, in any case, there is and could be no full remedy, short of the Last Judgment.)

What the modern republic is, in its own eyes, is simply a device for extending to every citizen, as far as it can, a full liberty to act as they choose, without thereby encroaching on the like liberty for any of their fellow citizens. It is a system of collective agency, which is also at the same time a system of equitable mutual restraint. This is an arduous, and inherently somewhat obscure, assignment. But no one could reasonably mistake it for a frontal assault on original sin. It is certainly reasonable to complain if the modern republic falls short of its self-assigned task. It is even more so to complain if one of its more fundamental features, the economic order on which it rests, is shown structurally to preclude the full discharge of this task. That complaint, too, is not obviated merely by demonstrating (if indeed that can be demonstrated) that no rationally preferable framework of economic life and political choice is practically available. A state form of which this is true is, *ex hypothesi*, the best state form we can now (or perhaps ever) have; but it is a state form permanently torn between a goal which it can never afford to abandon (yet never hope to reach) and one which it may indeed often attain (but can never frankly avow).

At present, as we have seen, this last predicament seems impossible to escape. This does not ground the state form on a structural conflict of interest. It does not identify it as the illegitimate victory of one set of narrow interests over another set of evidently broader interests. But, within a now all but mandatory political and economic frame, it shows even the best version of the way we live now to rest ultimately on the lavish nurturing of some, and on an altogether more niggardly care for others. (This is the disagreeable secret at the heart of John Rawls's painful inquiry into how it can now make sense for us to think about justice between fellow citizens: Rawls 1972 and 1993.) If this is the best which we can now coherently dream of for a society, we have come to set our sights very low. Is it really well seen, communitarians challenge, as a *society* at all?

THE LIMITATIONS OF THE MODERN REPUBLIC: STRUCTURE, INSTITUTIONS AND TIME

The modern republic is not a glorious state (Dunn 1994). It eschews grand goals and seeks to make itself fully at home in a deeply capitalist world. If there is something remediably amiss about it, this is not, as far as we can now tell, what or where or when it is. Rather, it is how it is organized.

There are at least three ways in which its organization may well be defective, none of which involves a commitment to grander goals or to a less morally and economically riven mode of life.

The first is in the bare structure of choice with which the modern republic confronts both its individual citizens and its contending career politicians. The second is in the miscellany of institutional settings within which each of these categories must seek to form and sustain the coalitions which are a precondition for acting effectively in politics. The third, more elusively but perhaps even more importantly, is in the state's capacity to confront the task of maximizing the freedom of all its citizens, not as a problem which arises and must be solved at one particular point in time, but as one which extends forward indefinitely through time.

It is easy here to see how infelicitous the state form might readily prove. At each particular point in time, the citizens of the modern republic collectively hold power over each other's freedom of action, and negotiate with one another just how that power is to be exercised. Each, notionally, has an equal power (and all certainly an equal right) to determine that outcome; and virtually none, palpably, have no power whatever to influence it. But, as time stretches inexorably into the future, more and more of those whose lives will be shaped by each decision have no power whatever to determine the outcome, no determinate right to influence it, and only on the most strained hypotheses much power to influence it. Most of those who have children no doubt have some concern for their own children's future. But no one can have much insight into what their great-grandchildren may want or need (certainly no one who is not directly acquainted with them).

The interests of the future are at the mercy of the present. The present has only the bleariest understanding of what they are; and, as they recede imaginatively in time, it does not, in truth, greatly care about them. Yet every community owes its present, for better or worse, to its ancestors. Such freedom as it has, such capacity to see and judge what use to make of that freedom, are gifts to it from those who have gone before. The modern republic, the political expression of what Edmund Burke christened 'the philosophy of vanity' (Burke, *Letter to a Member of the National Assembly* (1791): Burke 1989, 313), the politics of self-righteous present-tense self-absorption, has little feeling for its ancestors, and little care for its descendants. Nothing about its structure as a state compels it to have real regard for either. Yet its charter as a state implies as peremptory responsibilities to the latter, insofar as it can and will affect their future freedom, as it does to those who can speak and judge and act on their own behalf.

On slightly deeper thought, it might even be wise for this state form to recognize some measure of responsibility towards the past also – not because it can directly affect this, but because the failure to attend to it is likely also to mean a failure to understand it, and a failure to understand it is equally likely to lead to the squandering of whatever heritage it does happen to have left behind it. Edmund Burke was the great visionary of this process of depletion. He had little to offer in the way of political remedy; but his sense of what we permanently risk squandering is an essential complement to the operating routines, and the occlusive *imaginaire*, of the modern republic. With the prospect of irreversible ecological catastrophe, it now links, as never before, with a vision of natural punishment which just might at last endow the shadowy generations of the future with a mediated power of agency of their very own.

If this does indeed occur, the modern republic would find itself balanced in time as it has never been before, an experience as surprising as it would be salutary. To *expect* this to occur, however, would be not merely optimistic but also extravagant.

Over this deep issue neither analysts nor advocates of the modern republic have made detectable headway since Burke (who was emphatically *not* an advocate of the modern republic). Until very recently, indeed, they have shown exceedingly little interest in it. But over the bare structure of choice confronting citizens and politicians, and over the institutional settings for forming and sustaining politically effective coalitions, there has been endless inquiry, and many touted diagnoses and remedies. Each of these foci offers an alternative approach to the aetiology of recurrent political or economic mishaps: one which does not attribute the latter too hastily just to vice or folly (the intrinsically disreputable motives of all actual human beings, their invincible ignorance, or monumental practical stupidity).

Vice and folly we have ever with us. But structures of choice and institutional settings come and go. The modern republic today is democratic. It repudiates the purpose of excluding anyone from political choice or power merely on grounds of their ignorance or folly. Where the outcomes are clearly and determinedly chosen, or even when the acts of government themselves have been selected in blithe unawareness of how they were likely to come out, and when that choice has been made by a majority of the people, democrats cannot complain about this state of affairs. (It may well, to be sure, give them good reason to buffer the democratic authority they defend by other and countervailing power; but that is a qualification of their commitment to democracy, not a deepening or enhancement of this.) It is only where the acts of government were not (and would not have been) chosen by such a majority, or where the results of these acts were knowably (and known to be) unwelcome to a majority, that it is reasonable to assume that something must be amiss either in the choice procedures themselves or in the milieu in which citizens and politicians bargain and tussle together to amass the power to realize their political purposes.

SOCIAL CHOICE

It has been known for well over two centuries that there are some patterns of preference which preclude any choice procedure from generating outcomes which are plainly just or rational (Arrow 1963, extending Condorcet). But there is little reason to suppose that these relatively idiosyncratic patterns feature frequently or prominently in political life. What certainly does feature frequently and prominently is the broader set of circumstances in which agreeable outcomes can be reached by more than one chooser, if and only if all concerned fully understand what is at stake, can communicate freely with one another, and also know that they can (for one reason or another) trust each other to act just as they undertake. In a wide range of such cases, endlessly explored by students of the theory of games, neither clear mutual understanding nor dependable trustworthiness can reasonably be anticipated, whatever the facilities for communication; and what comes out must and will be determined by altogether more furtive (and perhaps necessarily self-protective) manoeuvre. When so determined, in many (though mercifully not all) cases, what comes out is far from agreeable.

The most intensively studied instance of such a structure is the famous Prisoner's Dilemma. The largest class of instances where the results are more encouraging than might reasonably be feared come in cases where the relations in question can be confidently anticipated to recur repeatedly over time, and the shadow of future hurt, disapproval and retaliatory suspicion hangs over, and perhaps penalizes, the prospect of clear and immediate gains. Game theorists call this the class of repeated games, a class in which it is less intuitively obvious just how it is rational to play, and why it is rational to play in that way, and not in any other (cf. Hardin 1995; Axelrod 1984). There is now much behavioural evidence that human agents do react differently in these predicaments, and do so essentially for just this reason.

All politics is largely a puzzle of collective action: a question of how it makes sense for each interested party (each individual agent) to act, given the fact that all the others whose actions may also affect the outcome must answer the same question too. Many potential political agents resolve this puzzle by paralysis – by simply giving up. More particularly, as political scientists discovered repeatedly in the 1950s and 1960s, those who know least and understand least about politics tend to resolve it in this way. This naturally modifies the balance of feasible coalitions among the poor, weak and uneducated, bleeding these of many of their natural supporters. (Their natural supporters, we may assume, are those who can reasonably anticipate benefiting from their success, if they have good chances of proving effective, and who could support them at an undismaying cost.) This, however, is a point not about the structure of choice but about its content and the strains of making it.

If the modern republic fails as a medium for resolving the puzzles of collective action, what causes it to do so, it is now reasonable to assume, is not principally the distorting impact of class structure – the crude and endlessly reinforced gap between the political advantages of the rich and the political obstructions which face the poor. For a long time in this century, and relatively openly, the modern republic in many settings moved firmly away from the outcomes preferred by the rich and towards those preferred by the poor. It did so avowedly, and as a result of clearly intended, and sometimes resolute and confident, political agency. If it has now moved rather a long way back, what has caused it to do so is not the intrinsic obstructiveness of the political form to the political purposes of the less advantaged, but the sheer difficulty of identifying sets of policies which will over time dependably serve their interests. This is a cognitive, not an institutional, obstacle (Dunn (ed.) 1990); and there is no good reason to attribute it to the structure within which individual citizens must make and register their political choices (Dunn 1984(a)).

Most forceful criticism of the modern republic as a political structure takes its ground from disapproval of one or other aspect of the perceived consequences of that structure: the outcomes which arise within it, and which it is therefore reasonable to attribute to it. But everything here hangs on the precision and cogency with which the causality at issue has been envisaged. There are at least three different types of causality which come under regular suspicion. One focuses on the gap between the claim to exemplify democracy and a practice of rule which utterly belies that claim: on a relation between enfranchised citizens and career politicians, in which the former should control the latter and very conspicuously cannot (cf. Schumpeter 1950, caps 20–3, esp. pp. 269–83: p. 285, 'democracy is the rule of the politician'; Manin 1997; Dunn (ed.) 1992, 239–66). A second focuses on the sheer difficulty of forming and implementing rational strategies either for individual citizens and groups or for their would-be political representatives. The last focuses principally on economic structure and process, on the perceived impact of these on amateur and professional political choice, or on the perceived impact of amateur or professional political choice, in turn, upon them. All three plainly affect, and react to, one another. But only the second, the choice and implementation of rational strategies for voters or career politicians, bears directly upon the choice structure provided by the modern republic as a state form. No one could now reasonably dispute that, as Joseph Schumpeter gleefully explained, modern republics are governed by competing teams of career politicians, and that they are democratic only insofar as these politicians are forced to compete for the people's vote (Schumpeter 1950, caps 20–3). No one can deny that this structure differs notably from the intimacy and participatory excitements of the Athenian Assembly (however unsentimentally these last are envisaged: Finley 1983; Ober 1989). Few, too, will wish to dispute that modern republics often govern extremely injudiciously, and frequently pursue economic policies which prove gravely misguided, in some instances for decades at a time. Look at the accumulated public debt of the Italian republic. But what is crucial is what exactly causes them to do so.

Do these untoward results emerge necessarily from the political gap between amateurs and professionals, rulers and ruled? Are they imposed by the limits set to the actions of each by the dynamics of global capitalist competition? Or do they arise, more interestingly and perhaps even more disturbingly, from the fact that for most citizens or groups of citizens there just are no patently rational political strategies of the faintest ambition in the first place, no lines of conduct the rational appeal of which is sufficiently robust and salient to carry to most potential agents, or stand up to critical assessment and the trials of experience? Unless such lines of conduct do exist, it may not greatly matter how democratic or undemocratic are the circumstances of rule, or how humanly frustrating or enabling the dynamics of global competition. In the most ideally democratic of political settings, within the gentlest and most generously permissive external economic environment, if human beings cannot see what it makes sense to do, they will still be hopelessly at sea. What they can and surely will do is to pursue one more or less confused or ill-judged idea after another; and what will result from what they do is yet further confusion and misjudgment.

This is certainly the political world with which we are familiar: the world of everyday political life (perhaps even a slightly laundered version of it). So why is it (why should it, or must it) be so hard for human beings to see what it makes sense to do politically, within, and in relation to, a modern republic? Where does the confusion and befuddlement come from?

Hobbes's answer to this question (admittedly asked about a very different Commonwealth) was that it mostly came from the vanity and intermittent malignity of individual human beings – above all, their incapacity to recognize the superiority of anyone else's judgment. These were more than enough to guarantee that democratic discourse would prove an endless nightmare (Hobbes 1983). It is easy to see that self-righteous partiality in judgment is a reliable intensifier of confusion, and that even institutions which secure genuinely democratic choice cannot be relied upon to dissipate such confusion effectively. But the suspicion remains that there is also a quite separate, and at least equally intractable, source of such confusion in the logical puzzles of collective action itself. If it lies there, it inheres in the very idea of what it is to have clearly good reason to act in one way rather than another, within a predicament shared in some respects by very many others, and at least partially constituted by still further others.

There are at least three separate components of such a predicament. One (which we have already seen to be distinctly murkier than most political discussion assumes) is the rational interests in possible outcomes held by different individuals or groups. The more carefully and reflectively you consider the question, the less easy it is to know just what is in your own interest. Groups, certainly in this sense, are in no way smarter than individuals. But this is a pall which hangs over all action: not something special to politics, or peculiarly pertinent to puzzles of collective action.

The other two, by contrast, are in some measure special to politics, and do bear distinctively on collective action. The first of these is the question of what outcomes it is reasonable even to hope to secure, and which, among the more acceptable of these, there is best chance of securing in practice by anything which one could readily do oneself. The second is how the costs of securing this outcome are likely to be distributed, and what proportion of them, if any, it is reasonable to consider bearing oneself.

The first is a matter of the comparative accessibility of potentially accessible outcomes: the probability space of possible, and remotely eligible, political futures. It is a nice metaphysical question whether there ever is more than one possible political future: the actual political future. But, even if there *is* only one, only God is privileged to know what it is going to be. For humans, there is always an endless miscellany of very vaguely conceived possible futures, political and otherwise.

The second is a matter of the rationality of contributing, as an individual or a group of whatever size, to the attempt to reach the chosen outcome.

FUTILITY, MEANNESS, INCOMPREHENSION

In allocating the costs of political endeavour, there are, once again, two very different considerations to be borne in mind: one a matter principally of efficacy, the other more one of relative generosity and clarity of understanding. The first, at its most abstract, turns on the probability of affecting the outcome at the margin by one's own personal contribution. Rationally considered, this must, in the great majority of significant cases, and for all but a handful of already well-positioned elite political actors, be negligible. (When did my vote ever swing a national election, or even a closely contested constituency struggle? You might never be able to prove that it in fact *had*. But here is an instance when proving a negative is pretty effortless from the experiences of virtually everyone.) What follows from this insight is the instrumental rationality, for almost everyone almost all of the time, of steady political inanition: the refusal to incur any costs at all in order to act politically for any outcome. To override this, some other kind of rationality has to be called into play: some degree of pride in and respect for the self as an agent, some schedule of motives which draws the self beyond its own discrete benefits and commits it at least partially to the interests of others, some sense of the action in question as a fulfilment, and not merely a cost. But this, of course, simply confuses these two very different sorts of consideration; and, by doing so, blurs, or even obliterates, the terms of the puzzle. If I act in politics to do what I can (usually nothing) for others, I no longer need to worry about what I can reasonably hope to derive from so acting on my own behalf. I act because I feel I should, not because of what I hope to get out of doing so. An over-polite (or perhaps just needlessly elaborate?) name for action so envisaged is expressively rational action: action which is rational, because and only because it articulates the agent's sense of what sort of a person they wish to be. But if the case against a particular action is that it is virtually certain to prove inefficacious, that case is scarcely met by noticing that the act in question resonates agreeably with one's own self-esteem. If an action is knowably futile, narcissism alone will not be sufficient to restore it to rationality. Heroism, for example, may be a great military good; but it can only be so in the right context. When the Six Hundred men of the Light Brigade rode at Balaclava into the valley of death, into the mouth of hell, what made their ride heroic was not its being a suicidal blunder, but its being someone *else's* blunder: its not being *suicidal*: 'Theirs not to reason why.'

In politics self-conscious heroism may be personally engaging. But it is rather seldom, on any defensible view, rational. Prospective efficacy is of the essence. In the arcane state, its rulers and ministers may have needed good nerves; but what was (and perhaps still is) supposed to guide their actions was its Reason, not their daring. In democratic states, at least overtly, it is everyone's responsibility to reason why. A rational, clear-headed and well-informed despondency at one's own political inefficacy is a decisive ground for political inanition. It may affront the confused priggishness of those who live off dreaming and gossiping about politics; but it is quite irrefutable as an estimate of what most of us most of the time can sanely hope to assist in bringing about, and hence of what we have any reason to do because, and only because, we desire some particular outcome.

In a more domestic political arena, with comparatively few political players and a high degree of continuity between games, this line of thought may come out very differently. There, the future can and will cast a long shadow. Much action is to some degree accountable, effectively signed by the agent in question, and open to memory, resentful or appreciative. (For the potential impact of such considerations over time see, very helpfully, Axelrod 1984 and 1997.) Many selves are to some degree engaged with fates distinctly wider than their own. Even costly and clear-sighted generosity need not be simply out of the question, though it will hardly be the modal experience. For most citizens, the routine politics of the modern democratic republic could scarcely be further from this degree of relative transparency and accountability. In it, most political action by most citizens is utterly unaccountable. All voting for public offices by ordinary citizens, for example, is unaccountable by definition (the ballot is secret).

When repeated games of any consequence occur, they occur principally between relatively small groups of career politicians; and, even in these, mutual accountability over time appears quite weakly developed. To be personally loathed (and loathed for good reason) may not quite be a net political asset. But to be loved (a relatively infrequent professional political experience) is not a dependable advance on being loathed. (Consider the career of Michael Foot, erstwhile leader of Britain's Labour Party. Compare the career, thus far, of the Conservative Michael Portillo.) *Oderint, dum metuant.* Let them hate, in the words of the second-century BC Roman dramatist, as long as they remain afraid.

Riding Free

In Mancur Olson's striking little study of *The Logic of Collective Action* (Olson 1965) something clear and intuitively compelling about what it is to act instrumentally as one among a great many came into focus. The answer depends on which of two conditions applies to what is at stake. Wherever the outcome, whether good or bad, will fall on all equally and whether or not they contribute to its costs, it will come out good only if its benefits exceed its costs for most contributors, or if most can be compelled to contribute. Otherwise, in these conditions, the reasonably adroit and moderately selfish will take the benefits (should these prove available), but evade contributing to the costs of securing them. They will use the public transport helpfully provided, whenever it suits them to do so; but they will do their level and ingenious best to ride upon it for free. Only if they can be stopped from riding upon it freely will it cross their minds to assist in paying for it. The result is that only if those who refuse to contribute can be excluded from the benefits will the benefits be provided. Most public services, including those whose overt purpose is ensuring the physical security of the population (police, armed forces, prophylactic public health) are of this character, and are therefore funded through the tax system. The ingenuity of free-riders, and especially of the wealthier among their number, is therefore unleashed at its most frenetic upon the workings of the tax system, inside, approximately parallel to and in uninhibited violation of the law. Much of the politics of the modern republic (especially in its democratic form) turns on the question of how far the citizens at large should be forced to furnish themselves, and one another, through the tax system with public goods of different kinds. Within this swirling competitive mêlée, it is characteristically unclear to all participants exactly what is going on: what bargains are really on offer, who can be trusted to stick to their offers when the time to pay comes, how far the constraints, on which any of the bargains in the end relies, can be effectively enforced in practice. On the whole, recent British survey and electoral evidence suggests that distinctly more voters are eager to express an enthusiasm for the provision of public goods than show themselves willing to vote to pay for them in the privacy of the polling booth. It is not completely clear whether what leads them to act in these fashions is that they think more clearly in the second setting or feel more nobly in the first. But the sceptical fear must be that their less clear thinking in the former setting is either a sign or a consequence of their success in deceiving themselves about their own character, while their comparative lucidity in the second is a product of the knowledge that no one else at all can see exactly what they are doing, let alone what is leading them to do it.

The appeals of free-riding, and the disabling recognition of the personal political ineffectuality of individual citizens, are formidable challenges to any vision of the modern democratic republic as a system which combines economic sanity, rationality and prospectively agreeable political outcomes in a dependable fashion. We may not at present be able to think of anything better. (Indeed we may *never* be able to think of anything better.) But we will always be able, quite effortlessly, to think of outcomes which we would vastly prefer to any which are likely to emerge from its workings, let alone to those which do in fact emerge. To view the fate of this regime form with any calm and judgment, the key point which we need to grasp is how very different these two threats are. The personal political ineffectuality of ordinary citizens is not a novel property of these regimes, nor one which has previously escaped notice. The main contrast between ancient and modern liberty, as Benjamin Constant explained (Constant 1988, 307–28), was that the personal freedoms of the latter – the liberty to live as we personally choose – are balanced by an inevitable sense, and a potentially perfectly accurate appreciation, of our own personal political inconsequence. There is nothing which can in general be done about this: certainly nothing at present which it might be sane to choose to do about it. We could, for example, have a permanent democratic equivalent of the old Polish *liberum veto* (the power of any individual citizen to ban any exertion of governmental power that they chose). But we would scarcely enjoy the consequences, if we did have this.

Any of us can choose, if we so wish, to go into politics: to join the competition to lead and represent the rest of us. Insofar as we succeed in forcing our way in, we may cross the line decisively between personal ineffectuality and real political power. But we cannot all cross that line; and the idea that we all might does not, on careful consideration, even make sense. Whether or not this really matters for political outcomes depends not on the tastes or anxieties of most citizens, but on the interaction between committed competitors to exercise political power, and on the structure of economic and social options which happens to be available at the time. There are circumstances in which it could matter (perhaps those of Germany between 1918 and 1933). But even in Germany in 1933, the most pregnant exercise of electoral choice in modern history, it is hard to defend the claim that what did the damage was in any sense the political ineffectuality of individual citizens. Through the democratic franchise and its simple ritual of electoral choice, the modern republic gives its citizens, while it lasts, a full power of collective veto: an opportunity to reject, and reject decisively. Where they fail to exercise this power and regret their failure acutely in retrospect, what leads them to fail is not their individual impotence, but vagaries in their judgment and attention, and opacities within, or more or less temporary distortions of, their desires. Not their individual impotence, but their collective folly. None of these are defects which institutional design can readily forestall: least of all in the case of institutions, the explicit point of which is to reflect the balance of judgment and desire across an entire population. On the economic theory of democracy, there could not be democracy because no reasonable elector would bother to vote; and the theory assumes all electors to be reasonable by this very criterion (Downs 1957; Olson 1965; Barry 1970). But this merely shows that the theory itself must be profoundly wrong. In the modern democratic republics which happen to exist, electors still vote in very large numbers (larger, of course, in some than others: fewer in America than in Britain). No doubt they have their reasons. What is clear is that at least some of these must be reasons which the economic theory of democracy fails to capture.

The appeals of free-riding are a more abrasive challenge. What is less evident is just what sort of a challenge, and precisely to whom. On this, again, there are two very different perspectives: essentially those of ancient political theory and those of its modern counterpart and supplanter. For ancient political theorists, any people sooner or later needs a Legislator, someone who can lick it into shape, and fashion for it an institutional frame and a structure of discipline which alone can give it the chance to live out a lengthy and honourable life together. In this view, the key prerequisite for effective political agency for any people must come from outside the motley ranks of ordinary citizens (or ordinary aristocrats). It must arrive on the scene in impeccable order; and it must reconstruct these ranks wholesale for purposes of collective agency – in effect imposing its own order upon them. Free-riding, on this view, is essentially a problem for those designing and implementing a scheme of public transport. It is *not* a problem for individual passengers, actual or potential. For the latter individually, if they are brave and sly enough to get away with it, free-riding, far from being a problem, is the perfect solution: to have one's cake and eat it. Even when enough of them prove sufficiently brave and sly to render public transport unworkable, and where public transport which did work would be decisively more convenient for its users than any available private counterpart, the problem at hand remains one of designing and implementing a scheme of public transport in the face of these obstacles.

For ancient political theorists, under these conditions, the natural response would be to work on the dispositions of recalcitrant travellers, to render them less fluently sly, or less offhandedly daring, or even less despicably indifferent to the public good. (On the view of the late Michel Foucault, this is just what the modern world, more surreptitiously, is doing all the time: Foucault 1979.) Modern political theorists tend to find this approach distasteful. They pride themselves on being clear-headed and disabused, and either taking their fellow citizens as these really are, or deferring politely to their all too apparent tastes and preferences. For them, the task of designing a public transport system is the epitome of modern politics (unless, to be sure, they happen to disapprove of public transport on principle). But they believe that the task must be discharged without assailing the souls of passengers. (One can see why they take this view.) It must and can be solved by designing and implementing systems of incentives which will price any attempt to ride free out of the market.

On this matter, the evidence goes both ways. On the one hand, most reasonably prosperous countries have functioning systems of public transport on which many of the passengers, for one reason or another, pay their fares. Endless ingenuity, and some force of will, goes into the task of ensuring that many (or that even more) will continue to choose to do so. At least comparable ingenuity, and even greater force of will, in a more dispersed manner, goes into the attempt to ride freely. It is a tense and endless struggle, and quite *rightly* seen as an epitome of modern politics. But what is its political lesson? What does it mean? The answer will depend a great deal on one's own temperament and personal experience. (It may depend quite a lot, too, on just where one happens to live.) What I wish to underline is the indiscretion of assuming that the perspective of modern political theory (the fare-enforcement system designer) will routinely capture most of the variance. Whether individuals choose to pay their fares may sometimes depend exclusively on whether they expect to be caught and penalized severely, if they do not. But for very many it also depends at least as much on their sense of what they would feel if they were to be caught. (Observe the careful wording of the notices on the London Underground.) Even a very small subjective probability of being caught may be quite enough to tinge the idea of choosing to ride freely with anticipatory humiliation: to poison it beyond recall. Here, soberly considered, the souls of potential passengers already feature decisively within the most austerely technical conception of the system of incentives. The same is very likely to prove true, in greater or lesser measure, right across the relation between most citizens and the criminal law.

COMMUNITARIAN AND LIBERAL RESPONSES TO FREE-RIDING

To understand the modern republic, accordingly, to see what we can reasonably hope to get it to do for us, modern political theory, with its self-consciously antiseptic preoccupations and routines, is most unlikely to prove sufficient. To make out, the modern republic still needs to handle the recesses of shame, or guilt, or fantasy, with which ancient political theory did not shrink from reckoning. It, too, is just as much at the mercy of the workings of the human imagination as the stuff with which ancient Legislators sought to work. It, too, would be well advised to draw as cunningly as it can on the insights of those who focused on the efforts of those Legislators, and sought to understand both the scope and the limits of their achievements. What has happened to this intellectual (but also eminently practical) agenda is less clear today than it might be. A despondent view would be that it has collapsed into pure farce, being replayed in an increasingly ludicrous, and narrowly academic, dialogue of the deaf between Communitarians and Liberals, with its epicentre in North America. (For the upper reaches of this see, for example, Sandel 1996; Rawls 1993.)

In that dialogue, the Liberals insist, each individual psyche must be left firmly to do its best (or worst) by its own lights, with politics mediating the potential collisions which inevitably ensue.

What the Communitarians insist on is plainly very different, but also somewhat inexplicit: perhaps just that it would be better if individual psyche and social setting dovetailed more intimately and neatly with one another, perhaps also that it would be better if they could dependably be made to do so, perhaps, more recklessly, that they *must* somehow be made to do so. (But does *must* necessarily mean can?) Everything, politically, turns on that 'somehow'. If they cannot in principle be made dependably to do so, any attempt to cause them to do so may easily go very far astray. What moves the Liberals in this debate is less an odd view of what it is to be human (a literal-minded pausing at the edges of the individual body), than a far from odd view of what is likely to result from treating that boundary too high-handedly, or from seeking to assail the soul with the instruments available to political authority. Certainly the history of armed assault upon the soul (give or take the Reformation or Counter-Reformation: Duffy 1992; MacCulloch 1996) has not been notably encouraging. It is not for nothing that the enemies of China's economic liberalization (and still more of its potential democratization) should stress so determinedly the evidence of 'spiritual pollution' that accompanies this (Tony Walker, 'Deng Reforms under Attack by Old Guard', *Financial Times* 30 November 1995, 10).

A more optimistic assessment is that the agenda of spiritual formation of a good society and polity has dispersed across the societies for which the modern republic seeks to defend a minimal and essentially procedural political shape. It has fractured and fragmented into an endless array of initiatives, none of which are necessarily restricted to the projects of single individuals, and all of which are, after their fashion, dedicated to enhancing the freedom of some range of persons to be more fully and authentically themselves, and to act more richly as they choose. It has dispersed into feminism, or the Green Movement, or into an altogether vaguer entity, Civil Society (in which it would be still more reckless to trust implicitly: cf. Dunn 1996 (c)).

There is something in this line of thought. But to take it at all literally, to see it as the direction of an essentially progressive

History, the contemporary version of what the German philosopher Hegel called *Geist*, the serene self-unfolding of the human spirit, is distinctly over-optimistic. Somewhere between the technical design and implementation of rational incentive systems to manage behaviour which is always potentially destructive and the free expression of long-subjugated and essentially benign human potentialities, the fate of the modern republic sways endlessly in the balance.

Both views raise more or less coherent and precise schedules of questions. Neither offers a trustworthy recipe for ensuring that its own future is in any respects good. Each, thought through carefully and honestly, provides some aid in understanding what is true about any particular modern republic here and now. But we cannot rely on either to tell us how to fashion a better home for ourselves in the years that lie ahead. Here we are still in the same predicament as the Legislators were. In the democratic version of the modern republic, too, one further thing is also true. Since in that setting it is everyone's political responsibility to reason why, a duty which is the simple reciprocal of the equal right to choose how, each of us bears a shadowy fading after-image of the responsibilities the Legislators faced. We are all permanently in complicity, whether we enjoy it or not, in an incessant flurry of Legislation, over which none of us has much real control, and on which few of us have even the most marginal intended purchase. (Consider the preoccupations of Dworkin 1986 from the viewpoint of an individual citizen.)

There is little reason to feel surprised that modern politics should prove so disagreeable and frustrating. No doubt it was much the same in the days of the Legislators (or shortly afterwards: Thucydides 1919–23; Finley 1983). But they, perhaps, saw less occasion for surprise at their frustrations.

It cannot really be said that any extant intellectual tradition offers us reasonably explicit and plausible guidance on how to settle down to handle these responsibilities. Somehow, as Plato long ago insisted, our souls will get formed (Lear 1998, cap. 10). They will be formed, to be sure, through the ways in which we see and feel, and through the choices which these perceptions and sentiments prompt us to make. But the ways in which we see and feel, in turn, will be shaped heavily by the importunities, enticements and menaces of our fellows. None of us can control these; and the selves which we try to fashion or control for ourselves in response to them will, over time, on any sane view, be far more a causal product of them than an effective monitor of them. It is possible to modify oneself over time by cunning and determined application (Aristotle 1926; MacIntyre 1981); but what carries through the modifying must be a self which was there in the first place: not something definite and hard-edged, but, in all its diffuseness and indefinition, nevertheless something there *before*.

What divides the Liberals from the Communitarians in the end is not that the latter know just what they wish (or dare) to do, but that the former are disinclined on principle to consider even attempting to do anything which requires the exertion of coercive power. In practice, of course, they often prove decidedly less disinclined, being as liable to horror, and even anger, as the next person. (The great intellectual hero of contemporary Liberals – certainly of contemporary male Liberals (Baier 1994) – Immanuel Kant, was also an especially careful and forceful exponent of the duty to punish the violation of rights.) But, whatever their own personal attitudes, no Liberal can accept the role of architect of others' souls. For them, education cannot in the end be an exercise of authority. It must be merely a provision of facilities, an opportunity for effective self-fashioning. There is endless dispute about the practical implications of such abstinence for the internal political and social architecture of a liberal society: the institutionalized forms and limits within which its members may, or may not, or should, or should not, seek to shape one another.

The favoured criterion, in Milton's phrase, the 'free and open encounter', remains evocative, but also, over much of the causally most decisive space, profoundly implausible. Who ever saw a free and open encounter of any great duration between an infant and its mother (or even, for that matter, its father)? Who ever saw a free and open encounter between the unborn and the greedy present-tense consumer? Some now at least affect to doubt whether anyone has ever seen a free and open encounter between a man and a woman. There is a lot of coercion about; and even what is not convincingly identifiable as coercion in the shaping of a person may be even less convincingly envisaged as free action or choice on their part.

These questions, naturally, are among the most pressing for feminists; and they have had some success in bringing out how deep and treacherous they are. (For feminists, however radical their proposals for reconstructing social and economic relations, and whether or not they happen to reject the term itself, the true seat of treachery is in the soul. Everything in the end hangs on how that soul comes to be as it is.) As yet, however, they have made little headway in showing any of us how to *answer* these questions.

The strongest case for attributing the less edifying and effective features of the modern republic in operation to the basic structures of choice with which it confronts its citizens or would-be rulers is a case not against that structure itself, but against the effect which it is natural for it to have on the dispositions of both citizens and rulers. This effect is, above all, to exacerbate mutual suspicion and erode mutual trust by underlining how little instrumental reason most of these can hope to have for adhering to the bargains, explicit or implicit, which they make. The purposeful attempt to avoid being a sucker would subvert human sociality more or less in its entirety (Dunn 1990, cap.3 and Williams 1988). What renders agreeable social life possible is a shared confidence that there are many worse fates than being a sucker: being morose, mean, heartless, brutal, cruel, cowardly.

On how we should seek to handle our relations with one another over time to avoid these disagreeable fates, modern political theory is massively discreet, or perhaps just endlessly evasive. No doubt it simply does not have a clue, but vaguely apprehends that it might prove disabling to admit this.

8

Explaining the Failings of the Modern Republic: Platonism versus Sociology

Incomprehension or Context?

If it is not the bare structure of choice with which it confronts its citizens and rulers which disables the modern republic, what does make its political performance today so unimpressive (so shabby, so confused)? Two sorts of answer might be genuinely illuminating. One attributes the misdirection essentially to incomprehension: to the fact that neither citizens nor career politicians really understand quite what they are doing, let alone grasp what they are inadvertently leaving undone. This is an ambitious diagnosis, and almost certainly right. But, to vindicate its correctness, it would be necessary to specify exactly what they really are doing and inadvertently leaving undone: what really is going on. Academic writers about politics frequently express themselves as though they were confident that they could meet this bill – that *they* at least have got to the bottom of things. But, in doing so, they are quite certainly deceiving either others or themselves. It is not humanly possible, in this sense, to know exactly what is really going on in politics on any scale, and it never will be – however impressive the future prowess of the social sciences. Much of what is really going on (and that, usually, the more important part) is simply not within our view: not a possible object for human sight.

The second answer is altogether less ambitious, and forms the principal stock in trade of political scientists, however generous or dim their view of the performance of those whom they study. It attributes the performance of politicians, above all, to the cognitive facilities and distortions which result from, and the more or less perverse incentives which are offered by, the institutional settings and social milieu in which they ply their trade. (See, for the US Congress, Mayhew 1974, or, in more relaxed mode for Westminster, Riddell 1996; see also Thompson 1998.) This is a simple-minded but, as far as it goes, vastly compelling picture. Any competent ethnography of a real political milieu will show all too clearly just why much inept and dismally unprepossessing behaviour is likely to occur within it. A simple but acute description of what goes on in the United States Congress is more than enough to explain many of the more lamentable features of the American polity in action. So too, no doubt, with the Houses of Parliament, the Elysée Palace, the European Commission, the Japanese Diet, as with the Court at Versailles in the days of Louis XIV in the Duc de Saint-Simon's stunning rendition, to say nothing of the last days of Hitler or Haile Selassie (Saint-Simon 1954–61; Le Roy Ladourie and Fitou 1997; Trevor-Roper 1947; Kapuscinski 1984).

IDENTIFYING THE REAL MOVERS

(Cf. Burke, *Reflections on the Revolution in France* (1790): Burke 1989, 59.) Most modern political science of any ambition, divides its professional labours according to two main criteria: where exactly it takes effective agency to be located within the sphere of politics, and what range of consequences, actual or potential, welcome or unwelcome, it regards as being peculiarly important. These two preoccupations are and must be intimately linked to one another. What makes political agency important (where it is important) is the consequences to which it may, or will, or could, or might, lead, not its intrinsic charm, or the spiritual qualities which inform it. In the classic Roman contrast, recurrently central to the political thinking of Western Europe for a good millennium and a half, it is the *utile*, not the *honestum*: the useful, not the honourable. In contrast with Roman political thinkers with their vividly aristocratic concern with the requirements for behaving grandly, modern political scientists, virtually without exception, are firmly utilitarian. Many, of course, in no way endorse utilitarian ethics as a technical analysis of the values which should rationally govern human choice; but even the fiercer critics of utilitarianism as a philosophical theory, if they choose to consider politics seriously at all, are apt to do so principally in terms of the types of outcome to which it is likely to lead under different conditions (cf. Williams 1973, 1981 and 1985).

It is possible, of course, to study political agency which is utterly inconsequential, and to do so in blithe indifference to its inconsequentiality: to study it for no better reason than the fact that it is there. The methodological doctrines of American behaviourists in the 1950s and 1960s could easily be read – and were in fact widely read at the time – as justifying, or even requiring, study of just this kind: study uncontaminated by, and hence undistorted by, human concern (MacIntyre 1971, cap. 22; cf. Taylor 1985, cap. 2). But these doctrines proved too confused and too flagrantly implausible to sustain belief for any length of time; and the shiftier, if plainly related, beliefs which have since replaced them in the profession give far fewer explicit hostages to fortune. To choose to study some human political practice simply because it is there is likely to impress few but fellow political scientists; and if that really is a full description of the grounds for selecting it, even among political scientists it is more likely to elicit complicity than to win admiration. Most substantial bodies of political study, in the 1950s as much as today, have plainly been prompted by some degree of political interest on the part of the inquirers. This is no occasion for regret.

It would be over-generous, however, to expect most works of political science to be principally concerned with matters of evident political importance, and ingenuous to be surprised that they are not. It is much easier to identify and study sites of political agency than it is to pin down the consequences which flow from them. It is also impossible in principle to pin down all the consequences which flow from them. (When, for example, do you stop looking for these? How do you ever know that you are right to have stopped?) It is inordinately hard, too, to judge which range of political consequences really is important. To pick out a political milieu, and inspect with some patience what those within it are up to, is a relatively simple task. To judge which political milieu it would be most instructive to pick out in relation to some item of pressing human concern is far harder; and to judge which items of human concern really are (or ought to be) most pressing is more baffling still. As political study moves from the behaviourally obvious towards the more grandly interpretative, it certainly gains in point, but it also loses in intellectual tractability. As it delves deeper into what is really going on, it strains ever more painfully the resources which human beings possess to apprehend this with any precision, dependability and control.

The idea of effective techniques of inquiry has been of enormous, if intermittent, importance in European thinking, ever since classical Greece (Lloyd 1990). It forms the core of the practice of the natural sciences: a building block of the world we now live in. In relation to politics, the idea of effective techniques of inquiry is as pertinent as in any other domain of interest. (Who could seriously wish to inquire into anything, but to do so ineffectually?) But, although pertinent enough, it is also pretty treacherous. The greater the preoccupation with modes of inquiry, the less fierce the pull of what needs to be understood. The more complete the commitment to follow inquiry into what needs to be understood wherever it leads, the slimmer the prospect of pursuing it throughout in reasonably good intellectual order. There are no strongly directive and wholly reliable techniques even for grasping what those who occupy a particular political milieu are really up to, still less what their activities signify for anyone else. But the more ambitious the political subject matter which we wish to understand, the less illuminating the conception of potentially effective techniques for enabling us to grasp it. The concern for epistemic control and the concern for political significance do not merely conflict with one another at intervals. They pull steadily and very powerfully in essentially opposite directions. Neither can reasonably be abandoned by anyone who seriously wishes to understand politics. But no one who is reasonably intellectually self-aware should expect to find a steady and comfortable equilibrium between them. In the study of politics, it requires great goodness of disposition (intellectual, and perhaps also moral) to withstand the baleful effect of professional socialization.

The conventional conception of the core of politics within any modern republic is its own routine politics: American politics if in the USA, French politics self-evidently if in France, New Zealand politics (no doubt) if in New Zealand, Japanese politics if in Japan. There is nothing necessarily muddled about this presumption. But it cannot be said to err on the side of sophistication or intellectual self-awareness. We need at this point to try to pin down the balance of advantage and disadvantage in this all too natural perspective. The advantages are not elusive. In the first place most people's interests are moderately parochial. They care more about, and initially know much more about, their own surroundings. It is easier for them to improve their understandings of these, should they so wish; and they more often do wish to. Nothing is easier to take in than simple repetition (the building blocks of our entire conception of natural causality: of how things work).

Expressed in these terms the perspective may seem a shade cowardly, even to someone who felt as strongly as Burke did for the fragility of a beloved political habitat. But it has more to be said for it than this allows.

In some ways, routine politics is appallingly easy to understand: the range of motives most potent within it, the obtusenesses which it reinforces and the treacheries which it endlessly calls forth. But the most routine politics there could possibly be remains full of surprises. These may more often be disagreeable than they are delightful. But this does nothing to diminish their significance. It is a drastic error to mistake jaded familiarity for cognitive command. The study of routine politics must be the core of political study, because it, and it alone, permits a reasonably high degree of cognitive mastery; and even it, as we have seen, precludes finality of understanding. *Et tu, Brute?* Julius Caesar's greeting to his least expected assassin (Meier 1995, 480–2) – is the paradigmatic moment of political awareness. To seek to understand politics at a disrespectful distance from routine politics would be not merely imprudent but intellectually and professionally ludicrous.

What, then, are the disadvantages of this impeccably reasonable focus? The disadvantages can be measured in two distinct dimensions, which may or may not coincide at any given point in time. The first is extremely practical, the second more fastidiously intellectual. The practical dimension is determined by the internal stability of the routines in question. But it is also determined by their external security, the degree to which they happen at the time to be effectively buffered against external disruption. Where routines are both relatively internally stable and well buffered against external disruption, there is no guarantee that their participants will understand them especially well. But there is at least no intrinsic obstacle to anyone else's understanding them, for all practical purposes, by studying them on their own. When they are not internally stable, however, or where there are few (if any) effective buffers between them and disruptive forces from the outside, far less of their potential fate can be reliably inferred from the ways in which they have recently operated. Under these conditions, any attempt to understand their political potentialities, however narrowly practical in intention, needs to think much harder and more adventurously about them. It needs to cease to take the routines for granted, and instead to grasp what made them possible in the first place, to judge just what (if anything) might sustain them under stormier conditions, and to assess how far they may and will be transformed, both from the inside and from without, under the very different conditions which now apply.

To think in this way is not a well-specified technical practice, though the attempt to do so is, of course, to some degree entrenched at the heart of every modern state, in its intelligence and defence agencies, the research departments of its ministry of finance or central bank, and the central advisory staffs of its political leaders. In these locales, it is a version of the practice at which Machiavelli hints, which Boccalini, Botero and Gabriel Naudé wrote up more elaborately in the subsequent century and a quarter, and which in their very different ways Cardinal Richelieu or Otto von Bismarck sought to practise: the reason of state (Meinecke 1957; Tuck 1993). Today, in the greatest power in the world, it is the continuing preoccupation of an army of state technicians and agencies: the White House staff, the National Security Council, the Bureau of the Budget, the Central Intelligence Agency.

Crisis and Routine Again

In conditions of acute political crisis, obviously enough, an understanding of local routine politics is likely to offer inadequate guidance. But in such circumstances there is no guarantee (and perhaps little probability) that any form of political understanding will offer adequate guidance. On 29 June 1789, a fortnight or so before the storming of the Bastille, the great Thomas Jefferson, then American ambassador to Paris, wrote home to report to his Secretary of State John Jay: 'This great crisis being now over, I shall not have matter interesting enough to trouble you with as often as I have done lately' (Jefferson Papers XV, 223: Davis 1990, 34).

In conditions of acute crisis, it is not hard to misjudge badly. What is practically misleading mainly in conditions of crisis may be intellectually misleading amid the staidest of routines. To assume the serene continuation of routines may prove an accurate prediction. But to assume that routines *must* continue (to take them unreflectively for granted) is always intellectually misleading. It is, to echo a familiar post-Romantic complaint, to reify the routines: to treat them as though they were a stable and inert physical object, and not, as they always are, a continuation of purposeful human action, resting on habit, the perception of advantage, anxiety and hope, on a relatively steady balance between obtuseness and convenience. In contrast to the French Revolution, many political routines before and since have been steady and well entrenched.

But it is fair to say that those who are most familiar, and most at home, with them have never been assured of understanding just why this should have proved so.

It is unlikely that professional students of politics (who have less at stake in the outcomes) often understand the dynamics of routine politics as well as its more adept practitioners. But they have more to gain (and usually nothing to lose) from viewing these routines from the outside as well as from within: from trying to pin down just what their conditions of existence are, and just what could or may transform these, or even subvert them entirely. It is even possible to hope that this externality of perspective may give them some comparative advantage from a strictly practical point of view. (From most practical points of view the comparative advantage of the practitioner here must be overwhelming. But from other practical points of view the advantage might to some degree be reversed. An instructive example to consider here might be the decision of a great multinational oil company on how to dispose of a huge, now obsolete and potentially highly polluting oil-extraction platform.)

In the late twentieth century, it seems reasonably clear, the balance of advantage is shifting quite insistently, even in the politics of the United Kingdom, from the world of Anthony Trollope's nineteenth-century novels, with their focus on Parliament and the great country houses, to the world of the World Trade Organization, an expanding post-Cold War NATO alliance, Brussels and Strasbourg, NAFTA, the Pacific Rim, the global currency markets. In Westminster and Whitehall themselves, the routines may often appear not to have shifted nearly far enough. But the forces which play on the activities of career politicians and high civil servants now very evidently derive from an endless variety of sources, most of them brusquely external to this little world and many of them emanating from very far away. No one of comparable intelligence could write today either of its present denizens or of their repertoire of responses with quite the ironic complicity which Trollope sustained. It is not that politics has become less petty in the interim. (Very far from it.) It is simply that the world which politicians volunteer to handle on our behalf has widened inexorably, and that all our lives from now on will be rather obviously in jeopardy within it.

HISTORY, ETHICS AND PRACTICE

If we ask what the professional study of politics can do to help us to grasp this jeopardy more accurately – what it means for us, and what we can hope to do about it – we need to consider the capacities of political study to furnish us with several different sorts of understanding. One conventional way of dividing these is to distinguish them into historical (explanation of how we have reached our present position and what this position now is), ethical (what we should value, and how valuing it should lead us in general to act), and practical (what sorts of policies we should favour in our rulers, and what courses of action we should seriously contemplate for ourselves in particular). We plainly need these three varieties of understanding, and each, to some degree, by appropriate intellectual effort, can be secured and made available to those who want it.

But this is too formal and passive a division of tasks to be at all directive in practice. It is more a format within which to register such political understanding as we do contrive to amass than a guide to how to search for such understanding in the first place. It conforms too comfortably to the conventional focus on routine politics, and is likely to squander the advantages of a more external approach for the less habituated, and hence more open-minded. For as long as it holds up, routine politics everywhere always is a tight little world, dominated by those who live largely for and off it; and the vastly greater range of lives on which it bears (often so painfully) have little steady capacity to modify it to their own prospectively very different conveniences.

This is why a focus on political elites is always politically instructive, even where the relations of power and responsibility between them and those who suffer (or benefit) at their hands are at their ugliest and most perturbing. It is just as much to the point where the political outcome takes the form of mass slaughter (as in

Burundi (Lemarchand 1996) or Bosnia) as it is where all that is at stake is the tenure of the leadership of a British Conservative government. But genocide is the polar opposite to routine politics: a dissolution of all the routines of shared social life. It would be hysterical (even paranoid) to see the potentiality for genocide lurking permanently beneath the surface of routine politics everywhere. But it would be less silly to do so than to be astonished that anything so ugly should ever disfigure our world. What good reason do we have to think of it as *our* world anyway, except by accident of temporary occupation and all too egoistic and naive appropriative effort? (Cf. Locke 1988; Dunn 1969; Runciman 1998.) Hobbes, we should remember, saw something very similar lurking permanently beneath this surface (Hobbes 1983 and 1991). No one in the three and half centuries since he wrote has proved a less silly interpreter of what politics really is, of what we can hope from it and what we must continue to fear. We must certainly seek to supplement his bleak picture, but who today really still has the gall to pretend to be able to replace it?

There is every reason (for us) to start from where and what we are. For most of those of us who live in the modern republics, this means starting by attempting to grasp what is really going on in their now rather well-established routine politics, and in those of our own state more particularly. But there is no reason whatever (no epistemic, or even practical, ground) to take these routines for granted. Instead, we need to see them from a very different angle: not as serenely and effortlessly reproducing themselves, from manifest desert or efficacy, or sheer force of habit, but as swamped increasingly by the irruptions of a vastly wider, and sometimes very turbulent, world beyond them. The point of doing so is not principally one of spiritual edification: replacing a focus on the habitual, the familiar and the comfortable with one on the disruptive, the alien and the frankly terrifying. Rather, it is epistemic and political: to give us a better sense of the world we really do live in, and of how we can reasonably hope to learn to cope with it better. Better will not necessarily mean more comfortingly. Understanding, as Max Weber pointed out a full century ago, may precisely mean abandoning certain sorts of hope (Weber, Freiburg Inaugural Address 1895: Tribe (ed.) 1989, 197).

This approach has its own hazards. (There are no risk-free options.) Humankind, as T. S. Eliot pointed out, cannot stand very much reality. What they cannot stand, they can be confidently expected to resist apprehending. It is an approach, we must remember, which Hobbes advised emphatically against. But Hobbes did not live in a modern republic, a republic in which it is always everyone's to reason why. He did not believe that such republics can have well-established routines: that they could create themselves and expect to last for centuries. (At the time, this was an eminently reasonable belief, though not one, perhaps, universally shared.) We now know that they can create themselves, and may last a very long time. We know that they are possible. We know of no better and more reliable mode of political organization within the modern capitalist world. For the imaginable future, our best option is to try to learn how to make them go as well as they can.

The professional study of politics has not been wholly obtuse to these considerations. One major genre of political analysis, international political economy (Gilpin 1987; Keohane 1984; cf. Brenner 1998), focuses precisely on the dynamics of the global economy, on the political mediations which sustain or impede these, and on the immediate impact of these dynamics on domestic governmental efforts and interest-group responses. Another, and somehat older, genre of international relations continues to focus extensively on problems of inter-state security and their handling. These two, taken together, supplement a focus on domestic routine politics of the modern republic, and do so in a well-institutionalized and practically reasonable division of professional labour. This, in the broadest outline, is how the routine understanding of the routine politics of our world is divided up, and how it works.

What falls outside that division is a motley array. It consists either of a string of anomalies or historical relicts (Saudi Arabia, Lichtenstein), or of a dismayingly broad swathe of territories in which little which could pass for publicly identifiable routines has been successfully established, and nothing which could be mistaken for a modern republic now exists, or of a distinctly smaller range of territories (pored over principally until recently by appreciative students of international political economy) which did appear, at least for a time, to have discovered how to handle the dynamics of the world economy, without submitting to the indignities of democratic scrutiny. It is analytically indefensible to lump these very disparate cases together as anomalous or pathological. It is also plainly culturally offensive to do so, especially to the set of states which then appeared to be coping more effectively with the dynamics of the world economy than most (or even any) of the modern republics. But, pathological or not, it is far from clear how to incorporate all (or any) of these into a common framework of understanding with their modern republican counterparts. (In the 1950s and early 1960s, at least for a range of North American political scientists (Apter 1963; Almond and Coleman (eds) 1960), matters temporarily seemed clearer. What was occurring over most of the world in all its variety, if at very different speeds, was modernization. The rest of it was becoming like us. Today, this seems unlikely, though just how unlikely remains controversial: Fukuyama 1992; Huntington 1997.) The task for the present, one which should unite professionals with amateurs and political practitioners, is to grasp just what this motley array of historical expedients has in common, and what has led it to be differentiated as it is: to recreate a common framework of understanding for a world which we are now compelled to share.

There are some obvious strategic questions for this framework of understanding to address. Why are there so many modern republics today? Why are those there are so widely felt by their ordinary citizens and state elites to be increasingly unsuccessful at present at handling the problems of their own populations (Dunn (ed.) 1995; Nye 1997)? How far is it really true that they are indeed increasingly unsuccessful at doing so? Is the perception that they are increasingly unsuccessful itself mainly a product of greater emancipation (or at least of impaired subjection) on the part of many of their subjects? (Women, for a start.) Why does the modern republic not work at all (why does it prove simply unsustainable) in so much of the world? What, if anything, works better (and by what criteria) in the settings where it cannot be sustained?

CONCEPTS AND CAUSAL JUDGMENT

In this common framework of understanding, there need to be at least two components: conceptual elements (instruments for potential understanding) and ambitious but relatively concrete causal judgment about politics. A supposedly scientific political science is a quest for the latter by means of the former. It attributes its extremely modest success (where it cares to acknowledge this at all) to some remediable degree of error in its selection or identification of the former. By now, however, it is hard to resist the conclusion that this way of seeing the matter is simply a mistake. The relatively concrete causal judgments can to some degree be tested by analytical instruments. But they cannot be generated by applying these. To be generated at all, they require a recklessness in the face of experience, not a practised docility. They cannot be fully domesticated.

The conceptual instruments, too, are not condensed instances of established understanding, in the way which scientific theories sometimes appear to those who are not scientists. Rather, they are devices through which such understanding may (or may not) be reached by those who seek it. They guarantee nothing whatever. Indeed, nothing within the domain of politics *guarantees* that any of it will ever be accurately understood. The natural sciences taunt seekers for political understanding with a cruel contrast: a zone of human experience where powerful and clearly cumulative understanding has been generated, and plainly will, for the reasonably near future, go on being so. There is something unmistakably instructive about this contrast. (This, for whatever reasons, is something truly different.) What the contrast is not and cannot be, however, is a source of directives on how to replicate the same degree of understanding in the very different zone of politics.

In that zone, we must do it with our bare minds, or not at all.

True, these minds have been formed in very complicated ways, which we still understand very poorly indeed. They draw on resources, as well as face obstacles, of which we still have barely a glimmering. Viewed soberly, each of them is a stunningly intricate genetic, cultural, historical, social and economic product: also a triumph of human power and will, in no way to be scorned. In the face of politics, however, none of them can ever be a vector of any self-guaranteeing cognitive procedure. In understanding politics, as in living a life, we are all of us, for all the plenitude of human effort and insight on which we may draw, always in the end on our own. There is an epistemic analogue here to the dialogue between Communitarians and Liberals on how we can hope to live well together: a dialogue about how we can hope to *know* how to live well together. It is not a technical puzzle, with a potential technical answer (though it encompasses technical puzzles, and therefore potentially technical answers, in some profusion). Rather, it is an existential challenge, to which there can be more or less felicitous existential responses.

Political scientists (even the most pusillanimous among them) cannot honourably refrain from making relatively ambitious causal judgments about politics. They must, and no doubt in general do, attempt such judgments as bravely as they dare, and as intelligently and imaginatively as they can. All of them are always at the mercy of their own pasts and of the ineluctable parochialisms of the milieu within which they live and work. To attempt such judgments is epistemically audacious. On a severe assessment, it even requires a degree of effrontery. (One of the deepest and most honest of such assessments is still given in John Locke's great *Essay Concerning Human Understanding*: Locke 1975; Dunn 1969; Ayers 1990.) Yet, if we want political understanding, we have no alternative but to make them as best we can. They are what political understanding ultimately consists of. There is nothing solider or more reassuring beneath them (only, if anything, the conceptually utterly irrelevant laws of nature). There is nothing sharper, or more elegant and imposing, above them, from which they can be painstakingly and precisely derived. In all their exposure, they are all we have, and, as far as we can now tell, all we can ever hope to have. They are where anyone who wants to understand politics must always begin.

The picture of political understanding which I wish to offer – of what it *consists* in – has just these two components: a modest set of conceptual elements, and an endless series of utterly exposed causal judgments. The former can help to order and clarify the latter. But nothing can substitute for the latter; and nothing external to them can generate or secure them. This is inordinately abstract, however, and shows us nothing at all about what political understanding is really like. To see more clearly what it is like, we need to turn back to the routine politics of an in some ways quite effectively (if always precariously) rationalized world (the world about which Max Weber was attempting to think, and Jürgen Habermas in our own day, so much less forthcomingly). If there were no political routines, there would be little practical hope of political understanding: only radical insecurity, and a wholly rational fear, reaching all the way out. All we could ever hope to understand with any accuracy would be the grim side of Hobbes's message. His confident remedy – the irresistible rationality of establishing such routines with a capacity to sustain and protect themselves – would be a hopeless delusion. (Hobbes himself, of course, vacillated over the question of whether it really was a delusion, and it remains controversial how far he ever managed to suspend his disbelief: Skinner 1996.) It is from pattern and recurrence that we begin to get our bearings in the universe, and to judge, however recklessly, what we can reasonably expect for the future, what we must continue for the present to fear, and what it may make sense to hope for. (This, very loosely speaking, was also where Aristotle began: Lear 1988.)

It is not, of course, the case that modern republics (even well-institutionalized modern republics) have an abundance of routines, while other contemporary polities do not. Still less is it true that the former belong in a single clear and causally determinate category, while the latter belong in another category, united only in causal indeterminacy. But, if political understanding is what we want, there is, for all the post-modern disarray and handwringing of cultivated circles within the modern republics, a clear elective affinity between this state form and the opportunity to acquire such understanding: not merely to look for it frankly, but to accumulate, develop, clarify and deepen it. Seen unsympathetically from the outside, American political science is in some ways ludicrously parochial. But it is also, for all its limitations, probably the largest, most densely populated and most protractedly sustained practical quest for political understanding in human history thus far. The parochialism has naturally qualified its success, especially beyond its own homeland. But it would be silly, as well as churlish, to overlook the scale and pertinacity of the quest. The American polity began, as Madison and Hamilton sought to think it through, in a remarkably vigorous and courageous quest for political understanding (Madison and Hamilton 1961). If it has seldom (or perhaps never) reached the same heights since, it has also never quite abandoned the search. In the last three-quarters of a century, more particularly, it has routinized the quest itself on a bewildering scale, seeking not merely to advance a myriad of professional careers, but also to extend and deepen a civic experience and commitment through the extension of political understanding itself. Unsurprisingly this has not altogether worked. To understand more in politics is often to forgive even less. In the less deeply democratic cultures of Britain or France, by contrast, the state has always had an edgier and more ungracious attitude to any wider diffusion of political understanding (cf. Farr 1995; Farr, Dryzek and Leonard (eds) 1995; Farr and Seidelman (eds) 1993, with Collini, Winch and Burrow 1983).

In this perspective, the role of political science within the modern republics looks suspiciously like a would-be 'science' of democracy (cf. Taylor 1985, cap.2): an introverted and distorted espousal of some of their cherished democratic practices. It cries out for complements: a clear-sighted and appropriately discomfiting putative 'science' of tyranny, or at any rate of a well-ordered and economically efficacious police state, a richly appreciative 'science' of unbridled corruption (Bayart 1993) or relentless criminality (Gambetta 1993). But today (unlike, perhaps, in sixteenth-century

Florence) even such complements draw much of their force from the opportunities open to, and perhaps even the cultural capabilities nurtured within, the habitat of this would-be science of democracy (or, at any rate, of its privileged heartlands, the well-institutionalized modern republics themselves). The modern republic is an Enlightenment idea (Fontana (ed.) 1994), and will not readily abandon its presumption of a privileged relationship to knowing or having the daring to know (Kant 1971, 54–60): of not being condemned to obscurantism in the first instance.

But the prudential force of grounding political understanding today on the routine politics of the modern republic does not depend on this perhaps over-allegiant and promiscuously generous way of seeing its routines. It rests simply on the recognition that these routines are the most extensively and accurately recorded instances of political behaviour we are likely to have available to us, and that they bear particularly directly and obviously on our own interests. We could scarcely have equally good reasons for focusing our attention principally elsewhere. Or rather, we could have such reasons, if and only if there was a body of understanding of a deeper and more serene kind which simply happened to derive from and focus upon quite different experiences elsewhere: a reservoir of esoteric knowledge which somehow trumped understanding which issued from our own opportunities and capacities to observe and judge. To the suspicious, however unjustly, something of the kind appears to be virtually the stock in trade of admirers of the late Leo Strauss. But a more charitable (and plausible) interpretation would view this, presumably, less as a potential substitute for contemporary causal judgments about politics than as a different set of conceptual elements for articulating such judgments, once they have been made.

At the heart of the politics of the modern republic there is a disturbing question. (Or is it perhaps just an endless struggle?) Not merely does this form of regime pride itself somewhat effusively on the opportunity it gives its denizens to think freely for themselves and speak freely to one another. Not merely have its most searching and sympathetic interpreters and advocates, from

Immanuel Kant in eighteenth-century Prussia to Jürgen Habermas in today's Federal Republic, always seen the quest for understanding, the promise of speaking clearly and freely together and the courage to know as its central mission. Any sanguine account of its prospects today or in future still depends on the judgment that it does indeed succeed in fostering and deepening political understanding: that its routine processes continuously generate, and even deepen, such understanding. (It is easier, naturally, to believe in the steady genesis than in any inbuilt tendency to deepening.)

Having rejected mystification so flamboyantly in the first instance, it has always been acutely vulnerable to the charge that in some way or other it suppresses, occludes and obliterates understanding, still more that it needs to do so in order to survive. Its great enemies have always understood this all too well: Edmund Burke, Joseph de Maistre, Lenin, after his fashion Adolf Hitler. There is very much at stake when we peer inside this now so familiar form of life. Is this a way of living together grounded ineluctably on vanity, deception and mendacity? Or is it (can it ever be) a space of freedom and light and well-considered practical activity, a comfortable and fitting home for the industrious and rational? And if it is, or even ever could be, the latter, what exactly does that signify for the less honest, the less industrious and the less rational?

Contemporary political scientists do not usually formulate their political intuitions with this degree of crudity or frankness. (How wise they are, you may think; or, perhaps, what cowards they are.) The less alert, indeed, may not even pause to wonder what causal role understanding or misunderstanding is playing in the routines which they study. But it would be unnatural for the more sensitive and attentive not to focus, sooner or later, on some aspect of this question. As it extends through time, accordingly, political science as a professional activity does not merely furnish employment on a substantial scale and occupy the time of many recipients of higher education, it also monitors, more or less discerningly, the political health or otherwise of the societies in which it is practised.

SOVEREIGN POPULAR MISJUDGMENT?

What is most distinctive about the modern republic is the degree to which it diffuses political responsibility. As its critics have been at pains to insist, this differs greatly from the the degree to which it diffuses power. But it has some implications for how power is in fact diffused, and may well have some too for what power in fact consists in: for what, among the population in question, it really is and means. On a cynical view, a political 'science' of democracy concerns itself with voters, their tastes and hopes and fantasies, because democracy, the official ideology of such republics, allots to voters an honorific but essentially illusory efficacy. But a less hasty judgment must recognize that that efficacy cannot be in any sense *aggregatively* inconsequential, since it determines at intervals just who can exercise the formal powers of government, and decide the content of legislation, and deploy the apparatus for enforcing that legislation in practice.

One great issue about the routine politics of these societies is always just what constraints the tastes and hopes and fantasies of their electorates, expressed through the institutional forms to hand at the time, do in fact place on how they can be governed, and what their laws are to be. A second great issue, intersecting with the first, is just what institutional forms really are to hand at the time: robustly present, being coaxed slowly into existence, or steadily fading away. The tastes, hopes and fantasies of the electorate, and the institutional forms through which these can hope to find expression, each have their own history. What explains their content at any time is always that history: the past from which they have emerged, however bumpily. But the two histories do not mesh neatly with one another; and neither presents a clear and undistorted image of the other. This is partly because the institutional forms are of several different kinds: legislative, executive, judicial, administrative, putatively representative, lobbies of interest or opinion. It is also because even those which must claim to be most intimately aligned with the tastes, hopes and fantasies of the citizenry are altogether denser than the judgments and sentiments on whose behalf they claim to act. They must live out their political lives in a more immediately obstructed space, and are inevitably shaped and reshaped by the imperatives of conflict and co-operation within that space.

A third great issue, underlying but also overarching the other two, is just what effects the intersection of these two causalities is actually having on the habitats within which each subsists: the economies and ecologies of the territories which they occupy. This is where the question of understanding becomes decisive. The histories of popular political perception and sentiments, and of institutionalized political conflict and co-operation go their own ways, often in serene incomprehension of what they are bringing about: the Second World War, the Cold War, global warming. But what they mean always turns in the end on what they are in fact bringing about: on their cumulative consequences.

It is easy for a narrowly professional political science of 'democracy' to over-domesticate itself. It can settle comfortably for a study of institutional forms and their current dynamics. It can bring in the citizenry at large only as and when the latter insist on intruding, and largely therefore as the bearers or withholders of votes. It can concern itself with their tastes and hopes and fantasies (a treacherous and elusive subject matter at the best of times) only as these can be shown at work in the giving or withholding of their electoral support. It can consign to others (economists, ecologists, cultural critics of self-consciously refined sensibility) the task of assessing the consequences of the ways in which these institutional forms, for the present, operate.

This is undeniably an understanding of politics (an interpretation of what it is and means). But it is not the understanding of politics which the modern republic requires. It is not, because it makes no attempt to bring home to the citizens at large the current content of their responsibilities, or the stake they have in how professional politics happens to be going. To furnish the modern republic with the understanding of politics which it needs, the most allegiant would-be 'science' of democracy must set its sights dramatically higher. It must ask, and attempt to answer, questions which cannot readily be either domesticated or professionalized.

It must try to survey and bring into focus an extraordinarily complicated and extensive skein of relations, which now stretches across the surface of the globe and takes in a bewildering variety of entities. A political understanding of the modern republic today must begin from the most conventional and obvious features of its politics. But it must reach out from these very far indeed: into the politics of very different times and places, and utterly different types of political unit, and into very many other domains which are in no sense overtly political at all. (What could be less political than the current plant stock of the Amazon jungle? What could be more political?) It can never comfortably sign off, never know that it has reached quite far enough.

PART III

9

Starting Again

The Components of Politics

At any point in its history, on this understanding, politics always has at least three constitutive components: the beliefs and sentiments of a given population, the institutional forms through which that population can (and, for the time, largely must) act, if it is to seek to realize its less personal purposes, and the cumulative consequences of the actions (individual, group or collective) which its members choose to perform. The relation between these components is always somewhat opaque; and the relation between intention and consequence, at any level from the single individual to the sovereign state, or the population of the globe as a whole, is always potentially unwelcome. Each component has a conceptually distinct history of its own, though all also affect one another to varying degrees throughout. Each can go well or badly. When any of the three goes well enough, it can come very close to justifying itself, vindicating a claim to be respected and protected for what it simply is. Any, too, can go extremely badly – show itself to be, for the present, deeply pathological and utterly beyond defence, even, at the limit, radically evil.

If actions had only intended consequences, and if institutions were frictionless transmission devices for conveying agency from individuals or groups to its intended destination (for securing the consequences at which they aim), political understanding could have a much simpler structure; and political causality would be far less opaque. The beliefs and sentiments of the population would be expressed accurately and faithfully through its institutions, and would issue in the consequences at which, on balance, they aimed. (Depending on the beliefs and sentiments in question, this might not be particularly encouraging. But it should in practice be relatively easy to understand, and must, *ex hypothesi*, be clearly intelligible in principle.) Since, however, actions characteristically have at least as many and important unintended as intended consequences, and since institutions are also very far from having only the type of consequence which their designers, builders or operators envisage, any understanding of politics needs to relate these three components systematically to one another, and can never confidently presume that the relations which it identifies between them will prove clear, stable or reassuring.

WHO NEEDS POLITICAL SCIENCE?

The relation between these three components gives the basic structure of political understanding. It picks out politics as a relatively distinct subject matter, varyingly tinged with coercion. But it does not define the content of political understanding. What defines that content is the relation between this subject matter and the purposes of those who wish to understand it. Political understanding, accordingly, is as various as the purposes of those who wish to obtain it; and this variety is an epistemic, and not merely a natural or historical, property of it. Actually existing human understandings of politics, of course, vary more simply and directly with the characteristics of those whose understandings they are. They are historically distinct and humanly embodied bits of the history of nature. A very large proportion of them will always consist of beliefs which are at least partially false. But political understanding, as an epistemic venture, cannot in itself consist of false beliefs at all, even if the purposes of the particular human beings who seek it are virtually certain to issue extensively from beliefs which are in fact false. The purposes themselves may well include an active determination to avoid acknowledging discomfiting truths. But the understanding which is being sought, however cramped or spiritually crippled its seeker happens to be, is always sought *as* true – as undeceptive and causally adequate.

The goal is to grasp what is occurring, and why, and to see how it bears on the purposes of those who seek it, whatever their purposes happen to be. Human beings at large produce, by their interaction with one another, a field of political causality, which any one of them at any moment might have good reason to wish to understand. This field is the subject matter of political understanding (its target). At some logically elusive level, human beings at large share an epistemic interest in grasping this causal field. (Certainly as much so as they share such an interest in understanding any other aspects of natural causality.) If there is, or could be, an absolute conception of reality (Williams 1978), this field would form part of it, and would be optimally comprehended within it. Political science as a profession might even volunteer (as it sometimes has) to supply its optimal comprehension.

Yet even if we confine our attention to the question of what is occurring and why, human purposes still play a prominent role within the subject matter of politics. Beliefs and sentiments lie behind these purposes, and prompt (and enable) their human bearers to form, discover, choose or adopt them. Existing institutions respond, or fail to respond, to them; and potential consequences issue, or fail to issue, from their active pursuit. The responsiveness (or otherwise) of institutions, and the attainment, or failure to attain, intended consequences in turn react back upon these purposes, chastening or emboldening them. The purposes themselves, too, it is safe to assume, have themselves issued earlier, at least in part, from beliefs about the historical capacity or incapacity of the population as a whole to secure or avoid particular types of consequences (the placing of women or men on the moon or at the end of a lengthy railway line, the provision of adequate nutrition and clean water to all human infants, the alleviation of pain, the eradication of lethal diseases, the destruction of the ozone layer, the warming or cooling of the globe).

Even a purely external view of the subject matter of politics as a single closed causal system must reckon constantly with causal chains in which the forming and modification of human purposes is strategically vital. There is nothing epistemically aberrant or flippant in inquiring how political causality bears upon our own purposes, and little epistemic promise in any conception of the subject matter of politics in which the bearing of apparent causality on current purpose or current purpose on real causality is firmly disregarded.

PURPOSE-RELATIVITY

We have, then, no reason to apologize for seeking political understanding for our own purposes, and no grounds for epistemic regret (or fear) that such a quest must contaminate or falsify whatever understanding we do secure. No extra-epistemic human purpose can be, in itself, an aid to understanding politics. But it is simply mistaken to think of such purposes as a kind of general obstacle to political understanding.

Political understanding is never simply constituted by historically given human purposes; but, to be determinate at all, it must always be purpose-relative. What bars it from being simply constituted by extra-epistemic purposes is the fact that it has a pre-given subject matter, which constrains all valid answers to the questions about it which humans may come to pose, but cannot, of itself, decide what any of those questions are to be.

The purpose-relativity of political understanding is easiest to see clearly where the purposes in question are most peremptory – in face of the question 'What is to be done?', and where it is clear that something drastic does need to be done. An assessment of the politics of anywhere which was adequate to the purposes of Saddam Hussein, for example, would never be one which was also adequate to my (or your) purposes (Al-Khalil 1990; Makiya 1993). The two might overlap in subject matter at some points (under what conditions he might be overthrown, by whom and with what prospective consequences in the short or medium term for most of his surviving subjects). But they would face in such different directions and dwell on such radically diverging schedules of issues that it would be absurd to think of them as cognitive disagreements about a common subject matter.

That purpose-relativity is appreciably less clear where the sole question under active consideration at least appears to be: 'What is occurring, and why is it occurring?' This is a question which always could be asked out of moderately idle curiosity, as many political scientists, political journalists, political historians and even newspaper readers often do ask it, and not a few of the former even pride themselves on doing. The contrast at issue here is that between moderately idle curiosity and radically idle curiosity (or blank indifference) – between desultory purpose and no purpose at all.

What if a political scientist chose to study a political phenomenon about which they happened to feel radically indifferent, for the good reason that they correctly supposed it of no political importance whatever: to be utterly politically insignificant? This would be an odd, but not a self-contradictory, choice. There is nothing logically incoherent about it. Real living political scientists, you may even judge, have at times come very close to making it. (Journalists, by contrast, being more immediately constrained by the need for an audience, or even historians, with their greater susceptibility to literary embarrassment, naturally tend to keep a safer distance.) The question which needs to be pressed is whether such a choice is naturally possible, whether any particular human being could ever quite make it: not whether it is logically coherent (which it plainly is), or whether it is intellectually fetching (which it perhaps isn't), but whether it is even causally coherent.

This I very much doubt. Political scientists certainly always could, and sometimes do, choose their research interests more for their methodological tractability than for their supposed political importance. They might care little enough about the consequences of politics for others, or be sufficiently radically despondent about those consequences, to choose their research interests without the slightest regard for what is at stake in politics. What is altogether less plausible is that they could do so in utter disregard of all the beliefs and sentiments of all their human fellows, or of the causal properties of every institution through which their own lives are organized. The most inhuman of political scientists has a career to pursue or a job to hold down, just like the most passionately committed. In pursuing that career, or even remaining in gainful employment, she or he must keep a wary eye on the beliefs and sentiments of many in the vicinity, and on the institutional constraints and opportunities which surround them. Between them, these will certainly provide grounds for focusing on some topics and areas of activity rather than others. The purpose-relativity may be confused, murky and, insofar as it is openly acknowledged, in pretty poor faith. But it will always, on sufficiently careful inspection, prove to be there. The most psychopathic of political scientists will always in the end have to lay off in respect of the perceptions, judgments, feelings and purposes of adjacent human beings. When you study politics, you can push human purposes very much to the margins of the imaginative field you choose to attend to; but, however far you push them, you cannot readily choose that field for no human reason whatsoever. (Even the *desire* so to choose it would turn out, on closer inspection, to be a discernibly human reason.) If you do your best to expel human purpose from political science with a pitchfork, it will still keep creeping back in.

It is at first sight plausible that it is easier to understand accurately where you do not much mind what your understanding implies for anything about which you care. It is less hard for some to believe what they keenly wish than what they direly fear. (Others, perhaps, find the reverse.) If wish-fulfilment (or fear-fulfilment) are real and widespread psychological phenomena, they may have strong implications for heuristics (for good or bad approaches to finding out what is the case). But they certainly do not imply that radical indifference is a precondition for comprehension. Indeed, unless wish-fulfilment and fear-fulfilment, between them, are more widespread and urgent than any compensating cognitive benefits which flow from the human propensity for interest in one another, there is no reason to suppose radical indifference even an aid in finding out what is the case. Some human purposes plainly inhibit political understanding. But those which inhibit it most severely bear more directly and fiercely on the prospects that particular lines of inquiry will be prosecuted with sincerity and urgency than on the prospects for carrying them through to a successful conclusion, once they are indeed undertaken. Many sorts of human purposes may certainly deter political inquiry. Some may, and very often do, obstruct it purposefully from the outside. What there is no reason whatever to suppose is that human purposes as such have any general tendency to obstruct it from the inside, once it is genuinely in train.

WHO CAN AFFORD POLITICAL SCIENCE?

A more likely (and equally perturbing) possibility is that political understanding, once it has been secured, will often (or perhaps always) corrode prior human purposes. Why might this be so? One possible answer is simple enough. Gratuitous hope plays a large causal role throughout human life, in child, adult and dotard, in the field of economics (Keynes assures us), as in that of politics. Insofar as we understand politics, we are likely to find (as Max Weber insisted: *Politics as a Vocation*: Weber 1948, 77–128) that many of the hopes which we bring to it are gratuitous. The measure of our comprehension may be precisely the degree to which we come to recognize ourselves forced to abandon them. *Tout comprendre c'est tout pardonner* is a discouraging maxim in personal life, since it threatens to deny us the option of combining the advantages of comprehension with the comforts of resentment (Strawson 1968). Its political extension (to, for example, the case of the Nazi regime) is, if anything, even less enticing than its application in private life. If we understand politics as a given field of ongoing causality – as what is simply going on, and why – it is easy to come to see it as virtually impermeable to our purposes, a closed and effectively self-sustaining causal system, over against our own ineffectual wills. A detached understanding of the political world has at least an elective affinity with fatalism: both with the causal judgment that the vast majority of individual human beings almost all the time are pre-condemned to political ineffectuality (that any political purposes that they are unwise enough to exert themselves to realize are foredoomed to frustration), and with the attitude, passive resignation, which that judgment readily fosters. Whatever will be will be (and whatever won't, won't); and there is effectively nothing we can do about it.

Gratuitous hope is no occasion for epistemic congratulation. But too little hope makes painful inroads into anyone's life. The pruning of hope by political comprehension sounds like a steady epistemic advance, and sometimes, and in detail, must plainly be of great human benefit. But how can we be sure that we will not cut too far, and wound the very lives which we wish to protect and foster? The point of insisting on the purpose-relativity of political understanding is to cut this fear down to size, and show us how to demarcate fantasy from comprehension within it. Insofar as we learn to understand politics, we need not expect to enjoy the experience. Some of what we learn is certain to be terrible news. But, for any given human individual, the world of politics directly encountered, however much it may endanger their physical survival, cannot be an intrinsic threat to their identity. It may threaten, brutalize or even kill them; but it cannot cancel their purposes (contrast George Orwell's *1984*: Orwell 1954), still less replace these with purposes of its own – this last, of course, not necessarily for want of trying. What it shows, at any point, is the limits of fatality, the edges to their freedom as agents, what they can or cannot hope to become or bring about, what their powers truly are. The true terrors of fatality lie not outside in the world within which we live, but inside us: not in our stars, but in our selves. Comprehending these, abandoning gratuitous hopes about them, may well be painful. It may even unhinge us. But it would be a very odd human being who could be unhinged merely by coming to understand politics. What political comprehension is far more likely to do, however, is to diminish political optimism. It is all but certain to lower our expectations of the chances of getting our very own political way and to lessen our estimate of the social or economic (let alone the spiritual) benefits that are likely to follow, if we do do so. If we understand how the political world now is, and why it is as it is, we cannot readily suppose that, at most times and places, it can be altered greatly for better or worse by anything which we ourselves might do, and do, not just personally, but even in active co-operation with very many of our fellows. Any serious attempt to understand politics must draw our attention insistently to the causal importance of existing institutions and habits, and to the logical obstacles to co-ordinating either the interests or the actions of individual agents.

However salutary this may be in discouraging foolish or irresponsible activism, it is hard for it not also to discourage a good deal else. Perhaps not logically, but certainly psychologically, it favours passivity over activity, narrowing over broadening of sympathies, greed and egoism at the expense of generosity or practical concern for more or less distant others.

One way of seeing the huge swing to the right politically across the world in the period of the long downturn (Brenner 1998) is as the working through, in the perceptions, beliefs and sentiments of hundreds (even thousands) of millions of people, of a shift in economic and political judgment with just these (readily predictable) consequences. In this vision, understanding better and being corrupted go hand in hand. With the decisive triumph of capitalism over all the political forces which have had the nerve to stand in its way has come the loss of any real grasp of what that triumph was always bound to mean.

In itself this is hardly an attractive outcome. Does it mean that political comprehension is somehow in complicity with the very active organization of power which has constructed the world in which we now live: that to comprehend all politically must be to connive at all?

This might be a more searching question if there were any danger of our ever comprehending all. In face of our severely limited capacities to comprehend politics at all, it has more the flavour of a malicious joke.

Except for those who are now extremely rich (and still more for those who have been extremely rich throughout it) the last twenty-five years of twentieth-century world politics have on the whole been pretty dismaying: a low dishonest quarter of a century. They have contained some emphatic political advances, above all the collapse of the Soviet empire and the effective abandonment of the global promises of Marxism–Leninism (Brown 1996). (Also some more subterranean shifts, as in gender perceptions and practices, which are hard to assess consequentially as yet but just *might*, in the long run, prove even more emphatic advances.) But they have also underlined the formidable power of capitalist economic organization to impose its conveniences on the huge variety of institutional expedients which human beings have devised in order to bring their sense of form, decency and justice to bear on its outcomes.

Where these institutions already were, or could readily learn how to become, effective servants of these conveniences they have drawn strength from this steady imposition. Where they have had no alternative but to fight back every inch of the way, they have largely been crushed. (The world of organized labour, familiarly, has always been poised somewhat opaquely between these two options.)

A world at last fit for capitalism will be a world in which those whose talents, good fortune and energy equip them to trade profitably profit handsomely, irrespective of where they happen to have been born. It will be a world in which property rights are highly secure, but other human claims have force only insofar as they fit comfortably with the security of property rights. In this sense, it will be a world of increasingly pure power, where the strong take what they can get and the weak endure what they have to (Thucydides 1919–23, Bk V, lxxxix: vol. 3, 158–9).

In some ways the features which have disfigured capitalism throughout its history are bound to appear even starker in a world made over in its image. Property requires political protection. But there cannot be political protection without political power; and where is political power to be drawn from? States can choose to protect property. But they can also choose to confiscate it. (So too, still more obviously, private protection agencies operating for their own profit: Gambetta 1993; cf. Nozick 1975.) In autocracies, the potential confiscator would be the autocrat. But in democracies, notoriously, it must be the demos itself. Over the last twenty-five years of the twentieth century capital has had some success in persuading the demos to feel less confiscatory towards property, or more devout about its standing. But this success, whether achieved by intimidation, mystification or rational persuasion over the content of their own interests, can scarcely be relied upon where their own experience increasingly demonstrates that they have no stake in defending property rights as these currently exist.

Even if the electorates of the OECD countries do not simply turn back the clock and revert to or persist in voting for (presumptively misguided) social democratic confiscation, they are most unlikely to continue to vote docilely as capital (they are assured) is telling them. If more voters are doing better than are doing worse, as the decades go by, that will be one thing. But there is nothing in the logic of a fully capitalist world to ensure that more voters in a country which is already wealthy will continue to do better than will not (cf. Brenner 1998). Already the workforces of the wealthier countries split disconcertingly into those who can individually take very good care of themselves on the market (because their tradeable powers can command a high price), those who can hold their own only because they belong to surviving units of collective action with a threat advantage out of all proportion to the value of individual members' labour, and those who are already going under, because no one would choose to pay much for their labour (cf. Wood 1994).

Those who can take very good care of themselves on the market plainly share an interest in protecting that market and what they can win from it. Those who can hold their own only by virtue of their membership of surviving units of collective action have at least as firm an interest in protecting the latter as they do in defending (or intensifying) the market. Those who are already going under have no clear interest in defending either the market or the property which it distributes, apart from the side-payments which the market's winners, or their own state, choose to pay out in mitigation. Social democratic parties, for much of the twentieth century, built (or aspired to build) welfare states in hope, or even confidence. But, insofar as the market's winners co-operated in this construction, they did so less in compulsive generosity than in prudent fear. The compression of welfare benefits, in explicit service of actual or potential winners on the market (for the scale in question see Esping-Andersen 1990; Pierson 1998), has been prompted less by aggravated meanness than by diminished fear. (Any noticeable increase in meanness – and there has perhaps been such an increase – is more a consequence than a cause of the compression.)

It will not be surprising if the fear (always in the end, Hobbes tells us (Hobbes 1991, cap. XIV, p. 99), the passion to be relied upon) revives. The distributive shape created by the market has never been one which most voters in a democratic state could be depended on to choose. As the capitalist world becomes ever more uncompromisingly international, the political task of securing an electoral majority for market outcomes in any particular state becomes ever more onerous. Capital has as little natural loyalty to territory as it docs to community. Where the local authority molests or impedes it, as Constant long ago pointed out (Constant 1988, 307–28), it is very apt to leave promptly for a more obliging domicile elsewhere.

The economic rationale for a fully capitalist world is to maximize the development of human productive powers and the exchanged value of what these powers produce. This yields a stronger case for consumers in the aggregate than it does for potential producers, or recipients of income, one by one. Where the numbers of producers fall sharply, and the incomes actually received by the majority (employed or disemployed) fall on average rather than rise, the economic rationale is unlikely to prove politically compelling. It is hard to imagine electorates welcoming such an outcome for any length of time. In democracies, what electorates consistently fail to welcome, and also mind about acutely, the state can hardly be expected to succeed in protecting. (But cf. Wilson 1997 for a telling contrast between the degree to which British and American political elites are compelled to defer to popular attitudes on methods for the control of crime against property.)

Looking for Political Understanding

In looking for political understanding, it is natural for us to look first for simple, clear conceptions with the widest practicable scope: for quick, cheap progress. But what we find on the whole, where we succeed in finding anything at all, is complicated, murky and often exceedingly local. The political choice between accepting and rejecting capitalism may seem clear and simple. But the better it is understood, the murkier and the more bafflingly complicated it is bound to turn out. The political history of socialism has centred on the hope that the political choice to accept or reject capitalism would, if only it was seen clearly enough (seen *correctly*), turn out to be clear, simple and virtually effortless. In itself this was a very natural hope; and for much of the intellectual history of socialism, it was also not a wholly unreasonable one. What is evident today, however, is that the more clearly and accurately (the more correctly) it is seen, the less clear, simple and humanly directive it will turn out to be (Dunn 1984(a); 1985). The startlingly rapid deflation of this simple hope has been of immense political importance; but it has also been intensely misleading.

Every epoch has its illusion. If socialism (democratic and otherwise) was the illusion of much of the twentieth century, the last quarter of that century replaced it with an illusion of its own, derived from very much the same sources: the illusion that a fully capitalist world might be chosen and rechosen indefinitely by the grateful consumers who populate it, acting individually and together, through all the institutional facilities open to them, to furnish it the protection which it will certainly continue to require. Even if this was a project of pure co-ordination (Lewis 1969), it would require singular felicity in communication and remarkable dependability in judgment to carry it through in practice. Since, all too obviously, it is more a problem of competitive strategy than a task of co-ordination (cf. Hardin 1995), the outcome can hardly fail to prove more ragged.

THE POLITICAL IMPLICATIONS OF THE TRIUMPH OF CAPITALISM

If the sole choice which we needed to make was the choice for or against a capitalist world, and if that choice itself was universally seen as both clear and simple, History might indeed have reached a kind of End. (One huge thing would have happened in history, as rationally incontestable as it was politically irresistible. To see this would be to accept it; and seeing it would in effect ride out, practically as well as epistemically, over all particular human purposes, since its recognition would be a precondition for pursuing any of these effectively in future.) As things are, however (cf. Chapters 6–8 above) the choice of what is to be done is as intricate, as differentiated and as baffling as it has ever been for human beings. The understanding of politics which each of us needs is as unmistakably purpose-relative as ever. History, we can be confident, is just beginning to get into its stride; and none of us can have the slightest idea of how far (let alone whither) it is going.

On its own terms a human world placed fully under the dominion of capital, with its full inventory of institutions serving the requirements of capital with fluency, precision and devotion, would be a single global public good (Olson 1965). The politics of the last quarter of the twentieth century has seen a drastic shift in this direction, and a deep imaginative impact of this vision of what is at stake in the construction and use of political power. What has driven this global shift, above all, has been the struggle to lay the ghost of socialism, to dissipate, supposedly for ever, the illusion that there is another and a better way. Insofar as the sole reason for presuming that another and better way existed was just that it would be good if one did, the loss of this illusion is no occasion for regret.

But with the illusion, for many, has gone the memory of what generated it in the first place, the formidably aversive experience for most human beings of living in a largely capitalist world. Perhaps there can be a way in which a fully capitalist world might be constructed, economically, politically, socially, as the best human world which truly is possible. But a species, patently susceptible to moral error, compulsively partial in judgment, historically situated within deeply conflicting structures of interest and baffled by the cognitive and practical challenges of collective action, will never see or experience a fully capitalist world in that light. If this were the verdict of Reason, Reason would never shine bright enough for all *our* purposes (Dunn 1989(b)). To the members of such a species, as they live their irremediably separate lives in one another's company and prepare to die alone, it will always seem an alien, profoundly untrustworthy and potentially deeply malign reality, a world in which they can never hope to be at home. Very many of their energies and endeavours are certain to go into the struggle, not to shore up and guarantee it, but to slip through its guard, elude its grasp, punish it for its massive indifference to their needs and feelings, even, if only they can, destroy it utterly.

In the short term, with the extraordinary dynamism of capitalist history, the political history of the world can seem to move (and even move in reality) dramatically in a single direction. For decades at a time, its friends or enemies can seem to sweep all before them. But the more accurately we understand the history which it has made and entered into, the more clearly will we come to recognize the permanence of the pressures in both directions, and the impossibility of lasting victory for either its friends or its enemies. If there proves to be a distant human future, this may well contain quite other options, and leave this ancient struggle and its narrow confines far behind. But, for the world in which you or I will live out all our lives and die alone, this is the setting of our politics (Hont 1995). This is what we must learn to comprehend, if we are to understand our fate and learn how to grasp the opportunities which are open to us. This is what is occurring, and what, for the moment at least, determines what can occur.

The basic capitalist dynamic constantly expands the range, scale and velocity of the consequences of capitalist production beyond the capacity of political institutions to recognize and bring under control their less welcome elements. Politics persistently lags economics, while being permanently required to sustain it. The trajectory from the Keynesian welfare state to globalized neo-liberal capital mobility may have looked to many participants at the time as a steadily rational sequence of change of belief. But it was clear as the twentieth century ended, with the incomparable benefits of hindsight, that no set of participants in any identifiable institutional site had a clear, well-founded and accurate understanding either of its implications or of its prospective effects. The view that we would have an overwhelming collective interest in learning (if only we could) how to control these consequences through political action is compelling enough. But the view that we readily *could* control these consequences in this way is deeply insensitive to the character of political institutions or processes. We would have such an interest if we could so learn, but what reason is there to believe that we can?

In a capitalist world, economics, in some sense, dominates politics. The politics which it prompts most readily (for a species like ours) is irritable, reactive and myopic: endlessly saturated with *ressentiment*. We have learnt over the generations to put a more prepossessing linguistic face on this politics, to describe and practise it with fluent and sometimes reasonable self-approbation (Skinner 1988). The compulsive partiality of individual (and group: Hardin 1995) judgment comes out in public political discourse in cunningly shared self-righteousness. (If you doubt this, read with care any reasonably professional academic articulation of how to conceive political virtue in relation to a topic of current concern: ecology, gender, distributive justice.) It is not hard to understand why politics should come out like this. What is difficult to judge is whether this is how it must come out: whether this is the best we can reasonably hope to do. Even if it is, this is not a fatalist conclusion. It still leaves each of us as very active agents, and leaves the felicity, or otherwise, of the consequences of our actions firmly to the future. But, in face of most of the history of political reflection in those civilizations where we can still hope to recover some of that history (China, Europe, the Islamic world, India, Japan), it would certainly be a most despondent conclusion (cf. for example Hao 1996; Metzger 1977). How far is such despondency justified? How far, indeed, is it rationally mandatory?

10

Doing Better: Fantasy and Judgment

Overt Resources and Covert Possibilities

I have tried so far to explain why politics today has come out broadly as it has. What I want to consider in the remainder of this book is what good reasons (if any) there may be to hope that we can learn to make it come out better in the future. If things do in due course turn out better, some of what has enabled them to do so will almost certainly be factors which perfectly well could be apprehended now (whether or not any of us happen to focus on them at present). Other factors, by contrast, will almost certainly not be apprehensible now, even in principle, because they will depend on intellectual inventions, or on scientific or practical discoveries, which have yet to be made. It will not be helpful to brood over the latter. Good reasons for hoping that things can be caused to go better must be reasons for us now, reasons which are potentially within our current cognitive reach. If these reasons are there, it would plainly be good to find them; and, unless and until we can tell dependably that there are no such reasons (which it is hard to see how we ever could), we have ample grounds for continuing to look for them.

The dynamism of human inventiveness, for example, now at the centre of economic development, would give good reason for optimism if we were to focus solely on its benign consequences. But no area of human practice has shown its impact more continuously or deeply than the organized effort to coerce or destroy (McNeill 1983; Kennedy 1988; Bracken 1982).

SPIRITUAL EDIFICATION AND ENHANCED RATIONALITY

Is this, then, the best we can reasonably hope to do? Despite Leibniz (Riley 1997), it is very hard to believe so. We might, for example, reasonably hope to do better in at least two dimensions: either morally or cognitively. We could, perhaps, learn to live and act more nobly, or at any rate less ignobly. (It is quite important that the vocabulary here carries the aspirations and pretensions of long-superannuated class structures: that it embodies, and is handing on, the preferred speech of politically defeated, and socially and economically anachronistic, aristocracies, usually of sword or brush, a language of feudal residues, an unmistakably pre-capitalist vision of the world and of human fate (compare, however, Cannadine 1998). But perhaps this need not be wholly to its disadvantage. Are you so sure that the women and men whom capitalism has made are in *every* respect a clear improvement?)

We could perhaps learn, too, to think and judge, and, with discretion, even to speak to one another, more lucidly and accurately, and to act accordingly with altogether greater instrumental rationality. (It is important that the vocabulary here is far more at home with capitalism, far less imaginatively at odds with it.) Very powerful attempts have been made in many of the world's great civilizations to show that these two dimensions of improvement are intimately linked to one another: to see cognitive advance as morally strengthening and edifying, and moral commitment and insight as direct aids to thinking clearly and seeing accurately. But the deep structure of these great historical endeavours of the human imagination has always involved the presumption of a world whose causality is finally under the sway of an essentially benign (or even benevolent) power. If we have no reason today to accept that presumption, we cannot expect to draw grounds from this immensely old, deep and intricate heritage for supposing that nobility of purpose and strictly cognitive insight have any natural affinity with one another, let alone any sure ties to bind them together. We must consider separately the possibilities that we might learn to live less ignobly and that we can learn to think and act more cunningly. And we must consider with the greatest care, as the theory of games encourages us to do, the possibility that ever greater individual instrumental cunning will make it harder rather than easier to act with even a moderate degree of collective prudence (Dunn 1990; Hardin 1993; but cf., more encouragingly, Axrelrod 1997).

In politics the historically given challenge is always to see how to get the consequences of our actions (or inaction) to come out better rather than worse. What it would be for them to do so, of course, depends on who we happen to be. It depends on how they will affect us in particular, and those whom we hold dear, or at least minimally care about. This is one reason why political understanding of any power and determinacy must always be purpose-relative. It is also why, however despondent it often may, or even should, be, it can never, short of the Last Judgment, simply collapse into fatalism.

PRECONDITIONS FOR IMPROVED PERFORMANCE

Our projects for causing the consequences of our actions (or passivity) to come out better depend effectively on three different factors. In the first place, they depend on the scope at the time of human power over the rest of the natural world (itself, of course, already very drastically modified by the past exercise of human powers). In the second, they depend on the current distribution and plasticity of our beliefs and sentiments. In the third, they depend on the contours and plasticity of our existing institutions of political, social and economic co-ordination. The task, in effect, is to do the best we now can to modify the consequences of our action and inaction for the better, by modifying as deftly and wisely as we can our own beliefs and attitudes, and the institutions through which alone we can hope to act effectively on any scale above that of single individuals. We can, of course, approach this task sometimes by devising and attempting to build quite new institutions; and this may well be the most economical approach to realizing many political goals. But it is also always a path which carries distinct costs of its own, in the huge resources of time, energy, patience and hope which must be devoted to the task of institutional construction itself. Consider, for example, the devastating struggles of the French Revolution, to say nothing of its still grimmer twentieth-century successors (Dunn 1989(a)).

In the political traditions of every major civilization there is extended and often passionate dispute as to whether the key site for enhancing the consequences of our performances is the modification of personal beliefs and sentiments, or the invention or reconstruction of institutions for co-ordination, co-operation and more effective conduct of the good fight. In a world already made over extensively for capitalist production, the prospects for large-scale transformation in a desired direction through redirecting sentiments have come to seem poor, not because the denizens of this world feel less intensely or more soberly than their predecessors, but because the operating economic logic of this world already takes feelings severely as given, and has seeped through pervasively into social life and political action. Socialism, while it lasted, was a final defiant bid to assert the dominance of belief and sentiment over a distinctively institutional causality, which it saw as profoundly alien, or, more romantically, to impose human will, choice and agency on a radically inhuman fate. (It is tempting here for feminism to volunteer to take over the mantle of socialism. But it is likely to find, where it does so, that it possesses even less effective expedients for acting than the socialism which it volunteers to replace or to raise to a higher level.)

It is wrong to exclude the possibility that the consequences of human action in several centuries' time may be far more deeply affected by changes in beliefs (and by changes in sentiment consequent upon these changes) than they prove to be by discrete alterations in the inventory and operating causalities of particular institutional sites (political, economic or even social). We cannot now know that this will not turn out to be the case. But to see this is to make a very general concession to scepticism, not to augment our current causal comprehension of anything in particular. What we can already see quite clearly is that, if such changes do derive from beliefs rather than from institutions we have no reason whatever to suppose that any given set of institutions (including, notably, the prevailing political institution of today) will contrive to pick out the more dynamic elements among them or direct their cumulative impact to the maximum.

Both the totalitarian project and the totalitarian nightmare were founded upon that anticipation. But the lessons of experience have vindicated neither project nor nightmare. Instead they have cut each firmly down to size, showing how much of the totalitarian hope was vitiated by the universal solvents of partiality, conflicting interest and the logical conundra of co-ordinating agency, and how much of the undeniable totalitarian terror was simply an extension and intensification of archaic brutalities or hypocrisies. If our beliefs and sentiments do change profoundly enough to transform the overall consequences of our actions for the better, we can be reasonably confident, this will not be because they are caused to do so somehow from the outside, but because we, severally, choose and act over time in such a way that they do. Here, once again, the likeliest antecedent to our choosing on balance in this direction is a growing comprehension of what we have already brought about, and are now bringing about, by our ways of acting: a change carried out and made possible by human reflexivity, but prompted by the most detached and disabused elements in human cognition (the elements most at home with an absolute conception of the world: Williams 1978).

Socialism, in retrospect, was a deeply romantic response to a human world disenchanted by capitalism and a natural world increasingly subordinated to the conveniences of industrial populations. Its key motif was to transpose enchantment from past or present to the future. As a practical orientation, this was inherently unstable. There is little reason to seek to revive it. We do not need an enchanted future (any more than we needed an enchanted past, or indeed an enchanted present). The question which we face is whether, by our own actions, we can make a future for ourselves and our descendants which is as good as (or better than) the present which we have inherited from our ancestors (cf. Dunn and Robertson 1973, esp. dedication page). There is no pre-guaranteed answer to this question across time and space. (Hardly so in the short run, for example, if a Bosnian Moslem in 1991.) But every generation in every human society has needed to face it and to work out as clear-headedly and boldly as it could what its own answer was to be.

Two Polarities: Voluntarism and Fatalism, Routine and Crisis

The main polarities of such answers lie in two distinct dimensions, one of attitude and the other of causal judgment. The polarity of attitude holds between voluntarism and fatalism; the polarity of causal judgment between routine and crisis. A fatalist vision of the human future need not be pessimistic (though probably it *should*). The enchanted future of socialism, while its spell lasted, was to be truly providential: to give us irresistibly and none too distantly an altogether better human world. What fatalism has in common is the presumption of a single integrated and strongly impacted causality, a logic of fate which, for better or worse, it makes no sense to dream of escaping. What it insists on is the need to see this causality as a whole and accept it (to internalize and respect it, if you cannot embrace or love it). For fatalists, human beings always face a single closed future, impermeable to their individual wilfulness or ingenuity. For voluntarists, inversely, the human future is always comprehensively open. It is always the product of what we wish and choose to do; and any of us, at any point, can always wish, or choose, or act, very differently from our recent habits.

The polarity of routine and crisis, by contrast, is a matter of would-be detached causal judgment. It may sometimes (perhaps always) in part depend upon attitudes (Dunn 1990, cap. 10); but in itself it is not a matter of attitude at all. Judging how far a given human practice or assemblage of practices is in a condition of routine or crisis will certainly be affected by temperament. But it must be predicated on the attempt to exclude temperament, to ascertain what is indeed the case, irrespective of what we would like or fear to be so. In the political history of socialism this relation was sometimes somewhat confused. Voluntarists readily confounded the judgment that a society, polity or economy was in crisis with the presumption that they might cause it to become so by their own actions, if only they acted with sufficient vigour, intelligence and daring (Dunn 1989(a)).

Fatalism, a condition which they tended to diagnose in the judgment of their political enemies, they saw as a powerful reinforcement of existing routines, an abjectly conservative political pressure. (Compare, for example, the assault on the Second International by Lenin, Luxemburg or Lukacs with a contemporary academic viewpoint like that of Roberto Unger: Lenin 1970; Lukacs 1970 and 1971; Harding 1977–81 and 1996; Nettl 1966; Unger 1986.) Voluntarism, by contrast, at least in their own case, could hope to be an equally powerful solvent of such routines. The social, economic and political world rebuilt in the aftermath of the collapsed routines would itself be fashioned, as well as made possible, by the vigour, intelligence and daring of those whose actions had caused them to collapse. It would be as free and humanly benign as they wished and chose it to be. Crisis, the collapse of hated routines, would thus be a time of pure opportunity, a leap into freedom from necessity. Where routines are cordially disliked, their end can readily appear an opportunity to transcend them, and, more incautiously, an assurance of the capacity to transcend them. But, of course, for human routines to collapse need not be a blessing. It will always have its hazards; and in some cases it is all too likely to prove a catastrophe.

At every point in time the human future can aptly be seen as a range of potentially attainable, and at least partially desirable, goals, and a set of concomitant dangers. What decides which of these goals are attained, and which of the dangers are incurred or avoided, is always, given the institutions available at the time through which to do so, how we choose and act. The best we can hope for is to modify the cumulative consequences of our actions for the better by modifying our own beliefs and attitudes, or by altering as effectively as possible the contours of the institutions through which we must act.

In this book I have been trying to press two main questions.

How fatalist an understanding should we have, not merely of our political, economic and social actions in the past, but also of their potential outcomes in the reasonably near future? How far should we see the routine institutional causality which largely makes up our political world as stable, pre-given and insulated against our wills and purposes? How far, rather, can we reasonably hope to modify that causality so that it induces less malign outcomes in the future?

These are very different sorts of questions. The first is a very general question about the relations between freedom and fatality across the entire human condition. The second is altogether more particular, focusing on the immediate dynamics of fixity or transformation. Because the first is such a general question, any significant contribution to answering it must be quite general too. It must rest on properties of human beings which have proved to endure over very long periods of time and on features of their political interaction (relations of rule and subordination, disagreements over what it is to live well or badly together) which have also been of some longevity. Because the second is so much more particular in focus and content, the main element of any answer to it must be a set of relatively concrete causal judgments about comparatively recent sections of history. Hence the shape of our inquiry thus far: its starting point in very general questions as to what politics is and why it occurs at all, and its insistent movement towards the question of what has been happening in the political history of the world as a whole over the last few decades (here and elsewhere), and why it has done so.

It is fair to note that this structure of inquiry arose for me from a particular political attitude: one of moderate dismay at most of what has taken place in the course of this epoch. But the same structure would have been just as apt if my attitude had been markedly different (if it had, for example, been one of moderate gratification, allied to a measure of anxiety over whether this could be confidently trusted to continue).

Two possibilities only would make this structure of inquiry categorically inappropriate. One would be a view of the depth of determination and the degree of closure of human political experience over time which simply precluded any important shift in the institutional format of political life from having the slightest real significance: a view of human political action as pure fatality or radical freedom, in no way modified by the history of institutional organization. The second would be a vision of the recent past as the site of an historical transformation radically and dependably for the human better: a shift too manifestly beneficial and too unambiguously welcome to face any continuing danger of political challenge (let alone political reversal).

RADICAL FATALISM: ORIGINAL SIN

The most starkly fatalist conception which we have considered is the idea of original sin: the view that all human beings, now and for the rest of their earthly existence, will continue to be driven to act in a manner deeply malign towards one another, and that what will compel them to do so is the cruelty, greed, pride and treachery at the very core of their personalities. (In the memorable vision of Joseph de Maistre: 'The whole earth, continuously steeped in blood, is nothing but an immense altar on which every living thing must be sacrificed without end' (Maistre 1965, 253). This is scarcely a soulless condition, but it is hard to imagine a more heartless world.) While in no way a frivolous hypothesis, this goes some little way beyond the evidence. As we have seen, too, there is reason to doubt how much of the human political experience to which it does apparently apply it really does illuminate.

THE ROOM FOR MANOEUVRE

In contrast, the further elements which we have considered (structural conflict of interest, partiality of judgment and the logical conundra of collective action), while more than sufficient to guarantee that political life remains uncomfortable, bemusing and dangerous, all give human agents far more room for manoeuvre, and also give their actions, for better or worse, far greater political significance. In particular epochs (Ming Confucianism, the construction of an orthodoxly Christian Western Europe, the communist world, perhaps the Enlightenment) the idea that partiality in judgment can be effectively overridden by changes in the institutional order (educational, economic or political) has won some credence for a time. But in the end, always, the sceptics have had much the better of this argument. There is certainly no reason at present to regard the eradication of partiality from human political judgment as a culturally accessible goal or a politically practicable achievement. And this, irrespective of whether it is even an epistemically coherent conception in the first place.

The cooler political judgments of today are more at home with the puzzles of collective action. Taking human beings very much as History happens to give them, the challenge which they offer is far more narrowly and obdurately one to institutional design or modification. How far can we hope to create and sustain a set of institutions which cause our interests to dovetail neatly with each other? How far, instead, must we simply accept, and learn to live with, conflicts between these interests which set us permanently and sometimes mortally at odds with one another? In Western political thinking, since at least the end of the seventeenth century, and in the increasingly global political theory of an increasingly globalized world, the key setting of these logical puzzles of collective action has come to be the analysis of economic causality. The conflicts or complementarities between human interests have come to be judged through modelling the dynamics of an increasingly globalized and intensive economy. The good or ill design of political institutions is seen to depend ever more radically and pervasively on the felicity with which they fit the operating requirements of that economy.

THE OPERATING REQUIREMENTS OF MODERN ECONOMIES

To tell what these requirements are is no easy task. The analysis of economic causality has not been one of the great success stories of modern intellectual history. The techniques which permit a high level of precision in economic analysis do not marry comfortably with attempts to identify what has been going on in the human world, let alone with efforts to assess what is likely to do so in the humanly relevant future. These techniques require idealization, and powerful and highly mathematized abstraction: the thinking away of almost all the clutter of human experience. (For a clear and courageous attempt to distinguish the prerequisites for precise understanding from the gratuitous ideological inferences which have been drawn so widely from these over the last two decades by economists and makers of governmental economic policy see Hahn and Solow 1995. Note especially the Conclusion at p. 154.)

What is clear is that the demands of these techniques strongly favour the stipulation of an economy theoretically and practically insulated from any other form of causality. They virtually rule out an analysis of an economy as a field of human interaction massively influenced by a rich variety of types of human preoccupation and purpose (political, cultural, spiritual), which are extremely volatile over time and in no sense constituted by economic categories themselves. If human beings were single-mindedly and efficiently concerned to maximize their current income or lifetime wealth it would be substantially easier to assess how they are likely to behave than it in fact is.

Stipulating an insulated economy, however, need not be an idle exercise. There has been very good reason since the days of Adam Smith or David Ricardo, and still better since those of Leon Walras, to explore the prospects for analysing the genesis and exchange of goods and money through an idealized model of a market. In the human world which capitalism has made, and in which all of us now live, it is quite unclear that there is any alternative strategic approach to understanding what, outside the narrowest of contexts, human beings have good reason to do. This globally intersecting set of markets gives a limit to modern politics, furnishing much of the architecture of its setting. But modern politics, equally, limits these markets in their turn. All the property rights traded on any market (and it is essentially property rights which are traded on every market), along with most of the terms on which buyers or sellers have access to and may trade on any given market, depend directly on politics, whether on the explicit and sovereign decisions of particular effective governments, or on the more informal and often flagrantly extra-legal practices of those who conspire to modify or elide these decisions. The economic interests of living human beings always depend at least as fundamentally on the political history within which their lives are immersed as they do on its economic counterpart. Within the human world, at any point in time, the economic history simply *is* a political history, and the political history, perforce, equally an economic history. The two histories and the two causalities jostle permanently against one another, obscuring to all the human agents concerned just what is in fact going on, and frustrating their efforts to muster a clear and accurate sense of what they can or cannot reasonably hope to achieve on their own behalf through their present or future actions.

It is not surprising that human beings should have found this experience discomfiting. It offers a more painful contrast to that sense of intensely personal political autonomy and efficacy which Constant diagnosed as the core appeal of ancient politics than the vision of effective and potentially self-protecting commitment to living as one pleases which he saw as the corresponding (and ever more potent) appeal of its modern counterpart (Constant 1988, 307–28, esp. 311). Today no one can reasonably anticipate that the opportunity to live as they please will be secured automatically by the economic or political dynamics of a global market economy; and no one at all can have well-founded confidence that they will enjoy such an opportunity, if the economic or political dynamics of that economy fail to secure it for them. More disturbingly still, no set whatever of political, economic and social agents, up to and including the present human population of the entire globe, can reasonably assume that they have the effective power to ensure that outcome by any set of actions which they might conceivably perform. When we consider how best to deal with this world, accordingly, the relations between routine and crisis, or between fatalism and voluntarism, are thus virtually certain to discourage rather than to reassure. Political routines and economic routines clash with, rather than sustain, one another. Fatalist visions of the implications of these clashes are most unlikely to see them as providential, and increasingly likely to view them as grounds for despair. Voluntarist visions, to be at all convincing, must either focus on very limited and short-term endeavours, or be even more severely abstract than general equilibrium models of a market, stressing formal freedom rather than substantive causality and focusing on what it is to act at all rather than on what prompts any given human being to act as they do. A voluntarist viewpoint can hope to identify and shape our awareness of precisely located spaces of practical freedom to choose and act, or take its stand instead, more sceptically but altogether undirectively, on the categorical freedom of all human agency. However voluntarist we may choose to be (or judge it appropriate to be), we cannot any longer hope, on the basis of practical understanding now at our disposal, to pick out robust, dependable and plainly mutually supportive practices, applicable on a national or global scale, which will *ensure* that the interests of present and future human beings are secured in a steady and effective manner. (The staffs of agencies like the World Bank and IMF, or for that matter the Japanese Ministry of Finance, would naturally dispute this judgment vigorously. But just look at the consequences of their actions in the last three years of the twentieth century.)

We can see how emphatically this must be so if we consider in relation to one another the terms of access to international trade, the politically and socially sustainable patterns of distribution within given populations or territories, and the sustainability or otherwise of existing forms of production and their currently implementable potential replacements. International trade can be analysed powerfully, in classical liberal manner (Bhagwati 1996 and 1998), through the idea of a single potential global market within which goods and services trade freely, and labour and capital move smoothly to the sites at which their use will add most value. This is a structure which could only be established by the use of enormous political power. It is unclear, too, that even if it could be established, it could also be sustained over time, either politically or socially, by any concentration of political power whatever. It is not an outcome which will readily commend itself at all steadily to the partial judgments of particular groups of human beings over time. So envisaged, it is a world of property rights effectively secured, without the aid of any redistribution whatever, yet somehow finding the political procedures and coercive capacities needed to secure them. Nothing about the political history of the last three hundred years suggests that this is a likely destination. Domestic political authority in the modern world has come more and more to require a plausible semblance of at least minimal accountability of rulers to ruled (Huntington 1991; Dunn (ed.) 1992; Dunn 1996(d)). The ruled, wherever such a semblance has been sustained for any length of time, have invariably insisted on some degree of redistribution of property rights away from the patterns produced by pure market operations. The prospects for constructing a monopolistic world political authority which had eluded these constraints, whether by conquest, by cumulative and spontaneous agreement or by iterative bargaining between units which remain fully sovereign, seem even more remote. Since all human beings are free agents, they could in principle choose to do this, and then succeed in carrying out their choice. But who can be fool enough to suppose that they in fact will, let alone that they would necessarily sustain their choice over time, if they ever, even briefly, did?

Each of these three elements is cognitively elusive and potentially inflammatory. How far a single economically frictionless world market in goods and services, with no external barriers to movement of labour or capital, would in fact maximize the welfare of the world's human population without further damaging that of the worst off is an extraordinarily difficult analytical and causal judgment, on which many thousands of intelligent women and men have long lavished much of their intellectual life. The balance of judgment among them has shifted drastically over time, by no means always in the same direction. We can confidently expect it to continue to shift for some time to come. If we look at these oscillations of judgment over the last three hundred years, the one thing which is clear is that there is no rival unifying conception of what is occurring within this space, or of how it can be better organized to further human welfare, with an intellectual power and simplicity to compare with the model of pure market competition. This is as important politically as it has proved to be intellectually. It means that the more obdurate intellectual enemies of the market must struggle to meet the challenge of Grand Strategy with a miscellany of (usually pretty inexplicit) micro-tactics. But, although the liberal conception of international trade thus carries great political potency, it is certain to continue to encounter acute political hostility. This hostility, furthermore, is not to be attributed merely to a succession of local sinister interests: mystificatory stakeholders in obstructions to freedom of trade or capital and labour mobility, and hence enemies to global human welfare as such. It arises just as insistently (and in what may well be just as politically consequential forms) from the moral sentiments and social imaginations of every human population, both domestically and internationally. Once partiality of judgment is recognized to be as much a property of imaginative habit or compulsion, as of neatly aimed instrumental quest for advantage, the prospect of ever imposing the (putatively impartial) liberal vision of free and unmolested international exchange in its entirety on the spiritedly partial populations of the globe seems fantastical.

It is hard to exaggerate the importance of this, since there is no corresponding unifying conception, of remotely comparable intellectual power or clarity of outline, of what is at stake in how we organize the sustaining or the enhancement of our productive powers, or of the range of patterns of distribution within a given territory or population which might prove to be sustainable socially or politically. The former question is one the scale and urgency of which we have only begun to grasp extremely recently. But the latter has been the core of the political history of the West for well over three hundred years. Our views about it have become enormously more intricate in the course of these extended quarrels. But it is far from clear that our strategic comprehension of what is at stake in them, or how far we can reasonably hope for them to be resolved peacefully and durably, is any better than Thomas Hobbes's in 1642.

POLITICS IN THE MAW OF A GLOBAL ECONOMY

Politics, in this understanding, has featured in the human world for a very long time; and it will continue to feature in any possible future of that world. It has always been confused, elusive and dangerous; and there is no reason whatever to expect it ever to cease to be any of these. Nothing about it guarantees the existence or viability of particular routines at any point in time. But, against the hypothesis of original sin, nothing precludes its occurring for long periods of time in particular places, in institutional settings of some fixity and apparent rigidity. If its hazards came solely from human malignity, as the hypothesis of original sin suggests, it is hard to see how such routines could ever become established, still less how they could hope to provide effective security for any length of time for most of their human participants. If its hazards came solely from purely epistemic partiality (an essentially perspectival egoism of judgment), it would still be hard to eliminate confusion from political interaction, or render the content of politics reasonably simple and obvious. But at least the target for institutional design would be relatively clear, and the protracted presence of essentially pacific routines a plausible index of some success in meeting it.

If its hazards came solely from structural conflicts of interest, the target might seem simpler still, and the remedy correspondingly direct: to conceive, and explore the internal causality of, schemes of human co-operation in which there are no continuing structural conflicts of interest, and all participants would therefore share a clear and stable interest in continuing to participate. There would still, of course, remain the problem of the transition (Dunn 1984(a)); and only a unique content to the scheme of common interest, and a single clear and unobstructed pathway towards it, would prevent the forces of partiality and the logical puzzles of co-ordination and cost-allocation from reintroducing confusion and obviating any prospect of steady movement towards it.

Transcending Politics?: Three Strategies

Seen in this light, politics is not an enviable predicament. As they have begun to see it in this light, accordingly, human beings have put great imaginative energy into the attempt to think their way through it and out the other side. They have tried above all to see how to replace malignity with goodwill, partiality, confusion and elusiveness with dispassion, clarity and determinacy, and danger with security. Their fundamental strategies for these replacements have been few in number; and both their potentialities and their limitations have probably altered rather little over time. What has altered greatly (and made much of the political and intellectual history of human societies by doing so) has been the level of imaginative energy, and the weight of hope or fear, invested in one strategy rather than another. The three principal strategies have been to clarify the causal character of human agency (what prompts it and what it can bring about), to clarify the scope and content of what is good or right for human beings, and to rectify the structures of interest. Most civilizations of any historical depth have given some attention to each. But it is probably fair to say that Christian and post-Christian Europe has made a longer and deeper attempt to combine the three than any other world civilization, and, by doing so, has left a deeper mark on the resources for understanding modern politics (Dunn 1996(a)) which are now available to anyone on the globe. It is worth underlining that this is a contentious and potentially self-serving judgment, coming from Europe; and that it may well mistake contingencies of the history of power for enduring necessities of the progress of human thinking (cf. Finer 1997). Contentious or not, however, it is very much the judgment behind this book.

The three strategies correspond to distinct diagnoses. The strategy of causal clarification issues from the view that we do not really know (but could in principle learn to understand) what we are doing. The strategy of normative clarification issues from the view that there is a way in which the human world ought or ought not to be which we recognize all too fitfully and heedlessly but could learn to apprehend altogether more steadily, and to which we would defer with patience and self-discipline, if only we did fully apprehend it. The strategy of the rectification of interests issues from the view that the manifest disparities of interest which structure our world are largely or wholly gratuitous, and could readily be replaced by an alternative in which all of us would then share a common stake. In the history of European Christianity and its more secular aftermath these strategies had natural imaginative links in the presumption that human beings were a divinely intended feature of a carefully designed and comprehensively divinely controlled universe whose interests and responsibilities could thus be perfectly apprehended from, and only from, God's point of view (Dunn 1984(b)). Suspending this last assumption leaves three quite dynamic modes of inquiry, each of which has great capacity for political clarification. But it destroys the presupposition that they arc in any way securely linked together, and hence destroys the grounds for supposing that the ongoing imaginative and analytical impetus of any of them must fit at all comfortably with that of either or both of the others. It also modifies sharply their relative weight.

Within a Christian framework, God's conception of what is good or right for human beings forms the fulcrum of any coherent understanding of how they have good reason to act. Capture this accurately, and everything else will in due course follow from it (certainly the acceptability or otherwise of every human goal, and the permissibility or otherwise of all institutionalized configurations of interest in particular human societies). In the absence of God, however, it is far less clear what status or human force conceptions of what is good or right for human beings can reasonably carry (Williams 1981 and 1985), and there are far less definite or peremptory side constraints on what configurations of interest particular groups of human beings should permit themselves to establish, defend or reproduce. The purely epistemic unclarity of each reinforces the political significance of the other in a strongly interactive psychological and political process. An epistemically ineradicable partiality of judgment draws malignity and motivational power from direct encounter with other groups of human beings actively pursuing what they take to be their own interests. In doing so, it sours the interaction itself and weakens the desire to recognize or understand the interests of others within the same framework of judgment as we use in identifying and interpreting our own. Under these conditions the very idea of rectifying configurations of interest to bring them into reflective equilibrium with our own (and others') conception of what is humanly good or right shrinks both in epistemic plausibility and in political appeal. What retains political appeal (and can safely dispense with epistemic vindication) is the idea of reconfiguring interests so that we ourselves benefit directly. It is not hard to see why the secularizing shift within the history of Christian and post-Christian Europe should yield a distinctly bleaker vision of what politics is and what it means. Nor is it hard, as we have seen, to grasp that none of the three central strategies for illuminating politics which have been pressed within that history can hope to offer us clear and authoritative guidance through the politics of the world which capitalism has made.

CAPITALISM AS FATE

It is clear that there are strong connections between the expansion of capitalist economic organization, ecological degradation and the limited pacification of property relations in every community in the world today. What is not clear is just how the practical causal connections between these three in our world and the cumulative imaginative and cognitive weight of the secularization of European Christianity bear on one another. On one familiar holistic and fatalist vision, the disenchantment of the world is itself a consequence of the triumph of capitalism, and the triumph of capitalism a sufficient condition for a politics of permanently irreconcilable, but also inherently unrectifiable, conflict of interest. On a rival and more voluntarist vision, the enchantment is far from over, and the triumph of capitalism itself far from complete. Impartiality still carries great imaginative force in our political and social institutions (cf. Barry 1989 and 1993); and our normative sensibilities still give us a real opportunity to recognize and reshape our practices to conform far better to their requirements. (Capitalism, however, may still set pretty stark limits to their prospective success in doing so.)

Fatalism is at its most convincing when we look at the shape and structure of the human world as a whole at any point in time (still more when we view it in intimate interaction with the habitat which it has changed so drastically). Voluntarism is at its most convincing when we view ourselves, or view one another, one by one, and ask with any urgency how often we really can choose to do one thing rather than another. It is very doubtful if, one by one, most human beings will ever have the imaginative option to cease to view themselves as agents making choices and altering their world importantly through the choices which they do make. It is just as doubtful if humans in the future could ever have good reason not to view their relations with all their living fellows and with the non-human world around them very much as fate, however much of it they recognize to be a product of the past agency of other human beings. The voluntarist and fatalist visions address different features of the human world and implicitly answer different questions about it. The voluntarist vision of politics tells us something enormously important about politics – that this consists comprehensively of an endless series of judgments and choices. But, although what it tells us is true and important, it is also, for political purposes, massively uninstructive. Nothing whatever follows from it as to what we ourselves should or should not do, or even consider doing. The fatalist vision is hard to formulate clearly without manifest error, and is always likely to mislead where it is formulated erroneously. But, unlike the voluntarist vision, it is quite imperiously directive. What it tells us is that very many bets are off – that there is always a huge range of desirable outcomes which we may be able to imagine coherently but cannot sanely hope to bring about through anything which we ourselves could do (or prompt others to do). This ugly narrowing of the horizon of hope is what gives political understanding a bad name. Where the narrowing, in retrospect, proves unwarranted, as for example with the sudden collapse of the Soviet Union, this bad name is plainly deserved. But there cannot be real thinking without the possibility of error. Judging the limits of fatality is what political thinking is for. It cannot be a sound case against trying to think politically that this sometimes issues in error. In thought, as in political agency, there are always limits to what can be done, distances that cannot be covered, strategies which will never work. But it can never make sense to equate thought itself with fatality, any more than it could make sense to view political agency in the same way.

CAPITALISM AND THE SPACE FOR POLITICAL CHOICE

An increasingly capitalist world sets very different limits to politics from those which were set by its productively more variegated (but also vastly less productive) predecessors. But, like all such predecessors and any possible successors, it itself is, throughout, a world of politics. The limits which it sets to politics are limits to the potential efficacy of agency. They are in no sense limits to the content of politics. Indeed they form, as I have tried to show, an increasingly large proportion of that content. They have come to do so, moreover, through what has been an unmistakably political process, a process in which sovereign decision and coercion, popular struggle and bemusement, and myriads of other agencies in no way explicitly political have all played highly consequential parts. Some of the dangers and opportunities posed by this world have been with us for a very long time. Others are comparatively novel. If political thinking is how we assess the resources of co-operation or potential struggle we possess with which to face these dangers or seize these opportunities, it needs to help us to see several things more clearly than we normally do. Above all, it needs to show us how we should view the existing institutions through which we seek to act collectively and on a large scale, and how far we can hope to replace any or all of them in the reasonably near future with other institutions which can serve us better. It needs to show us how far we are right to value what we at present value, in all our myopia and inattention, and how far we can and should learn to value more discriminatingly.

When it has taught us each of these as effectively as it can, it needs then, somehow, to put these two streams of instruction together, and show us what their confluence means, both more generally and in the sharpest historical detail, for how we have good reason to act in future.

Because political understanding has this structure, its standing is always elusive in relation to time. Some elements in it seem almost timeless. If we focus on these elements, it will be natural to see political understanding at its most robust as not merely vindicated by its evident longevity, but constituted by its impermeability to historical change, its stolid indifference to fashion. But other elements in it are focused above all on change, speed, daring, panic and danger: the capacity, above all, to see and seize the hour. Both of these elements are necessarily there: a slow silting down of wisdom and judgment across the generations, and the keen and steady eye and cool nerves of those who are most at home in dealing with their fellows day by day in organizing the human world and imposing their wills upon it. It is easy to be a snob of either mode of vision: a scholar or philosopher or stern unbending moralist, a person of the world.

But political understanding requires us to value both, and value each deeply, without succumbing to the glamour of either: to seek to know both the price *and* the value of everything. It must struggle ceaselessly against illusion, but it can never afford to relapse into cynicism. If this is right, it is easy to see that understanding politics should change a person, and potentially change most of us quite profoundly. It should sober, move, perhaps sadden and certainly embolden us: make us warier, but not less kind, more self-reliant, but also more grateful for what we do prove able to rely on in our fellows. It is a discipline of the heart as much as discipline of the mind. It is also a journey of the imagination which cannot hope to make itself fully at home in the busy market in self-advancement which dominates the life of modern academic institutions, as it increasingly dominates the thought world and public culture of the societies which capitalism has refashioned.

Conclusion

So where have we, for the moment, ended up?

Politics is the balance of conflict and co-operation between human purposes on any scale on which you care to look at it. You can mean endless other things by 'politics', and have good reasons for meaning a great many of them. But this is something which, whatever else we come to mean by it, and simply to understand what is really happening to our lives, every one of us needs to mean by it as well.

The balance of conflict and co-operation between our purposes depends, of course, on what those purposes at present are; but just as deeply it depends on how we judge we have good reason to act in order to realize our own purposes. Human purposes are very heterogeneous, and at least as likely to become more so as to become less so as time goes on. Likewise human judgments. For the members of a single animal species human beings are astoundingly plastic across time and space (Carrithers 1992). This bewildering diversity is more than enough in itself to ensure that there is a clear surplus of conflict over co-operation in human interactions and that there will always continue to be so.

By itself, too, that surplus alone will ensure that politics is always a site of danger for human beings, and that the experience of politics, for all but the most egotistical and resilient, will always be somewhat irritating and in the end all but invariably disappointing. In a human world increasingly dominated by the search for personal profit and monetary advantage the chances of human purposes and judgments converging on clear and convincingly public goods and shared preferences are very slight. There is nothing ingratiating in seeing others prosper more handsomely than we do ourselves, whether at home or abroad, and some real pain in sensing that their relative prosperity depends either on luck or on a sharper concentration on pursuing their own advantages than we manage to muster ourselves. Still more so when we recognize the costs our own relative competitive ineffectuality is inflicting on those who depend upon us and whom we love.

And yet in many ways the politics of an increasingly capitalist world is far less grim than this view of its kernel suggests. In many ways, on balance, and however erratically, capitalism has at last fashioned a world in which the conflicts between human purposes pose less lethal or disruptive threats to many than they have done for thousands of years. Not everywhere, of course: only in the economies which it has refashioned most thoroughly and the states which it has adapted to protect these, but notice too how many more there are of these today than there were in 1950. And even in these more fortunate cases, you might say, more by luck than by good judgment. But this just fails to recognize either the prodigious range of human energies and ingenuities which go into carving out the direction of History, or where that direction is in the end coming from. It is as humanly ungenerous as it is explanatorily obtuse.

Capitalism (the organized economic energies of humans producing for an increasingly global market) has selected, refined and diffused quite widely, a state form reconciled to human limitations (greed, quarrelsomeness, severely limited altruism) but still aimed at mitigating the vulnerability of its subjects and serving their more commonplace and insistent practical concerns. This state form has drawn its power from its success in implementing these two aims (always partial, but nevertheless cumulatively quite impressive in all the settings where it has held sway for more than a decade or two consecutively). There is nothing inspiring or morally commanding about this state form. It has had great difficulty across the centuries in establishing its power in face of other candidates which seemed far more urgent in their human (or supra-human) commitments or more exhilarating in the goals which they claimed to pursue.

But its power has come from its capacity to convince these subjects that it can and will protect them more reliably than its rivals, and recognize and respect what their purposes are to a degree which none of its rivals even pretends to try to. Above all it promises them that when and if the subjects themselves decide that enough is enough they will at least have a relatively prompt and reliable opportunity to remove their present rulers and replace them with what at the time appears the least forbidding alternative. This is a state form inured to human limitations, but neither vindictive nor hysterical in face of them. It has won its power by recognizing that human beings dislike and resent dependence and loathe slavery, but that all of them need to be subject to some degree of authority and none of them is fit to enjoy untrammelled power. It has kept and extended its power by recognizing and fully accepting the global economic matrix within which virtually all humans now decisively live. It has also learnt by now that this matrix is not a single clear destiny, but an infinite series of imponderable and bitterly contentious choices. The centrality of that fact ensures that we will continue to need the disabused and modest services of the modern republic just as permanently and insistently as the theological animosities of mid-seventeenth-century England proved to need its (seemingly so distant) ancestor.

We shall just have to see if this state form can muster the practical wisdom to rescue the world as a viable habitat for such vast numbers of humans in the centuries to come. We shall just have to see if it can continue to protect itself, co-operatively where possible but also in the end coercively when necessary, against the enemies which History will continue to send it. We owe it no veneration and we cannot reasonably expect to enjoy its ministrations over time. But we do owe it our loyalty, and perhaps also some of our limited stock of patience. Human beings have done many more fetching and elegant things than invent and routinize the modern democratic republic. But, in face of their endlessly importunate, ludicrously indiscreet, inherently chaotic and always potentially murderous onrush of needs and longings, they have, even now, done very few things as solidly to their advantage. Understanding politics, for now, must at least *begin* with recognizing that this is so.

NOTES

1. To describe bending the human world to our wills as mastery is to employ an obtrusively gendered language. Is that language simply misconceived: an indolently offensive residue of now mercifully challenged and increasingly discarded routines of gender subordination? Or does it show something startling and profoundly illuminating about the pervasive power of gender inequality in organizing the deepest and most consequential features of the milieu in which each of us lives? Does it reflect disparities in gender orientation which reach as deep as biology goes (the sinister or exhilarating power of testosterone to express itself everywhere human, from the most intimate etiquette of social relations to the design, production and deployment of battle tanks or thermonuclear weapons systems)?

   Who should you trust to tell you the answer to that question? Who indeed? Certainly, least of all yourself.

   Is it still true that boys are somehow taught in practice, virtually everywhere and for all the painfully correct effort to eliminate these disparities, to try to *master* their human (and indeed their non-human) environment, while girls somehow still learn to modify it by something a good deal subtler than direct assault?

   If it is true (insofar as it is true), whose fault precisely is this? What causes it to be so? Insofar as it is the fault of any of us, is that fault eradicable? Or is it in the end impossible to say where the fault stops and we start: to distinguish our faults from ourselves? Human beings, you might think, have been struggling with these faults for many thousand years, above all on the terrain of the Great Tradition religions of the world (Redfield 1960; Brown 1967; Eisenstadt 1986; Dumont 1972; Weber 1951, 1958(a) and (b), 1965). Think of Cain and Abel. Think of the Buddha. Think, less reassuringly, of Kali. Think of St Francis of Assisi.

   Have they (have we) at last begun to make real headway (here and there, in this field and that)? Or is the judgment that we have begun to do so just a complicated, if widespread, exercise in collective self-(or other-)deception? The rhetoric of public speech in many settings has altered quite far quite recently. The relative incomes and employment levels of men and women, often in much the same places, have altered appreciably, if somewhat less. But keep a watchful eye on the tanks and blue-water navies of the world; and note how very many small boys, however raised, continue to react to heavy earth-moving equipment or fast cars.

2. 'Comme s'il était permis d'oublier que c'est en ma personne seule que réside la puissance souveraine, dont le caractère propre est l'esprit de conseil, de justice et de raison; que c'est de moi seul que mes cours tiennent leur existence et leur autorité; que la plénitude de cette autorité, qu'elles n'exercent qu'en mon nom, demeure toujours en moi, et que l'usage n'en peut jamais être tourné contre moi; que c'est à moi seul qu'appartient le pouvoir législatif sans dépendance et sans partage; que c'est par ma seule autorité que les officiers de mes cours procèdent, non à la formation, mais à l'enregistrement, à la publication, à l'exécution de la loi, et qu'il leur est permis de me remontrer ce qui est du devoir de bons et utils conseillers; que l'ordre public entier émane de moi et que les droits et les interêts de la Nation, dont on ose faire un corps separé du Monarque, sont nécessairement unis avec les miens et ne reposent qu'en mes mains' (3 March 1766: Flammermont and Tourneux 1895, II, 557–8. For a rather cloudy discussion of the historical and ideological background to these claims, and the increasing strains to which they were subjected by the 1760s, see Van Kley 1996).

3. Much the largest and most carefully assembled body of information on comparative income distribution, especially in the relatively prosperous member countries of the OECD, is the data files of the Luxemburg Income Study. I was first introduced to the importance of this work in a careful and thoughtful paper by Vincent Mahler delivered at the Graduate School of International Studies at the University of Denver. I am very grateful both to him and to the generosity of my colleague Dr Jackie Scott in guiding me to the analytical work which has been done on the basis of these files. (See especially Gottschalk and Smeeding 1998, along with Gottschalk 1993, Danziger and Gottschalk 1995, Atkinson, Rainwater and Smeeding 1995.) Gottschalk and Smeeding 1998 emphasize especially the sharpness of income inequality in the United States, the dramatic increase in

income inequality in the United Kingdom between 1979 and 1995, and the very widespread character of increases in income inequality in the 1980s and 1990s, reversing in many cases trends in the opposite direction in the 1960s and 1970s. No observer of the politics of the last quarter of the twentieth century across the OECD countries would be likely to be surprised by these findings and few would regard them as an unintended outcome of the political activities of career politicians in government over this timespan in most of the countries concerned. This is the clearest and most important evidence for the swing to the right politically across most of the world in these two decades. It is also, I would claim, a plainly intended outcome of that swing.

4. 'His vote is not a thing in which he has an option; it has no more to do with his personal wishes than the verdict of a juryman. It is strictly a matter of duty. He is bound to give it according to his best and most conscientious opinion of the public good' (Mill 1910, 299).
5. Cf. note 3 above.
6. Cf. note 4 above.

BIBLIOGRAPHY

Abrahamian, Ervand 1995 *Khomeinism* London: I. B. Tauris

Addison, Paul 1977 *The Road to 1945: British Politics and the Second World War* London: Quartet Books

Al-Khalil, Samir (= Kanan Makiya) 1990 *Republic of Fear: The Inside Story of Saddam's Iraq* London: Hutchinson Radius

Allison, Graham T. 1971 *The Essence of Decision: Explaining the Cuban Missile Crisis* Boston: Little, Brown

Almond, Gabriel A. and Coleman, James S. (eds) 1960 *The Politics of the Developing Areas* Princeton: Princeton University Press

Althusser, Louis 1959 *Montesquieu: la politique et l'histoire* Paris: Presses Universitaires de France

Amiagada Herrera, Genero and Graham, Carol 1994 'Chile: Sustaining Adjustment during Democratic Transition' in Haggard and Webb (eds) 1994, 242–89

Amsden, Alice H. 1989 *Asia's Next Giant: South Korea and Late Industrialization* Oxford: Oxford University Press

Apter, David 1963 *The Politics of Modernization* Chicago: University of Chicago Press

Aristotle 1926 *The Nicomachaean Ethics* tr. H. Rackham, Cambridge, Mass.: Harvard University Press

Aristotle 1932 *The Politics* tr. H. Rackham, Cambridge, Mass.: Harvard University Press

Arrow, Kenneth 1963 *Social Choice and Individual Values* 2nd edn, New York: John Wiley

Atkinson, Anthony B., Rainwater, L. and Smeeding, T. M. 1995 *Income Distribution in OECD Countries: Evidence from the Luxemburg Income Study* Paris: OECD

Augustine 1884 *The City of God* tr. Marcus Dodds, 2 vols, Edinburgh: T. & T. Clark

Axelrod, Robert 1984 *The Evolution of Cooperation* New York: Basic Books

Axelrod, Robert 1997 *The Complexity of Cooperation: Agent-Based Models of Competition and Collaboration* Princeton: Princeton University Press

Ayers, Michael 1990 *John Locke: Epistemology and Ontology* 2 vols, London: Routledge

Baier, Annette 1994 *Moral Prejudices* Cambridge, Mass.: Harvard University Press

Balazs, E. 1965 *Political Theory and Administrative Reality in Traditional China* London: School of Oriental and African Studies

Ball, Terence, Farr, James and Hanson, Russell (eds) 1989 *Political Innovation and Conceptual Change* Cambridge: Cambridge University Press

Barber, William J. 1985 *From New Era to New Deal* Cambridge: Cambridge University Press

Barry, Brian 1965 *Political Argument* London: Routledge & Kegan Paul

Barry, Brian 1970 *Sociologists, Economists and Democracy* London: Collier-Macmillan

Barry, Brian 1989 *Theories of Justice* London: Harvester-Wheatsheaf

Barry, Brian 1993 *Justice as Impartiality* Oxford: Clarendon Press

Bayart, Jean-François 1993 *The State in Africa: The Politics of the Belly* London: Longman

Becker, Carl L. 1959 *The Declaration of Independence: A Study in the History of Ideas* New York: Vintage Books

Beer, Samuel H. 1965 *Modern British Politics* London: Faber & Faber

Beetham, David 1974 *Max Weber and the Theory of Modern Politics* London: George Allen & Unwin

Bell, Daniel 1976 *The Cultural Contradictions of Capitalism* London: William Heinemann

Bendix, Reinhard 1960 *Max Weber: An Intellectual Portrait* London: William Heinemann

Bentley, Roy, Dobson, Alan, Grant, Maggie and Roberts, David 1995 *British Politics* Ormskirk: Causeway Press

Berg, Maxine 1980 *The Machinery Question and the Making of Political Economy 1815–1848* Cambridge: Cambridge University Press

Bergounioux, Alain and Grunberg, Gérard 1996 *L'Utopie à l'épreuve: le socialisme européen au XXe siècle* Paris: Editions de Fallois

Berlin, Isaiah 1990 *The Crooked Timber of Humanity* London: John Murray

Berlin, Isaiah 1994 *The Magus of the North: J. G. Hamann and the Origins of Modern Irrationalism* London: Fontana Press

Berrington, Hugh (ed.) 1998 *Britain in the Nineties: The Politics of Paradox, Western European Politics* 21 (January special issue)

Berry, Mary Elizabeth 1989 *Hideyoshi* Cambridge, Mass.: Harvard University Press

Beveridge, William 1944 *Full Employment in a Free Society* London: George Allen & Unwin

Bhagwati, Jagdish 1996 *Fair Trade and Harmonization* Cambridge, Mass.: MIT Press

Bhagwati, Jagdish 1998 *A Stream of Windows* Cambridge, Mass.: MIT Press

Black, Antony 1992 *Political Thought in Europe 1250–1450* Cambridge: Cambridge University Press

Blackburn, Simon 1981 'Rule-Following and Moral Realism' in Holtzman and Leich (eds) 1981, 163–87

Bloch, Marc 1973 *The Royal Touch: Sacred Monarchy and Scrofula in England and France* tr. J. E. Anderson, London: Routledge & Kegan Paul

Bracken, Paul 1982 *The Command and Control of Nuclear Forces* New Haven: Yale University Press

Breiner, Peter 1996 *Max Weber and Democratic Politics* Ithaca: Cornell University Press

Brenner, Robert 1998 'The Economics of Global Turbulence: A Special Report on the World Economy 1950–1998' *New Left Review* 229, May–June 1998

Brewer, John 1989 *The Sinews of War: War, Money, and the English State 1688–1783* London: Unwin Hyman

Brown, Peter 1967 *Augustine of Hippo* London: Faber & Faber

Brown, Archie 1996 *The Gorbachev Factor* Oxford: Oxford University Press

Brownlee, W. Elliott (ed.) 1996 *Funding the Modern American State 1941–1995* Cambridge: Cambridge University Press

Brus, Wlodzimierz and Laski, Kasimierz 1989 *From Marx to the Market* Oxford: Clarendon Press

Bull, Hedley and Watson, Adam (eds) 1984 *The Expansion of International Society* Oxford: Clarendon Press

Burke, Edmund 1989 *Writings and Speeches* vol. 8, ed. L. G. Mitchell, Oxford: Clarendon Press

Butler, Anthony 1995 'Unpopular Leaders: The British Case' *Political Studies* 43, 48–65

Butler, David and Kavanagh, Dennis 1980 *The British General Election of 1979* London: Macmillan

Butler, David and Kavanagh, Dennis 1984 *The British General Election of 1983* London: Macmillan

Butler, David and Kavanagh, Dennis 1988 *The British General Election of 1987* Basingstoke: Macmillan

Butler, David and Kavanagh, Dennis 1992 *The British General Election of 1992* Basingstoke: Macmillan

Butler, David and Kavanagh, Dennis 1997 *The British General Election of 1997* Basingstoke: Macmillan

Caller, David P. 1995 'America's Federal Nation State: A Crisis of *Post-imperial Viability?*' in Dunn (ed.) 1995, 16–33

Campbell, John L. 1998 'Institutional Analysis and the Role of Ideas in Political Economy' *Theory and Society* 27, 377–409

Cannadine, David 1998 *Class in Britain* New Haven: Yale University Press

Canning, Joseph 1996 *A History of Medieval Political Thought 300–1450* London: Routledge

Carr, E. H. 1942 *Conditions of Peace* London: Macmillan

Carrithers, Michael 1992 *Why Humans Have Cultures: Explaining Anthropology and Social Diversity* Oxford: Oxford University Press

Church, William F. 1972 *Richelieu and Reason of State* Princeton: Princeton University Press

Clarke, Peter 1988 *The Keynesian Revolution in the Making 1924–1936* Oxford: Clarendon Press

Clausewitz, Karl von 1976 *On War* tr. Michael Howard and Peter Paret, Princeton: Princeton University Press

Cohen, G. A. 1978 *Karl Marx's Theory of History: A Defence* Oxford: Clarendon Press

Cohen, Joshua 1997 'The Arc of the Moral Universe' *Philosophy and Public Affairs* 26, 91–134

Colley, Linda 1992 *Britons: Forging of the Nation 1707–1837* New Haven: Yale University Press

Collini, Stefan, Winch, Donald and Burrow, John 1983 *That Noble Science of Politics* Cambridge: Cambridge University Press

Connolly, William E. 1974 *The Terms of Political Discourse* Lexington: D. C. Heath

Constant, Benjamin 1988 *Political Writings* ed. Biancamaria Fontana, Cambridge: Cambridge University Press

Coogan, Tim Pat 1995 *The IRA* London: Fontana

Cooper, John M. 1975 *Reason and Human Good in Aristotle* Cambridge, Mass.: Harvard University Press

Cowley, Philip and Garry, John 1998 'The British Conservative Party and Europe: The Choosing of John Major' *British Journal of Political Science* 28, 473–98

Crick, Bernard 1964 *In Defence of Politics* Harmondsworth: Penguin

Dahl, Robert 1953 *A Preface to Democratic Theory* Chicago: University of Chicago Press

Danziger, Sheldon and Gottschalk, Peter 1995 *America Unequal* New York: Russell Sage Foundation and Cambridge, Mass.: Harvard University Press

Davidson, Donald 1980 *Essays on Actions and Events* Oxford: Clarendon Press

Davis, David Brion 1966 *The Problem of Slavery in Western Culture* Ithaca: Cornell University Press

Davis, David Brion 1975 *The Problem of Slavery in the Age of Revolution 1770–1823* Ithaca: Cornell University Press

Davis, David Brion 1984 *Slavery and Human Progress* Oxford: Oxford University Press

Davis, David Brion 1990 *Revolutions: Reflections on American Equality and Foreign Liberations* Cambridge, Mass.: Harvard University Press

Dogan, Mattei 1997 'Erosion of Confidence in Advanced Democracies' in Dogan (ed.) 1997, 3–29

Dogan, Mattei (ed.) 1997 'Special Edition: When People Lose Confidence' *Studies in Comparative International Development* 32, 3

Dow, Christopher 1998 *Major Recessions: Britain and the World 1920–1995* Oxford: Oxford University Press

Downs, Anthony 1957 *An Economic Theory of Democracy* New York: Harper & Row

Dryzek, John 1990 *Discursive Democracy* Cambridge: Cambridge University Press

Duffy, Eamonn 1992 *The Stripping of the Altars* New Haven: Yale University Press

Dumont, Louis 1972 *Homo Hierarchicus: The Caste System and its Implications* tr. Mark Sainsbury, London: Paladin

Dunbabin, Jean 1985 *France in the Making (843–1180)* Oxford: Oxford University Press

Dunn, John 1969 *The Political Thought of John Locke* Cambridge: Cambridge University Press

Dunn, John 1980 *Political Obligation in its Historical Context* Cambridge: Cambridge University Press

Dunn, John 1984 (a) *The Politics of Socialism* Cambridge: Cambridge University Press

Dunn, John 1984 (b) *Locke* Oxford: Oxford University Press

Dunn, John 1985 *Rethinking Modern Political Theory* Cambridge: Cambridge University Press

Dunn, John 1989 (a) *Modern Revolutions* 2nd edn, Cambridge: Cambridge University Press

Dunn, John 1989 (b) '"Bright Enough for All Our Purposes": John Locke's Conception of a Civilized Society' *Notes and Records of the Royal Society* 43, 133–53

Dunn, John 1990 *Interpreting Political Responsibility* Cambridge: Polity Press

Dunn, John (ed.) 1990 *The Economic Limits to Modern Politics* Cambridge: Cambridge University Press

Dunn, John (ed.) 1992 *Democracy: The Unfinished Journey* Oxford: Oxford University Press

Dunn, John 1993 *Western Political Theory in the Face of the Future* 2nd edn, Cambridge: Cambridge University Press

Dunn, John 1994 'The Identity of the Bourgeois Liberal Republic', in Fontana (ed.) 1994, 206–25

Dunn, John (ed.) 1995 *Contemporary Crisis of the Nation State?* Oxford: Basil Blackwell

Dunn, John 1996 (a) *The History of Political Theory and Other Essays* Cambridge: Cambridge University Press

Dunn, John 1996 (b) 'The Transcultural Significance of Athenian Democracy' in Michel Sakellariou (ed.) *Democracy and Culture in Ancient Athens* Athens: Academy of Athens, 97–108

Dunn, John 1996 (c) 'The Contemporary Political Significance of John Locke's Conception of Civil Society' *Iyyun* 45, July, 103–24

Dunn, John 1996 (d) 'How Democracies Succeed' *Economy and Society* 25, 511–28

Dunn, John 1997 'Does Separatism Threaten the State System?' in Trude Andersen et al. (eds) *Separatism* Bergen: Ch. Michelsen Institute, 130–45

Dunn, John 1999 'How Politics Limits Markets: Power, Legitimacy, Choice' in Samuel Bowles, Maurizio Franzini and Ugo Pagano (eds) *The Politics and Economics of Power* London: Routledge, 85–100

Dunn, John and Robertson, A. F. 1973 *Dependence and Opportunity: Political Change in Ahafo* Cambridge: Cambridge University Press

Duverger, Maurice 1954 *Political Parties* tr. B. and R. North, London: Methuen

Dworkin, Ronald 1986 *Law's Empire* London: Fontana

Dworkin, Ronald 1996 'Objectivity and Truth: You'd Better Believe It' *Philosophy and Public Affairs* 25, 87–139

Easton, David, Gunnell, John G. and Stein, Michael B. (eds) 1995 *Regime and Discipline: Democracy and the Development of Political Science* Ann Arbor: University of Michigan Press

Eisenstadt, Shmuel N. 1986 *The Origins and Diversity of Axial Age Civilizations* Albany: State University of New York Press

Elison, George 1988 *Deus Destroyed: The Image of Christianity in Early Modern Japan* Cambridge, Mass.: Harvard University Press

Elliott, John H. 1984 *Richelieu and Olivares* Cambridge: Cambridge University Press

Elster, Jon 1975 *Logic and Society* Chichester: John Wiley

Elster, Jon 1979 *Ulysses and the Sirens* Cambridge: Cambridge University Press

Elster, Jon 1985 *Making Sense of Marx* Cambridge: Cambridge University Press

Ertman, Thomas 1997 *Birth of the Leviathan: Building States and Regimes in Medieval and Early Modern Europe* Cambridge: Cambridge University Press

Esping-Andersen, Gosta 1984 *Politics against Markets* Princeton: Princeton University Press

Esping-Andersen, Gosta 1990 *The Three Worlds of Welfare Capitalism* Cambridge: Polity Press

Farr, James 1995 'From Modern Republic to Administrative State: American Political Science in the Nineteenth Century' in Easton, Gunnell and Stein (eds) 1995, 131–67

Farr, James, Dryzek, John S. and Leonard, Stephen T. (eds) 1995 *Political Science in History: Research Programs and Political Traditions* Cambridge: Cambridge University Press

Farr, James and Seidelman, Raymond 1993 *Discipline and History: Political Science in the United States* Ann Arbor: University of Michigan Press

Farrar, Cynthia 1988 *The Origins of Democratic Thinking* Cambridge: Cambridge University Press

Ferejohn, John 1995 'The Development of the Spatial Theory of Elections' in Farr, Dryzek and Leonard (eds) 1995, 253–75

Finer, S. E. 1997 *The History of Government* 3 vols, Oxford: Oxford University Press

Finley, M. I. 1980 *Ancient Slavery and Modern Ideology* London: Chatto & Windus

Finley, M. I. 1983 *Politics in the Ancient World* Cambridge: Cambridge University Press

Flammermont, Jules and Tourneux, Maurice 1888–98 *Rémontrances du Parlement de Paris au XVIIIe siècle* 3 vols, Paris: Imprimerie Nationale

Fontana, Biancamaria (ed.) 1994 *The Invention of the Modern Republic* Cambridge: Cambridge University Press

Forbes, Duncan 1975 *Hume's Philosophical Politics* Cambridge: Cambridge University Press

Ford, Franklin D. 1953 *Sword and Robe* Cambridge, Mass.: Harvard University Press

Fortes, M. and Evans-Pritchard, E. E. 1940 *African Political Systems* Oxford: Oxford University Press

Foucault, Michel 1979 *Discipline and Punish: The Birth of the Prison* tr. Alan Sheridan, Harmondsworth: Penguin

Franklin, Julian 1973 *Jean Bodin and the Rise of Absolutist Theory* Cambridge: Cambridge University Press

Fukuyama, Francis 1992 *The End of History and the Last Man* London: Hamish Hamilton

Gallie, W. B. 1978 *Philosophers of War and Peace* Cambridge: Cambridge University Press

Gambetta, Diego (ed.) 1988 *Trust: Making and Breaking Cooperative Relations* Oxford: Basil Blackwell

Gambetta, Diego 1993 *The Sicilian Mafia: The Business of Private Protection* Cambridge, Mass.: Harvard University Press

Gamble, Andrew 1996 *Hayek: The Iron Cage of Liberty* Cambridge: Polity Press

Garnsey, Peter 1996 *Ideas of Slavery from Aristotle to Augustine* Cambridge: Cambridge University Press

Gauthier, David 1969 *The Logic of Leviathan* Oxford: Clarendon Press

Gay, Peter 1959 *Voltaire's Politics: The Poet as Realist* Princeton: Princeton University Press

Geertz, Clifford 1983 *Local Knowledge* New York: Basic Books

Gellner, Ernest 1998 *Language and Solitude: Wittgenstein, Malinowski and the Habsburg Dilemma* Cambridge: Cambridge University Press

Getty, John A. 1985 *Origins of the Great Purges* Cambridge: Cambridge University Press

Geuss, Raymond 1980 *The Idea of a Critical Theory* Cambridge: Cambridge University Press

Gilmour, Ian 1992 (a) *Riot, Risings and Revolution* London: Hutchinson

Gilmour, Ian 1992 (b) *Dancing with Dogma: Britain under Thatcherism* London: Simon & Schuster

Gilmour, Ian and Garnett, Mark 1997 *Whatever Happened to the Tories?* London: Fourth Estate

Gilpin, Robert 1987 *The Political Economy of International Relations* Princeton: Princeton University Press

Goethe, Johann Wolfgang 1970 *Italian Journey (1786–1788)* tr. W. H. Auden and Elizabeth Mayer, Harmondsworth: Penguin

Gottschalk, Peter 1993 'Changes in Inequality of Family Income in Seven Industrialized Countries' *American Economic Review* 83, 2, 136–42

Gottschalk, Peter and Smeeding, Timothy M. 1998 'Empirical Evidence on Income Inequality in Industrialized Countries' (Luxemburg Income Study Working Papers 154, June 1998 – final draft to appear in Anthony B. Atkinson and Francis Bourguignon (eds) *The Handbook of Income Distribution*: Working paper available from Luxemburg Income Study website http://lissy.ceps.lu/wpapers.htm)

Gray, John 1986 *Hayek on Liberty* Oxford: Basil Blackwell

Gray, John 1995 *Enlightenment's Wake* London: Routledge

Gray, John 1998 *False Dawn* London: Granta

Griffin, James 1986 *Well-Being: Its Meaning, Measurement and Moral Importance* Oxford: Clarendon Press

Gwyn, W. B. 1965 *The Meaning of the Separation of Powers (Tulane Studies in Political Science*, IX) The Hague: Martinus Nijhoff

Haggard, Stephen and Webb Steven B. (eds) 1994 *Voting for Reform* Oxford: Oxford University Press

Hahn, Frank and Solow, Robert 1995 *A Critical Essay on Modern Macroeconomic Theory* Cambridge, Mass.: MIT Press

Hall, Peter A. (ed.) 1989 *The Political Power of Economic Ideas: Keynesianism across Nations* Princeton: Princeton University Press

Hampton, Jean 1986 *Hobbes and the Social Contract Tradition* Cambridge: Cambridge University Press

Hansen, Mogens 1991 *The Athenian Democracy in the Age of Demosthenes* Oxford: Basil Blackwell

Hao, Chang 1996 'The Intellectual Heritage of the Confucian Ideal of *Ching-Shih*' in Tu Wei-Ming (ed.), *Confucian Traditions in East Asian Modernity: Moral Education and Economic Culture in Japan and the Four Mini-Dragons* Cambridge, Mass.: Harvard University Press, 72–91

Hardin, Russell 1982 *Collective Action* Washington, DC: Johns Hopkins University Press

Hardin, Russell 1993 'The Street-Level Epistemology of Trust' *Politics and Society* 21, 505–29

Hardin, Russell 1995 *One for All: The Logic of Group Conflict* Princeton: Princeton University Press

Harding, Neil 1977–81 *Lenin's Political Thought* 2 vols, London: Macmillan

Harding, Neil 1992 'The Marxist–Leninist Detour', in Dunn (ed.) 1992, 155–87

Harding, Neil 1996 *Leninism* Basingstoke: Macmillan

Harrington, James 1977 *The Political Works of James Harrington* ed. J. G. A. Pocock, Cambridge: Cambridge University Press

Hart, H. L. A. 1961 *The Concept of Law* Oxford: Clarendon Press

Hintze, Otto 1975 *The Historical Essays* ed. Felix Gilbert, New York: Oxford University Press

Hirschman, Albert O. 1970 *Exit, Voice and Loyalty* Cambridge, Mass.: Harvard University Press

Hirschman, Albert O. 1977 *The Passions and the Interests: Political*

Arguments for Capitalism before its Triumph Princeton: Princeton University Press

Hirschman, Albert O. 1991 *The Rhetoric of Reaction* Cambridge, Mass.: Harvard University Press

Hobbes, Thomas 1969 *Behemoth* ed. F. Toennies, 2nd edn, London: Frank Cass

Hobbes, Thomas 1983 *De Cive: the English Version* ed. Howard Warrender, Oxford: Clarendon Press

Hobbes, Thomas 1991 *Leviathan* ed. Richard Tuck, Cambridge: Cambridge University Press

Holtzman, Steven and Leich, Christopher (eds) 1981 *Wittgenstein: To Follow a Rule* London: Routledge

Hont, Istvan 1990 'Free Trade and the Economic Limits to National Politics: Neo-Machiavellian Political Economy Reconsidered' in Dunn (ed.) 1990, 41–120

Hont, Istvan 1993 'The Rhapsody of Public Debt: David Hume and Voluntary State Bankruptcy' in Nicholas Phillipson and Quentin Skinner (eds) *Political Discourse in Early Modern Britain* Cambridge: Cambridge University Press, 321–48

Hont, Istvan 1994 'Commercial Society and Political Theory in the Eighteenth Century: The Problem of Authority in David Hume and Adam Smith' in Willem Melching and Wyger Velema (eds) *Main Trends in Cultural History* Amsterdam: Rodopi, 54–94

Hont, Istvan 1995 'The Permanent Crisis of a Divided Mankind: Contemporary "Crisis" of the Nation State in Historical Perspective' in Dunn (ed.) 1995, 166–231

Hont, Istvan and Ignatieff, Michael (eds) 1983 *Wealth and Virtue* Cambridge: Cambridge University Press

Hume, David 1911 *A Treatise of Human Nature* 2 vols, London: J. M. Dent

Hume, David 1985 *Essays Moral, Political and Literary* ed. Eugene F. Miller, Indianapolis: Liberty Classics

Hundert, E. J. 1993 *The Enlightenment's Fable* Cambridge: Cambridge University Press

Huntington, Samuel P. 1991 *The Third Wave: Democratization in the Late Twentieth Century* Norman: University of Oklahoma Press

Huntington, Samuel P. 1993 'The Clash of Civilizations?' *Foreign Affairs* 72, 22–49

Huntington, Samuel P. 1997 *The Clash of Civilizations and the Remaking of World Order* London: Simon & Schuster

Irwin, Douglas 1996 *Against the Tide* Princeton: Princeton University Press

Jolliffe, J. E. A. 1955 *Angevin Kingship* London: A. & C. Black

Jordan, Winthrop D. 1968 *White over Black* Chapel Hill: University of North Carolina Press

Kaase, Max and Newton, Kenneth (eds) 1995 *Beliefs in Government* Oxford: Oxford University Press

Kant, Immanuel 1971 *Political Writings* ed. H. Reiss, Cambridge: Cambridge University Press

Kapuscinski, Ryszard 1984 *The Emperor* tr. W. R. Brand and K. Mroczkowska-Brand, London: Pan

Kavanagh, Dennis 1998 'Power in Parties: R. T. Mackenzie and After' *Western European Politics* 21, 28–43

Kennedy, Paul 1988 *The Rise and Fall of the Great Powers* London: Unwin Hyman

Keohane, Robert 1984 *After Hegemony: Cooperation and Discord in the World Political Economy* Princeton: Princeton University Press

Khilnani, Sunil 1997 *The Idea of India* London: Hamish Hamilton

King, Anthony et al. (eds) 1993 *Britain at the Polls 1992* Chatham, Jersey: Chatham House Publishers

Kingston, Rebecca 1996 *Montesquieu and the Parlement of Bordeaux* Geneva: Droz

Klingemann, H.-D. and Fuchs, D. (eds) 1995 *Citizens and the State* Oxford: Oxford University Press

Kolakowski, Leszek 1978 *Main Currents of Marxism* 3 vols, Oxford: Clarendon Press

Lal, Deepak and Myint, H. 1996 *The Political Economy of Poverty, Equity and Growth: A Comparative Study* Oxford: Clarendon Press

Lear, Jonathan 1988 *Aristotle: The Desire to Understand* Cambridge: Cambridge University Press

Lear, Jonathan 1998 *Open-Minded: Working Out the Logic of the Soul* Cambridge, Mass.: Harvard University Press

Lemarchand, René 1996 *Burundi: Ethnic Conflict and Genocide* Cambridge: Cambridge University Press

Lenin, V. I. 1970 *What Is to be Done?* ed. S. V. Utechin, London: Panther Books

Le Roy Ladourie, Emmanuel and Fitou, Jean-François 1997 *Saint-Simon, ou le système de la cour* Paris: Fayard

Levack, Brian P. 1987 *The Formation of the British State: England, Scotland and the Union 1603–1707* Oxford: Clarendon Press

Levi, Margaret 1988 *Of Rule and Revenue* Berkeley: University of California Press

Levi, Margaret 1997 *Consent, Dissent and Patriotism* Cambridge: Cambridge University Press

Lewis, David 1969 *Convention: A Philosophical Study* Cambridge, Mass.: Harvard University Press

Lichtheim, George 1961 *Marxism: An Historical and Critical Study* London: Routledge

Lichtheim, George 1969 *The Origins of Socialism* New York: Frederick A. Praeger

Lloyd, G. E. R. 1990 *Demystifying Mentalities* Cambridge: Cambridge University Press

Locke, John 1975 *An Essay concerning Human Understanding* ed. Peter H. Nidditch, Oxford: Clarendon Press

Locke, John 1979 *Correspondence of John Locke* ed. E. S. de Beer, vol. IV, Oxford: Clarendon Press

Locke, John 1988 *Two Treatises of Government* ed. Peter Laslett, Cambridge: Cambridge University Press

Lukacs, G. 1970 *Lenin: A Study on the Unity of his Thought* tr. Nicholas Jacobs, London: New Left Books

Lukacs, G. 1971 *History and Class-Consciousness* tr. R. Livingstone, London: Merlin Press

Lukes, Steven 1974 *Power: A Radical Analysis* London: Macmillan

Lukes, Steven 1985 *Marxism and Morality* Oxford: Clarendon Press

Lund, William R. 1992 'Hobbes on Opinion, Private Judgment and Civil War' *History of Political Thought* 13, 448–69

MacCulloch, Diarmaid 1996 *Thomas Cranmer: A Biography* New Haven: Yale University Press

McDowell, John 1981 'Non-Cognitivism and Rule-Following' in Holtzman & Leich (eds) 1981, 141–62

McDowell, John 1996 *Mind and World* Cambridge, Mass.: Harvard University Press

McGinn, Colin 1982 *The Character of Mind* Oxford: Oxford University Press

Machiavelli, Niccolò 1988 *The Prince* ed. Quentin Skinner and tr. Russell Price, Cambridge: Cambridge University Press

MacIntyre, Alasdair 1971 *Against the Self-Images of the Age* London: Duckworth

MacIntyre, Alasdair 1973 'Ideology, Social Science and Revolution' *Comparative Politics* 5, 321–42

MacIntyre, Alasdair 1981 *After Virtue: A Study in Moral Theory* London: Duckworth

Mackenzie, Robert 1963 *British Political Parties* 2nd edn, London: William Heinemann

Mackie, J. L. 1977 *Ethics: Inventing Right and Wrong* Harmondsworth: Penguin

McNeill, William H. 1983 *The Pursuit of Power: Technology, Armed Force and Society since AD 1000* Oxford: Basil Blackwell

Macpherson, C. B. 1962 *The Political Theory of Possessive Individualism* Oxford: Clarendon Press

Macpherson, C. B. 1973 *Democratic Theory: Essays in Retrieval* Oxford: Clarendon Press

Madison, James and Hamilton, Alexander 1961 *The Federalist Papers* ed. Jacob E. Cooke, Cleveland: Meridian Books

Maistre, Joseph de 1965 *The Works* tr. Jack Lively, New York: Macmillan

Maistre, Joseph de 1994 *Considerations on France* ed. and tr. Richard A. Lebrun, Cambridge: Cambridge University Press

Makiya, Kanan 1993 *Cruelty and Silence: War, Tyranny, Uprising, and the Arab World* London: Jonathan Cape

Manin, Bernard 1994 'Checks, Balances and Boundaries: The Separation of Powers in the Constitutional Debate of 1787', in Fontana (ed.) 1994, 27–62

Manin, Bernard 1997 *The Principles of Representative Government* Cambridge: Cambridge University Press

Mann, Michael 1986–93 *Sources of Social Power* vols 1 and 2, Cambridge: Cambridge University Press

Mann, Michael 1988 *States, War and Capitalism* Oxford: Basil Blackwell

Marx, Karl and Engels, Frederick 1975 (a) *Collected Works* vol. 3, London: Lawrence & Wishart

Marx, Karl and Engels, Frederick 1975 (b) *Collected Works* vol. 4, London: Lawrence & Wishart

Mayhew, David R. 1974 *Congress: The Electoral Connection* New Haven: Yale University Press

Meek, Ronald 1976 *Social Science and the Ignoble Savage* Cambridge: Cambridge University Press

Meier, Christian 1995 *Caesar* tr. D. McKlintock, London: Fontana

Meinecke, Friedrich 1957 *Machiavellism* tr. Douglas Scott, London: Routledge & Kegan Paul

Metzger, Thomas A. 1977 *Escape from Predicament: Neo-Confucianism and China's Evolving Political Culture* New York: Columbia University Press

Michels, Robert 1959 *Political Parties* tr. E. and C. Paul, New York: Dover

Mill, James 1992 *Political Writings* ed. Terence Ball, Cambridge: Cambridge University Press

Mill, John Stuart 1910 *Utilitarianism, Liberty, Representative Government* ed. A. D. Lindsay, London: J. M. Dent

Miller, William L., Timpson, Annis May and Lessnoff, Michael 1996 *Political Culture in Contemporary Britain: People and Politics, Principles and Practice* Oxford: Clarendon Press

Mommsen, Wolfgang J. 1974 *The Age of Bureaucracy: Perspectives on the Political Sociology of Max Weber* Oxford: Basil Blackwell

Montesquieu, Charles-Louis de Secondat, Baron de 1989 *The Spirit of the Laws* ed. Anne Cohler, Basia Miller and Harold Stone, Cambridge: Cambridge University Press

Moore, Barrington Jr 1978 *Injustice: The Social Bases of Obedience and Revolt* London: Macmillan

Morgan, Kenneth O. 1985 *Labour in Power 1945–1951* Oxford: Oxford University Press

Mottahedeh, Roy 1987 *The Mantle of the Prophet: Religion and Politics in Iran* Harmondsworth: Penguin

Munro, Donald J. 1969 *The Concept of Man in Early China* Stanford: Stanford University Press

Nairn, Tom 1977 *The Break-up of Britain* London: New Left Books

Nettl, J. P. 1966 *Rosa Luxemburg* 2 vols, Oxford: Oxford University Press

Newton, Kenneth 1993 'Caring and Competence: The Long, Long Campaign' in King et al. 1993, 129–70

Nippel, Wilfried 1995 *Public Order in Ancient Rome* Cambridge: Cambridge University Press

Nove, Alec 1983 *The Economics of Feasible Socialism* London: George Allen & Unwin

Nozick, Robert 1975 *Anarchy, State and Utopia* Oxford: Basil Blackwell

Nozick, Robert 1993 *The Nature of Rationality* Princeton: Princeton University Press

Nussbaum, Martha A. 1985 *The Fragility of Goodness* Cambridge: Cambridge University Press

Nye, Joseph 1997 'In Government We Don't Trust' *Foreign Policy* 108, 99–111

Oakley, Francis 1984 (a) *Natural Law, Conciliarism and Consent in the Later Middle Ages* London: Variorum Editions

Oakley, Francis 1984 (b) *Omnipotence, Covenant and Order* Ithaca: Cornell University Press

Oakley, Francis 1995 'Nederman, Gerson, Conciliar Theory and Constitutionalism: *Sed Contra*' *History of Political Thought* 16, 1–19

Ober, Josiah 1989 *Mass and Elite in Democratic Athens* Princeton: Princeton University Press

Okimoto, Daniel I. 1989 *Between MITI and the Market: Japanese Industrial Policy for High Technology* Stanford: Stanford University Press

Olson, Mancur 1965 *The Logic of Collective Action* Cambridge, Mass.: Harvard University Press

Olson, Mancur 1982 *The Rise and Decline of Nations* New Haven: Yale University Press

Ooms, Herman 1985 *Tokugawa Ideology: Early Constructs 1570–1680* Princeton: Princeton University Press

Orwell, George 1954 *Nineteen Eighty-Four* Harmondsworth: Penguin

Ostrogorski, M. 1964 *Democracy and the Organization of Political Parties* ed. & abridged S. M. Lipset and tr. F. Clarke, 2 vols, Garden City, New York: Doubleday

Parfit, Derek 1984 *Reasons and Persons* Oxford: Clarendon Press

Pascal, Blaise 1962 *Pensées* ed. L. Lafuma, Paris: Editions du Seuil

Pasquino, Pasquale 1994 'The Constitutional Republicanism of Emmanuel Sieyés', in Fontana (ed.) 1994, 107–17

Passmore, John 1974 *Man's Responsibility for Nature* London: Duckworth

Philp, Mark 1997 'Defining Political Corruption' *Political Studies* 45, 436–62

Pierson, Christopher 1998 'Contemporary Challenges to Welfare State Development' *Political Studies* 46, 777–94

Pinkney, David H. 1972 *The French Revolution of 1830* Princeton: Princeton University Press

Plato 1930–5 *The Republic* tr. Paul Shorey, 2 vols, Cambridge, Mass.: Harvard University Press

Pocock, J. G. A. 1972 *Politics, Language and Time* London: Methuen

Proust, Marcel 1983 *Remembrance of Things Past* tr. C. K. Scott Moncrieff and Terence Kilmartin, 3 vols, Harmondsworth: Penguin

Przeworski, Adam 1985 *Capitalism and Social Democracy* Cambridge: Cambridge University Press

Ralston, David B. 1990 *Importing the European Army* Chicago: University of Chicago Press

Ramsden, John 1998 *An Appetite for Power: A History of the Conservative Party since 1830* London: HarperCollins

Rawls, John 1972 *A Theory of Justice* Oxford: Clarendon Press

Rawls, John 1993 *Political Liberalism* New York: Columbia University Press

Redfield, Robert 1960 *Peasant Society and Culture* Chicago: University of Chicago Press

Richelieu, Armand Jean du Plessis, cardinal de 1947 *Testament Politique* ed. L. André, Paris: Robert Laffont

Riddell, Peter 1996 *Honest Opportunism: How We Get the Politicians We Deserve* 2nd edn, London: Indigo

Riley, Patrick 1997 *Leibniz' Universal Jurisprudence* Cambridge, Mass.: Harvard University Press

Robertson, John 1985 *The Scottish Enlightenment and the Militia Issue* Edinburgh: John Donald

Rorty, Richard 1979 *Philosophy and the Mirror of Nature* Oxford: Basil Blackwell

Rousseau, Jean-Jacques 1962 *Political Writings* ed. C. E. Vaughan, 2 vols, Oxford: Basil Blackwell

Rousseau, Jean-Jacques 1964 *Discours sur les sciences et les arts* ed. François Bouchardy, Paris: Gallimard

Rousseau, Jean-Jacques 1986 *The First and Second Discourses* ed. and tr. Victor Gourevitch, New York: Harper & Row

Rowen, Herbert H. 1962 'L'Etat c'est à Moi: Louis XIV and the State' *French Historical Studies* 2, 83–98

Rowen, Herbert H. 1980 *The King's State: Proprietary Dynasticism in Early Modern France* New Brunswick: Rutgers University Press

Runciman, David 1997 *Pluralism and the Personality of the State* Cambridge: Cambridge University Press

Runciman, W. G. 1967 *Relative Deprivation and Social Justice* London: Routledge & Kegan Paul

Runciman, W. G. 1998 *The Social Animal* London: HarperCollins

Ryan, Alan 1988 'A More Tolerant Hobbes?' in Susan Mendus (ed.) *Justifying Toleration* Cambridge: Cambridge University Press, 37–59

Saint-Simon, Louis de Rouvroy, duc de 1954–61 *Mémoires* ed. G. Truc, 7 vols, Paris: Gallimard

Sandel, Michael J. 1996 *Democracy's Discontent: America in Search of a Public Philosophy* Cambridge, Mass.: Harvard University Press

Sanders, David 1993 'Why the Conservative Party Won – Again' in King et al. 1993, 171–222

Sansom, Sir George 1963 *A History of Japan 1615–1867* London: Dawson

Sartori, Giovanni 1976 *Parties and Party Systems: A Framework for Analysis* 2 vols, Cambridge: Cambridge University Press

Scanlon, T. 1982 'Contractualism and Utilitarianism' in Amartya Sen and Bernard Williams (eds) *Utilitarianism and Beyond* Cambridge: Cambridge University Press, 103–28

Schapiro, Leonard 1972 *Totalitarianism* London: Macmillan

Schmitt, Carl 1996 *The Concept of the Political* tr. George Schwab, Chicago: University of Chicago Press

Schumpeter, Joseph 1950 *Capitalism, Socialism and Democracy* London: George Allen & Unwin

Schwoerer, Lois 1974 *No Standing Armies: The Antiarmy Ideology in Seventeenth Century England* Baltimore: Johns Hopkins University Press

Scott, James C. 1998 *Seeing Like a State* New Haven: Yale University Press

Selby, Ian 1995 *Government and Politics: Concepts and Comparisons* London: Nelson

Shackleton, Robert 1961 *Montesquieu: A Critical Biography* Oxford: Clarendon Press

Shaviro, Daniel 1997 *Do Deficits Matter?* Chicago: University of Chicago Press

Shklar, Judith N. 1984 *Ordinary Vices* Cambridge, Mass.: Harvard University Press

Silberman, Bernard S. 1993 *Cages of Reason: The Rise of the Rational State in France, Japan, the United States and Great Britain* Chicago: University of Chicago Press

Skidelsky, Robert 1992 *John Maynard Keynes: the Economist as Saviour 1920–1937* London: Macmillan

Skinner, Quentin 1978 *The Foundations of Modern Political Thought* 2 vols, Cambridge: Cambridge University Press

Skinner, Quentin 1988 'Some Problems in the Explanation of Political Thought and Action' in Tully (ed.) 1988, 97–118

Skinner, Quentin 1989 'The State' in Ball, Farr and Hanson (eds) 1989, 90–131

Skinner, Quentin 1996 *Reason and Rhetoric in the Philosophy of Hobbes* Cambridge: Cambridge University Press

Skocpol, Theda 1979 *States and Social Revolutions* Cambridge: Cambridge University Press

Skocpol, Theda 1994 *Social Revolutions in the Modern World* Cambridge: Cambridge University Press

Skowronek, Steven 1982 *Building the New American State* Cambridge: Cambridge University Press

Smith, Adam 1976 *An Inquiry into the Nature and Causes of the Wealth of Nations* ed. R. H. Campbell, A. S. Skinner and W. B. Todd, Oxford: Clarendon Press

Smith, Adam 1978 *Lectures on Jurisprudence* ed. R. L. Meek, D. D. Raphael and P. G. Stein, Oxford: Clarendon Press

Sonenscher, Michael 1997 'The Nation's Debt and the Birth of the Modern Republic: The French Fiscal Deficit and the Politics of the Revolution of 1789' *History of Political Thought* 18, 64–103 and 267–325

Spitzer, Alan B. 1957 *The Revolutionary Theories of Louis Auguste Blanqui* New York: Columbia University Press

Strawson, P. F. 1968 'Freedom and Resentment' in P. F. Strawson (ed.) *Studies in the Philosophy of Thought and Action* Oxford: Oxford University Press, 71–96

Swann, Julian 1995 *Politics and the Parlement of Paris under Louis XV 1754–1774* Cambridge: Cambridge University Press

Swedberg, Richard 1991 *Schumpeter: A Biography* Princeton: Princeton University Press

Taylor, Charles 1985 *Philosophy and the Human Sciences* Cambridge: Cambridge University Press

Taylor, Charles 1989 *Sources of the Self* Cambridge, Mass.: Harvard University Press

Taylor, Michael 1982 *Community, Anarchy and Liberty* Cambridge: Cambridge University Press

Taylor, Robert H. 1987 *The State in Burma* London: Hurst

Thompson, E. P. 1993 *Customs in Common* Harmondsworth: Penguin

Thompson, Helen 1996 *The British Conservative Government and the European Exchange Rate Mechanism 1979–1994* London: Pinter

Thompson, Karl M. 1998 'The Logic of Modern Prudence: Practical Political Judgment in Modern Representative Democracies' unpublished PhD dissertation, University of Cambridge

Thucydides 1919–23 *History of the Peloponnesian War* tr. C. F. Smith, 4 vols, Cambridge, Mass.: Harvard University Press

Tierney, Brian 1982 *Religion, Law and the Growth of Constitutional Thought 1150–1650* Cambridge: Cambridge University Press

Tierney, Brian 1983 'Tuck on Rights: Some Medieval Problems' *History of Political Thought* 4, 429–41

Tierney, Brian 1989 'Origins of Natural Rights Language: Texts and Contexts 1150–1250' *History of Political Thought* 10, 615–46

Tilly, Charles (ed.) 1975 *The Formation of National States in Western Europe* Princeton: Princeton University Press

Tolstoy, Leo N. 1957 *War and Peace* tr. Rosemary Edmonds, 2 vols, Harmondsworth: Penguin

Tolstoy, Leo N. 1960 *The Death of Ivan Ilyich and Other Stories* tr. Rosemary Edmonds, Harmondsworth: Penguin

Trevor-Roper, H. R. 1947 *The Last Days of Hitler* London: Macmillan

Tribe, Keith (ed.) 1989 *Reading Weber* London: Routledge

Tuck, Richard 1979 *Natural Rights Theories* Cambridge: Cambridge University Press

Tuck, Richard 1989 *Hobbes* Oxford: Oxford University Press

Tuck, Richard 1990 'Hobbes and Locke on Toleration' in Mary Dietz (ed.) *Thomas Hobbes and Political Theory* Kansas: University of Kansas Press, 153–71

Tuck, Richard 1993 *Philosophy and Government* Cambridge: Cambridge University Press

Tuck, Richard 1999 *Political Thought and the International Order from Grotius to Kant* Oxford: Oxford University Press

Tully, James (ed.) 1988 *Meaning and Context: Quentin Skinner and his Critics* Cambridge: Polity Books

Ulam, Adam B. 1969 *Lenin and the Bolsheviks* London: Collins Fontana Library

Ullmann, Walter 1946 *The Medieval Idea of Law* London: Methuen

Ullmann, Walter 1961 *Principles of Government and Politics in the Middle Ages* London: Methuen

Underdown, David 1985 *Revel, Riot and Rebellion: Popular Politics and Customs in England 1603–1660* Oxford: Clarendon Press

Unger, Roberto Mangabeira 1986 *False Necessity* Cambridge: Cambridge University Press

Van Deth, Jan W. and Scarborough, Elinor (eds) 1995 *The Impact of Values* Oxford: Oxford University Press

Van Kley, Dale 1996 *The Religious Origins of the French Revolution* Princeton: Princeton University Press

Vile, M. J. C. 1967 *Constitutionalism and the Separation of Powers* Oxford: Clarendon Press

Viollet, Paul 1912 *Le Roi et ses ministres pendant les trois derniers siècles de la monarchie* Paris: Librairie de la Société du Recueil Sirey

Voltaire (François-Marie Arouet) 1968 *Candide* ed. J. H. Brumfitt, Oxford: Oxford University Press

Wade, Robert 1990 *Governing the Market: Economic Theory and the Role of Government in East Asian Industrialization* Princeton: Princeton University Press

Waltz, Kenneth N. 1959 *Man, the State and War* New York: Columbia University Press

Walzer, Michael 1978 *Just and Unjust Wars* London: Allen Lane

Weber, Max 1948 *From Max Weber: Essays in Sociology* ed. H. H. Gerth and C. Wright Mills, London: Routledge

Weber, Max 1951 *The Religion of China* ed. and tr. H. H. Gerth, New York: Macmillan

Weber, Max 1958 (a) *The Religion of India* tr. H. H. Gerth and D. Martindale, New York: Free Press

Weber, Max 1958 (b) *The Protestant Ethic and the Spirit of Capitalism* tr. Talcott Parsons, New York: Charles Scribner's Sons

Weber, Max 1965 *The Sociology of Religion* tr. E. Fischoff, London: Methuen

Weber, Max 1968 *Economy and Society* ed. Guenther Roth and Claus Wittich, 3 vols, New York: Bedminster Press

Whiteley, P., Seyd, P. and Richardson, J. 1994 *True Blues: The Politics of Conservative Party Membership* Oxford: Oxford University Press

Williams, Bernard 1973 'A Critique of Utilitarianism' in J. J. C. Smart and Bernard Williams, 1973 *Utilitarianism For and Against* Cambridge: Cambridge University Press 77–150

Williams, Bernard 1978 *Descartes: The Project of Pure Inquiry* Harmondsworth: Penguin

Williams, Bernard 1981 *Moral Luck* Cambridge: Cambridge University Press

Williams, Bernard 1985 *Ethics and the Limits of Philosophy* London: Fontana

Williams, Bernard 1988 'Formal Structures and Social Reality', in Gambetta (ed.) 1988, 3–13

Wilson, James Q. 1997 'Crime and Justice in England and America' *Bulletin of the American Academy of Arts and Sciences* Jan.–Feb., L, 43–50

Womack, John Jr 1968 *Zapata and the Mexican Revolution* London: Thames & Hudson

Wood, Adrian 1994 *North–South Trade, Employment and Inequality* Oxford: Clarendon Press

Wood, Gordon P. 1991 *The Radicalism of the American Revolution* New York: Alfred Knopf

Young, Hugo 1998 *This Blessed Plot: Britain and Europe from Churchill to Blair* London: Macmillan

Zagorin, Perez 1982 *Rebels and Rulers 1500–1660* 2 vols, Cambridge: Cambridge University Press

INDEX